Deception in Markets

Deception in Markets

An Economic Analysis

Edited by Caroline Gerschlager

palgrave
macmillan

First published 2005 by
PALGRAVE MACMILLAN
Houndmills, Basingstoke, Hampshire RG21 6XS and
175 Fifth Avenue, New York, N. Y. 10010
Companies and representatives throughout the world

PALGRAVE MACMILLAN is the global academic imprint of the Palgrave Macmillan division of St. Martin's Press, LLC and of Palgrave Macmillan Ltd. Macmillan® is a registered trademark in the United States, United Kingdom and other countries. Palgrave is a registered trademark in the European Union and other countries.

ISBN 1–4039–4345–1 hardback

This book is printed on paper suitable for recycling and made from fully managed and sustained forest sources.

A catalogue record for this book is available from the British Library.

Library of Congress Cataloging-in-Publication Data

Deception in markets: an economic analysis / edited by Caroline Gerschlager.
p. cm.
Includes bibliographical references and index.
ISBN 0–4039–4345–1
1. Information theory in economics. 2. Fraud. 3. Business ethics.
4. Institutional economics. 5. Economics. I. Gerschlager, Caroline.

HB133.D43 2004
330′.01′154–dc22 2004058335

10 9 8 7 6 5 4 3 2 1
14 13 12 11 10 09 08 07 06 05

Printed and bound in Great Britain by
Antony Rowe Ltd, Chippenham and Eastbourne

Contents

Acknowledgements

This book presents the results of a research project on "Exchange, Deceptions and Self-Deceptions," which was directed by the editor and financed by the Austrian Federal Ministry of Education, Science and Culture (bm:bwk). Intermediate results of the project were presented at a workshop in December 2001 at Maison des Sciences de l'Homme/MSH and Maison Suger in Paris. I am pleased to acknowledge their financial support for the workshop.

Firstly, I would thank the authors of this book and all participants in the workshop in Paris for having contributed to this project. For me, personally, this book also presents an enduring souvenir of our workshop in Paris where the topic was first addressed from a variety of approaches.

In addition, I would like to gratefully acknowledge the help of numerous (anonymous) referees who – with their comments and criticisms on the individual chapters – have helped to contribute to this book.

The project was institutionally located at the Institute of Economics at the Vienna University of Economics and Business Administration (Wirtschaftsuniversität Wien) and I am grateful to Leonhard Bauer and Hanns J. Pichler for their warm welcome.

List of Contributors

Joshua Coval
Harvard Business School
Finance Department
Morgan Hall 491
Soldiers Field Road
Boston, MA 02163
USA
jcoval@hbs.edu

Rachel T. A. Croson
University of Pennsylvania
OPIM
The Wharton School
Philadelphia, PA 19104-6340
USA
crosonr@wharton.upenn.edu

Paul Dumouchel
Graduate School of Core Ethics and Frontier Science
Ritsumeikan University
56-1 Toji-in Kitamachi, Kita-ku
Kyoto, 603-8577
Japan
dumouchp@gr.ritsumei.ac.jp

Caroline Gerschlager
Vienna University of Economics and Business Administration
Institute of Economics (III)
Augasse 2-6
A-1090 Vienna
Austria
caroline.gerschlager@wu-wien.ac.at

Paul van der Grijp
Université de Provence
Maison Asie Pacifique
3 place Victor Hugo
F-13003 Marseille
France
pvdgrijp@up.univ-mrs.fr

Alan Hamlin
University of Southampton
Department of Economics
Southampton SO17 1BJ
UK
aph@soton.ac.uk

Marcel Hénaff
University of California, San Diego
Department of Cultural and Religious Studies
UCSD 0410
La Jolla, CA 92093
USA
mhenaff@ucsd.edu

Ellen Hertz
Université de Neuchâtel
Institut d'ethnologie
Rue Saint-Nicolas 4
CH-2000 Neuchâtel
Switzerland
Ellen.Hertz@unine.ch

David Hirshleifer
The Ohio State University
Department of Finance
740A Fisher Hall
2100 Neil Avenue
Columbus, OH 43210-1144
USA
hirshleifer_2@cob.osu.edu

Gisela Kubon-Gilke
Evangelische Fachhochschule Darmstadt
Zweifalltorweg 12
D-64293 Darmstadt
Germany
kubon-gilke@efh-darmstadt.de

Vincent-Antonin Lépinay
Sociology Department, Columbia University (New York)
& Centre de Sociologie de l'Innovation, Ecole des Mines (Paris)
val2003@columbia.edu

Laurence S. Moss
Babson College
Economics Department
Mustard Hall, MA 02457-0310
USA
Lmos@aol.com

S. Abu Turab Rizvi
University of Vermont
Department of Economics
Old Mill, 94 University Place
Burlington, VT 05405-0114
USA
abu.rizvi@uvm.edu

Esther-Mirjam Sent
University of Nijmegen
Nijmegen School of Management
PO Box 9108
6500 HK Nijmegen
The Netherlands
e.m.sent@nsm.kun.nl

Siew Hong Teoh
The Ohio State University
Department of Finance
740A Fisher Hall
2100 Neil Avenue
Columbus, OH 43210-1144
USA
teoh_@cob.osu.edu

Introduction

Caroline Gerschlager

The present book offers a summary and focused discussion of deception in markets from the point of view of modern economic theory. It presents a systematic account of how different approaches to modern economics deal with dishonesty and cheating in the marketplace.

While deception is a common component of military strategy and battle and also occupies criminologists, for economists it is a relatively novel concern. The reason for this is that competitive markets have traditionally been assumed to detect, punish, and finally eliminate cheats. In a curious reversal of Gresham's law, honest traders are meant to drive out dishonest ones. In bimetallic times, Gresham observed that "bad" money drove out the good, consequently inflating the economy. In markets, however, it is assumed that merits will be gained only by those deserving it. The false and "bad" ones will be detected, their reputations spoiled, and nobody will want to trade with them any longer. In this way, cheats are assumed to disappear from the marketplace. The general idea is that the mechanisms inherent in markets will rid them of liars and cheats.

Since the burst of the new economy bubble in 2001, an ongoing series of economic and financial fraud has placed the spotlight on markets as sites of dishonesty. To mention some prominent examples reported worldwide:

- CEOs at Enron, WorldCom Tyco,[1] Parmalat in Italy, and other leading companies in Europe[2] looting their firms.
- Analysts in leading investment firms such as Merrill Lynch and Citigroup misleading and deceiving (potential) investors.[3]
- Managers in the mutual funds industry skimming money from millions of investors through illegal trading practices.[4]
- Illegal trading of foreign currencies on Wall Street.[5]

From the point of view of economic theory, fraudulent activities should not have happened on that scale at all.

In economic theory, deception is typically associated with the imperfect or non-functioning of markets, such as with market failures. In the case of asymmetric information, for example, it has been shown that competitive markets may not always be sufficient to prevent fraud. This is the case when buyers are unable to verify the quality of the good or only at a very high cost. Credence goods, such as medical services, are a case in point (Darby and Karni 1973).

What Darby and Karni suggest in their analysis is that under specific circumstances, deception may indeed spread in markets. Thus, one reason why the market view outlined above does not apply is the existence of market imperfections, such as asymmetrical information.

In these cases, institutional views in economics contend that when markets fail to detect deception, as is the case with credence goods, institutions will arise to counter the deception. Oliver Williamson, a prominent representative of this view, claims that liars and cheats can be constrained only by appropriate institutional arrangements (Williamson 1985, 2000).

By effectively constraining lying and cheating, institutions are certainly important features of the marketplace. Since Enron, however, it has become clear that a number of key institutions designed to safeguard the functioning of the economy are clearly ineffective. The unprecedented extent of fraudulent activities, some of which were mentioned above, also reminds us of the fact that what applies to markets is also likely to apply to institutions: like markets, institutions may fail to hold cheats in check.

When we look at the current debates on institutional reform in relation to financial and economic scandals, the difficulty in identifying an appropriate institutional form becomes evident.

- Stock options, for example, were long considered an appropriate incentive to make the management of modern corporations act in the corporate interest. However, by inciting a short-term interest in the rise of share prices, it also seems that stock options have triggered a general response by executives to plunder their companies. Fraudulent practices that occur with such frequency immediately invoke basic questions about human behavior: are people cheats or are they honest? While it seems obvious that these questions are at the foundation of all trade and exchange, the role of the human element in economic concepts today is again an open question.
- The historical wave of economic and financial fraud has come to light following an era of massive deregulation, which was long advocated by regulatory authorities. Questions of principle on the relation between markets and the state may be invoked in this context: are private attempts at self-control, such as internal auditing or remuneration committees, effective? Can markets eliminate cheats on their own? Or are requirements and new regulations needed in order to enhance corporate governance? Is intervention by the law, such as the Sarbanes-Oaxly Act currently advocated by regulatory authorities, sufficient to safeguard the economy?

These examples of institutional reform indicate how hard it is to understand the problem when it comes to markets. There is much disagreement on effective ways of dealing with cheating and defrauding in markets. What these examples should have made clear, though, is that the problem of deception also concerns fundamental questions at the conceptual level of economic theory.

The present book offers an interrogation of fundamental economic concepts and their application to deception. There is a clear emphasis on rationality and behavior in relation to deception. In particular, the authors highlight the conceptual strengths and limitations of economic theory and models in dealing with deception. Deception is analyzed within standard economic frameworks (game theory, new institutional economics, new classical macroeconomics), and recent behavioral insights are referred to, challenging the basic economic concepts of rationality and self-interest. Finally, anthropological findings are used to contrast these economic conceptions of deception.

Deception in economic theory

In the traditional economic view, economists see competitive forces operating through Adam Smith's invisible hand as rendering price-taking individuals unable to benefit from information. General equilibrium theory (formalized by Arrow and Debreu in the 1950s), which is the prototypical economic model, thus reflects the ideal – perfectly competitive – exchange in which people do not get in each other's way in their respective pursuit of self-interest. In these models, in which information is perfectly spread among all individuals, deception simply does not exist.

The advent of the information paradigm in the 1970s challenged this view and generated a new understanding of markets: information is unequally, or better still, asymmetrically distributed among the agents in the economy.[6]

With the introduction of asymmetric information, any exchange *ipso facto* could also be modeled as an occasion for deception. Since Akerlof's article on "lemons" and the market for used cars, models with asymmetric information have become a standard consideration in economics (1998 [1984], p. 5). While the competitive paradigm (of general equilibrium) left no role for deception, the information paradigm could be said to impose it on the economic agenda. In asymmetric information models, the cheat "misrepresents the information he [or she] has at his [or her] disposal so as to persuade another individual ... to choose a course of action he [or she] would not have chosen had he [or she] been properly informed" (Karni 1987, p. 416).

Using the emblematic case of the market for used cars, Akerlof has shown how private information may cause inefficiency. The problem is that the buyer does not have access to the information concerning the true quality of the goods, such as the used car. In cases where information is hidden from one party, it is likely that the exchange will not take place at all. Alluding to Gresham's law that, according to Akerlof, "had made a modified reappearance ... [f]or most cars traded will be the 'lemons,' and good cars may not be traded at all. The 'bad' cars tend to drive out the good (in much the same way that bad money drives out the good)" (Akerlof 1998 [1970], p. 9).

The rationality of cheating seriously affects the functioning of the market system. The "economic costs of dishonesty" (7) include the loss by the victim of deception, as well as the loss incurred from driving legitimate business out of existence. The point Akerlof makes is that business may become extremely difficult if not impossible in situations where deception is eminent, such as in situations of asymmetric information.

With the introduction of asymmetric information, for the first time it was possible to explicitly relate the concept of the market to the problem of deception and to enable deception to be perceived at all in markets. Clearly, the requirement for deception is asymmetric information: one agent is better informed than the other and in a position to use his or her superior knowledge to affect the partner's actions so as to increase his or her own share of the total benefit at the partner's expense (Karni 1987, p. 416).

However, the point is not to systematically fool people. Referring to models of asymmetric information typical of the used car market, Molho emphasizes that a form of "rational expectation" is usually taken for granted to weaken or destroy the economic mechanism that makes lying a success (1997, p. 10). People are said to "make correct assessments *on average* (for example, about the likely quality of a used car) although they may be wrong in specific cases" (ibid.). Once cheated, they are expected to know better next time. The idea in these models is that a person may well fall victim to deception once but not all the time.

For example, when used cars dealers lie about their products, trying to pass off bad cars for good ones, this will be met with considerable suspicion by potential buyers. In the end, the seller's claims won't be taken seriously, because it is commonly known among the agents that the informational asymmetries between buyer and seller (with regard to the product quality) are an incentive for the seller to lie. This is why the seller's claims are said to be "meaningless." Thus typically, even if there is an interest in it, deception cannot succeed in models of asymmetric information.[7] Perfectly rational agents are indeed 'uncheatable.'

This analysis of asymmetric information leaves us with one crucial question: why does exchange work in spite of deception? Or, in other words, given the possibility of deception, why does exchange take place at all?

The crucial role of social institutions has been acknowledged in this context. In his article on market inefficiencies, Akerlof, for example, highlighted "counteracting institutions" (1998 [1970], p. 21) such as brand names, guarantees, and licensing, which all serve to offset the effects of uncertainty about quality.

Institutions thus facilitate trade and exchange. They serve as restrictions for individuals, among other things, preventing deception and the exchange problems resulting from it. Institutional arrangements, such as contracts and governance structures, are seen as having evolved to discourage malfeasance. Institutional arrangements – "non-markets" in Williamson's terms – will avert deception by making it too costly to engage in it (Williamson 1985).[8]

The example of the market for used cars is ideal for our purposes, because it shows that when information is distributed asymmetrically, the market mechanism is ineffective even in the presence of rational agents. The lesson to be drawn from this example is incompatible with the inference from the competitive paradigm in economics in which cheats are detected, penalized, and eliminated from the market. Akerlof's claim was that when information is hidden, the exchange will not take place, or only at very high cost.

- The issue of deception dealt with in the present book raises important questions for conceptual economic thinking, which will continue to stimulate further revision and progress in the field:
- Can economic agents be manipulated? Are they continually prone to deception by themselves and by others? Or, are they perfectly rational in making their decisions, and thus have to be considered 'uncheatable'?
- How have frauds and swindlers managed to survive and flourish in markets? What incentives to cheat exist in the marketplace? What institutional rules are favorable for deception?[9]
- What kind of market inefficiencies may arise as a result of the existence of 'cheat-able' and 'lie-able' individuals? How can the quality of regulation and control be enhanced? Can the effectiveness of political measures be improved by psychological insights?

Guide to the chapters

The Rationality of Deception

The first part of the book discusses conceptual difficulties of rationality. The authors deal with the conceptual difficulties arising when the economic concept of rationality is applied to deception. In their chapters, Paul Dumouchel and S. Abu Turab Rizvi focus on insights from game theory and Esther-Mirjam Sent puts the spotlight on new classical macroeconomics.

When we leave competitive markets, the rationality of exchange outlined in the prototypical economic model becomes threatened, because perceptions of others, in particular of their rationality, become part of our own rationality and conceptual difficulties of rationality arise (Arrow 1954, p. 70). In (normative) game theory (and rational choice), it is usually assumed that agents are perfectly rational.[10] The models analyzed are purely deductive and characterized by strong rationality principles. "The players are assumed to know what they want, to be exclusively motivated to obtain what they want, and to have an unbounded, costless, calculating ability to analyze any situation. In addition, the theory supposes that these players analyze the situation by means of a common model. The rules of the game are assumed [to be] common knowledge, i.e. everybody knows that everybody knows that [such and such] are the rules" (Van Damme 1999, pp. 184–5).[11] It is further assumed that the antagonists (in a strategic game) neither err nor cheat.[12] Investigation into tricks and turns is left to experts in individual games and consciously excluded in the assumptions of the game theorist (Davis 1993, p. 20).[13]

This is not to say that game theory does not care about deception. Given the existence of opportunistic and self-interested agents, cheating is a serious obstacle to social cooperation (Kliemt 1986, pp. 16–7) and has always been a concern in the theory of strategic decision making.[14]

Against this background, and because "it deals with differences in information, knowledge, and belief among people, game theory seems to be ideally situated to address matters involving deception." In his chapter, **S. Abu Turab Rizvi** challenges this intuition. He shows that game theory models have difficulties in establishing equilibria that allow for deception to take place. According to him, this is due to the inconsistency between the rationality assumptions (that knowledge is widely available, for example) required to show that game theory models have equilibria on the one hand, and the very existence of deception, which requires that knowledge is hidden, on the other. To this end, Rizvi inquires into the concepts of mutual and common knowledge in as much as they are imposed on the rationality of agents with a view to establishing game theoretic solutions. In particular, he discusses Aumann's "agreeing to disagree" result (Aumann 1976) and the related common prior assumption. He argues that deception cannot occur in Aumann's settings, because the players cannot end up with differences in belief. This is because when agents propose to act on the basis of privately held information, they reveal that information, causing others to revise their beliefs. According to Rizvi, asymmetric information is clearly negated by common knowledge. In the author's view, this result runs counter to the intuition that game theory can handle deception well. He therefore concludes that "game theory has failed to provide an interesting advance in dealing with some important information asymmetries among agents, however promising it may have seemed on a heuristic or common sense basis."

Paul Dumouchel also inquires into the difficult relationship between deception and rationality. He stresses that paradoxes of rationality such as those analyzed in some models of game theory and rational choice indicate conceptual problems of rationality when applied to deception. Also referring to the prisoner's dilemma, which is a clear case of a paradox, Dumouchel shows that deception is represented as irrational. In the traditional prisoner's dilemma, perfectly rational agents both lose out, although they would have been better off cooperating. Although it appears as perfectly rational for the agents to deceive, when we look at it from an individual perspective, the social dilemma arising from it makes it impossible to represent deception as rational. Against this background, Dumouchel draws on examples taken from anthropology and history and asserts that a distinction between "on-going deception" and "final deception" is necessary. He claims that because game theory and rational choice view deception exclusively in terms of final deception, they consider it to be irrational. If, in turn, deception is considered as ongoing, it may appear to be perfectly rational, resulting in dynamic equilibria. What is characteristic for ongoing deception is that the agents, including the one that is deceived, consent to it. Deception in this view does not put an end to the exchange, as suggested by the social dilemma literature, but supports it. Consequently, cooperation, far from being considered irrational by the agents, appears as a rational strategy. Indeed, in spite of deception there can be cooperation, such as exchange. The idea with ongoing deception is that being deceived can be in the interest of the agents and this is why they consent to it. Although self-deception is involved, the conclusion to be taken from this is not that we deal with irrational agents. Dumouchel claims to relax the constraints on the rationality of agents so that ongoing deception can be modeled as a form of rational behavior within an (evolutionary) game theoretic framework.

Esther-Mirjam Sent deals with the rationality concept at the foundation of new classical macroeconomic models, focusing on the (in)effectiveness of government intervention, which is said to rest on the deception of economic agents, namely rational expectations. She analyzes the claim of these models to render deception ineffective by introducing agents who are able to form rational expectations. In other words, not only do agents learn from their past mistakes (which is what previous models had assumed by supplying their agents with "adaptive expectations"), but agents forming "rational expectations" are able to anticipate future actions of the government: they anticipate that monetary policy measures (for example, the decision to lower interest rates) amount to inflation, and hence won't believe in it. They will therefore regard these measures as "meaningless," which is why they also remain ineffective. The general idea here is that any attempts to manipulate rational agents ultimately fail because the agents are fully knowledgeable, and are assumed to be "on an equal footing" (Sargent 1993, p. 21) with the manipulating agencies. Following Simon (1982), Sent claims that rational expectation models are not adequate for the needs of policy and opts to replace the assumption of rational expectations with psychological insights into behavior and the concept of bounded rationality. In behavioral approaches, it is acknowledged that agents, far from being perfectly rational, may systematically "act against their own interest." Behavioral economists put the emphasis on empirical and experimental insights into human behavior acknowledging that agents systematically commit errors in judgment (caused, for example, by organizational over-identification or cognitive dissonance). Sent concludes that it is particularly in their approval of self-deception that behavioral approaches challenge the rationality assumptions underlying macroeconomic models, lending support to the development of viable alternatives to mainstream economics.

Behavior and Incentives to Deceive: The Success of Deception in Markets

The second part of the book focuses on deceptive behavior. In order to explain and make predictions, modern economics regularly invokes the self-interest assumption. Recent research in behavioral economics questions the validity of the strict selfishness assumption. Fehr and Gächter (2000), for example, criticize Williamson for his assumption of unrestrained opportunism. Partly following Rabin (1993),[15] who argues for the incorporation of fairness into game theory and economics, they concentrate on behavior guided by social norms of fairness and reciprocity. While following these norms, agents may also act against their own self-interest,[16] and this is why they are different from the economic man at the center of standard economic theory. It has thus been shown that the egoistic image of homo economicus is deficient and needs to be completed by a more altruistic version, namely that of homo reciprocans, the cooperator.[17]

While fairness and reciprocity are clearly important, there is also another – more wicked – side to the coin. In real markets, not only fair and honest people, but also deceivers, liars and cheats, come together. As we have seen, some of them even loot their own companies. The contributions on deceptive behavior in markets in part two of this book should therefore be understood in the spirit of the above line of reasoning, namely as a challenge to the basic assumptions of economic theory.

In her chapter **Caroline Gerschlager** takes the Enron case as a point of departure in order to discuss economic incentives to deceive. Fraud and deception are relatively novel concerns in economics, and Gerschlager offers an informal discussion on how modern economics typically accounts for these phenomena. The study of incentives is crucial because in an economic context people are seen as responding to them in a particular way. Economics is typically concerned with the study of incentives that induce people to work, trade, consume or save. Against this background, Gerschlager emphasizes incentives in terms of perverse incentives, i.e., incentives that have an opposite effect to that intended. She exemplifies economic incentives to deceive in corporations and markets by drawing on recent examples in which economic mechanisms encourage people to act to the detriment of others, i.e., to the detriment of their company or the state. In particular, the focus is on stock options and looting strategies in the savings and loan crises of the 1980s in the US. In conclusion, deception is discussed as an issue of economic policy.

Rachel T. A. Croson's contribution on deception in economics experiments has to be seen in relation to a number of recent papers that concentrate on lying, in particular (for example Crawford 2003, Charness 2000). With reference to signaling and bargaining games, she points out that deception succeeds to a greater extent than equilibrium theory predicts. She argues that agents can be cheated because they are gullible. In this approach, agents are regarded as overconfident of their abilities to detect deception and insufficiently skeptical of statements they receive from others. As a consequence, "they are prone to deception by others." In accordance with standard economic theory predictions, experiments have also shown that agents do in fact lie when it is in their interest. In this view, 'lie-able' agents cannot be conceived of as rational in the sense of the self-interest postulate of economic theory, and this is why the likelihood of becoming a victim of deception is attributed to irrationalities in human behavior such as overconfidence and gullibility.

Following the pioneers of psychological approaches to human behavior (Simon 1982; Katona 1968a,b; 1980; Festinger 1957; Kahneman and Tversky 1974; 1979; 1982), these and other biases (regret avoidance, conservativeness, and representativeness, for example) have been applied to problems in economics by authors such as Thaler (1991; 1992), Laibson et al. (1998a,b) Mullainathan et al. (2000), Loewenstein et al. (2000a,b), Camerer (1995) and Rabin (1998). In this chapter, the behavioral finance theorists **Joshua Coval**, **David Hirshleifer,** and **Siew Hong Teoh** apply biases of emotions and beliefs to capital markets in order to explain various aspects of the behavior of investors and of prices in capital markets.[18] They argue that these biases should be seen in terms of self-deception and conclude that individuals who are sensitive to these biases are more likely to be victims of deception, too.[19] According to the authors, it is in fact the tendency toward self-deception that can make it easier for predators to deceive and exploit investors. In particular, overconfidence in the ability to interpret signals transmitted by others can lead to excessive credulity. With regard to the disclosure policy of companies, they claim that due to overconfidence, "individuals will fail to discount fully for the fact that they are ignoring some of the considerations relevant for their decision. As a consequence, investors may be fooled by actions firms can take to manipulate perceptions." In this view, excessive credulity also led analysts and investors to misinterpret information released by Enron prior to its 2001 collapse.

Behavioral finance approaches suggest that if investors are excessively credulous, they are likely to be exploited in markets. The overall tenet is that deception is successful in markets. Why do these biases persist? Why aren't they penalized and selected against? The authors stress an evolutionary explanation: if agents fool themselves, they will also have an advantage in deceiving others. So, on the one hand, self-deception gives an evolutionary advantage to the cheat. On the other hand, overconfident individuals may also be selected because they have a greater tendency to venture innovative solutions. Coval, Hirshleifer, and Teoh maintain that these arguments may also apply to the environment of financial markets, where individuals can prosper in spite of their biases. The authors conclude that market forces such as competition, arbitrage, and learning on the part of decision makers will not completely eliminate fraud and cheating.

Because of the existence of 'cheat-able' and 'lie-able' individuals, inefficiencies in the workings of the market mechanism may arise.

Subjectivism and Deceptive Behavior in Markets

In the third part of the book, **Laurence S. Moss** analyzes deceptive behavior in markets from the perspective of Austrian subjectivism. The Austrians, and in particular Friedrich von Hayek, ignored the fact that information is not always accurate but is often manipulated. A great deal of deception is neither anticipated nor noticed. In fact, bargainers are not always aware of the machinations of their counterparts. Moss explains that by crediting markets with producing rules of fair dealing and basic honesty, modern Austrian School writers have a tendency to rule out the problem of deception. When agents are assumed to adhere to a pre-existing rule of law, "*homo economicus* conman" is clearly disregarded. If considered at all by these writers, Moss shows that deception is seen as being imposed on the market order. The mismanagement of money and credit by the central banks denounced by Hayek is a case in point. By contrast, Moss contends that deceptive behavior is naturally created by the market processes. Drawing on many examples, partly with reference to the pioneers of modern game theory and information economics, he shows that deceptive strategies are crucial and emphasizes that they alter the division of the gains from the trade. In conclusion, he makes the case for a renewed interest in the role that subjective ideas about language, promises, and alleged product characteristics play in relation to price formation processes in markets. He claims that instead of being eliminated by the workings of the competitive market, deception should be seen as naturally arising as part of the market process itself.

Social Institutions and Regulation: How to Control Deception

The topic of deception has not received much separate attention within economics. In most cases, it is simply inferred from the regular assumption that economic agents unemotionally follow their self-interest. If the pursuit of self-interest requires the use of deception, *homo economicus* will use it. Institutions are a given to the economic agent and either constrain or facilitate deception. The authors of part four of this book put the emphasis on the analysis of institutional safeguards designed to control *homo economicus* willing to use guile and deceit. They outline the standard economic approach to human behavior, which is said to be controlled by appropriate incentive structures. Here the idea is to ban deception by making it too costly for the agent to engage in it. Concepts such as incentive compatibility and the associated truth revelation principle are key in this context. They are either explained or applied by the authors in the following chapters.

Is the threat of deception more overwhelming than the institutional analysis admits it to be? Are the economic mechanisms effective? In the fourth part of the book, it is shown that the quality of regulation and control can be extended. **Alan Hamlin** reminds us of the fact that the standard economic view of deception ignores the fact that people are also influenced by normative concerns. According to him, economic models (for example models used for the regulation of a monopoly) should account for motivational heterogeneity and admit the "intrinsic" values of honesty or trust. Indeed, he claims that some individuals "reliably tell the truth, reveal information, keep promises, and so on, even when it is not in their own narrowly conceived interest to do so." In contrast to the standard view of the economic agent who is supposed not to care about normative concerns at all, Hamlin asserts that like honesty and trust, deception, too, "is a normatively charged concept."[20] The presence of positive virtues of the agent such as trust and honesty acts as an efficient barrier to "the negative act of deception (which can be thought of as arising in the absence of trust and honesty)." Drawing on the reliance predicament, a dynamic game version of the prisoner's dilemma, Hamlin demonstrates that the institutional solutions resulting from the invisible hand mechanism (that is, focusing on controlling unemotional self-interested agents via incentives) are rather limited, as they usually transfer the problem to a higher level without solving it. In turn, the recognition of honesty and trust as a normative concern means that the problem of deception can be tackled at its source. According to Hamlin, the introduction of normative concepts into economic models may be a solution to the problem of the general unreliability of agents. To recognize that some individuals are motivated by normative concerns means to substitute internal virtue for external mechanisms and devices on which the standard economic approach is based. Hamlin concludes that building on these internal virtues can be more effective than economizing on them, an insight which he believes to be of particular value in regulation and politics, where deception is central.

Gisela Kubon-Gilke states that the focus on incentives in the standard approach reduces the range of human motivations. She holds that the standard approach by assumption is egocentric and does not allow for "real behavior." Kubon-Gilke claims that a psychological foundation of economics can extend our understanding of the mechanisms that make commitments credible and also produce a different understanding of the term deception. Drawing on cognitive psychology, she shows that when we deal with deception, it is of analytical importance to consider the relationships between laws of perception, emotions, motivations, and behavior of individuals.

According to Kubon-Gilke, the psychological concept of requiredness is particularly revealing because it focuses on the fact that human behavior is influenced by the objective character of a social situation, that is, motivational processes often find their origin in perceived structures of the environment and its imperfections. In this sense, she holds that beyond the egocentric motives, people "have a need to live with others truthfully, to establish relations of trust, good faith, and cooperation. They have a need to act according to what they perceive as inherently fitting." Kubon-Gilke concludes that further research is needed to analyze the relevance of psychological considerations for the effects of political measures.

Preconditions of Markets and Deception: An Anthropological Perspective

While deception is a novel concern for economists, anthropologists have always appreciated that deception is essential to understanding exchange processes (Gerschlager 2001). When he was analyzing the all-compounding character of gift exchange in the 1920s, Marcel Mauss in his "Essai sur le don" clearly acknowledged the necessity for social simulation to create and reproduce the social bond (Mauss 1924). Hence, numerous observations on the ubiquitousness of deception by which social life is characterized can be found in anthropological treatises (for example, Needham 1972, pp. 100–1; Bailey 1971). And this is why analyses of markets from the perspective of social anthropology are finally introduced, helping to contrast the economic conceptions.

The anthropological understanding of markets concentrates on their "social embeddedness" (Polanyi 1944; 1957; Granovetter 1985; Callon 1998, pp. 1–57). Here, we leave the economic approach. The authors of part five contrast the individual economic (and psychological) focus on individual motivation to deceive by examining what exactly conditions the agent to deceive. While the approaches adopted in this part of the book partly diverge and also differ in what they actually stress, their common focus is on institutions[21] and personal social interaction.

Drawing on the actor-network approach (Callon 1998) and based on ethnographic fieldwork (participant observation, formal and informal interviews) with a large Parisian bank active in financial markets, **Vincent-Antonin Lépinay** and **Ellen Hertz** pursue an empirical approach. From an anthropological point of view, deception is viewed as a form of communication. The authors show that this communicative act often fails in financial markets, because of the opaqueness of technologically highly equipped, anonymous, and rapidly changing markets. They claim that because of the set of particular social conditions that are necessary for successful deception to take place and that are less often met in financial markets than one might suspect, the imputation of deception is rare. Contrary to many popular accounts, according to the authors' analyses, deception is not a pervasive activity on these markets, or at least market participants do not act and speak as if it were. They conclude that the consideration of deception must move away from the human-centered perspective common in the social and economic sciences. Instead, detailed examinations of the technical and institutional environments in which trading takes place are central to allowing for different forms of exchange behavior.

In his contribution, **Paul van der Grijp** refers to the concept of asymmetrical exchange which was used in anthropological studies of "Big Man, Great Man" and chiefly exchange systems (Sahlins 1963, Godelier 1982, White and Lindstrom 1997). The concept of asymmetrical exchange, according to Van der Grijp, is characterized by "unequal access to material resources and knowledge, and linked to a certain type of socially shared ideas or ideology." It is associated with "social inequality"[22] and "can be gauged from an interaction between individuals or groups which has the form of an unequal exchange of goods or services." Drawing on observations from Western and non-Western countries, he applies the concept of asymmetrical exchange to exemplary cases on trade and exchange where deception is present (for example, a prosperous supermarket owner in western Polynesia; two entrepreneurs in France; the arts market in St. Louis). Pointing to the victims that are left behind (for example, relatives in western Polynesia who are left without their legitimate inheritance; a disappointed and bankrupt entrepreneur in France; an uncompensated artist in St. Louis), he highlights that deception has to be seen in terms of a moral concept that always involves value judgments. He claims that this moral dimension of (deception in) trade and exchange should be understood in light of a contemporary dilemma referred to as the "trader's dilemma" in recent economic anthropology. This dilemma is characteristic of a globalized world, where different ethical systems meet.

Marcel Hénaff analyses deception in relation to trust, which is still "the central question of our modern societies and constitutes for them the main way to relate to traditional ones." Drawing on original forms of gift exchange, he presents a broad argument on deception as a problem existing at the personal level of social interaction. As Hénaff's analysis of the ceremonial gift exchange shows, it is always the creation or refusal of trust that is at stake in interpersonal relationships. He reminds us of the frequency of breach and conflict in these relationships characterized by risk and uncertainty. While the establishment of the contract (and the law) in modern societies has reduced these risks, the problem of deception cannot be solved by these institutions and thus prevails. Hénaff argues that the problem consists in the fact that institutions cannot create trust. Trust is an experience and refers to interpersonal relations, where emotions (not subject to direct rational control) are crucial. He offers a contrasting perspective to the model of *homo economicus*, which accounts for deception in terms of a strategic option, contesting that trust is seen in terms of a risk that can be rationally calculated. He concludes that deceptive strategies may instead undermine the trust in terms of an emotional experience on which all trade and exchange is built.

Notes

1 At Enron, the case was set up by the company's CEOs, who made an attempt to misrepresent the company's financial condition with a view to benefiting from the high share price by cashing in their stock options. At WorldCom, executives hid costs and inflated profits and revenues in order to keep the good times rolling as the telecom world collapsed. At Tyco, CEOs were accused of looting their company of tens of millions of dollars.

2 At Deutsche Bank, the CEO was accused of having granted himself too high compensation in connection with the takeover of Mannesmann by Vodafone (*Frankfurter Allgemeine Zeitung*, 17 January 2004, No 14); at Libro (Austria), the CEO has been prosecuted (Himmelbauer, M. and Nikbakhsh, M. 2004, pp. 48–52). There are other similar cases.

3 They did so by issuing fraudulent research reports and initial public offerings to executives. Stock analysts allegedly issued overly rosy recommendations to win investment-banking business. They produced fraudulent research reports and IPO (initial public offerings to executives) "spinning." At Merrill Lynch the executives inflated the Internet stock bubble for their own benefit. The U.S. brokerage firm and its former star Internet analyst issued overly optimistic research reports about dot-com businesses to boost investment banking fees (BBC News 2002).

4 Mutual funds managers were charged with fraud because of illegal trading practices: "late trading" of the fund's shares after the official 4 p.m. deadline and "market timing" (such as the rapid trading in and out of the fund to exploit the difference in the fund's price and the fluctuating value of its underlying shares). Both practices gave insiders a trading advantage at the expense of millions of outsiders

who had entrusted their money to the funds. Market timing may not have been banned by law, but most funds had promised not to do it, and so were committing fraud when they did. Moreover, both practices breach the basic obligation of the fund manager to treat all their investors the same (*The Economist*, 8 November 2003, pp. 13–4).

5 Forty-seven traders were arrested and leading companies such as JP Morgan, UBS, Société Générale, Dresdner Kelinwort Wasserstein, and Israel Discount Bank were involved. They have been operating in this way for the last 30 years. There is no regulator or other control of foreign securities (Liebert 2003, p. 25).

6 The price system is seen as imperfect because prices do not aggregate and disseminate all bits of information.

7 Pooling equilibria are an exception to that rule, because in them, incentives to deceive exist. In pooling, cheats mimic signals of their honest rivals. However, the people who suffer from the mimicry are not the potential targets of deception, but those that may be imitated (Molho 1997, p. 78.)

8 The analysis of institutions has become intimately related with the analysis of transaction costs, such as costs that are incurred in the process of exchange, costs of the search for prices or trading partners, costs of contract negotiation and enforcement, and costs of breach (Landa 1994, p. 22). In this view, exchange is not considered free of charge (Coase 1937), as is the case with general equilibrium theory, and institutions are supposed to reduce transaction costs. In this approach, deception appears as a point of friction adding extra costs to exchange and therefore resulting in inefficiencies, such as market failures.

9 Spectators observing other agents gaining money by taking advantage of their partners learn quickly to lie and cheat.

10 Normative game theory analyzes the consequence of strategic behavior by super-rational players and is based on strong rationality principles. The common knowledge assumption underlies all of game theory and much of economic theory. The model itself must be assumed common knowledge, otherwise, it is insufficiently specified and the analysis incoherent. The basic task of game theory is to tell us what strategies rational players will follow and what expectations they can rationally entertain about other rational players'strategies. It is obvious that the theory of rationality should not be self-destroying; hence, in a society of people behaving according to the theory, there should be no incentive to deviate from it. In consequence, normative

theory has to prescribe the play of a Nash equilibrium (Van Damme referring to Aumann, Harsanyi, and Selten (1999, p. 185)

11 In order to guarantee coordination, such as the predictability of behavior, economic agents need to share common knowledge or have the same points of reference (such as shared rules, procedures, routines, and conventions).

12 It is worth noting here that in situations with some minimal positive probability, agents may also slightly err, hence playing bad moves, for example Selten's concept of trembles (Selten 1975).

13 According to Morton Davis, there is a pragmatic reason for "these unrealistic assumptions": it is much easier to point to distortions than to develop a general and systematic theory, which allows us to take advantage of these (Davis 1993, pp. 19–20). In their critical introduction to game theory, Hargreaves Heap et al. question the rationality concept implied here, because it requires that each person believes that neither will make a mistake in a game. He argues that everyone who has talked to good chess players will testify that rational persons pitted against equally rational opponents (whose rationality they respect) do not immediately assume that their opposition will never make errors. On the contrary, the point in chess is to engender such errors. With this argument, Hargreaves Heap et al., also emphasize the difference in approaches between real games and game theory. It resides in the fact that the former think it is "rational for players to think that they might outwit their opponent, in the sense that they act on a belief that their opponent thinks they will do something other than what they are going to do," while game theorists think that it is not. (Hargreaves Heap et al. 2002 [1995], pp. 57–8).

14 Fraudulent practices (such as opportunists pursuing their own self-interest) are potentially threatening to cooperation, resulting in the well-known social dilemma, in which no exchange takes place at all.

15 There are numerous departures from the self-interest postulate in modern economics putting the stress on so called "social preferences," such as altruism, fairness, and equity of distribution of resources, beyond ways that it increases total direct well being. People are also concerned about intentions and motives, and want to reciprocate the good and bad behavior of others (Rabin 1993, pp. 665ff).

16 According to Fehr and Gächter, people "take revenge even in interaction with complete strangers and even if it is costly for them

and yields neither present nor future material rewards" (Fehr and Gächter 2000, p. 159).

17 Fehr and Gächter refer to an environment in which people face strong material incentives to free ride, and – very much in contrast to the self-interest model that predicts no cooperation at all – reciprocal types punish free riders even when the punishment is costly for the punisher. As a consequence of the punishing behavior of the reciprocal types, a very high level of cooperation can in fact be achieved. According to Fehr and Gächter, "the power to enhance collective actions and to enforce social norms is probably one of the most important consequences of reciprocity" (Fehr and Gächter 2000, pp. 159–60).

18 Contradicting the classical approach where agents are supposed to be fully rational and markets efficient, they cast doubt on the validity of the efficient market hypotheses. According to the efficient markets theorists, professional investors may police the market so efficiently that they drive the prices of all issues to fully reflect all information that is "knowable" about the company, its industry, or the general economy. Agents trade financial assets only when their prices are going away from their equilibrium values, and by doing so, prices are pushed back to their fundamental levels. In this view, markets are rational and speculation is stabilizing.

19 Following Rabin (2002), in the future, the major task of behavioral economics will be to show the economic relevance of these insights and, in particular, to highlight the role of economic incentives and their impact on behavior.

20 According to Hamlin, motivational heterogeneity matters in an environment in which at least some of the individuals are influenced by normative concerns. Thus, the "intrinsic" values of honesty or trust should be admitted.

21 Anthropologists consider formal (such as property and contract) and informal institutions (such as norms, customs, mores, traditions, beliefs, and superstitions). While the former are accounted for by economists, the latter are regarded as given by most economists (see Williamson 2000).

22 Van der Grijp highlights that social inequality is present "at various levels within a society," such as, the relation between the sexes, age and kinship categories, classes, or between societies at the international level, such as the relations between Third World countries and the highly industrialized countries of the West.

References

Akerlof, G. A., 'The Market for "Lemons": Quality Uncertainty and the Market Mechanism' [1970]. Reprinted in G. A. Akerlof, *An Economic Theorist's Book of Tales* [1984] (Cambridge: Cambridge University Press, 1998), pp.7–22.

Akerlof, G. A., 'Introduction', in G. A. Akerlof, *An Economic Theorist's Book of Tales* [1984] (Cambridge: Cambridge University Press, 1998), pp. 1–6.

Arrow, K. A. and Debreu, G., 'Existence of an Equilibrium for a Competitive Economy', *Econometrica*, 22 (1954), 265–90.

Arrow, K. J., 'Economic Theory and the Hypothesis of Rationality', in J. Eatwell et al. (eds), *The New Palgrave: A Dictionary of Economics* (New York: The Stockton Press, 1987), pp. 69–74.

Aumann, R., 'Agreeing to Disagree', *Annals of Statistics*, 4 (1976), 1236–39.

Bailey, F. G., *The Prevalence of Deceit* (Ithaca: Cornell University Press, 1971).

BBC News, 'Enron at-a-glance', 22 August 2002 (http://news.bbc.co.uk/1/hi/business/1780075.stm).

Callon, M. (ed.), *The Laws of the Markets* (Oxford: Blackwell, 1998).

Camerer, C., 'Individual Decision Making', in J. H. Kagel and A. E. Roth (eds), *The Handbook of Experimental Economics* (Princeton, NJ: Princeton University Press, 1995), pp. 587–703.

Camerer, C., 'Behavioral Economics', *CSWEP Newsletter* (Winter 1999) (www.cswep.org/camerer.html).

Charness, G., 'Self-Serving Cheap Talk: A Test of Aumann's Conjecture', *Games and Economic Behavior*, 33/2 (2000), 177–94.

Coase, R. H., 'The Nature of the Firm', *Economica*, 4 (1937), 386–405.

Crawford, V. P., 'Lying for Strategic Advantage: Rational and Boundedly Rational Misrepresentation of Intentions', *American Economic Review*, 93/1 (2003), 133–49.

Darby, M. R. and Karni, E., 'Free Competition and the Optimal Amount of Fraud', *Journal of Law and Economics*, 16 (1973), 67–88.

Davis, M. D., *Spieltheorie für Nichtmathematiker* (Munich et al.: Oldenbourg Scientia Nova, 1993).

The Economist, 'Mutual Funds: Skimming' (8 November 2003), 13–4.

Fehr, E. and Falk, A., 'Joseph Schumpeter Lecture: Psychological Foundations of Incentives', *European Economic Review*, 46 (2002), 687–724.

Fehr, E. and Schmidt, K., 'A Theory of Fairness, Competition and Co-Operation', *Quarterly Journal of Economics*, 114 (1999), 769–816.

Fehr, E. and Gächter, S., 'Fairness and Retaliation: The Economics of Reciprocity', *Journal of Economic Perspectives*, 14/3 (2000), 159–81.

Festinger, L., *A Theory of Cognitive Dissonance* [1957] (Stanford, CA: Stanford University Press, 1966).

Forsythe, R., Lundholm, R., and Rietz, T., 'Cheap Talk, Fraud, and Adverse Selection in Financial Markets: Some Experimental Evidence', *Review of Financial Studies*, 12/3 (1999), 481–518.

Frankfurter Allgemeine Zeitung, 'Mannesmann-Prozeß' (No. 14, 17 January 2004) (www.faz.net/s/mannesmann).

Gerschlager, C. (ed.), *Expanding the Economic Concept of Exchange: Deception, Self-Deception and Illusions* (Boston, Dordrecht and London: Kluwer Academic Publishers, 2001).

Granovetter, M., 'Economic Action and Social Structure: The Problem of Embeddedness', *American Journal of Sociology*, 91/3 (1985), 481–510.

Godelier, Maurice, *La production des grands hommes* (Paris: Fayard, 1982).

Hargreaves Heap, S. P. and Varoufakis, Y., *Game Theory: A Critical Introduction* [1995] (London and New York: Routledge, 2002).

Harsanyi, J. C., *Rational Behaviour and Bargaining Equilibrium* (Cambridge: Cambridge University Press, 1977).

Himmelbauer, M. and Nikbakhsh, M., 'Der fliehende Holländer', *Profil* (9 February 2004), pp. 48–52.

Kahneman, D. and Tversky, A., 'Judgment under Uncertainty: Heuristics and Biases', *Science*, 185 (1974), 1124–31.

Kahneman, D. and Tversky, A., 'Prospect Theory: An Analysis of Decision under Risk', *Econometrica*, 47/2 (1979), 263–91.

Kahneman, D., Slovic, P. and Tversky, A., *Judgment under Uncertainty: Heuristics and Biases* (Cambridge and New York: Cambridge University Press, 1982).

Karni, E., 'Fraud', in J. Eatwell et al. (eds), *The New Palgrave: A Dictionary of Economics* (New York: The Stockton Press, 1987), pp. 416–17.

Katona, G., 'On the Function of Behavioral Theory and Behavioral Research in Economics', *American Economic Review*, 58/1 (1968a), 146–9.

Katona, G., 'Consumer Behavior: Theory and Findings on Expectations and Aspirations', *American Economic Review*, 58/2 (1968b), 19–30.

Katona, G., *Essays on Behavioral Economics* (Ann Arbor: Institute for Social Research, University of Michigan, 1980).

Kliemt, H., *Antagonistische Kooperation* (Freiburg and Munich: Verlag Karl Alber, 1986).

Laibson, D. and Zeckhauser, R., 'Amos Tversky and the Ascent of Behavioral Economics', *Journal of Risk and Uncertainty*, 16 (1998a), 4–47.

Laibson, D. I., Repetto, A. and Tobacman, J., 'Self-Control and Saving for Retirement', in *Brookings Papers on Economic Activity*, 1 (1998b), pp. 91–172.

Landa, J. T., *Trust, Ethnicity, and Identity: Beyond the New Institutional Economics of Ethnic Trading Networks, Contract Law, and Gift Exchange* (Ann Arbor: University of Michigan Press, 1994).

Liebert, N., 'Devisenhändlern drohen lange Haftstrafen', *Financial Times Deutschland* (21 November 2003), p. 25.

Loewenstein, G. and Adler, D. A., 'Bias in the Prediction of Tastes' [1995], in D. Kahneman and A. Tversky (eds), *Choices, Values, and Frames* (Cambridge, New York and Melbourne: Cambridge University Press; New York: Russell Sage Foundation, 2000a), pp. 726–34.

Loewenstein, G. and Prelec, D., 'Anomalies in Intertemporal Choice: Evidence and an Interpretation' [1992], in D. Kahneman and A. Tversky (eds), *Choices, Values, and Frames* (Cambridge, New York and Melbourne: Cambridge University Press; New York: Russell Sage Foundation, 2000b), pp. 578–96.

Mauss, M., 'Essai sur le don. Forme et raison de l'échange dans les sociétés archaïques', *L'année sociologique, nouvelle série*, 1 (1923/24), pp. 30–186.

Molho, I., *The Economics of Information: Lying and Cheating in Markets and Organizations* (Oxford: Blackwell, 1997).

Mullainathan, S. and Thaler, R. H., *Behavioral Economics*, NBER Working Paper 7948 (Cambridge, MA: NBER, 2000) (www.nber.org/papers/w7948.pdf).

Needham, R., *Belief, Language, and Experience* (Oxford: Blackwell, 1972).

Polanyi, K., *The Great Transformation* (New York: Rinehart & Co., 1944).

Polanyi, K., *Trade and Markets in the Early Empires*, ed. C. Arensberg and H. Pearson (New York: The Free Press, 1957).

Rabin, M., 'Alfred Marshall Lecture: A Perspective on Psychology and Economics', *European Economic Review*, 46 (2002), 657–85.

Rabin, M., 'Incorporating Fairness into Game Theory and Economics', *American Economic Review*, 83 (1993), 1281–302.

Rabin, M., 'Daniel Kahneman and Amos Tversky', in W. J. Samuels (ed.), *American Economists of the Late Twentieth-Century* (Cheltenham: Edward Elgar, 1996).

Rabin, M., 'Psychology and Economics', *Journal of Economic Literature*, 36 (1998), 11–46.

Sahlins, M., 'Poor Man, Rich Man, Big Man, Chief: Political Types in Melanesia and Polynesia', *Comparative Studies in Society and History*, 5 (1963), 285–303.

Sargent, T. J., *Bounded Rationality in Macroeconomics* (Oxford: Oxford University Press, 1993).

Selten, R., 'Re-examination of the Perfectless Concept for Equilibrium in Extensive Games', *International Journal of Game Theory*, Physica Verlag Vienna, 4 (1975), 22–5.

Simon, H. A., *Models of Bounded Rationality*, I and II (Cambridge, MA: MIT Press, 1982).

Thaler, R., *Quasi-Rational Economics* (New York: Russell Sage, 1991).

Thaler, R., *The Winner's Curse* (Princeton, NJ: Princeton University Press, 1992).

Tversky, A. and Kahneman, D., 'Rational Choice and the Framing of Decisions', in R. M. Hogarth and M. W. Reder (eds), *Rational Choice: The Contrast between Economics and Psychology* (Chicago, IL: University of Chicago Press, 1987), pp. 67–94.

Van Damme, E., 'Game Theory: The Next Stage', in A. Kirman et al. (eds), *Economics Beyond the Millennium* (Oxford: Oxford University Press, 1999), pp. 184–214.

White, G. M. and Lindstrom, L. (eds), *Chiefs Today: Traditional Pacific Leadership and the Postcolonial State* (Stanford, CA: Stanford University Press, 1997).

Williamson, O. E., *The Economic Institutions of Capitalism: Firms, Markets, Relational Contracting* (London: The Free Press and Macmillan, 1985).

Williamson, O. E., 'The New Institutional Economics: Taking Stock, Looking Ahead', *Journal of Economic Literature*, 38 (2000), 595–613.

Part I

The Rationality of Deception

1

Deception and Game Theory*

S. Abu Turab Rizvi

Abstract

Because game theory deals with differences in information, knowledge, and belief among people as they interact, it seems ideally suited to address matters involving deception. The purpose of this chapter is to see if this intuition is justified. The conclusion is that it is not. The main impediment is an inconsistency between what is required to show that game theory models have equilibria (widely available knowledge, for example) and what deception rests on (privately held knowledge). There are also difficulties in game theory models in establishing equilibria that allow for deception to take place. It seems that game theory is not, in its present state, able to offer a good way to study deception.

Introduction

In order for deception to take place, there must be differences in belief; or, there might be differences in one person's knowledge of something and another's belief of that thing. So if I am a cheat and believe I am one, I might portray myself as fair and honest. For you to be deceived by my dissembling, you have to believe I am fair and honest. Thus, my deception is based on differences in your belief and mine about my fairness.

Deception therefore concerns matters such as information, knowledge, evidence, and belief. Because there is a deceiver and others who are deceived, deception also involves interactions that are likely to be strategic in nature. Since game theory addresses all of these matters, it can be seen as a natural way to illuminate issues of deception.

To look into this matter, we need to arrive at a definition of deception in a strategic setting. What is best for each player typically will depend on the actions of the others. Since all aspects of the game might not be transparent, and players might well have different knowledge of the game and of each other's motivations, the possibility arises that players will deceive one another in order to gain an advantage. Deception then involves a player causing another to accept as true or valid what is false or invalid in an attempt to gain the upper hand.

In 1921, Émile Borel began mathematical investigations in game theory (Fréchet 1953). He used poker as an example and discussed bluffing and outguessing the opponent in a game of imperfect information. Poker involves imperfect information since each player only knows her own hand. Chess, on the other hand, involves perfect information since all relevant game details are known to both players. Bluffing in poker, which involves playing as if you have a hand that you do not, clearly involves deception. Poker was also an inspiration to von Neumann when he proved the minimax theorem (von Neumann 1928). Von Neumann wanted to formalize the concept of bluffing and did so. In fact, the optimal strategy for poker was eventually demonstrated and it indeed involved bluffing (Cutler 1975; see Binmore 1990, pp. 96–103). However, actual poker players do not use this strategy, since it is safe to assume that your opponent will deviate from the predictions of game theory, and so you should also deviate from the "optimal" strategy. Indeed, many aspects of the strategy seem odd to seasoned poker players (Rizvi 1994, p. 13). Because of this situation, what has occurred in game theory more recently is a concentration on when it makes sense to play a "rational" or "optimal" strategy. This thought has led to an investigation of the epistemic or knowledge assumptions that players make of each other. Here we can see that what at first glance seems to be a straightforward application of game theory to the problem of deception – bluffing in parlor games – becomes quite complicated and leads to a discussion of knowledge assumptions.

Before discussing these knowledge assumptions (in the next sections), it is worth stressing that, for economics, the cited example of poker is quite relevant. There are many important situations, falling under the heading of information economics (Stiglitz 1985), that represent games of imperfect information, and in that sense are akin to poker: insurance and moral hazard (since the insurer and the insured will have differing knowledge of the insured person's chance of collecting insurance); principal-agent problems (in which, for example, a supervisor and a worker have differing knowledge of the worker's diligence at the job); and auctions and negotiations (where different bidders or agents have very uneven knowledge about each others' range of acceptable bids or offers). Situations involving only buying and selling, or pure exchange, may also be analyzed as falling under information economics. For instance, the seller of a used car has more knowledge of its quality than does a buyer (Akerlof 1970). (The pure exchange case untainted by information asymmetries is one in which buyers and sellers have perfect information.) In all of these situations involving asymmetric information, it is insufficient to demonstrate that a game-theoretic solution exists, just as it is insufficient in the case of poker. The solution will not be used unless it can be shown that it makes sense to use it. We need to investigate the conditions under which agents will actually want to use game theoretic prescriptions in situations of imperfect information.

Game theory makes significant assumptions about the rationality and knowledge of players. Because of these assumptions, I will argue that it is quite difficult for game theoretic models to encompass deception, precisely because it is hard for them to treat differences in belief, which as we have seen, are necessary for deception to take place. There are also other difficulties, such as equilibria that do not involve deception or non-existence of any equilibrium. I begin with a discussion of models with asymmetric information, particularly those having to do with signaling and screening. This introduces us to some of the issues involved. At this point, I do not explicitly consider knowledge issues, but focus on whether the models can encompass deception on their own terms. I then turn to issues of knowledge for the rest of the chapter, specifically exploring what sort of knowledge is important to the establishment of game theoretic solutions. At that point, I introduce the notions of mutual and common knowledge. It happens that common knowledge under certain circumstances also implies that players cannot end up with differences in belief. This is Aumann's agreeing to disagree result. I then discuss whether the premises of Aumann's result should be questioned, and whether this allows for a place for deception in game theory after all.

As the reader can tell already, the purpose of this investigation is circumscribed: it does not cover many of the areas of intersection between deception and game theory that would be possible to consider. However, this focus highlights a fundamental question: is it possible to encompass deception in game theory models?

Asymmetric information: signaling and screening games

There is a class of game theory models that seems to have deception at its crux. These are games involving asymmetric information: for example, games that deal with adverse selection, signaling, and screening. As we just saw, with asymmetric information, buyers and sellers do not have complete information about the characteristics of commodities.

Specifically, either the buyer or the seller has more or better information. In the presence of asymmetric information, market equilibria will tend to be inefficient. The tendency toward inefficiency is exacerbated by adverse selection. Adverse selection occurs when an agent's privately held information makes his behavior worse for uninformed agents. Thus, an insured individual is more likely to want insurance coverage when she knows she will use it. Or, if someone knows his car is not of high quality, he is more likely to bring it to market. Adverse selection may lead markets to function very poorly, or to work not at all, even when buyers want to buy and sellers want to sell.

Given this situation, informed agents may want to signal to uninformed agents that they have certain information through observable actions. Thus, an agent might acquire an education available only, or more easily, to skilled workers to signal publicly what she already knows about her skill but which is otherwise unobservable. By this means, the worker tries to overcome the problems arising from the informational asymmetry; in particular, she distinguishes herself from workers of lesser ability. In a similar way, the uninformed party may want to distinguish the characteristics of agents with different individuals by screening. A possibility for the insurance company is to offer two policies, one with no deductible but a high premium, the other with a high deductible but a low premium. Those wanting insurance sort or self-select, with high-risk individuals opting for a no-deductible policy and low-risk individuals choosing the high-deductible policy.

The original investigations of models with asymmetric information were published in the 1970s (Akerlof 1970, Rothschild and Stiglitz 1976, Spence 1973, Wilson 1977). Since the issues in markets with asymmetric information involve strategic interaction between at least two agents, economists continued to develop game-theoretic models involving asymmetric information. Some of the important papers are Kreps and Wilson (1982b) and Milgrom and Roberts (1982b). Points that are relevant to deception arise in signaling and screening games and we turn to these next, relying on the exposition of Mas-Colell, Whinston and Green (1995, ch. 13).[1]

To study signaling, we might consider a situation where workers may choose to demonstrate that they are of high quality by acquiring more education, where both the average and marginal cost of education are lower for high-ability workers. This cost assumption is based on the idea that acquiring education is easier for a high-ability worker. A random move of nature determines which workers are high quality and which are low quality. Next, they choose how much education to acquire, and then enter the job market. Firms observe the levels of education and make offers to workers. The workers then decide whether to work and for which firm, whereupon the game ends. In the exposition of Mas-Colell, Whinston and Green (1995), the equilibrium concept employed is one of weak perfect Bayesian equilibrium with an added condition that firms have common beliefs about each other's wage offers. (We will return to this assumption about beliefs.) In this setting, there are two types of equilibria that might arise: separating equilibria, in which the two types of workers choose different levels of education and pooling equilibria, in which they choose the same levels of education. From the point of view of deception, we can characterize these two sorts of equilibria in another way. In a separating equilibrium, deception is not possible because the high-ability workers get a higher wage than the low-ability workers (given the lower cost of education for high-ability workers, they are more willing to acquire education for a given wage increase). The two sorts of workers are distinct and cannot be confused with one another. In a pooling equilibrium, on the other hand, the two sorts of workers cannot be distinguished because their observable characteristics (levels of education) are the same. In our initial look at deception in game theory, then, the possibility of deception rests with the existence of pooling equilibria. It happens that in a signaling model, both separating and pooling equilibria may arise, suggesting that deception is possible in a game theoretic model of asymmetric information.

However, there are complications concerning the pooling equilibria. High-ability workers do not want to deceive. They would like to take measures, in fact, that allow clearer knowledge of their true status. It is the low-ability workers who have an advantage in keeping their low-ability status unobserved. They indeed will earn more in a pooling equilibrium than in a separating equilibrium. How much they and the high-ability workers will earn, though, is not determined. This is because a wide range of equilibria is possible as solutions to the model. "As we have seen, we can have separating equilibria in which firms learn the worker's type, but can also have pooling equilibria where they do not; and within each type of equilibrium, many different equilibrium levels of education can arise. In large part, this multiplicity stems from the great freedom that we have to choose beliefs off the equilibrium path. Recently, a great deal of research has investigated the implications of putting 'reasonable' restrictions on such beliefs..." (Mas-Colell, Whinston, Green 1995, p. 457). In other words, as has been common in game theory, an approach to multiple equilibria is to use various criteria to "refine" the equilibria and thus to select a unique equilibrium or, at least, a smaller group of equilibria. One reason to do this is that multiple equilibria, besides not being able to give us a crisp prediction as to the outcome of the model, are particularly problematic in an interactive setting. If there is more than one equilibrium, what is to prevent a player from playing a strategy according to one equilibrium, only to have the other players playing strategies according to another? In other words, there is a problem of coordinating play so that players choose the same equilibrium when there is more than one equilibrium to begin with. Finding a set of multiple equilibria is not enough.

As Mas-Collel, Whinston and Green suggest, part of the problem seems to be the freedom in the model to choose the beliefs of firms. Perhaps there are more reasonable beliefs that might generate different outcomes. One particularly influential refinement employed in this setting is the one discussed by Cho and Kreps (1987). If there are two types of workers, Cho and Kreps showed that according to their "intuitive" criterion on beliefs, there would be a unique outcome to the signaling model, one that ruled out all pooling equilibria; in fact, only the separating equilibrium with the least amount of costly signaling survives. If there are three or more worker types, other, stronger, refinements can yield a similar outcome (Fudenberg and Tirole 1992, pp. 446–60).

What should we make of this situation? We can see that signaling models, while they allow for pooling equilibria and the possibility of deception, are intuitively problematic since they have a plethora of equilibria. When a refinement of reasonable beliefs is applied to the model, the pooling equilibria are ruled out and with them, the possibility of deception. Whether we agree with the intuitive criterion of Cho and Kreps,[2] it is clear that pooling equilibria in signaling models present problems. Either we have multiple pooling equilibria, which are intuitively problematic, or we use a plausible refinement that rules them out. To the extent that other approaches are possible, we get widely different predictions based on minor changes in modeling choices.

The difficulties in game theoretic models of asymmetric information persist and deepen in treatments of screening. In screening models, the uninformed party tries to distinguish between individuals. Rothschild and Stiglitz (1976) and Wilson (1977) studied this possibility in the context of insurance markets, but here (again following Mas-Colell, Whinston and Green 1995) we consider a labor market. We can study the subgame-perfect Nash equilibria of a two-stage game. Two firms announce offers of work. In the second stage, workers decide which contract to accept, if any. As in the signaling game, there is the possibility of separating outcomes (where the two types of workers select different contracts) and pooling outcomes (where all workers choose the same contract). A key result is that if equilibria exist, there will be no pooling equilibria. In other words, in the important class of screening games, deception – in the sense that workers are indistinguishable by their observable choices – is not possible. It further turns out, though, that for a significant range of parameter values, even a separating equilibrium may not exist (Mas-Colell, Whinston and Green 1995, p. 465).

Given this review of game theoretic models with asymmetric information, we are left with little support for the idea that they handle deception convincingly. The possibility of deception rests with pooling equilibria. In the screening models we reviewed, pooling equilibria do not arise. Moreover, equilibrium existence is also problematic. In signaling models, there are multiple equilibria which, when a plausible refinement is applied, reduce to a separating equilibrium, again ruling out pooling. If other modeling choices are used, we are left with the fragility of game theoretic predictions: the model predictions are very sensitive to the precise specification of modeling details. If we maintain a focus on multiple equilibria, we are left with an intuitively implausible situation since it is unclear how participants should play in that setting. We might conclude that deception is not handled well in what might be considered the promising setting of asymmetric information games. Yet we considered this class of models explicitly because they seemed to be promising vehicles for incorporating deception.[3]

We can now turn to somewhat more fundamental issues regarding games and deception, those having to do with the knowledge requirements of players. In our discussion of games with asymmetric information, these issues were left in the background. Yet we would like to determine what players need to know to find equilibrium and whether they need to know so much that deception is not possible. We can begin with a discussion of mutual and common knowledge.

Knowledge and game theoretic solutions

Mutual knowledge differs from common knowledge. Something is *mutual knowledge* for a group of people if everyone in the group knows that thing. But mutual knowledge does not say anything about what knowledge anyone in the group attributes to others. Since game theory seems to involve just this figuring out of what others know, mutual knowledge might be seen to be insufficient to address the concerns of ratiocination in game theory. If mutual knowledge extends to infinitely many tiers (each knows that each knows – and so on, *ad infinitum* – that each knows something), then we have *common knowledge*.

Common knowledge has an interesting history (Vanderschraaf 1999). David Hume, in *A Treatise of Human Nature*, related mutual knowledge and convention. He argued that members of a society need to know what to expect from one another in order for conventions to be upheld. Thus, Hume held that the structure of knowledge in a society could sustain important conventions. More than 200 years later, it was also in a treatment of convention that the philosopher David Lewis first gave a formal treatment of common knowledge (Lewis 1969). Prior to this work, J. E. Littlewood, the mathematician, had discussed some situations involving common knowledge (Littlewood 1953), and both Thomas Schelling (1960) and John Harsanyi (1967; 1968) argued that something similar to common knowledge is needed to say why people in strategic settings can figure out what others are thinking. Following on Lewis's work on convention, Stephen Schiffer (1972), a philosopher, and Robert Aumann (1976), a mathematician, gave other formalizations of common knowledge. Schiffer employed a system of epistemic logic adapted to use knowledge operators (which say someone knows something); he then defined common knowledge within this expanded logical system. Aumann gave an alternative set-theoretic definition of common knowledge, which I will discuss later on. However, these two approaches are equivalent (Fagin, Halpern, Moses and Vardi 1995).

Game theorists have explored in detail how knowledge and game theoretic solutions are related. Bernheim (1984) and Pearce (1984) considered the consequences of knowledge of rationality. Aumann and Brandenburger (1995) studied the relation between knowledge and Nash equilibrium. Investigations by Armbruster and Boge (1979), Boge and Eisele (1979), Bonanno and Nehring (1999), Mertens and Zamir (1985), Nehring (2001), Samet (1999; 2000), and Tan and Werlang (1988) contributed to this literature. Brandenburger (1992), Bicchieri (1993), Dekel and Gul (1997) and Battigali and Bonnano (1999) survey work in this area. With these investigations as background, we can now turn to the relation between knowledge and game theoretic solution concepts. What knowledge assumptions are needed to find a solution to a game?

In this section we will be concerned with games in normal form. On the other hand, games that involve players moving sequentially and can be represented as a tree with decision nodes are games in extensive form. For many purposes generally, and for many purposes having to do with deception, an extensive form game is appropriate. So, for example, it might be important to study when actions by players reveal information in a study of deception. Thus, a word on these games seems appropriate here. One way to solve such finite games with perfect information is to use backward induction, by looking at the best choice of the last mover, and working backwards to see what the first move should be. Selten introduced this method in his definition of subgame-perfect equilibrium.

This framework, though very simple, continues to arouse controversy. Researchers differ on the relation between rationality and the backward induction method and the equilibrium based on it. For some (for example, Aumann, 1995), common knowledge of rationality is held to be a consistent concept in this setting and one that implies the backward induction solution. Others disagree. They argue that common knowledge of rationality does not imply backward induction or that common knowledge of rationality is not a coherent or non-contradictory term in this setting (Reny 1987; 1992; Basu 1988; 1990; Binmore 1987; Bicchieri 1989; 1993; Rizvi 1994). What this means is that there is no established theory of sequential rationality.[4] On the most optimistic account, such a theory will at least involve common knowledge of rationality and likely further assumptions. On a more pessimistic account, rationality itself is not defined in such games. We might note that the screening games we reviewed, for example, involve subgame perfection. In general, most models of asymmetric information are sequential in nature.

Thus these difficulties with games in extensive form are a problem for the study of deception. We can turn to other issues as well, where more consensus has been achieved. We might want to answer several questions. Are problems only there for extensive form games? What does common knowledge of rationality imply? What assumptions are needed for Nash equilibrium?

For some time, game theorists identified the epistemic requirements for Nash equilibrium to entail or to be closely related to common knowledge, as Aumann and Brandenburger (1995) point out. Thus, Kreps and Wilson wrote, "An equilibrium in Nash's sense supposes that strategies are 'common knowledge' among the players" (1982a, p. 885). Similarly, Milgrom and Roberts wrote that they are troubled that in games of strategy "the equilibrium is common knowledge" (1991, p. 82). This seemed to make sense. In Nash equilibrium, a player plays the equilibrium strategy because the other does, the other does because the first does, and so on. Brandenburger and Dekel (1989) demonstrated a result along these lines. It turns out, however, that while common knowledge is involved, Nash equilibrium is not tied to common knowledge in a straightforward manner.

But let us begin with common knowledge of rationality rather than Nash equilibrium.[5] To proceed, we need to introduce the concept of iterated deletion of dominated strategies. A strategy is dominated if, regardless of what others do, it earns a smaller payoff than some other strategy. Once a dominated stragey has been eliminated from the game, players can review the resulting sub-game, and seek to eliminate further dominated strategies, continuing until, perhaps, only one strategy profile remains. But there is no guarantee that any strategies can be eliminated from a game in this manner, or that a unique outcome result will be found.

Nevertheless, the important result here is that if there is common knowledge of rationality, players will choose strategies that survive the iterated deletion of dominated strategies. The justification is along the following lines. If players know they and other players are rational, they know that dominated strategies, if present, will not be chosen, since this would make players worse off. After this first round of deletion of dominated strategies, players will again not play any strategies that are dominated, giving two rounds of deletion. If players know that they know they are all rational, they will again not choose the dominated strategies that remain, giving three rounds of deletion. If we continue this process, we get the result that common knowledge of rationality leaves players with those strategies that survive iterated deletion.

This is not all. It turns out that there are no strategies beyond these that can be eliminated by common knowledge of rationality. Thus, common knowledge of rationality and iterated deletion of dominated strategies are closely connected. If players have common knowledge of rationality, we know they will choose a strategy that survives iterated deletion. And, if all we know is that players have common knowledge of rationality, this is all we can say.

There may be no strategies in a game that are dominated, and even if there are, the iterative process may not yield a unique equilibrium. In other words, this is a weak solution concept and so it seems that common knowledge of rationality does not imply much. Nash equilibrium is a stronger concept. Nash equilibrium is a set of strategies such that each player's strategy is optimal for the player, given the strategies of the others. All Nash equilibria survive deletion of dominated strategies, but there may be strategy choices that survive iterated deletion that are not Nash equilibria. With this in mind, we can turn to the knowledge requirements for Nash equilibrium, and the key investigation of Aumann and Brandenburger (1995). They identify the knowledge assumptions needed to underpin the idea of Nash equilibrium. Let us begin with an observation (Aumann and Brandenburger 1995, p. 1161, whose discussion I follow in this paragraph). Suppose each player is rational, knows his or her payoff function, and knows the strategies chosen by others; then the players' choices of strategies will constitute Nash equilibrium. This follows from, or is nearly identical to, the definition of Nash equilibrium. Only mutual knowledge of strategy choices and of rationality, without a need for others to know that each knows strategies chosen (or for any higher level of knowledge) needs to be assumed. Thus, common knowledge (the idea that all players know, all know that all know, and so on forever) need not be assumed. This is true of pure strategy equilibrium, but Nash equilibrium need not exist in pure strategies for finite games. It is also true of mixed strategies, for which Nash equilibrium exists in finite games, as long as they are interpreted as conscious random choices of strategies. This result follows very closely from the definition of Nash equilibrium, so much so that, because mutual knowledge of payoffs is assumed, and other players' strategies are known, there is also mutual knowledge of the strategies forming the Nash equilibrium. Thus, one way of saying this is that each player knows the Nash equilibrium.

Yet common knowledge makes its appearance in another way, having to do with mixed strategies. Since few people choose consciously to randomize, the use of mixed strategies has been problematic, whatever its convenience in allowing solutions to be demonstrated. It is also troubling conceptually. Players have no incentive to choose mixed strategies. They never gain by randomizing since they get the same expected payoff in a mixed strategy equilibrium that they would have had they chosen one of the pure strategies over which they are randomizing. Given this, and following a suggestion by Harsanyi, an alternative interpretation of mixed strategies has arisen, one in which the probabilities refer to the conjectures players make about the choices of others, and those choices are actions that are not randomly chosen (Harsanyi 1973). In this setting of a mixed-strategy Nash equilibrium involving conjectures, when there are more than two players, knowledge requirements increase. Other players must have the same assessment about what a given player will do. Conditions that guarantee this are that players have a common prior (an assumption that is discussed below) and that their conjectures are common knowledge (Aumann and Brandenburger 1995).

We have now considered the knowledge requirements for the most popular solution concept in game theory, Nash equilibrium. With a view to studying deception, the results are not encouraging. Even if we consider just pure strategy equilibria, which are not guaranteed to exist, players need mutual knowledge of each other's rationality and strategies. It is difficult to see the possibility of deception if we assume that players know each other's strategy choices and that they are rational. What is left to hide? More deeply, it is difficult to understand how players come to acquire this knowledge. Even if there were common knowledge of rationality, we know that this would only imply that iteratively dominated strategies would not be played, and this does not generally leave us with a unique strategy. We thus really have no basis for thinking that players will know each other's strategies. When we move to the conjectural equilibrium interpretation of mixed strategies, in the general case of more than two players, we need to assume common knowledge of conjectures, a yet more dubious assumption (and also that players have a common prior).

In the two cases we have covered – strategies that survive iterated deletion of dominated strategies and Nash equilibria – our understanding of the necessary knowledge assumptions seems fairly complete. In general, we need to rely on common knowledge (of rationality or conjectures) for these cases. We began the section with a review of the situation with extensive form games involving backward induction, which are not as well understood. Yet even here, in the best scenario (Aumann's), we need to assume common knowledge of rationality. Alternatively, rationality is not well defined in this setting. So in general, for all of these situations, common knowledge seems needed in order to guarantee equilibrium solutions. Even where we can assume mutual knowledge is sufficient, for example, in cases where we can demonstrate that there is Nash equilibrium in pure strategies, it seems incongruous (especially if we are to study deception) to have players whose knowledge extends to knowing others' strategy choices as a matter of course. We now turn to the importance of privately held information.

Impossibility of agreeing to disagree

It has long been thought, and intuitively makes sense, that differences in information – information that is privately held – leads to differences in belief and therefore in behavior. Buyers and sellers have different information about the product being sold, for example.

In our own case, the deceiver and the person being deceived have different beliefs about the deceiver's straightforwardness: this is because the deceiver knows better and the person being deceived does not know any better. Asymmetric information is, of course, the cornerstone of a large body of work in economics, for which the Nobel Prize was awarded in 2001. However, in well-defined circumstances, this intuition – that privately held information leads to differences in belief – proves to be ill founded. This result, known as the impossibility of agreeing to disagree, was established by Aumann (1976).

Aumann's approach to common knowledge, as we have seen, was based on set theoretic notions rather than on systems of logic. Here is how he proceeds There are possible *states of the world* and one of them will actually occur. Thus it may rain tomorrow, be cloudy without rain, or it may be sunny; only one of these eventualities will actually take place.

These states of the world form a set, which can be partitioned into mutually exhaustive and exclusive subsets. An *information partition* for a person is used frequently in the economics of information. An information partition shows subsets of the states of the world such that the person knows which of the subsets contain the true state, but might not know which among the states in a particular subset is true. For example, you might believe that it will rain or be cloudy without rain tomorrow, and assign no likelihood to its being sunny. But you cannot say within the subset, {rain, cloudy without rain}, which of the components will actually transpire. This confusion may actually occur due to differences in perception. So if you are indoors, you might be able to see that it is not sunny, but you might not be able to tell if it is just cloudy, or if rain is also falling.

The example shown in the following figure can be used to appreciate the intuition behind Aumann's result (Nau 2001).

State	*a*	*b*	*c*	*d*	*e*	*f*
Prior Prob.	0.1	0.15	0.2	0.1	0.15	0.3
Ann's Partition	------------------		------------------		------------------	
Bob's Partition	-------	-------	-------------------------------------			
Meet	------------------		-------------------------------------			
A's P (E | Info)	0	0	0.33	0.33	0.33	0.33
B's P (E | Info)	0	0	0.33	0.33	0.33	0.33

Suppose there are six states, indicated by the letters *a* through *f*. Ann has the information partition {*a*, *b*}, {*c*, *d*}, and {*e*, *f*}. Thus, if state *a* or *b* actually occurs, Ann knows that one of them has occurred but can not say which one. Similarly, she cannot distinguish between states *c* or *d*, or between states *e* or *f*. Bob's information partition is {*a*}, {*b*}, and {*c*, *d*, *e*, *f*}. In this case, if state *a* or *b* occur, Bob can say exactly which state has occurred, but cannot distinguish among states *c* through *f*.

Information partitions model what agents know. They can be used to show common knowledge. Aumann realized that an event is common knowledge at a particular state if it is contained in the element of the *meet* that contains that state. The meet is the *finest common coarsening* of the players' information partitions: the smallest information partition that is as large as the largest individual information partition. In the example, the meet of Ann's and Bob's information partitions is {*a*, *b*}, {*c*, *d*, *e*, *f*}. It is common knowledge that either state *a* or *b* has occurred if one of them actually occurs. Only Bob knows for sure which one has occurred, however. It is also common knowledge that one of the states *c*, *d*, *e*, or *f* has occurred if one of them actually occurs; Ann additionally knows whether the actual state is *c* or *d* or if it is *e* or *f*.

In demonstrating his result, Aumann additionally supposes that agents begin with a common prior distribution over the states of the world. This *common prior assumption* (CPA) was introduced into the economics literature by Harsanyi (1967; 1968). Even though agents begin with common priors, they will later receive different information as indicated by their information partitions. When they learn about other players holding different beliefs, each person will update personal probabilities according to Bayes's Theorem. Since information partitions are assumed to be common knowledge, agents know each other's posterior distributions over the states of the world. So the posterior probabilities of agents can be common knowledge for events that contain a state that actually occurs. This implies that every agent's posterior probability for this event must be constant (and, for that matter, the same) for the part of the meet that contains the actual state.[6]

This can be seen using the example we considered. Ann and Bob both have common prior probabilities, {0.1, 0.15, 0.2, 0.1, 0.15, 0.3}, for states *a* through *f* respectively. Perhaps the event they are interested in is E = {*d*, *e*}, which occurs if either *d* or *e* occurs. First, suppose *c* or *d* actually occurs. Then Ann knows (judging from her information partition) that state *c* or *d* occurred but not which one. E will be true only in the event that *d* has occurred. Ann can compute the posterior probability of this possibility: 0.1/(0.1 + 0.2) = 0.33, which is the probability that state *d* has occurred divided by the probability that either state *c* or *d* has occurred. Next, suppose that state *e* or *f* actually occurs. Then E will be true if state *e* occurs. Ann's posterior probability for E is then the probability that state *e* has occurred divided by the probability that either state *e* or *f* has occurred: 0.15/(0.15 + 0.3) = 0.33. Thus, Ann's posterior probability for E is the same no matter which of the four states, *c*, *d*, *e*, or *f*, has occurred. These probabilities incorporate the information contained in her information partition.

Bob's situation is a little less complicated since he knows less about states *c*, *d*, *e*, and *f*. If one of these states occurs, his posterior probability for E is the probability that either *d* or *e* occurs divided by the probability that one of them occurs: (0.1 + 0.15)/(0.2 + 0.1 + 0.15 + 0.3) = 0.33. Since {*c*, *d*, *e*, *f*} is part of the meet, the players' posterior probabilities are common knowledge if one of these states has occurred; this is not an assumption but is rather a consequence of the other assumptions. In the example, Ann and Bob's posterior probabilities for E are calculated to be the same. Aumann proved that this will always be the case.

What leads to this situation? By acting on the basis of differentially held information, agents reveal this information, leading others to revise their beliefs. This process ends with posterior beliefs being the same, as long as players seek to take advantage of their information. As a consequence of this dynamic, if agents begin with a common prior distribution, then having differential information held privately does not lead to different posterior probabilities and agents cannot agree to disagree about the probability of events. It is true that if agents choose not to act on their privately held information, beliefs can differ. But then nobody is using deception to gain an advantage on the basis of that information.

This is an important result. We have seen that the validity of game theoretic solutions may depend sensitively on common knowledge. Thus in the game settings for which this is true, if Aumann's assumptions are accepted and agents become aware of information differences, you cannot have agents disagreeing even if they have different information.[7] The implications for information economics are profound. Most models with asymmetric information are thereby affected. Startling among the applications of this result are the no-trade theorems. They assert that new information cannot induce trade between rational agents, even in the presence of asymmetric information (Milgrom and Stokey 1982). As soon as it is public information that agents wish to trade, their probabilities for the value of the asset in question are recalculated and become the same, negating the basis for trade. This is indeed a startling result since it is a common intuition that exchange, for example in speculative assets, occurs precisely because buyers and sellers have heterogeneous beliefs about the worth of what is being transacted. Many other authors, whose papers do not invoke the CPA, have buttressed Milgrom and Stokey's investigations (Bacharach 1985, McKelvey and Page 1986, and Dow, Madrigal and Werlang 1990).

The result is also important for our concern with deception. Recall that deception depends on heterogeneity of beliefs: the deceiver and the person being deceived have different beliefs about the deceiver's honesty. Moreover, deception can work because the two parties have differing amounts of information. Game theory, particularly its asymmetric information variant, seems to be a natural way to understand deception since games involve strategy. Yet, as we have seen, solutions for games often involve common knowledge assumptions, or other assumptions that are similar. When common knowledge is assumed, and agents reveal information by acting on this basis, Aumann has shown that posterior beliefs will be the same and that agents cannot agree to disagree. Plainly, this means that deception cannot occur in these settings. This is not to say that deception does not occur; just that it cannot be encompassed in such a game theoretic model.

Of course, Aumann's result is based on assumptions and, in order to test the robustness of the conclusion just reached, we need to examine these. Perhaps the assumptions are doubtful and game theory can incorporate deception after all.

Common priors

Aumann's theorem is based on two assumptions: (1) common knowledge of information partitions, and (2) the common prior assumption (CPA) that agents have the same probability distribution regarding states of the world before they receive information. Aumann defends the first assumption on the procedural grounds that it is always possible to define states of the world in such a way that the assumption will be correct. But, substantively, what matters is what agents believe their and others' information partitions to be. Many economists have argued that the first assumption can be defended since public events in a society are common knowledge. If something is published on the front page of the *Wall Street Journal*, and all speculators read it, then that event will be common knowledge for them. Economic variables such as prices will tend to be commonly known for this reason, it is argued. Note that this defense puts emphasis on public rather than private information. Yet more controversy attends the CPA.

There are basically two arguments in favor of the CPA: one is a defense as a positive description of agents' belief formation, and the other is based on convenience for modeling.[8] Aumann, and Harsanyi before him (referring to Savage), has argued that prior to receiving information, agents should have the same beliefs. Thus, someone does not think that stock prices will rise just because she is an optimistic person, but because she has some information that gives her reason to think that way. Once differential information comes in, agents will form different beliefs. But prior to information, beliefs are best treated as being the same. Another way of thinking about this is that if agents have the same information, they will have the same beliefs, but as soon as information is available privately and differs, their beliefs will diverge. The controversy over this defense surrounds the artificiality of the thought experiment. Faruk Gul (1998) has recently been forthright in attacking the CPA for this very reason. For people receive different information throughout their lives and there is no reason to think that there is a coordinated moment in the lives of any group of agents where they are empty vessels waiting to receive information. Aumann (1998) has replied that game theory is replete with instances of thought experiments used to justify its constructs. Indeed, Nash equilibrium is often justified this way. Additionally, there are many constructs outside of game theory proper in economics that are similarly hard to justify and they are used all of the time. Given preferences in microeconomics would be one of many examples. Aumann adds that people who do not like the CPA are free not to use it. And this brings us to the convenience argument.

There are not very many deviations from the CPA in the formal literature on information economics. Harsanyi (1967; 1968) introduced the CPA precisely because he wanted to model situations where agents are differentially informed but have beliefs that are consistent in some manner. Prior to Harsanyi's work, economists had to assume that agents knew each other's utility functions. Harsanyi's model allowed for uncertainty concerning these functions. The situations that result, with incomplete information, have had numerous applications in game theory. But this complication led to a difficulty that was resolved by Harsanyi by further assumptions. In what is now a common approach, Harsanyi limited uncertainty over utility functions by allowing for a number of types of utility functions (see also Mertens and Zamir 1985). This set of types was common knowledge, just as information partitions are for Aumann. Also, beliefs had to be made consistent in order for players to reason about each others' behavior. Thus, Ann and Bob are uncertain about each others' types, but Ann's beliefs about what Bob believes about her type, given his own type, should be consistent with what he really believes, and so on. Harsanyi assumed that agents have the same distribution over types from which a posterior distribution for each player concerning the types of others can be arrived at by conditioning on her own type. This is, of course, the CPA that Harsanyi invoked. Then the equilibrium is one of the strategies chosen by types of players.

This framework has been used in hundreds of applications of game theory to situations of incomplete information (Aumann and Heifetz 2001, Ausubel, Cramton and Deneckere 2001). Consequently, while there are examples of consistent beliefs that do not use the CPA (one is given in Gul 1998), it is fair to say that the CPA is used extensively and nearly exclusively in game theory models with incomplete information. Consequently, a fair amount of its appeal rests on grounds that it is convenient to use – that it allows the enterprise to move forward. In its absence, there are serious tractability problems. Thus, returning to our case, while it is strictly possible to dispense with the CPA, it is a quite different task to construct an analysis of deception or any other situation of incomplete information without it. That would seem to be quite daunting since not only are the "agreeing to disagree" and "no-trade" results possible to prove in frameworks broader than those used by the originators of those theorems, but the CPA is used precisely because it is useful. It is hard to do information economics without it.

Conclusion

We are left to conclude that game theory does not handle matters of deception well. When we look at signaling and screening models of asymmetric information, depending on which model we are considering, there are no equilibria, equilibria that involve no deception, or too many equilibria. When a plausible refinement is applied in the multiple equilibrium case, the equilibria with deception disappear. If multiple equilibria remain, it is difficult to see how players should act. Moreover, outcomes are very sensitive to minor changes in modeling details, giving little confidence in the model's predictions.

Nash equilibrium in pure strategies does not require common knowledge, but it does require mutual knowledge of strategy choices. This is difficult to reconcile with deception. Importantly, it is also difficult to understand how this could ever come about. Even with common knowledge of rationality, the most we can say is that dominated strategies will not be played; yet we cannot presume that a unique strategy will be played. In the more credible interpretation of mixed strategy Nash equilibrium, whenever there are more than two players, we do have to resort to common knowledge of conjectures, which is even more implausible. Yet this is important because mixed strategy equilibria in finite games are guaranteed to exist, unlike the case with pure strategy equilibria. In the key category of extensive form games, either we need to assume common knowledge of rationality or rationality is itself hard to define.

Given the significance of common knowledge to game theory equilibria, it is important to determine its consequences. When there is common knowledge of information partitions and there is a common prior assumption (CPA) on beliefs, agents cannot agree to disagree about the likelihood of an event even if they had differential information to start with. This is because when an agent proposes to act on the basis of privately held information, she reveals that information, causing others to revise their beliefs. Thus, here, asymmetric information is negated by common knowledge. Since privately held information seems to be at the base of deception, this result runs counter to the intuition that game theory can handle deception well. Moreover, while the CPA does not seem to have a good justification, it is used in nearly all models of asymmetric information for tractability reasons. Thus, it is not easy to dispense with either: jettisoning it would remove the basis on which information economics has been built.

Consequently, it seems possible to conclude that game theory has failed to provide an interesting advance in dealing with some important information asymmetries among agents, however promising it may have seemed on a heuristic or common sense basis. Deception is one of those asymmetries.

Notes

* I would like to thank an anonymous referee for comments, responses and suggestions, participants at the workshop on "Exchange, Deceptions and Self-Deceptions," Maison des Sciences de l'Homme, Paris, December 7-8, 2001, for their comments, and the Austrian Federal Ministry of Science (bm:bwk) for financial support.

1 It is best to turn to some unified treatment, because the literature on games of asymmetric information is sprawling and does not follow a single path. After Rothschild and Stiglitz's (1976) demonstration that the equilibrium may not exist in markets with asymmetric information, various approaches have been tried. Some authors, such as Wilson (1977) and Riley (1979) use non-Nash equilibrium methods. Others, such as Cho and Kreps (1987) and Hellwig (1987) use Nash equilibrium refinements in multistage games. As Crocker and Snow (2000, p. 2) point out, while each of these approaches predicts an equilibrium in pure strategies, these predictions do not agree. As I mention below, equilibrium existence remains a problem for screening games, leading some to seek mixed-strategy equilibria (Dasgupta and Maskin 1986) or to reformulate the problem more fundamentally, again leading to situations where model predictions are very sensitive to the precise formulation of the problem. Mas-Colell, Whinston and Green (1995, p. 467) state: "Given that our models are inevitably simplifications of actual market processes, if market outcomes are really very sensitive to issues such as this our models may provide us with little predictive ability."

2 Cho and Kreps emphasize that the intuitive criterion has been criticized as being unintuitive to some (1987, p. 203). However, they argue that their criterion makes sense. Nevertheless, they caution that their arguments should not be used to focus only on the one equilibrium that remains (Cho and Kreps 1987, p. 214). Indeed,

precise details of the model's constitution have large effects on the model's outcome (Cho and Kreps 1987, p. 215, n. 13), as is common in game theory models.

3 An anonymous referee emphasized this point, leading me to include this whole discussion. The referee stressed that in these models, agents can be differentiated by their payoff functions in addition to the information they possess. It is important to find out, then, how these models fare in showing deception in equilibrium.

4 As an anonymous referee points out, it may be argued that there is even no good theory of sequential decision making (Kreps 1979).

5 The following exposition is close to that of Board (2002).

6 An anonymous referee points out that Aumann's result assumes an interactive situation. Players may hold different beliefs as long as they are not aware that beliefs differ. However, whenever a player tries to take advantage of private information, say by betting a certain way, other players will become aware of that player's beliefs and will update their own. Thus, in any situation where a player seeks to take advantage of differentially held information, posterior beliefs will become the same.

7 Aumann's result has been extended to more general settings (Bacharach 1985; Geanakoplos 1989; 1994; Rubinstein 1988; Rubinstein and Wolinsky 1990; Samet 1990; Shin 1993). For example, strict adherence of the CPA can be relaxed. However, for simplicity, I will stick to Aumann's original presentation.

8 Morris (1995) provides a critical and more detailed examination of the CPA.

References

Akerlof, G. A., 'The Market for "Lemons": Quality Uncertainty and the Market Mechanism', *Quarterly Journal of Economics*, 84 (1970), 488–500.

Armbruster, W. and Boge, W., 'Bayesian Game Theory', in O. Moschlin and D. Pallaschke (eds), *Game Theory and Related Topics* (Amsterdam: North-Holland, 1979).

Aumann, R, 'Agreeing to Disagree', *Annals of Statistics*, 4 (1976), 1236–39.

Aumann, R., 'Backward Induction and Common Knowledge of Rationality', *Games and Economic Behavior*, 8 (1995), 6–19.

Aumann, R., 'Common Priors: A Reply to Gul', *Econometrica*, 66 (1998), 929–38.

Aumann, R. and Brandenburger, A., 'Epistemic Conditions for Nash Equilibrium', *Econometrica*, 63 (1995), 1161–80.

Aumann, R., and Heifetz, A., 'Incomplete Information', in R. Aumann and S. Hart (eds), *Handbook of Game Theory with Economic Applications*, III, ch. 43 (Amsterdam: North-Holland, 2001).

Ausubel, L., Cramton, P. and Deneckere, R., 'Bargaining with Incomplete Information', in R. Aumann and S. Hart (eds), *Handbook of Game Theory with Economic Applications*, III, ch. 50 (Amsterdam: North-Holland, 2001).

Bacharach, M., 'Some Extensions to a Claim of Aumann in an Axiomatic Model of Knowledge', *Journal of Economic Theory*, 37 (1985), 167–90.

Basu, K., 'Strategic Irrationality in Extensive Games', *Mathematical Social Sciences,* 55 (1988), 247–60.

Basu, K., 'On the Non-Existence of a Rationality Definition for Extensive Games', *International Journal of Game Theory*, 19 (1990), 33–44.

Battigali, P. and Bonnano, G., 'Recent Results on Belief, Knowledge and the Epistemic Foundations of Game Theory', *Research in Economics*, 53 (1999), 149–225.

Bernheim, B., 'Rationalizable Strategic Behavior', *Econometrica*, 52 (1984), 1007–28.

Bicchieri, C., 'Self Refuting Theories of Strategic Interaction: A Paradox of Common Knowledge', *Erkenntnis*, 30 (1989), 69–85.

Bicchieri, C., *Rationality and Coordination* (Cambridge: Cambridge University Press, 1993).

Binmore, K., 'Modelling Rational Players, I', *Economics and Philosophy*, 3 (1987), 179–214.

Binmore, K., *Essays on the Foundations of Game Theory* (Oxford: Blackwell, 1990).

Board, O., 'Knowledge, Beliefs and Game-Theoretic Solution Concepts', *Oxford Review of Economic Policy*, 18 (2002), 433–45.

Boge, W. and Eisele, T., 'On Solutions of Bayesian Games', *International Journal of Game Theory*, 8 (1979), 193–215.

Bonnano, G. and Nehring, K., 'How to Make Sense of the Common Prior Assumption under Incomplete Information', *International Journal of Game Theory*, 28 (1999), 409–34.

Brandenburger, A., 'Knowledge and Equilibrium in Games', *Journal of Economic Perspectives*, 6 (1992), 83–101.

Brandenburger, A. and Dekel, E., 'The Role of Common Knowledge Assumptions in Game Theory', in F. Hahn (ed.), *The Economics of Missing Markets, Information, and Games* (New York: Oxford University Press, 1989), pp. 46–61.

Cho, I.-K. and Kreps, D. M., 'Signaling Games and Stable Equilibria', *Quarterly Journal of Economics*, 102 (1987), 179–221.

Crocker, K. and Snow, A., *Efficiency and Existence of Nash Equilibria with Multidimensional Screening*, Working Paper (Ann Arbor: University of Michigan Business School, November 2002).

Cutler, W., 'An Optimal Strategy for Pot-Limit Poker', *American Mathematical Monthly*, 82 (1975), 368–76.

Dasgupta, P. and Maskin, E., 'The Existence of Equilibrium in Discontinuous Economic Games', *Review of Economic Studies*, 46 (1986), 1–41.

Dekel, E. and Gul, F., 'Rationality and Knowledge in Game Theory', in D. Kreps and K. Wallis (eds), *Advances in Economics and Econometrics*, I (Cambridge: Cambridge University Press 1997), pp. 87–172.

Dow, J., Madrigal, V. and Werlang, S. R., *Preferences, Common Knowledge, and Speculative Trade*, Working Paper (Rio de Janeiro: Fundaçao Getulio Vargas, 1990).

Fagin, R., Halpern, J., Moses, Y. and Vardi, M., *Reasoning About Knowledge* (Cambridge, MA: MIT Press, 1995).

Fréchet, M., 'Emile Borel, Initiator of the Theory of Psychological Games and its Application', *Econometrica*, 21 (1953), 95–6.

Fudenberg, D. and Tirole, J., *Game Theory* (Cambridge, MA: MIT Press, 1992).

Geanakoplos, J., *Game Theory Without Partitions, and Applications to Speculation and Consensus* (New Haven, CT: Cowles Foundation Discussion Paper No. 914, Yale University, 1989).

Geanakoplos, J., 'Common Knowledge', in R. Aumann and S. Hart (eds), *Handbook of Game Theory*, II (Amsterdam: North-Holland, 1994).

Gul, F., 'A Comment on Aumann's Bayesian View', *Econometrica*, 66 (1998), 923–28.

Harsanyi, J., 'Games with Incomplete Information Played by "Bayesian" Players, I: The Basic Model', *Management Science*, 14 (1967), 159–82.

Harsanyi, J., 'Games with Incomplete Information Played by "Bayesian" Players, II: Bayesian Equilibrium Points', *Management Science*, 14 (1968a), 320–24.

Harsanyi, J., 'Games with Incomplete Information Played by "Bayesian" Players, III: The Basic Probability Distribution of the Game', *Management Science*, 14 (1968b), 486–502.

Harsanyi, J., 'Games with Randomly Disturbed Payoffs: A New Rationale for Mixed Strategy Equilibrium Points', *International Journal of Game Theory*, 2 (1973), 1–23.

Hellwig, M., 'Some Recent Developments in the Theory of Competition in Markets with Adverse Selection', *European Economic Review*, 31 (1987), 319–25.

Hume, D., *A Treatise of Human Nature* [1740], ed. L. A. Selby-Bigge, 2nd rev.edn, ed. P. H. Nidditch (Oxford: Clarendon Press, 1976).

Kreps, D., 'A Representation Theorem for "Preference for Flexibility"', *Econometrica*, 47 (1979), 565–77.

Kreps, D. and Wilson, R., 'Reputation and Imperfect Information', *Journal of Economic Theory*, 27 (1982a), 253–79.

Kreps, D. and Wilson, R., 'Sequential Equilibria', *Econometrica*, 50 (1982b), 863–94.

Lewis, D., *Convention: A Philosophical Study* (Cambridge, MA: Harvard University Press, 1969).

Littlewood, J., *Mathematical Miscellany*, ed. B. Bollobas (London: Methuen, 1953).

Mas-Colell, A., Whinston, M. and Green, J., *Microeconomic Theory* (Oxford: Oxford University Press, 1995).

McKelvey, R. and Page, T., 'Common Knowledge, Consensus and Aggregate Information', *Econometrica*, 54 (1986), 109–27.

Mertens, J.-F. and Zamir, S., 'Formulation of a Bayesian Analysis for Games with Incomplete Information', *International Journal of Game Theory*, 14 (1985), 1–29.

Milgrom, P. and Roberts, J., 'Limit Pricing and Entry under Incomplete Information', *Econometrica*, 50 (1982a), 443–60.

Milgrom, P. and Roberts, J., 'Predation, Reputation and Entry Deterrence', *Journal of Economic Theory*, 27 (1982b), 280–312.

Milgrom, P. and Roberts, J., 'Adaptive and Sophisticated Learning in Normal Form Games', *Games and Economic Behavior*, 3 (1991), 82–100.

Milgrom, P., and Stockey, N., 'Information Trade and Common Knowledge', *Journal of Economic Theory*, 26 (1982), 17–27.

Morris, S., 'The Common Prior Assumption in Economic Theory', *Economics and Philosophy,* 11 (1995), 227–53.

Nau, R., *Beyond Nash Equilibrium* (2001) (http://faculty.fuqua.duke.edu/~rnau/ choice/choice07.pdf).

Nehring, K., 'Common Priors under Incomplete Information: A Unification', *Economic Theory*, 18 (2001), 535–53.

Pearce, D., 'Rationalizable Strategic Behavior and the Problem of Perfection', *Econometrica*, 52 (1984), 1029–50.

Reny, P., 'Rationality in Extensive Form Games', *Journal of Economic Perspectives*, 6 (1992), 103–18.

Riley, J. G., 'Informational Equilibrium', *Econometrica*, 47 (1979), 331–59.

Rizvi, S., 'Game Theory to the Rescue?', *Contributions to Political Economy*, 13 (1994), 1–28.

Rosenthal, R., 'Games of Perfect Information, Predatory Pricing, and the Chain Store Paradox', *Journal of Economic Theory*, 25 (1981), 92–100.

Rothschild, M. and Stiglitz, J. E., 'Equilibrium in Competitive Insurance Markets: An Essay in the Economics of Imperfect Information', *Quarterly Journal of Economics*, 80 (1976), 629–49.

Rubinstein, A., *Modeling Bounded Rationality* (Cambridge, MA: MIT Press, 1988).

Rubinstein, A. and Wolinsky, A., 'On the Logic of "Agreeing to Disagree" Type Results', *Journal of Economic Theory*, 51 (1990), 184–93.

Samet, D., 'Ignoring Ignorance and Agreeing to Disagree', *Journal of Economic Theory*, 52 (1990), 190–207.

Samet, D., 'Coherent Beliefs are Not Always Types', *Journal of Mathematical Economics*, 32 (1999), 475–88.

Samet, D., 'Quantified Beliefs and Believed Quantities', *Journal of Economic Theory*, 95 (2000), 169–85.

Savage, L., *The Foundations of Statistics* (New York: Wiley, 1954).

Schelling, T., *The Strategy of Conflict* (Cambridge, MA: Harvard University Press, 1960).

Schiffer, S., *Meaning* (Oxford: Oxford University Press, 1972).

Selten, R., 'Spieltheoretische Behandlung eines Oligopolmodells mit Nachfragentragheit', *Zeitschrift fur die gesamte Staatswissenschaft*, 12 (1965), 201–324.

Shin, H., 'Logical Structure of Common Knowledge', *Journal of Economic Theory*, 60 (1993), 1–13.

Spence, A. M., 'Job Market Signaling', *Quarterly Journal of Economics*, 87 (1973), 355–74.

Stiglitz, J. E., 'Information and Economic Analysis: A Perspective', *Economic Journal*, 95 (1985), 21–41.

Tan, T. and Werlang, S., 'The Bayesian Foundations of Solution Concepts of Games', *Journal of Economic Theory*, 45 (1988), 370–91.

Vanderschraaf, P., 'Common Knowledge', in E. Zalta (ed.), *The Stanford Encyclopedia of Philosophy* (Fall 1999) (http://plato.stanford.edu /entries/common-knowledge).

Von Neumann, J., 'Zur Theorie der Gesellschaftsspiele', *Mathematische Annalen*, 100 (1928), 295–320. Translated as 'On the Theory of Games of Strategy', in A. W. Tucker and R. D. Luce (eds), *Contributions to the*

Theory of Games, IV (Princeton, NJ: Princeton University Press, 1959), pp. 13–42.
Wilson, C., 'A Model of Insurance Markets with Incomplete Information', *Journal of Economic Theory*, 16 (1977), 167–207.

2

Rational Deception*

Paul Dumouchel

> En somme, on ne peut que ruser avec un partenaire d'échange, le prendre en traître serait saper les fondements de l'échange.
>
> R. Hamayon *La chasse à l'âme*

> But the emperors, and other Christian sovereigns, under whose government these errors, and the like encroachments of ecclesiastics upon their office, at first crept in, to the disturbance of their possessions, and of the tranquility of their subjects, though they suffered the same for want of foresight of the sequel, and of insight into the designs of their teachers, may nevertheless be esteemed *accessories to their own, and the public damage.*
>
> Hobbes *Leviathan*

Abstract

This chapter inquires into the relationship between deception and rationality. First, I argue that many models in game theory and rational choice theory make it impossible to represent deception as rational. Second, with the help of examples taken from anthropology and history I show that it is necessary to distinguish between ongoing deception and final deception. In conclusion, I argue that it is because game theory and rational choice theory view deception exclusively as final deception that they consider it to be irrational. Ongoing deception, to the contrary, can allow agents to reach correlated equilibria that are otherwise unattainable.

Deceit and rationality

Caroline Gerschlager (2001, p. 3) argues that in "the neo-classical model of exchange, deception violates the optimality conditions and is thus regarded as an irrationality." At the end of that same book, she remarks that in standard neo-classical approaches, "economists traditionally treat deception as an irrationality, as a flaw in a perfectly rational process" (p. 237); that of exchange. Yet there are, as she reminds us, many reasons to believe that deception is at times rational and that it plays a fundamental role in both exchange and in human societies. Furthermore, the essays collected in that volume (Gerschlager 2001) bear impressive witness to the truth of both suggestions. In this paper, I want to see if this difficulty in describing deception as a rational process is in any way related to our conception of rationality. By "our" conception of rationality, I mean the view of rationality that is shared by most economists and which has been adopted by numerous philosophers: rationality as it is defined by rational choice theory in terms of maximizing expected utility and the associated axioms concerning preferences and beliefs.[1] My guiding hypothesis is that the difficulties that neo-classical economic theory has in dealing with deception come from the fundamental role it gives to that concept of rationality, or at least to the importance it gives to one interpretation (or one family of interpretations) of rational choice theory. In other words, I argue that the problem comes from the understanding of rational behavior that is taken for granted in many parts of economic theory. Yet, even if this is true, does anything important follow from it? Does the failure of economic theory or rational choice theory to give a coherent account of deception entail any significant consequences?

I suggest that it does. I link certain well-known paradoxes in which rational behavior leads to sub-optimal results with the inability to conceive of deception as a rational option. My argument will be that in these situations, given certain conditions related to the rationality of the agents, deception is impossible and agents end up with sub-optimal payoffs. Under different conditions, deception becomes a viable option for them and they can avoid sub-optimal results. However, this does not entail that they attain these superior results through deception; instead, the possibility of deception makes these results possible. Furthermore, when these conditions are changed, the structure of the situation is modified. The temporal horizon of the situation is extended and, as we will see, this raises important epistemological issues. I subsequently turn my attention to two theories of self-deception: paradoxical self-deception and self-deception as a cognitive mistake. In spite of their many differences, both theories assert that self-deception is rationally impossible for reasons closely related to those at work in interpersonal deception. This will help us discover which particular aspect of rationality is at fault here.

In what follows, I analyze three examples of deception: one taken from literature (Homer's *Iliad*), another from anthropology proper (India), and the last from the history of political thought (Machiavelli). I distinguish two different forms of deception, which I call *ongoing deception* and *final deception.* The first form of deception has two important characteristics: One is that it takes into account further interactions between the agents involved, the other is that it entails self-deception on the part of the deceived agent, at least, and perhaps both agents. In other words, *ongoing deception* as a form of interpersonal deception requires intrapersonal deception. *Final deception,* on the contrary, neither requires self-deception, nor takes into account further relations between the agents.

Armed with these notions of deception, I then return to the situations initially analyzed. I argue that in game theory and rational choice theory, we usually model deception as *final deception* and that this is inseparable from the interpretation of rationality that prevents us from avoiding sub-optimal results in the paradoxes analyzed earlier. In closing, I suggest that with different constraints on the rationality of the agents, it is possible to model *ongoing deception* as a form of rational behavior.

Interpersonal deceit

At first sight, our economic and social theories deal with many situations in which deception plays a fundamental role. It can even be argued that in the last 30 or 40 years these situations have become central in our conceptions of rationality and social cooperation. For example, the free-rider problem has shaped our views on collective action and the prisoner's dilemma has transformed our understanding of the social contract. From the layperson's point of view, both phenomena involve deception. In the free-rider problem, this is because you can succeed in getting a free ride only if you can hide the fact that you are not paying your due, in other words, by cheating. In the prisoner's dilemma, this is because defecting is equivalent to squealing and letting the other take all the blame for a crime of which you are also responsible. Yet, once these problems are formulated within the context of rational choice theory or game theory, deception disappears. The economic theory or game specialist will answer that this is not a problem and should not surprise us. Technically, these dilemmas or problems are different from what the layperson spontaneously understands by free riding or defection. That difference, she will argue, is precisely what creates the great theoretical interest of these paradoxes, for they describe situations in which things go wrong even in the best of circumstances, that is, when everybody is acting perfectly rationally. The layperson, on the contrary, and even the traditional philosopher[2] falsely diagnose these situations as failures of rationality and consequently do not see the fundamental problems they pose for our theories of rationality.

It is certainly the case that the issue as it is conceptualized by the theorist is different from what the layperson understands by the free-rider problem or defection. Nonetheless, it is far from clear that the latter is simply confused when seeing deception where the theorist does not. Let us look at two famous examples of situations where common sense would think deception is at work but where the theorist will demonstrate that it is absent. However, first a few words about deception. We can take for granted that the layperson has an intuitive understanding of what deception is, but the theorist may want something a bit more rigorous. As an anonymous referee suggested, for the rational choice model a natural definition of deception could be: "A deceives B when A creates an expectation of 'x' in B's mind and 'x' does not occur." In other words, deception in this context is naturally conceived as creating false expectations that move agents to act in ways that contradict their best interest.

The free-rider problem

If free-riding is to take advantage of a public good without paying your share of the expense involved in producing it, then it seems at first sight that deception is necessary to attain that goal, either in order to avoid the sanction associated with free riding and/or in order to continue enjoying the good in question. But that is not quite what the theorist understands by the "free-rider problem." Given a situation where free riding is possible, then every rational agent should free ride. The reasoning behind this conclusion is the following: if the other agents do not free ride then I will maximize my expected utility if I do. If, on the contrary, they free ride then it is to my advantage to do so also. This time, the reasoning is in order not to be alone to pay the cost of the public good. In any case, no matter what the other agents do, free riding constitutes every agent's dominant strategy. As a result, the public good will not be produced and through their perfectly rational behavior the agents will fail to obtain a public good, which, in principle, everyone desires. Deception does not take place in the free rider problem. Given that all the agents involved are similarly rational, and that they know it, what happens is precisely what everyone expects. More precisely, deception is (theoretically) impossible here. If deception took place, the public good would be produced and this specific problem and paradox would not arise.

The prisoner's dilemma

In the classical two-person prisoner's dilemma with perfect information, deceit is impossible once again and for the same reason as in the free-rider problem described above. The only Nash equilibrium is double defection, but this involves no deceit. Each prisoner expects that the other will defect and that is why he too defects. It is also why they end up with a sub-optimal outcome. The perfect transparency of the game excludes any possible deceit, yet it is not enough to ensure trust and cooperation. On the contrary, it condemns both players to a strategy that leads to a second-rate result. It may also be argued that because there is a dominant strategy in both the prisoner's dilemma and the free-rider problem: expectations about other agents' behavior are irrelevant. Therefore, deceit construed as manipulation of an agent's expectations by another agent is certainly ruled out. What may partially obscure these results in the eyes of the layperson is that, in the two examples above, the rational agents' prescribed actions are not different from what they would have been had they intended to deceive partners who were less than perfectly rational. That is, the analysis of both the free rider problem and the prisoner's dilemma suggests that deceit involves a failure of rationality. In such situations, it is only when (some) agents are not perfectly rational that deceit is possible, and of course when that is the case the paradoxes do not arise: the rational agent does not obtain a sub-optimal outcome. But when all the agents are rational, the rational behavior that excludes deception is also conducive to sub-optimal outcomes. Is there any relationship between these two things? Let us look at two other examples:

Newcomb's paradox

This paradox is generally viewed as belonging to the same class of problems as the prisoner's dilemma and other social dilemmas, such as the free-rider problem (Campbell and Sowden 1985). Imagine a quasi-omniscient predictor, an agent who in the past has always successfully predicted other people's behavior. He offers you the following choice. There are two boxes in front of you, one is opaque, the other transparent. The transparent box as you can clearly see contains $1000. You may take both boxes, in which case (says he) I will have predicted it and the opaque box will be empty. If you take the opaque box only, I will have predicted that and it will contain $1,000,000. What do you chose? Theorists have been divided into two camps concerning this paradox, respectively named "one boxers" and "two boxers." "Two boxers" argue that when it is the agent's turn to choose, the predictor has already put either $1,000,000 or nothing in the black box. Therefore, whatever the case may be, one cannot lose by taking both boxes. An agent who takes two boxes will end up at worst with $1000 and at best with $1,001,000. If she does as the (quasi) omniscient predictor urges her and takes only the opaque black box, she will gain at best $1,000,000 and at worst nothing at all. The choice, they claim, is clear; taking both boxes is the dominant strategy. "One boxers" argue, on the contrary, that the predictor will have anticipated the "two boxers'" decision and left the black box empty. Therefore one should choose only the black box, because given the predictor's track record, he will have anticipated that and put $1,000,000 in it. A (slightly) religious mind could argue that forgoing the $1,000,000 is the price that "two boxers" pay for not trusting the predictor. The question is: Can the (quasi) omniscient predictor be deceived? If not, then we should pity "two boxers." It is generally assumed that the predictor is not out to trick the agents. Therefore, if the agent chooses only the black box and finds it empty, we should conclude that this was the result of an innocent mistake on the part of the predictor. If it makes sense, as I believe it does, to see those in favor of taking two boxes as trying to deceive the predictor in Newcomb's paradox, then that problem turns out to have a structure similar to that of a simple sequential choice problem, for example.[3] The following classical example is depicted in Figure 1 below.

Sequential choice problem

If Peter and Mary can succeed in exchanging, they will both be better off, but they must do so sequentially rather than simultaneously and each must trust the other in order to move first. Therefore, the question arises: Can they exchange? Peter has first choice: he can either exchange or not (O2). If he does not exchange, then he gets his second least preferred outcome and Mary her worst. If he moves, then it is Mary's turn. She can either reciprocate (exchange) or not. If she does not (04), then she gets her preferred outcome and he gets his worst. If she reciprocates (O3), then he gets his preferred outcome and she gets her second-best outcome, which is nonetheless much better than (O2). The agents' outcome preferences are: Peter 03 > 02 > 04 and Mary 04 > 03> 02. The difficulty is usually expressed in the following way: Peter will refuse to exchange because he predicts that when Mary's turn comes she will choose 04, which is her favored outcome, but his worst. He is therefore better off with 02. Consequently, he will not move and, as a result, Mary and he will be worse off than they would have been had they cooperated and reached 03. Once again, these predictions are based on the assumption that both agents are perfectly rational and, once again, the perfect rationality that prevents them from deceiving and from being deceived is what condemns them to a sub-optimal outcome.[4]

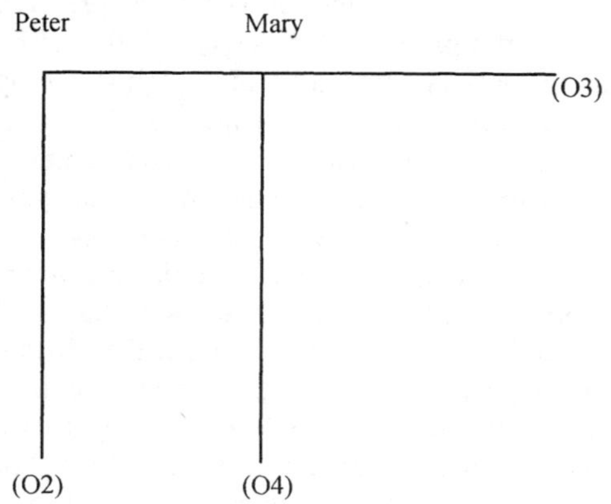

Figure 1: The Sequential Game

Peter moves first. He can either cooperate, in which case it is Mary's move, or he can defect. If he defects, Mary does not get to play and they end up in O2, which is his second best result and Mary's worst. When Mary's turn comes (if it does) she can either cooperate and both players end up in O3, which is Peter's most favored outcome and her second best, though much better than O2. She can also defect in which case O4 is the result; that is her best outcome and Peter's worst.

The inequalities then are the following:

Peter O3 > O2 >> 04

Mary O4> O3 >> O2

The structure of Newcomb's paradox can be seen as similar to this problem with only one difference: when Mary moves she does not know what the predictor (Peter) has done. At the first node of the game, the predictor can either refuse to exchange and leave the black box empty or exchange and put $1,000,000 into it. At node two, the agent has to choose without knowing what the predictor has done. She can either be a "two boxer" and choose 04, in which case the predictor will have predicted the defection (just as Peter does in the standard game) and the agents will end up in 02, or she can be a "one boxer," at which point she obtains 03, which is her second-best outcome, and, since the predictor is not out to trick her, it must also be the predictor's preferred outcome. In Newcomb's paradox, the players' preferences are the following: the preferences of one who moves first, that is, the predictor (or Peter), are 03 > 02 > 04. This means that the predictor prefers above all that you choose only the black box and earn $1,000,000. (By definition, this must be the case, otherwise, given that he is not out to trick you, he would not have made the proposition.) The predictor's second-best outcome is that you take both boxes and that he has predicted it and you get $1000; his worst outcome is that you take both boxes and that he failed to anticipate your move. The second agent's preferences, like Mary's, are 04 > 03 > 02; that is, $1,001,000 is better than $1,000,000, which is better than $1000.

What would be the equivalent of the "one boxer" for the sequential choice problem? Clearly it would be for Mary not to choose her most preferred outcome, 04, when it is her turn to move. Why should she do this and is it rational? In Newcomb's problem, the one boxer bases his decision on the past performance of the predictor. Given the predictor's success at predicting the agents' choices, the expected utility of choosing the opaque box only is far greater than that of taking both boxes, but this is not the case for Mary. The utility of choosing 04 is greater than that of ending up in 03. What can change her decision is that Peter and Mary may interact again in the future. If such is the case, it may be rational and to Mary's advantage to reciprocate. If she fails to do so, Peter, who unlike the predictor does not have the capacity to punish in anticipation, could nonetheless make her pay dearly tomorrow for today's treason. One boxers take into account a past history of interaction that is crystallized in the predictor's reputation for accurate predictions, and they base their decision on this. In repeated games, Mary takes into account future interactions with Peter. In both cases, what is crucial, it seems, is the extension of the time frame within which we judge the rationality of each strategy. Cooperation can be rational in social dilemmas, and the dilemmas solved, if we take into account repeated interactions between agents rather than one-shot games only. Furthermore, when we do this, deception becomes a live option for the agents once again. Interestingly enough, we will encounter a similar result when we study deception in anthropology.

Intra-personal deceit (self-deception)

Attitudes toward self-deception or intra-personal deceit are not unrelated to those we have seen when studying interpersonal deceit in the context of social dilemmas. Here again, as we will see, (self-)deception is viewed as irrational and logically impossible. Interestingly enough, some authors, that is, Mele (1997), have claimed that the reason for this is that intra-personal deceit has been modeled on inter-personal deceit. Deception, which he thinks can be understood in a very straightforward way at the inter-personal level, becomes paradoxical at the intra-personal level when it is conceived as a phenomenon similar to inter-personal deceit but taking place within an individual agent. He states that self-deception should instead be viewed as a form of cognitive mistake. Here are these two notions of self-deception

The paradox of self-deception

From one point of view, self-deception seems impossible given that it appears to involve an insuperable logical contradiction. In order to deceive herself, an agent would have to lie to herself. Now, if she is to do this successfully, she must, it seems, both know that p is true and believe that p is not true, and hence hold contradictory beliefs. (If she does not know that p is true while believing that not p is true, then she is not lying to herself, she simply has a false belief [for whatever reason]. If she does not believe that p is not true, then she is not lying to herself, either.) Therefore, self-deception is impossible because it involves a logical contradiction. In order to avoid the above conclusion, which cries out against our intuition that self-deception exists and that it is frequent, one solution has been to split the self into two, more-or-less, isolated parts (Davidson 1998), one of which contains p and the other not-p. The difficulty with this type of solution, as many authors have noticed, is that it ultimately replaces self-deception (intra-personal deceit) with inter-personal deceit or inter-selves deceit. The paradoxical result of this strategy is that the price to pay in order to understand the possibility of self-deception is the self itself (Ogien 1993). In an attempt to make self-deception possible, the self is reduced to a collection of independent agents, and the self can neither be said to be one of those independent agents nor the whole collection of them. Self-deception is then impossible, either because it is logically contradictory or because the self does not exist.

"Although," as J. Foss (1997, p. 112) notes, "it is logically impossible for contradictory propositions to both be true, there is no logical problem in their both being believed. If there is any mystery here, it is psychological rather than logical." The point is well taken. Whether or not self-deception is possible depends on just how rational we want the psychology of our agents to be.

Self-deception as a-rationality

In this case, self-deception is viewed as a particular form of cognitive mistake, for example, of wishful thinking or of even more innocent types of errors which we often make when we review the evidence in favor of or against a particular belief or when we ascertain the probability of an event. An agent comes to adopt a false belief because of bad epistemic discipline. However, in the case of self-deception it just so happens that the belief in question is often a particularly important personal concern, for example, it concerns whether or not his spouse is having an extra-marital affair. The problem is that, in this case, "self-deception" is nothing more than a particular instance of a general class of cognitive error. That is to say, wishful thinking about one's spouse's sexual behavior does not require mechanisms different from those involved, for example, in wishful thinking about the effect of greenhouse gases on the ozone layer. As a result, there is nothing special about "self-deception" compared with any other form of cognitive failure. This means that the prefix "self" in "self-deception" does not refer to a particular form of deceit, but to the content of the beliefs involved, or, to put it in another way, every form of deceit is self-deception, for it is always the agent who is deceived. [5]

It may be that some cases of self-deception correspond to breakdowns of more general cognitive mechanisms and the actual extent of this phenomenon is an empirical question. Mele calls this approach the "deflationary" account of self-deception, because he believes it dissolves the logical paradoxes that have exercised and entertained many philosophers.

It is time to bring the argument of the first part of the text to an end. In the very simple models of social dilemmas we looked at, deception is impossible for the same reason as in paradoxical self-deception. In these models, we assume perfect/symmetric information as well as common knowledge (CK) and common knowledge of rationality (CKR). Consequently, everything that is in the mind of one player is also in the mind of the other, as well as in the mind of the game theorist. In order for deception to be possible, these postulates would need to be contradicted. In this case we can inverse Mele's claim and say that it is deception that is made to resemble self-deception. What I mean is this: Self-deception is seen as impossible because the self is viewed as an agent who is, as we say, closed under deduction or at least an agent whose rationality requires complete transparency of what she believes. Similarly, deception is impossible among agents whose rationality requires them to have complete and perfect knowledge of each other and the world. The price they pay for this perfect rationality and their imperviousness to deception is sub-optimal results in certain situations. Relax these requirements concerning the agents' rationality and they can avoid the poor results to which their perfect rationality condemns them. They also become susceptible to deceit, potential victims of deceivers. A fault here, I suspect, is the interpretation of rational choice theory as a normative theory of subjective rationality. Why? Because, it is only within that interpretation that we need to make such unrealistic hypotheses concerning the rationality of agents.

Deceit in anthropology

The range of phenomena that (possibly) fall under the heading of deceit is extremely wide and, conceptually, one of the problems raised by the use of the term is whether we are dealing with one type of phenomenon only or with a family of loosely related types of events. I do not think that it is possible at this point to provide a satisfactory solution to this difficulty. Therefore, I will give three different examples of deceit: one from history (literature), one from anthropology (India in the 1950s) and one from the history of political thought (Machiavelli). I will then try to identify a few characteristic features of these phenomena to determine whether the deceit involved is similar or radically different. In conclusion, I will compare the results of this "anthropological analysis" of deceit with those obtained from our inquiry into the relationship between deceit and rationality.

Antilochus's race

The first example is taken from Homer's *Iliad* (Canto XXIII) and is partially analyzed in Detienne and Vernant's *Les ruses de l'intelligence: la "métis" des grecs* (1974). After he has killed Hector, Achilles organizes a chariot race among the Greeks to celebrate his victory. It is to take place on the plain in front of Troy. Antilochus, a young nobleman, has slower horses than Meneleas, King of the Greeks, but he succeeds in robbing Meneleas of second place through ruse and deceit, or, as Meneleas says later in the agora, by cheating. Here is the original incident: Antilochus and Meneleas, who have distanced the pack, are now vying for second place, but the latter's horses are faster and he is progressively gaining on his opponent. As the chariots come to a narrow passage made even more impractical by recent rainfall, Antilochus urges on his horses and Meneleas shouts to him (more or less, this is my modern rendering of Homer): "Slow down you fool or you'll kill yourself and me too! We can't go through there together!" (Remember that

Meneleas is an older king, who has responsibilities and Antilochus a fiery young man). However, Antilochus (who has read Thomas Schelling's *The Strategy of Conflict* [1960]) pushes on as if he hasn't heard and forces Meneleas to reign in his horses in order to avoid a crash. Thanks to the advantage he has gained through this stratagem, Antilochus succeeds in finishing before Meneleas. The reader knows that this is no accident and no mistake on the part of an inexperienced driver, as Meneleas is supposed to believe because the whole incident has been rehearsed in advance between Antilochus and wise Nestor, his father.

Antilochus deceives Meneleas by making him believe that he has lost control of his horses, thereby forcing him to assume his responsibility as king and as an older driver. He then takes advantage of the restrictions imposed in this way on Meneleas in order to rob him of second place. This is how Detienne and Vernant (1974) analyze the incident. However, there is more to it, which to my knowledge they do not take into account. Interestingly, the deceit does not stop here.

Once the race is over, Meneleas challenges Antilochus in the agora, that is to say, in front of all the warriors who have been watching the race. "You won by cheating," he says to him, "but I, who am King, do not want to be seen as taking the prize for second place (a wild horse) from you simply because I am jealous and more powerful. So, let the warriors assembled here judge if you have won fairly or not. Are you ready to swear in front of all that you really lost control of your horses at that narrow spot where you overtook me?" Actually Meneleas is giving Antilochus a rather hard choice: either renounce the prize and admit that you cheated, or recognize in front of all that you are a bad driver and that you did not even win by chance, but through incompetence. However, it is not for nothing that Antilochus is the son of Nestor. He answers: "Dear Meneleas, there is nothing I would hate more than to lose your love and respect, therefore it is gladly that I give you the second prize and I am ready to give you more if you wish in order to win back your friendship. Please forgive me, I am still young and because of that I have been more rash than prudent." Meneleas, then says "I will not be less generous than you and I give you back your prize, but, remember, in the future do not defy warriors who are more powerful than you."

Antilochus, I think, is pretty good at what he is doing: deceiving. In his short reply to Meneleas, he has succeeded in doing three things. First, he has kept his prize. Second, he has avoided saying that he is an incompetent driver. Third, by recognizing that he is a rash young man he subtly passes on the message that he has successfully deceived and defied a more powerful warrior! There are many different forms of deceit involved here, indeed, so many that it raises the question of who is being deceived? This question can be put in a different way: would the solution that was finally reached in the contest between Antilochus and Meneleas be unstable or unavailable if we supposed that the above analysis is clear to both main actors and to everyone else? My guess is that this solution is stable under *mutual knowledge* but not under *common knowledge* in the technical sense.[6] There are many indications in this passage, and elsewhere in the *Odyssey*, that Meneleas is an idiot. Nonetheless, let us assume that he is intelligent enough to grasp what Antilochus is doing: making a fool of him to some extent. Yet, in his reply, Antilochus has saved appearances. He has publicly recognized Meneleas's superior power and his own reluctance to enter into conflict with him. Thus, the young man's explicit statement allows the King to believe he may be the only one to recognize his rival's deviousness. Furthermore, if Meneleas now presses the point, not only will he show that he is vindictive and lacking generosity, but he will also publicly recognize that Antilochus has challenged his authority twice with relative impunity. He will transform what is *mutual knowledge* into *common knowledge*. On the contrary, if Antilochus's deceit is already *common knowledge*, then the conflict is of a different nature and it becomes all important to Meneleas not to let Antilochus "get away with it." In the next example, we will also see a form of deceit in which it is all important to "save appearances."

Collusive lying: Indian peasants and government representatives

This example is taken from F. G. Bailey's *The Prevalence of Deceit* (1971, pp. 46–52), a book that I recommend to anyone who is interested in deceit. The story takes place in the Indian village of Bispira in the State of Orissa during the 1950s. At that time, in every region of the country, the government of India had created agricultural cooperatives that provided improvement loans to peasants. One day in Bispira, the government employee responsible for the cooperative ran away with the money and the records of the loans. Shortly thereafter, the government sent officials to inquire into the incident and attempt to recover the loans. When the officials questioned villagers, they would invariably get the following answer: "I know some money was borrowed, but I did not borrow any myself and I do not know anybody who did or how much money was borrowed." Of course this was false. Every villager knew who had borrowed and had a good idea how much. The government officials stayed on for a while, trying to find out more about the loans and the money that had disappeared, but they did not order in the police, who had means of making the villagers more talkative. In the end, the peasants won and got away without having to pay back the money they had borrowed. Bailey also reports that the villagers would say among themselves, though not to the government officials, that the whole incident was ultimately the government's fault because the government had hired an outsider to manage the cooperative instead of a local man, and everyone knows that foreigners cannot be trusted.

Bailey points out that the villagers' silence is not the only aspect of deceit here. Throughout the whole incident, the peasants behaved toward the government officials as if the latter had infinite power, as if they were traditional lords, who had powers of life and death and as if they themselves had no power whatsoever. (Clearly government officials had enough power to make the life of the villagers unpleasant, but, as the result of the conflict shows, their power was nonetheless quite limited.) The peasants adopted a code of conduct in which they acted toward petty government officials as if they were great lords. The officials, in turn, treated the peasants as if they were abject slaves. They forced older villagers to wait standing up for hours while they discussed topics among themselves as if the peasants did not exist. It seems likely that everyone knew that this was a false pretence, yet all tacitly agreed to abide by it. We therefore have (at least) two levels of deceit or lying: the peasants' silence embedded in the collective pretence concerning the power relationship. The officials could have called in the police and looked the other way while the representatives of the law "strongly encouraged" one or two villagers to become more talkative. They also could have bribed a rich peasant. It is not known why they did not resort to any of these tactics, but is likely that the villagers were not entirely unaware of these possibilities.

Some similarities

The most striking similarity between these two examples is that in both cases deceit takes place with, to some extent, the consent of those who are deceived. What I mean is that in the cases of both Antilochus and Bispara, there is a pretence or lie that is offered to the deceived in order to deceive, yet the deceived accept the lie even when (at least partially) aware of the deceiver's lack of sincerity. Here we must ask; why would anyone knowingly agree to be cheated? The short answer is: Because he or she cannot do otherwise. However, this is probably a bit too short. Neither Meneleas nor the Indian government officials would agree to be cheated in all circumstances. In both cases, the lie they are offered is a payoff or bribe, and part of the reason they agree to be deceived. The Indian peasants, like Antilochus, pay their respects to the superiority of those they deceive, and this payment is part of the reason the "deceit" is accepted. Of course, this raises the question of whether what we are really dealing with here is deceit.

The other interesting similarity between the two cases is that self-deception seems to be involved in both. If the above analysis is correct, Meneleas is deceived by Antilochus because he is vain (and not too intelligent). He is ready to believe either Antilochus's lie or that he is the only one who can see through it. In any case, it is hard to imagine that Meneleas does not know better, at least to some extent. In the Bispara story, this is even clearer. The government officials must have known that the peasants were lying to them. Apparently they were ready to be tricked in order to maintain, despite evidence to the contrary, their prejudices, according to which peasants are a sorry lot of incompetent fools, and the illusion of their own power. It seems that, as Hobbes said, both may be "esteemed accessories to their own damage." But is there damage here? This is a question to which we will return later on.

Moreover, in both examples, though neither of the parties involved wants to lose, it seems that both give paramount importance to the possibility of continuing to interact with each other. By offering Meneleas the horse he has won and saying that he does not want to lose his friendship, Antilochus stresses how important it is to him that he and the King maintain their relationship, even as he tries to get away with both the symbolic and material spoils of his deceit. Meneleas lets him do this, perhaps because he is an idiot (as the whole story suggests), but certainly because, in his speech, Antilochus is wise enough to indicate that the outcome of these two contests (the race and the debate in the agora) would not upset the power hierarchy of the antagonists.

Clearly, the same can be said about the Bispira villagers, who made sure that the government officials were convinced that they, the peasants, were not taking any pride in their treachery. Consequently, they framed the whole incident as another example of their own stubbornness and general incompetence, re-affirming the stability of the government's power while at the same time defying it. The officials could therefore close their eyes to the whole affair because it did not seem to imply any lasting consequences for future relations between the government and the peasants. Again, what both parties were saying was not only that they were ready to respect the existing power hierarchy, despite the fact that it clearly was challenged by the conflict, but mainly that they wanted to keep on interacting in accordance with the established rules.

A last similarity between these two examples is that in both cases the interaction takes place in front of external observers and can be understood by this "third party" in a way that is different from how it is evaluated by either of the two principals. This is the difference between the two parts of the contest between Meneleas and Antilochus. What takes place on the racetrack is for the most part known by the two rivals only, but in the middle of the agora everything is obvious to each and every warrior. Similarly, in the Bispara case, the government officials, at least, are acting in front of a third party, which is the authority that has sent them to Bispara. It may be that what gives the peasants an edge in this conflict is that they constitute their own audience. It could also be that Antilochus's advantage in front of the assembled warriors is that he has less to lose than Meneleas.

For all these reasons, I propose calling this form of deceit *ongoing deceit*, not simply because it does not rule out further interaction, but because its main characteristics can be derived from the fact that it is turned toward further interactions.

A final form of deceit

However, as we all know, there are other forms of deceit. One, in particular, is much more definitive than the collusive lie of the Indian peasants or the ruse of Antilochus. It is a form of deceit that puts an end to the relationship between the agents involved either because it is fatal to the deceived party or because none of those involved want to interact with the others again. In Chapter VII of Machiavelli's *The Prince*, there is a remarkable example of such *final deceit* (Machiavelli 1950). After Ceasar Borgia had conquered Romagna, a province that had previously been ruled by many small lords of little power, he realized that these had not governed but robbed their subjects and that consequently it was full of thieves, brigands, and highway robbers. In order to bring back peace, he called upon the services of Messer Remirro de Orco, a cruel and able man. To Messer de Orco's merit, it must be admitted, says Machiavelli, that a few months later Romagna was completely peaceful. However, the people complained loudly about de Orco's cruelty. Borgia therefore instituted a civilian tribunal with a wise president and, in order to prevent the people's justified resentment from working its way back to him, had de Orco executed in secret. One morning his body, cut in half, was found in the piazza of Cesena next to an executioner's block and a bloody knife. "The ferocity of this spectacle," says Machiavelli, "caused the people both satisfaction and amazement" (1950, p. 27).

This example is interesting partly because of its complexity, for it contains two different forms of deceit embedded in each other. Let us start with the way Ceasar Borgia deceived Messer Remirro de Orco. This clearly is *final deceit*, not only because of the death of his lieutenant, but mainly because, contrary to the Indian peasants' collusive lie and Antilochus's ruse, it neither aims at nor takes into account any further relationship between the principals. This is a one-shot game. As a result, such deceit can succeed only if it escapes the notice of the deceived party.

Though he may deceive himself because he is overly confident in his master, Ceasar Borgia,[7] Remirro de Orco does not know before it is too late that he is being deceived and, if he did, would not consent to it. Similarly, this deceit does not take place in front of third parties who could influence the outcome of the encounter. When it becomes public, it is over: de Orco is dead. The other type of deceit, in which Ceasar Borgia's deceit of Remirro de Orco is embedded, is Borgia's deceit of the people of Romagna. In this case, there are good reasons to think that the deceit does take place to some extent with the assent of the deceived party. Actually, it seems that Borgia's strategy will be optimally successful if the people of Romagna *can* believe that the cruel treatment they received was not ordered by their Prince, given that he has punished his minister, and yet know, given de Orco's horrible death, that Borgia is a cruel master. Confronted with a choice between a truth that means repression and a lie that means peace, they choose peace. Once again, it is not clear how much self-deception is involved in the deceit. Furthermore, this deceit takes place in front of an audience, a third party, toward which it is largely aimed, for there are many who form public opinion but were not victims of the repression. They, like the warriors in the agora, influence the decisions of the principals.

At first sight it may seem that these two forms of deceit are radically opposed. One rests to some extent on the assent of the deceived party, and therefore entails self-deception to a point. The other one excludes it. One has a view to future relationships. The other has none. One takes place in front of an audience. The other can succeed only if it remains secret. Notwithstanding these contradictory characteristics, it seems that one type of deceit can easily be transformed into the other. First, we should note that *final deceit* is also present in our two first examples of deceit and then, that in each of the three examples, the relationship between the two types of deceit is different. In our last example, *final deceit* was embedded in *ongoing deceit*. In the Bispara example, *final deceit* involves a different agent; the agricultural cooperative employee who runs away with the money and the records. His deceit must remain secret until it is over, excludes the agreement of those who are deceived, and rules out any further relationship. Finally, in Antilochus's case, the two forms of deceit constitute two successive moments of a unique process rather than being distributed over different agents. That, at least, is what I would now like to suggest.

Interestingly, in the contest between Meneleas and Antilochus, *final deceit* apparently comes first and leaves Meneleas fuming. The race is a one-shot game and Antilochus has tricked him into thinking that he had lost control of his horses. This is not deceit to which Meneleas can assent.

It is too much, and Antilochus must now make amends or all is over. Next comes *ongoing deceit.* Antilochus, for whatever reason, cannot afford to lose Meneleas's friendship, but he does not want to relinquish what he has already won. Thus, he endeavors to make Meneleas an accessory to his own damage, and it is likely that, in the process, Antilochus gains even more in the eyes of the assembled warriors. Now, there is a sense in which here there are not two incidents, but only one, which begins on the racetrack and ends in the agora. If such is the case, then it seems that there is no clear-cut distinction or intrinsic characteristics that allow one to distinguish between *final* and *ongoing deceit* before the game is over. Any reader of the *Odyssey* knows that the debate between Meneleas and Anticholus could have had a much less pleasant ending for Antilochus. If it had, we might have considered that he had cheated and only got what was to be expected in such a violent society. In other words, it is only the future of the relationship that decides what type of deceit it was and the future of the relationship is in the hands not only of the deceiver, but also of the deceived. This is why it makes sense to say that in *ongoing deceit*, the deceit rests to some extent on the assent of those who are deceived. The story of Antilochus shows that it is sometime possible to transform what at first was (or was seen as) *final deceit* into *ongoing deceit.* The violent end of Messer Remirro de Orco indicates the limits of such retrospective transformation.

The rationality of deceit

Let us first compare *ongoing deception* and *final deception* with our original sketch of a definition of deceit in relation to rational choice theory: A deceives B when A creates an expectation of "x" in the mind of B and "x" does not occur. It seems that in *final deception*, what is going on may be described in those terms or in closely related terms. Both the clerk in charge of Bispara's agricultural loan co-operative and Cesar Borgia created false expectations in the minds of the others. This is not quite as clear when we come to the chariot race. Antilochus does not create any false expectation in Meneleas's mind. It may appear at first sight that the race is a game of chicken. If such is the case, Antilochus's so called "deception" would then consist of making a credible threat and this would involve something like changing Meneleas's subjective probability assessment concerning future events or perhaps his assessment of Antilochus's responsiveness to his own strategic choices. But this need not be the case, as a bit of psychology will show. Suppose that Antilochus did not resort to the stratagem of pretending he had lost the control of his horses and that Meneleas was convinced that the young driver was not going to back down in response to Meneleas's own strategy of "full speed ahead." In other words, suppose that Meneleas's probability distributions over outcomes remain the same, but that Antilochus now appears in perfect control of what is happening. In that case, given what we know of Meneleas's psychology, we can expect that Meneleas's behavior would have been different. If he had thought Antilochus was in control, he would have attempted to go through the narrow passage at the same time. Why? Because he assigns to losing face a disutility that is greater than what he attributes to the dangers of a violent crash. Antilochus's stratagem offers Meneleas the opportunity of foregoing the second prize without losing face. His ruse is not to change any of Meneleas's expectations or to modify his probability distribution concerning various events; it consists of transforming the apparent value of the different outcomes for Meneleas. When the king later challenges Antilochus in the agora, he is asking for confirmation of this new evaluation of the outcomes. If such is the case then it seems that the first part of the race incident was not *final deception*, contrary to what was suggested earlier, but *ongoing deception.* The success of Antilochus's trick on the racecourse also required some sort of agreement on the part of Meneleas and it already took into account future interactions between the principals.

Ongoing deception not only does not imply, but excludes manipulating the other agent's expectations. This is because such manipulation implies that the agent will be wiser after the fact, that the event will contradict her expectations. This outcome puts an end to the deception. As long as deceit is guided by the event of that revelation, of when things turn out to be different than expected, it is *final deception.* Because of that, *final deception* cannot lead to a result that is in equilibrium. At least one of the agents is always in a situation where she could have done better. On the contrary, *ongoing deception* can sometimes lead to a dynamic equilibrium.

From the point of view of an external observer, it is not clear that Meneleas and Antilochus could have done better. Without Antilochus's repeated deceptions, Meneleas and he were heading for a crash, or clash, that could have left them both much worse off. The reason for this is that, at least on the racetrack, each agent views yielding to the other as less valuable than the perspective of a possibly fatal crash. That is to say, the game is symmetrical and the agents' preferences are the following: Each one prefers (1) that he charge on and that the other one yield (c/y); (2) that they both attempt to cross the narrow passage together (c/c); (3) that he yield and let the other go first; (4) that both yield, as this may allow another driver to overtake them (y/y), that is, (c/y) > (c/c) > (y/c) > (y/y). Given this, each agent's dominant strategy is to keep charging (c) and the end result is that they will crash. Yet, this preference structure does not reflect the utilities of the outcomes. Let us assume these are (c/y) > (y/c) > (y/y) > (c/c). Deception then allows both players to obtain a result that they could not have reached otherwise in view of their distorted preference structure. It also plays another role. In the new game, if the other agent plays c, my best strategy is y and if she opts for y I should go for c. This is now a partially co-operative game and some sort of co-ordination or way of breaking the symmetry is needed in order to avoid the pitfalls of (c/c) or (y/y). In the above example, it is also what Antilochus's deception does: it allows the players to reach a correlated equilibrium.

This brings us back to the conclusion made in the first part of the text. Viewed as a normative theory of subjective rationality, rational choice theory requires that the point of view of the agents involved in the decision correspond to that of an external observer. This constraint reduces the number of equilibrium points accessible to the agents. This constraint also makes deception impossible. Once you relax this requirement, the equilibrium points become accessible as is shown by evolutionary game theory (Danielson 1998) and deception can turn out to be to everybody's advantage.

Is it deceit then? If everybody is better off being deceived and if even the deceived party agrees to the deception, in what sense is this *really* deception? Here is one possible answer: Rational choice theory interpreted as a normative theory of subjective rationality assumes that the only interesting equilibrium points are those that are accessible under the condition that the point of view of the deciding agents be equivalent to that of the rational choice theorist.[8] Social dilemmas indicate that this is not always the case. Mutually advantageous *ongoing deception* fails to satisfy this condition just as much as *final deception* does. In both cases, there is no description of the situation that could be accepted by all those involved as well as by the external observer. Even though *ongoing deception* often takes place in front of an audience of external observers, there is no description of the situation that can be shared by all the parties involved. That is to say, if Meneleas, Antilochus, and the warriors assembled in the agora shared the same description of the situation, then the conflict between the two main protagonists could not be solved in such a gentlemanly way. Deception is involved here because it is part of our conception of truth that if a true description of a situation exists, then it can and should be accepted by everyone involved. If the situation is such that cooperation requires that some agents be prevented from having access to this true description of the situation, then cooperation rests on a lie, on deception, even if it is to everyone's advantage, for example, in terms of expected utility. In the cases of *ongoing deception* that we have seen, if the protagonists shared the same description of the events, the mutually advantageous point on which they are presently co-coordinated would be unavailable.

Notes

* I wish to thank Jean-Pierre Dupuy, Caroline Gerschlager, Don Ross, Lucien Scubla and an anonymous referee for useful comments on previous drafts of this paper. I also gratefully acknowledge financial support from the Austrian Federal Ministry of Education, Science and Culture (bm:bwk).

1 For example: E. Eells 1982, J. Elster 1979, I. Levy 1986, L. Savage 1972.

2 For example Hobbes (1651, p. 90), at least that is how J. Hampton (1986, pp. 64–9) interprets the passage where Hobbes defends the rationality of keeping one's contract in the state of nature.

3 Jean-Pierre Dupuy (1998a; 1992) has also argued that there is a similarity in structure between Newcomb's paradox and the sequential trade problem.

4 Concerning this sequential choice problem, see (Dupuy 1998b) and (McClennen 1998).

5 See Mele (1987) and (1998).

6 A statement S is mutual knowledge in a population P if it is known by every member of P. It is common knowledge if 1) it is mutual knowledge, if 2) everyone in P knows that all members of P know S, if 3) everyone in P knows that every member of P knows that every member of P knows S, and so on ad infinitum.

7 Though nothing in the text suggests that such is the case. Actually, the difference between ongoing deceit and final deceit, with respect to self-deception, is best expressed in the following way: ongoing deceit entails paradoxical self-deception, whereas final deceit allows but does not require self-deception in either of its forms, but excludes the consent of the deceived party.

8 Concerning this condition and its role in social explanations, see Dumouchel (1992).

References

Aumann, R. J., 'Irrationality in Game Theory', in P. Dasgupta, D. Gale, O. Hart and E. Maskin (eds), *Economic Analysis of Markets and Games (Essays in Honour of Frank Hahn)* (Cambridge, MA: MIT Press, 1992).

Bach, K., '(Apparent) Paradoxes of Self-Deception and Decision', in J. P. Dupuy (ed.), *Self-Deception and Paradoxes of Rationality* (Stanford, CA: CLSI Publications, 1998), pp. 163–89.

Bailey, F. G., *The Prevalence of Deceit* (Ithaca, NY: Cornell University Press, 1971).

Campbell, R. and Sowden, L. (eds), *Paradoxes of Rationality and Co-operation* (Vancouver, BC: Vancouver University Press, 1985).

Danielson, P. A. (ed.), *Modelling Rationality, Morality, and Evolution* (Oxford: Oxford University Press, 1998).

Davidson, D., 'Who is Fooled?', in J. P. Dupuy (ed.), *Self-Deception and Paradoxes of Rationality* (Stanford, CA: CLSI Publications, 1998), pp. 1–18.

Detienne, M. and Vernant, J. P., *Les ruses de l'intelligence: la 'métis' des grecs* (Paris: Flammarion, 1974).

Dumouchel, P., 'Systèmes Sociaux et Cognition', in D. Andler (ed.), *Introduction aux sciences cognitives,*(Paris: Gallimard, 1992), pp. 472–88.

Dupuy, J. P. (ed), *Self-Deception and Paradoxes of Rationality* (Stanford, CA: CLSI Publications, 1998a).

Dupuy, J. P., 'Rationality and Self-Deception', in J. P. Dupuy (ed.), *Self-Deception and Paradoxes of Rationality* (Stanford, CA: CLSI Publications, 1998b), pp. 113–49.

Dupuy, J. P., 'Two Temporalities, Two Rationalities: A New Look at Newcomb's Paradox', in P. Bourgine and B. Waliser (eds), *Economics and Cognitive Science* (Oxford: Pergamon Press, 1992).

Eells, E., *Rational Decision and Causality* (Cambridge: Cambridge University Press, 1982).

Elster, J., *Ulysses and the Sirens: Studies in Rationality and Irrationality* (Cambridge: Cambridge University Press, 1979).

Foss, J., 'How Many Beliefs can Dance in the Heads of the Self-Deceived?', *Behavioral and Brain Sciences*, 20/1 (1997), 111–2.

Gerschlager, C., *Expanding the Economic Concept of Exchange Deception, Self-Deception and Illusions* (Boston, MA: Kluwer Academic Publishers, 2001).

Hamayon, R., *La chasse à l'âme* (Paris: Société d'Ethnologie, 1990).

Huizinga, J., *Homo Ludens: A Study of the Play Element in Culture* (Boston, MA: Beacon Press, 1950).

Jeffrey, R., *The Logic of Decision*, 2nd rev. edn (Chicago, IL: Chicago University Press, 1983).

Levy, I., *Hard Choices: Decision Under Unresolved Conflicts* (Cambridge: Cambridge University Press, 1986).

Machiavelli, N., *The Prince and the Discourses* [1513] (New York: The Modern Library, Random House, 1950).

McClennen, E. F., 'Rationality and Rules', in P. A. Danielson (ed.), *Modelling Rationality, Morality, and Evolution* (Oxford: Oxford University Press, 1998), pp. 13–40.

Mele, A., 'Real Self-Deception', *Behavioral and Brain Sciences*, 20/1 (1997), 91–102.

Mele, A., *Irrationality* (Oxford: Oxford University Press, 1987).

Ogien, R., *La faiblesse de la volonté* (Paris: PUF, 1993).

Satz, J. and Ferejohn, J., 'Rational Choice and Social Theory', *Journal of Philosophy*, 41 (1994), 71–87.

Savage, L., *The Foundations of Statistics*, 2nd edn (New York: Dover, 1972).

Schelling, T, *The Strategy of Conflict* (Cambridge, MA: Harvard University Press, 1960).

Skyrms, B., *Evolution of the Social Contract* (Cambridge: Cambridge University Press, 1996).

3

A Deceptive Journey from Rational Expectations to Bounded Rationality*

Esther-Mirjam Sent

Abstract

In economics, deception manifests itself in many guises at multiple levels. This paper is concerned with deception in the sense of outwitting, which involves efforts to exploit asymmetry between economists and the agents they study and between these agents and the governments they elect, as well as with self-deception in the sense of making decisions that are contrary to one's interests. It shows how the move from rational expectations to bounded rationality involved an accompanying change from deception to self-deception. In particular, the second section of the text shows how rational expectations economics has sought to remove deception in the sense of outwitting from the relationships among economists, agents, and governments. In the face of obstacles to do so, rational expectations economists moved toward bounded rationality, as discussed in the next section, which also illustrates the accompanying change from deception to self-deception.

Introduction

In economics, deception manifests itself in many guises at multiple levels. When their effort cannot be accurately observed by employers, workers may shirk. When insurers cannot costlessly monitor their precautions to reduce the probability of accidents or damages due to them, the insured may become more risk-taking. An argument along these lines also holds for criminal activity. Whereas the actions of experts such as lawyers, repair persons, and managers may be costlessly observed by those they serve, these agents cannot know with certainty whether the actions were in their interest. Without some device for buyers to identify good products, bad products will always be sold along with the good products. When banks are uninformed about individual borrowers' probability of default, market equilibrium on the credit market will involve an excess demand for loans. To reduce expected inflation, the Fed might announce that low inflation is the paramount goal of monetary policy. Yet, once households and firms have formed their expectations of inflation and set wages and prices accordingly, the Fed has an incentive to renege on its announcement and implement expansionary monetary policy to reduce unemployment.

This paper is concerned with deception in the sense of outwitting, which involves efforts to exploit asymmetry between economists and the agents they study and between these agents and the governments they elect,[1] as well as with self-deception in the sense of making decisions that are contrary to one's interests. It shows how the move from rational expectations to bounded rationality involved an accompanying change from deception to self-deception, as defined here. In particular, the second section of the text shows how rational expectations economics has sought to remove deception in the sense of outwitting from the relationships among economists, agents, and governments. In the face of obstacles to do so, rational expectations economists moved toward bounded rationality, as discussed in the next section, which also illustrates the accompanying change from deception to self-deception.

Rationality and deception

Economists vs. agents

Our journey starts with deceptions in the relationship between economists and agents under the adaptive expectations hypothesis and leads to the rational expectations approach. The hypothesis of adaptive expectations, which was used heavily up until the late 1960s, postulated that individuals used information on past forecasting errors to revise their current expectations (see, for example, Begg 1982, Cagan 1956, Friedman 1968, Nerlove 1958). In particular, agents were presumed to rely on mechanistic, backward-looking, extrapolative rules. As a result, economists and econometricians outwitted agents by fitting models that forecast better than agents. The reason is that the economists and econometricians were presumed to be fully knowledgeable, while the agents were postulated as making systematic forecasting errors period after period. This gave economists and econometricians an edge to be exploited in making policy recommendations, as discussed in what follows. By starting with the idea that individuals were inspecting and altering their own forecasting records just like economists and econometricians in their attempts to eliminate systematic forecasting errors, some argue, the concept of rational expectations was able to banish this deception. It embodied the idea that economists and econometricians, on the one hand, and the agents they are modeling, on the other hand, were placed on an equal footing by postulating that the forecasts made by the agents within the model were no worse than the forecasts by the economist or econometrician who has the model (see, for example, Kantor 1979, p. 1429; Sargent 1987a, pp. 411 and 440; 1987c, p. 76; 1993, pp. 21 and 39). In a paper first circulated in 1973 and subsequently published in 1976, Nobel-laureate Robert Lucas (1976) drew attention to the fact that if the agents are put on an equal footing with economists and governments and if estimated coefficients of observable equations implicitly contain policy parameters that have entered through their role as predictors of the future, then these parameters will change when a new policy is adopted. Hence, parameter estimates derived under old policies would be inappropriate in simulating new policies. We will return to this shortly.

One of the main motivations behind the rational expectations hypothesis, then, was to remove deception in the sense of one agent outwitting another. In Sargent's (1993, p. 21) words: "The idea of rational expectations is ... said to embody the idea that economists and the agents they are modeling should be placed on an equal footing: the agents in the model should be able to forecast and profit-maximize and utility-maximize as well as the economist – or should we say econometrician – who constructed the model."[2] Or: "The concept of a rational expectations competitive equilibrium ... has the attractive property that ... [the agents] in the model forecast ... as well as the economist who is modeling them" (Sargent 1987a, p. 411).

The elimination of deception between agents and economists in the sense outlined above encountered a few stumbling blocks. First, if there is no deception among agents, then there is no reason for them to trade with each other, even if they possess different information. Second, agents and econometricians have to outwit each other in order to justify the error term. Let us consider each obstacle in turn.

The first question is how there can be trade among agents who do not deceive each other. One suggestion, following a line of research started by Lucas (1972a), is that equilibrium probability beliefs differ and that agents actually trade on the basis of this different information. However, a whole series of "no-trade" theorems overrule this commonsense intuition (see Hakansson et al. 1982, Milgrom and Stokey 1982, Rubinstein 1975,

Tirole 1982, Varian 1987). Instead of there being a hive of activity and exchange, Tirole (1982) proved that a sharp no-trade theorem characterizes rational expectations equilibria. Consider a purely speculative market, meaning that the aggregate monetary gain is 0 and that insurance plays no role. When it is common knowledge that traders are risk-averse, are rational, and have the same prior and that the market clears, then it is also common knowledge that a trader's expected monetary gain given her information must be positive in order for her to be willing to trade. In other words, if one agent has information that induces her to want to trade at the current asset price, then other rational agents would be unwilling to trade with her, because they realize that she must be trying to outwit them because she has superior information. The equilibrium market price fully reveals everybody's private information at zero trades for all traders.

Hence, in order to examine models with different equilibrium beliefs and nonzero trading volume, the only solution is to consider models that lack one of the necessary hypotheses for these no-trade theorems. First, there may be some risk-loving or irrational traders; the problem with pursuing this approach lies in deciding what kHinds of irrational behavior are plausible. Second, insurance and diversification considerations may play a significant role. However, after a single round of trading based on hedging and insurance considerations, there is no further reason to trade when new information arrives for exactly the same reasons described by Tirole: In a market of rational individuals there would be no one with whom to trade. Third, agents may have different prior beliefs. Now, if differences in prior beliefs can generate trade, then these differences in belief cannot be due to information as such, but rather can only be pure differences in opinion. Allowing for differences of opinion in this sense can be viewed as allowing for a certain kind of irrational agents.

The second obstacle encountered by rational expectations economists involved error term justification. In particular, close scrutiny of the justification of error terms revealed that the econometrician needed to be outwitted by the agents. As Lucas and Sargent (1981, p. xxii) explained: "Errors in the estimated equation crop up perhaps because the econometrician has less information than the agents, in some sense, or else because the model is misspecified in some way."[3] Initially reluctant to explore the misspecification route, rational expectations economists instead incorporated deception between econometricians and agents. Under this interpretation, error terms can have a variety of sources. There could be shocks observed by agents but not by the econometrician, there could be interactions with hidden decision variables simultaneously chosen by agents but unobserved by the econometrician, agents could be using larger information sets than the econometrician as a result of data limitations à la Shiller (1979),[4] or the econometrician could have data sampled at a coarser interval than the agents.[5] Later, rational expectations economists also explored the errors-in-variables justification of error terms. The problem with this interpretation is that error is not confined to the single dependent variable, making it hard to settle on the correct method to model these equations.[6]

Recalling that rational expectations economists and econometricians had earlier challenged adaptive expectations advocates for fitting models that forecast better than agents, we now observe a reversal of the contested deception. When implemented numerically or econometrically, rational expectations models impute more knowledge to the agents within the model (who use the equilibrium probability distributions in evaluating their Euler equations) than is possessed by an econometrician, who faces estimation and inference problems that the agents in the model have somehow solved.

Before elaborating on efforts to eliminate these differences, we will first discuss deception between agents and governments.

Agents vs. governments

Some have argued that the treatment of policy in the Keynesian tradition led inevitably toward rational expectations (see, for example, Keuzekamp 1991; Sargent 1987a, p. xxii). The reason is that Keynesian policy analysis, extending back to Tinbergen, pursued the idea of applying optimal control theory to models in order to make precise quantitative statements about optimal policies. In these policy experiments, the government was imagined to behave precisely as an agent with rational expectations. Therefore, in an effort to eliminate deception, it was only natural that economists would eventually apply these ideas to private agents' decision rules as well as those of the government. Outwitting between government agents and private agents was eliminated by assuming that both types of agents had rational expectations and solved rich dynamic optimization problems that took into account all the constraints that they faced.

The supposed, inevitable move from the Keynesian tradition to rational expectations hypothesis was facilitated by the failure of traditional Keynesian policies in the 1970s. The ensuing observation that government policy did not seem to work, some argue, lent a certain credibility to the rational expectations school's insistence that the government could not fine-tune the economy. Specifically, the rational expectations postulate gave rise to a skeptical attitude about how much economists knew and how much the government could accomplish, and a suggestion that both economists and the government had overreached themselves to society's detriment (see, for example, Barro 1976; Buiter 1980; Hoover 1988, pp. 65-73; Lucas 1972a; 1972b; 1975; 1976; McCallum 1979a; Sargent and Wallace 1975; 1976). Recognizing the limitations of their profession, rational expectations economists maintained that the economy would basically be stable if it were not subjected to the shocks repeatedly administered by the government. Since nobody understood deeply how the economy responded, they argued that it was best not to try anything fancy. Instead, rational expectations economists claimed that they should recommend policy rules.

In addition, proponents of the rational expectations hypothesis argued that government tinkering could be not only dangerous, as outlined above, but also ineffective. They replaced the old view that the government could manage the economy through deceiving people by the idea that people can foil government policy makers. By taking seriously the observation that people learned from their mistakes, rational expectations economists showed that orthodox prescriptions of economic policy crumbled, since much of the effectiveness of these policies relied on the government's ability to deceive people indefinitely. In particular, as people wised up to the government scheming to manage the economy, they forestalled the very results that the government sought when it tried to alter the economy's course through fiscal or monetary interventions. In the end, rational expectations economists contended, the interventions would prove worse than useless, because people would change their strategies when the government changed its strategies.[7]

The obstacle rational expectations encountered here in their efforts to eliminate deception is that there can be no policy recommendations if there is no outwitting (see, for example, Lucas and Sargent 1981; Sargent 1984; Sargent 1987a, pp. 435–36; 1987c; Sargent and Wallace 1976). If there is a rational expectations equilibrium with optimal policy, then there is no room for improvement in government policy. The reason is that the system cannot be influenced. Making the assumption that in the historical period the system was in a rational expectations equilibrium raises the question of why we study a system that we cannot influence. On the other hand, if there is no rational expectations equilibrium with an optimal policy, then there is room for improvement in government policy. However, this presumes that agents' expectations about government policy are deceptive in that they do not properly take the policy advice into account. Hence, if government policy is believed to have room for improvement, any rational expectations model always misspecifies the economic structure.[8]

In the face of these conundrums, rational expectations economists moved toward bounded rationality, as outlined in the following.

Transition

Subsequent to the difficulties outlined so far, rational expectations economists tried to remove deception among the agents, economists, and econometricians by making them all boundedly rational. Sargent (1993), for example, made a "call to retreat from ... rational expectations ... by expelling rational agents from our model environments" (p. 3) and "to create theories with behavioral foundations by eliminating the asymmetry that rational expectations builds in between the agents in the model and the econometrician who is estimating it" (pp. 21–2). The hope was that boundedly rational traders would escape no-trade theorems, that boundedly rational agents and economists did not need to outwit each other, and that policy recommendations could be made without the need for the government to deceive agents. Unwilling to relinquish rational expectations altogether, Sargent and his companions further felt that the rational expectations equilibrium would be more attractive if learning would drive the system toward this equilibrium and were led to focus on convergence to the rational expectations fixed point. In addition, they hoped that incorporating bounded rationality would allow them to deal with some of the problems associated with rational expectations. First, rational expectations models sometimes have too many equilibria. At the same time, a system with boundedly rational agents could be used to select an equilibrium path. Second, rational expectations models were incapable of dealing with regime changes, which could be analyzed through the incorporation of learning. Finally, rational expectations equilibria might be difficult to compute. At the same time, incorporating learning could assist in the computation of equilibria by suggesting algorithms for performing this.

Ironically, in their efforts to make the agents in their model more boundedly rational, rational expectations economists had to be smarter because their models became larger and more demanding econometrically: The reason is that an econometric consequence of replacing rational agents with boundedly rational ones is to add a number of parameters. This is because many decisions need to be made about how to represent decision-making processes and the ways that they are updated. This returned rational expectations economists to the situation in which adaptive expectations had previously found itself, namely that economists were outwitting agents. Hence, their efforts at eliminating deception were not entirely successful. At the same time, the move to bounded rationality involved an embracement of self-deception, as discussed in the following.

Bounded rationality and self-deception

Bounded rationality

Instead of using bounded rationality to try to strengthen the concept of rational expectations, Herbert Simon pointed out in his theory of bounded rationality why the basic assumptions of neoclassical economics did not always work in practice. Simon (1975) foresaw difficulties along three steps of the way to a decision: "(1) the listing of all the alternative strategies; (2) the determination of all the consequences that follow upon each of these strategies; (3) the comparative evaluation of these sets of consequences" (p. 67). According to Simon (1975), "the subject, in order to perform with perfect rationality in this scheme, would have to have a complete description of the consequences following each alternative strategy and would have to compare these consequences. He would have to know in every single respect how the world would be changed by his behaving one way instead of another, and he would have to follow the consequences of behavior through unlimited stretches of time, unlimited reaches of space, and unlimited sets of values" (p. 69). Hence, Simon's bounded rationality differed in three important respects from rational expectations economics.

First, instead of assuming a fixed set of alternatives among which the decision-maker chose, Simon's theory of bounded rationality postulated a process for generating alternatives. Appealing to studies in modern cognitive psychology on the processes that human subjects used to choose among given alternatives and to find possible course of action, Simon argued that under most circumstances it was not reasonable to talk about finding "all the alternatives." The generation and evaluation of alternatives was a lengthy and costly process and one where, in real-world situations, even minimal completeness could seldom be guaranteed. Second, Simon detected another weakness associated with the basic assumptions of neoclassical economics in the fact that individuals had difficulty coming up with original solutions to problems. Cognitive limits – lack of knowledge and limits of ability to forecast the future – played a central role in the evaluation of alternatives. These cognitive limits were not simply limits on specifich information. They were almost always also limits on the adequacy of scientific theories that could be used to predict the relevant phenomena. Such observations led Simon to speculate that the mind mostly functions by applying approximate or cookbook solutions to problems. Finally, instead of assuming the maximization of a utility function, Simon's bounded rationality theory postulated a satisficing strategy. It sought to identify, in theory and in actual behavior, procedures for choosing that were computationally simpler and argued that individuals picked the first choice that met a pre-set acceptance criterion. Simon (1978b) concluded that "neoclassical theory, even with the help of 'rational expectations' (more accurately described as 'consistent expectations'), is far from adequate to the needs of policy" (p. 471; also see Simon 1976, pp. 437–8; 1978a, pp. 445 and 453; 1979, pp. 485–6; 1982a, pp. 3 and 405; 1996, pp. 23–4, 38–9, 154).

Self-deception

Whereas rational expectations economics sought to eliminate deception, bounded rationality approaches embraced self-deception, in the sense of making decisions that are contrary to one's interests. Let us illustrate this by considering Simon's insights on organizational identification (see Cyert and March 1963; Simon 1997; 1998). In Simon's approach, organizations are viewed as devices, alternative to the market, by which individuals acting with incomplete knowledge and information can satisfactorily reduce their uncertainty and make their decisions. At the same time, the bounded rationality of the members of the organization restricts their ability to achieve optimality in the pursuit of their goals. As a result, theories of bounded rationality see organizations as setting targets and looking for alternatives that satisfy those targets, rather than trying to find the best imaginable solution. The typical administrator will follow rules-of-thumb to consider only those solutions that will satisfy reasonable goals with as few complications as possible. Furthermore, she will attend to goals sequentially, rather than simultaneously. These theories and observations on decision making in organizations have been applied to the systems and techniques of planning, budgeting, and control that are used in business and public administration.

According to Simon, organizational identification, which has a motivational and a cognitive component, colors and distorts individuals' decisions. The motivational component involves the observation that individuals become attached to group goals and develop a willingness to support these even at some sacrifice of personal goals. In other words, organizational identification implies self-deception. The cognitive component concerns the fact that information, conceptions, and frames of reference are different within an organization, thereby adding to the self-deception. In Simon's opinion, this was a natural extension of the insight that individuals need to form a simplified picture because they cannot handle the complexity of the world. In Simon's (1997, p. 295) words: "Through identification, organized society imposed upon the individual the scheme of social values in place of his personal motives." This self-deception prevents individuals from making correct decisions when the restricted area with which they identify themselves must be weighed against other values outside that area. Yet, leading individuals to pursue organizational goals at the expense of their own interests is essential for organizational effectiveness. Because of the powers of identification to tie people to organizational goals, organizations are far more coherent and play a far more central role in economic life than mainstream economic theory supposes. In other words, self-deception is essential to the role of organizations.

Whereas such appeals to self-deception have not yet appeared in the rational expectations literature, they are an integral part of other research that develops Simon's original bounded rationality program, most notably behavioral economics.[9] Starting from empirical and experimental counter-evidence to the strong rationality assumptions employed in mainstream economics, behavioral economists formalize and test psychological predictions. After identifying ways in which behavior differs from the mainstream model, they show how alternate theories can explain apparent anomalies. Along the way, they argue that market forces such as competition and arbitrage, learning on the part of decision makers, and some sort of evolutionary mechanism cannot eliminate the importance of their insights.

Sendhil Mullainathan and Richard Thaler (2000) identify three ways in which this new behavioral economics deviates from the standard model. First, under bounded rationality conditions, humans are faced with limited cognitive abilities that constrain their problem solving abilities, and are therefore subject to the self-deception that accompanies organizational identification. Second, bounded willpower illustrates that people sometimes make choices that are not in their long-run interest. Before elaborating on the self-deception involved in bounded willpower, let us complete our brief overview of behavioral economics. Finally, bounded self-interest shows that humans are often willing to sacrifice their own interests to help others, which does not necessarily involve self-deception. The size of the deviation determines the extent to which economics' conception of human choice needs to be modified. Matthew Rabin (1998) suggests three "degrees of deviation." First, there is evidence requiring relatively small modifications of the utility functions economists employ. This includes data illustrating that preferences are determined by changes in outcomes relative to a certain reference level. That is, decision makers' dislike for losses outweighs their desire for gains. Also, evidence that people pursue "other-regarding" goals such as fairness, reciprocal altruism, and revenge might not require a complete overhaul of the mainstream model. The next set of insights focuses on biases in judgment under uncertainty and calls for a more radical challenge to the standard model. They show that humans often infer too much from too little evidence and misread evidence as conforming to their hypotheses. Finally, the most radical critique includes support for the insight that people have difficulties evaluating their own preferences. There is also confirmation of framing effects, preference reversals, and related phenomena. And there is evidence of self-control problems and a focus on short-run gratification inconsistent with long-run preferences. In other words, the more self-deception, the bigger is the overhaul required of the mainstream model, which brings us to the promised closer look at bounded willpower.

The most prominent example of people making choices that go against their self-interest concerns cognitive dissonance (see Earl and Wicklund 1999), which focuses on forms of behavior that appear to involve ignoring information that potentially conflicts with cherished beliefs. These insights were first developed in psychology by Leon Festinger (1957, p. 3), who advanced two hypotheses:

The existence of dissonance, being psychologically uncomfortable, will motivate the person to try to reduce the dissonance and achieve consonance.

When dissonance is present, in addition to trying to reduce it, the person will actively avoid situations and information that could increase the dissonance.

In economics (see Earl and Wicklund 1999), these hypotheses were first picked up by Albert Hirschman (1965) in understanding the successes and failures of underdeveloped countries. Shlomo Maital (1982) employed cognitive dissonance to explain debt accumulation through credit cards and his insights were further extended by Amitai Etzioni (1986). Stanley Kaish (1986) appealed to self-deception in the sense of cognitive dissonance to explain why participants in a bull market ignore crash warnings. Finally, George Akerlof and William Dickens (1982), in perhaps the best-known contribution among the ones mentioned here, argue that the prevalence of self-deception calls for arrangements such as compulsory old age insurance as well as safety regulation.

In the spirit of Simon, and not of appeals to bounded rationality on the part of rational expectations economists, the self-deception associated with cognitive dissonance calls into question the core assumptions of mainstream economics, which brings us to our concluding evaluation of the transition from rationality to bounded rationality, as well as from deception to self-deception.

Conclusion

While models of bounded rationality have not always appeared as attractive as the axiomatized certainties of neoclassical economics, more and more economists are embracing one form or another of bounded rationality. Models of bounded rationality owe their revival partly to attempts to develop a viable alternative to neoclassical economics and partly to attempts to strengthen neoclassical economics. As we have seen, the move from rational expectations to bounded rationality may be understood as an effort to eliminate deception in the sense of outwitting. At the same time, it involved a transition to self-deception, thereby undermining efforts to support the mainstream. Self-deception as defined in this paper challenges several core orthodox insights (see Earl and Wicklund 1999, Elster 1983). Sunk costs that have been mistakenly incurred require extensive justification efforts on the part of a decision maker who seeks to avoid cognitive dissonance. Opportunity costs are best forgotten by self-deceptive agents who endeavor to ignore the sacrifices they have made as a result of their choices. Finally, "given preferences" are undermined by agents who actively seek alternatives in accordance with their choices, once the decisions have been made. These consequences, then, weaken attempts to strengthen neoclassical economics through appeals to bounded rationality, while at the same time lending support to efforts on the part of bounded rationality theorists, behavioral economists, and the like to develop viable alternatives to mainstream economics.

Returning to the deception with which this paper started, let us briefly touch on the realization that analysts of economics, including the author of this piece, are also prone to deception. Whereas (epistemological) symmetry between social scientists and the agents they study has only recently begun receiving attention from economists, it is an issue that has long exercised the minds of science studies scholars. If science studies scholars and the scientists they study are truly distinct in an epistemological sense, then science studies scholars can only claim some kind of epistemic privilege in understanding the scientists' quandaries more deeply than they do themselves by using some criteria of superiority. However, the source of these criteria is unclear. If, on the other hand, science studies scholars and the scientists they study are not distinct epistemologically, their interdependence suggests that the science studies scholars' research processes assume (at least part of) the answers they set out to find. Yet, supposing the science studies scholars are able to reproduce the scientists' reasoning in their own terms, then it is unclear why one should take their word over the scientists'. Thus, science studies scholars' voices either undermine their own assertions or become indistinguishable from the voices they wish to observe. If the scientists are unintelligible, then how come science studies scholars can make sense out of them? If the scientists are intelligible, then why would we listen to science studies scholars? We are all, science studies scholars, economists, agents, and governments alike, involved in similar efforts at dealing with (self-)deception.

Notes

* The author gratefully acknowledges comments from Caroline Gerschlager, participants of the Workshop on Exchange, Deceptions, and Self-Deceptions, as well as an anonymous referee. She is also very appreciative of the support of the Netherlands Institute for Advanced Study in the Humanities and Social Sciences (NIAS).

1 In other words, it has an informational as well as a motivational component.

2 Also see Sargent (1987c): "[R]ational expectations possesses the defining property that the forecasts made by agents within the model are no worse than the forecasts that can be made by the economist who has the model" (p. 76).

3 Lucas and Sargent (1981) also noted that the "model misspecification route seems less likely to deliver error terms with the good statistical properties – namely, certain orthogonality properties" (p. xxii).

4 The idea of replacing the information set with a subset, thereby adding an error term, was suggested by Shiller (1979) in his study of the term structure of interest rates.

5 Taking this idea to the limit, economic agents perceive and process information in continuous time, whereas econometricians only have discrete time data. This is known as the problem of aggregation over time.

6 It could be argued that the errors-in-variables justification has never been taken seriously by econometricians, because they display very little interest in the process of the generation of their data.

7 I should note that the more specific claim is that policies that alter nominal aggregate demand do not affect real variables. It was later argued that this claim follows not from rational expectations, except

to the degree that rational expectations prevents money illusion from encouraging people to make real mistakes, but from the classical dichotomy built into the notion of continuous market clearing.

8 In particular, making policy recommendations required that the government had better information than everyone else, or was able always to do the unexpected and catch people off guard.

9 Also note that mainly through Williamson's (1975; 1985) insistence, the notion of bounded rationality has played a prominent role in transaction cost economics. Williamson sought to link the idea of conflict of interest with the idea of information limitations and saw organizational forms as implicit or explicit solutions to the problems of decision and control created by opportunism and bounded rationality. In Williamson's (1985, p. 47) words: "By opportunism I mean self-interest seeking with guile." And: "[O]pportunism refers to the incomplete or distorted disclosure of information, especially to calculated efforts to mislead, distort, disguise, obfuscate, or otherwise confuse." This deception can occur both actively and passively, as well as both ex ante and ex post, before and after contracting takes place. However, this interpretation of deception falls outside of the main focus of this paper, so is not pursued in further detail here.

References

Akerlof, G. A., 'The Market for "Lemons": Quality Uncertainty and the Market Mechanism', *Quarterly Journal of Economics*, 84 (1970), 488–500.

Akerlof, G. A. and Dickens, W. T., 'The Economic Consequences of Cognitive Dissonance', *American Economic Review*, 72 (1982), 307–19.

Barro, R. J., 'Rational Expectations and the Role of Monetary Policy', *Journal of Monetary Economics*, 2 (1976), 1095–117.

Begg, D. K. H., *The Rational Expectations Revolution in Macroeconomics* (Baltimore, MD: Johns Hopkins University Press, 1982).

Bray, M. and Kreps, D., 'Rational Learning and Rational Expectations', in G. Feiwel (ed.), *Arrow and the Ascent of Modern Economic Theory* (New York: New York University Press, 1987), pp. 597–625.

Buiter, W. H., 'The Macroeconomics of Dr. Pangloss: A Critical Survey of the New Classical Macroeconomics', *Economic Journal*, 90 (1980), 34–50.

Cagan, P., 'The Monetary Dynamics of Hyperinflation', in M. Friedman (ed.), *Studies in the Quantity Theory of Money* (Chicago, IL: University of Chicago Press, 1956), pp. 25–117.

Cyert, R. M. and March, J. G., *A Behavioral Theory of the Firm* (Englewood Cliffs, NJ: Prentice-Hall, 1963).

Earl, P. E. and Wicklund, R. A., 'Cognitive Dissonance', in P. E. Earl and S. Kemp (eds), *The Elgar Companion to Consumer Research and Economic Psychology* (Cheltenham: Edward Elgar, 1999), pp. 81–8.

Egidi, M., Marris, R., Simon, H. A. and Viale, R. (eds), *Economics, Bounded Rationality and the Cognitive Revolution* (Brookfield, VT: Edward Elgar, 1992).

Elster, J., *Sour Grapes: Studies in the Subversion of Rationality* (Cambridge: Cambridge University Press, 1983).

Etzioni, A., 'The Case for a Multiple-Utility Conception', *Economics and Philosophy*, 2 (1986), 159–84.

Festinger, L., *A Theory of Cognitive Dissonance* (Stanford, CA: Stanford University Press, 1957).

Friedman, M., 'The Role of Monetary Policy', *American Economic Review*, 58 (1968), 1–17.

Hakansson, N. H., Kunkel, J. G. and Ohlson, J. A., 'Sufficient and Necessary Conditions for Information to Have Social Value in Pure Exchange', *Journal of Finance*, 37 (1982), 1169–81.

Hirschman, A. O., 'Obstacles to Development: A Classification and a Quasi-Vanishing Act', *Economic Development and Cultural Change*, 13 (1965), 385–93.

Hoover, K. D., *The New Classical Macroeconomics* (New York: Blackwell, 1988).

Kaish, S., 'Behavioral Economics in the Theory of the Business Cycle', in B. Gilad and S. Kaish (eds), *Handbook of Behavioral Economics*, B (Greenwich, CT: JAI Press, 1986).

Kantor, B., 'Rational Expectations and Economic Thought', *Journal of Economic Literature*, 17 (1979), 1422–41.

Keuzekamp, H. A., 'A Precursor to Muth: Tinbergen's 1932 Model of Rational Expectations', *Economic Journal*, 101 (1991), 1245–53.

Lucas, R. E., 'Expectations and the Neutrality of Money', *Journal of Economic Theory*, 4 (1972a), 103–24.

Lucas, R. E., 'Econometric Testing of the Natural Rate Hypothesis', in O. Eckstein (ed.), *The Econometrics of Price Determination Conference* (Washington, DC: Board of Governors of the Federal Reserve System, 1972b), pp. 50–9.

Lucas, R. E., 'An Equilibrium Model of the Business Cycle', *Journal of Political Economy*, 83 (1975), 1113–44.

Lucas, R. E., 'Econometric Policy Evaluation: A Critique', in K. Brunner and A. H. Meltzer (eds), *The Phillips Curve and Labor Markets*, Carnegie-Rochester Conference Series on Public Policy, I (Amsterdam: North-Holland, 1976), pp. 19–46.

Lucas, R. E. and Sargent, T. J., 'Introduction', in R. E. Lucas and T. J. Sargent (eds), *Rational Expectations and Econometric Practice* (Minneapolis: University of Minnesota Press, 1981), pp. xi–xl.

Maital, S., *Minds, Markets, and Money: Psychological Foundations of Economic Behavior* (New York: Basic Books, 1982).

McCallum, B. T., 'The Current State of the Policy Ineffectiveness Debate', *American Economic Review*, 69 (1979a), 240–5.

McCallum, B. T., 'Rational Expectations and Macroeconomic Stabilization Policy', *Journal of Money, Credit, and Banking*, 12 (1979b), 716–46.

Milgrom, P. and Stokey, N., 'Information, Trade and Common Knowledge', *Journal of Economic Theory*, 26 (1982), 17–27.

Mullainathan, S. and Thaler, R. H., 'Behavioral Economics', NBER Working Paper 7948 (Cambridge, MA: NBER, 2000).

Nelson, R. R. and Winter, S. G., *An Evolutionary Theory of Economic Change* (Cambridge, MA: Harvard University Press, 1982).

Nerlove, M. L., 'Adaptive Expectations and Cobweb Phenomena', *Quarterly Journal of Economics*, 72 (1958), 227–40.

Rabin, M., 'Psychology and Economics', *Journal of Economic Literature*, 36 (1998), 11–46.

Rubinstein, M., 'Securities Market Efficiency in an Arrow-Debreu Economy', *American Economic Review*, 65 (1975), 812–24.

Sargent, T. J., 'Autoregressions, Expectations, and Advice (with discussion)', *American Economic Review*, 74 (1984), 408–21.

Sargent, T. J., *Macroeconomic Theory*, 2nd edn (Boston, MA: Academic Press, 1987a).

Sargent, T. J., *Dynamic Macroeconomic Theory* (Cambridge, MA: Harvard University Press, 1987b).

Sargent, T. J., 'Rational Expectations', in J. Eatwell et al. (eds), *The New Palgrave: A Dictionary of Economics* (London: Macmillan, 1987c), pp. 76–85.

Sargent, T. J., *Bounded Rationality in Macroeconomics* (Oxford: Oxford University Press, 1993).

Sargent, T. J. and Wallace, N., '"Rational" Expectations, the Optimal Monetary Instrument, and the Optimal Money Supply Rule', *Journal of Political Economy*, 83 (1975), 241–54. Reprinted in R. E. Lucas and T. J. Sargent (eds), *Rational Expectations and Econometric Practice* (Minneapolis: University of Minnesota Press, 1981), pp. 215–28.

Sargent, T. J. and Wallace, N., 'Rational Expectations and the Theory of Economic Policy', in R. E. Lucas and T. J. Sargent (eds), *Rational Expectations and Econometric Practice* (Minneapolis: University of Minnesota Press, 1981), pp. 199–213. Reprinted from *Journal of Monetary Economics*, 2 (1976), 169–84.

Shiller, R. J., 'The Volatility of Long-Term Interest Rates and Expectations Models of the Term Structure', *Journal of Political Economy*, 87 (1979), 1190–219.

Sent, E.-M., *The Evolving Rationality of Rational Expectations: An Assessment of Thomas Sargent's Achievements* (Cambridge: Cambridge University Press, 1998).

Simon, H. A., 'A Behavioral Model of Rational Choice', *Quarterly Journal of Economics*, 69 (1955). Reprinted in H. A. Simon, *Models of Man* (New York: Wiley 1957), pp. 241–60 (page references to reprint).

Simon, H. A., 'Rational Choice and the Structure of the Environment', *Psychological Review*, 63 (1956). Reprinted in H. A. Simon, *Models of Man* (New York: Wiley, 1957), pp. 261–73 (page references to reprint).

Simon, H. A., *Models of Man* (New York: Wiley, 1957).

Simon, H. A., *The New Science of Management Decision* (New York: Harper & Row, 1960).

Simon, H. A., 'Thinking by Computers', in R. G. Colodny (ed.), *Mind and Cosmos: Essays in Contemporary Science and Philosophy* (Pittsburgh, PA: University of Pittsburgh Press, 1966). Reprinted in H. A. Simon, *Models of Discovery* (Dordrecht: D. Reidel Publishing Company, 1977), pp. 268–85 (page references to reprint).

Simon, H. A., 'The Logic of Heuristic Decision Making', in N. Rescher (ed.), *The Logic of Decision and Action* (Pittsburgh, PA: University of Pittsburgh Press, 1967a), pp. 1–20. Reprinted in H. A. Simon, *Models of Discovery* (Dordrecht: D. Reidel Publishing Company, 1977), pp. 154–75 (page references to reprint).

Simon, H. A., 'Reply to Professor Binkley's Comments', in N. Rescher (ed.), *The Logic of Decision and Action* (Pittsburgh, PA: University of Pittsburgh Press, 1967b), pp. 32–3.

Simon, H. A., 'The Theory of Problem Solving', *Information Processing*, 71 (1972), 261–77. Reprinted in H. A. Simon, *Models of Discovery* (Dordrecht: D. Reidel Publishing Company, 1977), pp. 214–44 (page references to reprint).

Simon, H. A., *Administrative Behavior*, 3rd edn (New York: The Free Press, 1975).

Simon, H. A., 'From Substantive to Procedural Rationality', in S. J. Latsis (ed.), *Method and Appraisal in Economics* (Cambridge: Cambridge University Press, 1976), pp. 129–148. Reprinted in H. A. Simon,

Models of Bounded Rationality, II (Cambridge, MA: MIT Press, (1982b), pp. 424–43 (page references to reprint).
Simon, H. A., *Models of Discovery* (Dordrecht: D. Reidel Publishing Company, 1977).
Simon, H. A., 'Rationality as Process and as Product of Thought', *American Economic Review*, 68:2 (1978a), 1–16. Reprinted in H. A. Simon, *Models of Bounded Rationality*, II (Cambridge, MA: MIT Press, 1982b), pp. 444–59 (page references to reprint).
Simon, H. A., 'On How to Decide What to Do', *Bell Journal of Economics*, 9 (1978b), 494–507. Reprinted in H. A. Simon, *Models of Bounded Rationality*, I (Cambridge, MA: MIT Press, 1982a), pp. 460–73 (page references to reprint).
Simon, H. A., 'Rational Decision Making in Business Organizations', *American Economic Review*, 69 (1979), 493–513. Reprinted in H. A. Simon, *Models of Bounded Rationality*, I (Cambridge, MA: MIT Press 1982a), pp. 474–94 (page references to reprint).
Simon, H. A., *Models of Bounded Rationality*, I (Cambridge, MA: MIT Press, 1982a).
Simon, H. A., *Models of Bounded Rationality*, II (Cambridge, MA: MIT Press, 1982b).
Simon, H. A., 'Behavioral Economics', in J. Eatwell et al. (eds), *The New Palgrave: A Dictionary of Economics* (London: Macmillan, 1987a), pp. 221–25.
Simon, H. A., 'Bounded Rationality', in J. Eatwell et al. (eds), *The New Palgrave: A Dictionary of Economics* (London: Macmillan, 1987b), pp. 266–8.
Simon, H. A., *Models of My Life* (New York: Basic Books, 1991).
Simon, H. A., 'Introductory Comment', in M. Egidi et al. (eds), *Economics, Bounded Rationality and the Cognitive Revolution* (Brookfield, VT: Edward Elgar, 1992), pp. 3–7.
Simon, H. A., 'The Human Mind: The Symbolic Level', *Proceedings of the American Philosophical Society*, 137 (1993), 638–47.
Simon, H. A., *The Sciences of the Artificial*, 3rd edn (Cambridge: MIT Press, 1996).
Simon, H. A., *Administrative Behavior*, 3rd edn (New York: The Free Press, 1997).
Steinbruner, J. D., *The Cybernetic Theory of Decision* (Princeton, NJ: Princeton University Press, 1974).
Stiglitz, J. and Weiss, A., 'Credit Rationing in Markets with Imperfect Information', *American Economic Review,* 71 (1981), 393–410.
Tirole, J., 'On the Possibility of Speculation under Rational Expectations', *Econometrica*, 50 (1982), 1163–82.

Varian, H. R., 'Differences of Opinion in Financial Markets', *Financial Risk: Theory, Evidence, and Implications* (Proceedings of the 11th Annual Economic Policy Conference of the Federal Reserve Bank of St. Louis, 1987), pp. 3–37.

Williamson, O. E., *Markets and Hierarchies* (New York: The Free Press, 1975).

Williamson, O. E., *The Economic Institutions of Capitalism* (New York: The Free Press, 1985).

Part II

Behavior and Incentives to Deceive: The Success of Deception in Markets

4

Deception in Markets: The Enron Case

Caroline Gerschlager

Abstract

This chapter takes the Enron case as a point of departure in order to discuss one type of perverse incentive, namely, the incentive to deceive. Deception is a relatively novel concern in economics, where the study of incentives under conditions of information asymmetries is crucial in accounting for the possibility of deception in markets. By acting in a particular way, people are seen as responding to economic incentives. Economists are typically concerned with the study of incentives that induce people to work, trade, consume, or save. Against this background, the chapter discusses economic incentives to deceive by drawing on financial scandals in which economic mechanisms encourage people to act to the detriment of others whether these others constitute a company or the state. In conclusion, problems of controlling deception are addressed.

Introduction

On 2 December 2001, when Enron filed for bankruptcy (under Chapter 11), the swindle came to an end. It was the first evidence of a case of ongoing economic and financial fraud. In the first section of the chapter, the Enron case is taken as point of departure for a discussion of economic incentives to deceive. Fraud and deception are relatively novel concerns in economics, and the second section provides a basic discussion of how modern economics typically accounts for these phenomena. The study of incentives, and the question of how they make people act in a particular way in the context of the economy, is crucial in this connection. The third section focuses on deception in terms of perverse incentives in corporations and markets. Finally, incentives to deceive are discussed as an economic policy issue. Can markets get rid of liars and cheats unaided?

The Enron case[1]

Enron was a leading energy company that sought to transform itself into the world's largest energy trader. Led by its dynamic chairman Kenneth Lay, who had extensive political connections, during a 15-year period Enron became America's seventh largest company, employing a staff of 21,000 in more than 40 countries. It embraced new technologies and established new methods of trading in energy, in particular trading futures in energy contracts between suppliers and consumers in the deregulated energy world, where prices have become more volatile. It thus became a major player in the US energy market. It offered companies the chance to hedge against the risk of adverse price movements and seemed to be a shining example of American corporate success.

But the firm's success turned out to be based on an elaborate scam. Enron lied about its profits and stood accused of a range of shady dealings, including concealing debts by setting up shell companies that didn't show up in the company's accounts. As the depth of the deception became clear, investors and creditors retreated, forcing the firm into Chapter 11 bankruptcy in December 2001. When Enron's financial manipulations finally became public, its stock collapsed. In three months, Enron went from being a company worth almost US$111 billion to bankruptcy. Its share price collapsed from about US$95 to less than US$1.

Enron's concealment of debts and dubious credit-raising practices amounted to a huge Ponzi scheme, with the collusion of a network of individuals and institutions. The Enron case has been analysed from different perspectives. Some commentators have seen it as an accounting scandal (putting the blame on lax accounting standards), or have interpreted it as a consequence of an era of massive deregulation and laissez-faire. It has also been diagnosed as a case of regulatory failure (it was said that the regulatory authorities had insufficient financial resources to perform their task). Others blamed the breakdown of Enron on greed and the chief executives' excessive salaries.[2] While these factors have all contributed to the corporation's failure, the Enron scandal should also be seen as a deception scandal. Enron is significant primarily as an example of deception, and the scandal revolves around the story of who was deceived by whom.

The CEOs misrepresented the company's financial condition in order to benefit from the high share price by cashing in their stock options.[3] There were abundant opportunities to conceal the firm's actual ills in the financial reports. Enron was overvalued by means of the accounting firm's deceptive reporting. This overvaluation, which resulted from not expensing stock options, long remained unnoticed by the markets. Shareholders were led to believe that stock options were cost-free and therefore harmless. Stock options are a good example of how accounting can provide misleading information. An important aspect of the deception scandal is that the CEOs distorted information, thereby exploiting investors' ignorance of the cost of stock options to the company issuing them.[4]

In their effort to hide debts, Enron executives colluded with respected banks that were key players in a series of fraudulent transactions.[5] Enron manipulated its taxes and accounting in order to abuse the tax system. The report said Enron profited from 12 large tax deals from 1995 to 2001, which saved the corporation more than US$2 billion. Thus, not only investors but also the state were cheated and defrauded. The Senate Finance Committee found that the energy giant paid no income tax between 1996 and 1999.

Why did investors, accountants, and the state expose themselves to such abuse? With the help of modern economics, it is possible to unravel parts of the scandal to get a better understanding of deception in corporations and markets.

Deception in modern economics

How are cheats and frauds perceived from an economic point of view? What specific pictures do economic models draw when they are applied to deception? We make these questions more precise by reference to new developments in modern economics.

General equilibrium theory, as first proclaimed by Walras in the 1870s and then formalized by Arrow and Debreu in the 1950s, is fundamental to economic thought, because it demonstrated the very possibility of economic order founded on the individual pursuit of self-interest. These models gave a prominent role to the idea of the invisible hand, which can be traced back to Adam Smith (1976 [1776]). This is the idea that the pursuit of individual self-interest need not conflict the overall good of the society (as theologians claimed), but can promote it. The central idea here is that "private vices" generate "public benefits" (Mandeville 1924

[1714]) by stimulating growth, or, to adopt Smith's terminology, by stimulating the "wealth of nations".

The basic characteristics of the economic agent are, then, rationality and self-interest (Hirshleifer 1985, p. 54). Typically, economic man is characterized by self-interested goals and a rational choice of means.[6] Yet in general equilibrium theory, despite the assumption that human beings tirelessly promote their self-interest, deception simply does not exist. This is because the model's assumption of rationality derives its force from other basic concepts such as equilibrium, competition, and the completeness of markets. In particular, it is the assumption of perfect competition in this model that prevents people from getting in each other's way in their pursuit of self-interest (Arrow 1987, p. 70). In this perfect world, information is complete: agents are conceived as omniscient, that is, equipped with complete certainty about the world – or at worst having full probability distributions for uncertain events (Simon 1982 [1978], pp. 281ff.). What is important for our problem is that these models simply do not accommodate anything like the Enron fraud.

Asymmetries of information

When the assumption of perfect competition in markets is relaxed, agency problems arise, such as exploitation of shareholders by CEOs. These problems have an important impact on the perfect functioning of markets. Within the framework of agency relationships, it is axiomatic that principal and agent have conflicting interests and differential information. Asymmetric information is the most obvious requirement for deception. As Hamlin points out "in a world in which all individuals are fully informed so that there is both full information and common knowledge of that fact, there can be no deception. Even where information is incomplete, so that there is genuine uncertainty, deception cannot occur if all individuals confront the world with identical information resources (and know that this is the case). So, by definition, there can be no deception unless information is (or is believed to be) distributed across individuals asymmetrically" (see Hamlin, Chapter 8 in this book). Deception is therefore as prevalent and as persistent as the asymmetrical information necessary to support it.

Oliver E. Williamson correctly reminds us that there is nothing in the image of the economic man that hinders him or her from "embezzle[ing] funds" or "robb[ing] banks" (Williamson cites Diamond, 1985, p. 49fn), provided he or she can gain an advantage. The self-interest postulate, according to Williamson, can therefore best be captured by the term "opportunism". Opportunism includes "lying, stealing, and cheating ... [and] ... more often involves subtle forms of deceit" (Williamson 1985,

p. 47). In other words, economic man will cheat if he can, that is, in the absence of constraints.

An opportunistic agent is thus a cheat when he or she "misrepresents the information he has at his disposal so as to persuade another individual (principal) to choose a course of action he would not have chosen had he been properly informed. ... The agent is better informed than the principal and in a position to use his superior knowledge to affect the principal's actions so as to increase his own share of the total benefit at the principal's expense" (Karni 1987, p. 416).

In the principal-agent framework (which can thus be used to study problems of deception), it is assumed that the agent has an informational advantage over the principal. Owing to conflicting interests, the agent could use his or her informational advantage to further his or her own interests at the expense of those of the principal. If the opportunity for deception presents itself, it is likely to take place. Therefore, it is assumed that the potential victim of deception needs protection in the form of a contract governing the relationship between the parties. In many contexts, where the interests of the contracting parties diverge, agency problems arise, typically in contracts governing the relationships between debtholders and/or stockholders and managers, owners and employees, banks and debtors, and so on. Opportunism manifests itself as adverse selection, moral hazard, shirking, and other forms of strategic behavior (Williamson 2000, p. 601).

Moral hazard is used as a synonym for "hidden action." It involves monitoring problems that arise after the conclusion of a contract. It is crucial when the actions taken by one party to the contract (the agent) are unobservable for the other party (the principal). The term "moral hazard" traditionally referred to hidden actions in the insurance industry, where the problem is particularly relevant. For example, in the case of a fire insurance contract where the insurance claim (following the complete destruction of a building by fire) exceeds the market value of the building (that is, in cases of 100 percent coverage), the owner has a strong incentive to be inattentive, or even to torch his or her own building (Campbell 1995, p. 104).

In the literature, similar problems are reported in the credit market, for example, where an act of investment is hidden, because banks are unable to observe the project in which an entrepreneur invests. The problem is that there is no credible way of transmitting the relevant information (the entrepreneur may make a wrong investment decision; he may be incompetent or even lie). This often leads to the bank selecting "bad" debtors. The bank in this case is subject to adverse selection because it can never possess all the relevant information on the debtor's capacity and willingness to repay his or her debts. As a consequence, the problem of credit rationing may occur in capital markets (Hillier 1997, pp. 50–1).

While typically the invisible hand is meant to work with a view to uniting the interests of individuals and society, modern economics has shown the limitations of markets. The emphasis of modern economics in this view is not on showing how markets can function perfectly but on how our understanding of market imperfections can be improved. One of the central insights of modern economics is that the price mechanism does not always work. Under conditions of asymmetric information, market inefficiencies arise, and it can no longer be taken for granted that the individual pursuit of self-interest automatically contributes to creating wealth. The possibility of deception under conditions of asymmetric information certainly is one important element in market failure.

Biases of human behavior

In most of these economic models a form of rational expectations is assumed (for a discussion of knowledge assumptions and equilibrium models, refer to Rizvi, Chapter 1, and Croson, Chapter 5, in this book). While the approaches cited above share the rationality assumption in explaining deception, economists exploring a psychological foundation for economic theory have adopted a different approach. Experiments have confirmed that deception works and that agents are in fact 'cheatable', an insight that conflicts with the assumptions of rationality and self-interest postulated by the traditional model of economic man. Croson, for example, in her review of experiments (Chapter 5 in this book), concludes that agents can be cheated because they are gullible; she holds that agents are overconfident in their ability to detect deception and insufficiently skeptical of statements they receive from others. As a consequence, they are "prone to deception by others". Croson's analysis has to be seen in the context of a number of recent papers that concentrate on lying, in particular (for example, Crawford 2003, Charness 2000). In accordance with standard economic predictions, Croson claims that agents do in fact lie when it is in their interest to do so. On the other hand, experiments also show that deception works because targets are "'lie-able' to a greater extent than equilibrium theory predicts" (ibid.). Lie-able agents cannot be conceived of as rational in the sense of the self-interest postulate of economic theory, and this is why, from the vantage point of economic theory, gullibility (a "weakness" that is related to other behavioral biases discussed by this approach) is a clear case of irrationality. Coval, Hirshleifer, and Teoh (Chapter 6 in this book) also write in this tradition, assuming that these biases in human behavior explain why deception works in the marketplace. The authors also cite the process of evolution as a reason for the persistence of deception (and self-deception). In their study on financial markets they conclude that (overconfident and biased) investors easily become targets of deception (ibid.).

According to this approach, the gullibility of human beings can be seen as an additional explanation of how deception may occur in economic settings.

Incentives to deceive

In modern economic approaches, the study of incentives is crucial (Laffont and Martimort 2002). Economic incentives are seen as a response to the question of what makes people act in a particular way. This part of the chapter discusses perverse incentives, that is, incentives that have the opposite effect to that intended. Incentives to deceive in corporations and markets are discussed. Examples are given whereby economic mechanisms encourage people to act at the detriment of others, that is, to the detriment of their company or the state. In particular, the focus is on stock options and looting strategies in the savings and loan crises of the 1980s in the US.

Deception in corporations

In the Enron fraud, the ideal situation, in which the CEO is the controlling shareholder, clearly failed. We saw that stock ownership increased the CEO's incentive to engage in fraud because fraud creates fictional income and increases stock prices. With hindsight, the increase in their satisfaction due to stock options – much in contrast to what was assumed – did not increase loyalty, but seems to have triggered a general tendency by executives to plunder their firms.

The problem of diverging interests inherent in the modern corporation has already been focused on by Berle and Means (1991 [1932]) who saw in the divorce of ownership from the control of the modern corporation a serious problem, because management might possibly occupy a position of (absolute) power. Berle and Means foresaw a possible development whereby "the controlling group is given free rein, with the corresponding danger of a corporate oligarchy coupled with the probability of an era of corporate plundering" (ibid., p. 311).

Berle and Means were already aware of modern agency theory in which the interests of the directors and managers are seen as diverging from those of the owners of the firm. The theory of the modern corporation later placed emphasis on the opportunities for the exploitation of shareholders by unfaithful managers. What has become known as "the agency problem" is the propensity for agents (that is, managers) to cheat their principals (that is, shareholders) to their own advantage if they can evade detection or, if caught, without suffering a penalty greater than their gain.

In economic theory, an agency relationship is a contract under which one or more persons (the principal[s]) engage another person (the agent) to perform some service on their behalf, which involves delegating some decision making authority to the agent. If both parties to the relationship are utility maximizers, there is good reason to believe that the agent will not always act in the best interests of the principal. The idea here is that the principal can limit damage to his or her interest by establishing appropriate incentives for the agent and by incurring monitoring costs designed to limit the aberrant activities of the agent (Jensen and Meckling 1976, p. 308).

The use of stock options as a form of compensation went hand in hand with shareholder value development of the 1980s. In theory, stock options are meant to solve the corporate governance problem outlined above. In this view, options should align the interests of managers and the interests of shareholders. Generally, stock options are favored in contract theory as a means to solve the problem of divergent interests between management and shareholders in publicly traded corporations. CEOs, for example, are supposed to work harder if they know they might benefit from an increase in their company's stock. Easterbrook and Fischel (1991), for example, two leading theorists of corporate governance, recommend that executives be encouraged by stock options to hold substantial quantities of the firm's stock (ibid., p. 282). They hold that these would act as "built-in guarantees of the buyer's good intentions" and "act as a bond for honest conduct" (ibid., p. 133). Stock options are generally seen as appropriate incentives to prevent shareholder-CEOs from harming their companies, as this would mean harming themselves too.

One commonly accepted incentive for the over-reporting of corporate income, which came to light in 2002, was the granting of stock options as part of executive compensation packages. As a result of corporate scandals this view of stock options has come under scrutiny. Far from solving the agency problem, stock options may – under specific circumstances – contribute to exacerbating it. The problem with stock options is that they set an economic mechanism in place that provides an incentive for managers to distort information (Stiglitz 2003, pp. 118ff). In this sense, rewards are given for "bad" behavior. Stock options were a means of concealing the CEOs' income, and consequently also of concealing the actual profits (or losses) the company was making; hence it was not clear what the company was really worth. CEOs clearly gained from distorting information on their real income because if "shareholders had known what was being given to their executives, they would have recognized that there was less left for themselves" (ibid., p. 120).[7]

With the rise of stock prices, options became more valuable and induced managers to present Wall Street with the figures it wanted, whatever the reality of their businesses. This is not to say that stock options cannot also be desirable if tied to long-term development of the company; but as they were set in place, inciting a short-term rise in share prices, they generated consequences that were not originally intended in the optimal contracting framework.

Some authors have recently been working on an alternative to the contracting approach in order to explain stock options, putting forward the "managerial power approach" (Bebchuk, Fried, and Walker 2002). In this approach executive pay reflects managerial rent-seeking rather than the provision of effective incentives.

The above discussion of stock options as providing incentives to deceive (or perverse incentives) shows that they should be seen as part of the agency problem and not as their solution (Bebchuk and Fried 2003).[8]

Deception in markets

The series of corporate scandals subsequent to Enron bears testimony to a cumulative increase in deception, which was located not exclusively, but most importantly, in finance and high-tech industries. We know from experience that the deception scandal at the core of Enron was not the first in corporate and economic history. The savings and loan scandal of the 1980s was already significant in showing how agency problems may lead to managerial looting, of both shareholders and the state (Krosnzner and Strahan 1996).

In their analysis of the savings and loan crisis of the 1980s in the United States, Akerlof and Romer (1993) argue that the observed behavior came close to a Ponzi scheme. They claim that a fraudulent scheme existed: CEOs and their partners (in deceit) were not only taking excessive risks, but directly taking advantage of insurance guarantees. Akerlof and Romer particularly stress distorted and "perverse incentives" (ibid., p. 3). In their view, "looting" or "bankruptcy for profit will occur if ... owners [have] an incentive to pay themselves more than their firms are worth and then default on their debt obligations" (ibid., p. 2). These opportunities to loot, according to the authors, occur when management can profit from the failure of the firm. Akerlof and Romer show that, when a firm has little or negative capital, it can be a wealth-maximizing strategy for the CEO to plunder other people's money, typically deposits in financial institutions or insurance funds, with the guarantor of the assets, "typically the government and its taxpayers, left holding the bag" (ibid., pp. 6–7).

With this analysis they also challenge the standard explanation of the banking crisis in terms of moral hazard.[9] According to Akerlof and Romer, the problem was that firms had incentives "to go broke for profit at society's expense (to loot) instead of to go for broke (to gamble on success)." The authors focus, not on excessive risk-taking (ibid., p. 4), but on empirical evidence that profit opportunities from looting were exploited. "Bankruptcy for profit occurs most commonly when a government guarantees a firm's debt obligations" (ibid., p. 2). In Akerlof and Romers's analysis, the CEOs were definitely not unaware of what they were doing; it is not their particular incompetence, or herd behavior, which led them to conclude bad deals, they intentionally took advantage of the company at the expense of others (that is, the creditors). The general idea is that looting rather than incompetence was responsible for the general harm that the savings and loan debacle caused (Hall 1993, p. 62).

A decade later, we can observe similarities between the savings and loan scandal and the recent scandals: both cases were characterized by perverse incentive structures.

Are the markets enough to control deception?

In discussions of fraud and deception, it is often claimed that the most effective way to control deception is not control markets. In the law and economics theory of corporate governance, for example, it is the authority of the market that checks deception. Easterbrook and Fischel (1991) argue that the dynamics of the market drives managers "to act as if they had investors' interests at heart" and not to enrich themselves at the investors' expense (ibid., p. 4). Markets are said to offer information that can distinguish value-increasing control transactions from others in which looting or mismanagement may be involved (ibid., p. 116). Once looters have plundered a firm, the damage to their reputation prevents them from doing so again. Deception is therefore seen as "one-time transaction" (ibid., p. 130). Once frauds are detected, markets exclude them, because other market participants will refuse to deal.[10] This view is part of the idea that markets also provide a solution to their own imperfections.[11]

Other authors adopt a similar view with regard to the savings and loan crisis of the 1980s; it has been argued that looting was not really decisive in this context, and that the cause of the crisis was not underregulation but rather, excessive and bad regulation (Mankiw 1993).[12]

These approaches assume that individuals' pursuit of their own interests contributes to the public good. As has been shown above, this is not always the case. Due to asymmetric information, CEOs will not necessarily have an interest to honestly disclose, and the efforts that were undertaken not to expense stock options (and thus to provide transparency with regard to the firm's actual worth) can be seen as a case in point. Markets can function only if the information provided by economic agents is truthful, and not manipulated. Good accounting standards and practices therefore reduce asymmetries of information, and help make capital markets work better (Stiglitz 2003, p. 128). Modern economics has shown that information asymmetries (and biases in behavior) affect the workings of the market. When information is not distributed equally among the agents (between the shareholders and the management, for example), incentives to deceive can arise, subsequently harming workers, investors, and the state. These modern economic insights suggest that markets cannot always get rid of cheats and deceivers on their own.

Is any protection against abuse at all possible? In his article on the savings and loan crisis of the 1980s referred to above, Akerlof also suggested that there is a chance that people would learn from the crisis and be able to recognize the problem. However, today, after the experience of another series of economic and financial frauds, unprecedented in scale, it seems, on the contrary, as if history has repeated itself. The question that comes to mind is whether we can possibly learn how to protect the market from abuse.

This question aside, further research is needed to improve theoretical and empirical knowledge of the specific conditions under which a higher rate of intensified fraud and deception is likely to occur in the economy.

Notes

1. The following discussion is based on BBC News, "Enron at-a-glance," (2002). For a detailed description of the Enron case also see Fox (2003).
2. For a discussion of some of these reasons see Berenson (2003).
3. Among the major victims of the scheme are the employees and pension holders, investors and shareholders, and the state. As to the first group, thousands of people were left redundant. In addition, thousands lost their personal investments and pensions as Enron's stock plunged. Many employees had personal pension funds made up

of Enron shares, a common situation in corporate America. As to the second, the losses in the shareholders class action of the plaintiffs, who purchased Enron equity and debt securities between 19 October 1998 and 29 November 2001, are estimated at more than US$25 billion. The company's finance manager defrauded not only investors but also Enron itself through a number of complex financial deals. He created and managed the web of partnerships that disguised the true state of affairs in the firm and is alleged to have made a personal fortune in kickbacks from the partnerships. He was charged with fraud, money laundering and conspiracy in connection with Enron's multi-billion dollar collapse. Among the victims is the state: according to the investigation by the Senate Finance Committee the energy giant paid no income tax between 1996 and 1999. There were week-long programs of wining and dining, tennis, fishing and golf as part of the strategy to ease the relationship between bankers and Enron's tax research department. Enron made efforts to manipulate its taxes and accounting in order to abuse the tax system. The report said Enron profited from 12 large tax deals from 1995 to 2001 that saved the corporation more than US$2 billion

4 Not expensing stock options contributed to leaving investors in the dark about the depleted value of their shares. This ignorance in turn increased incentives to provide more and more pay in this non-transparent manner (Stiglitz 2003, p. 127); and, with more and more compensation depending on the short-run stock value, stock options provided an opportunity for the firms to inflate their numbers. In turn, stock options, which are gratifying when stock prices rise, also produce incentives for executives to give Wall Street the predictable earnings reports it wants, regardless of whether they correspond to the actual situation of their companies.

5 With the help of such collaboration, they were able to deceive investors by moving billions of dollars of debt off Enron's balance sheet and artificially increasing the value of Enron stock. Loans that should have counted as debt were made to look like profits from sales. They hid loans, set up false investments and facilitated phantom Enron sales. They tricked investors with double deception: first, by helping to set up clandestinely controlled Enron partnerships, using offshore companies to disguise loans, and second, by facilitating the phoney sale of overvalued Enron assets. In addition, the banks made inside deals for themselves and a number of bank executives profited personally from the schemes. First-tier auditing

firms such as Anderson contributed to the investor's deception by routinely giving Enron clean bills of health.

6 Rationality is mainly understood as an instrumental concept; that is, the agent is rational, if – in the light of his goals (preferences) – the means chosen (actions) are appropriate; if not, the agent is irrational. "Appropriate" here refers to method rather than the result. Rational behavior is action calculated on the basis of the rules of logic and other norms of validity (Hirshleifer 1985, p. 54). Consequently, in standard models, violations of the self-interest postulate are seen as failures of rationality.

7 This is where Stiglitz goes as far as characterizing the accounting practices in relation with stock options as a form of "corporate theft", that is, they deprive unwary shareholders of what was theirs (ibid., p. 122).

8 They focus on a different link between the agency problem and executive compensation: executive pay is seen not as a potential solution to the agency problem but as part of the problem itself.

9 In which it is argued that savings and loans engaged in very risky investments in desperation. Given an unhealthy financial situation, the only (and improbably) chance of success lies in taking on risky investments (Campbell 1995, pp. 87–90).

10 Also, the market mechanism provides incentives for honest firms to distinguish themselves from fraudulent ones, which is why Easterbrook and Fischel claim that cheating does not work in markets in the long term. The focus of this approach is clearly on the markets and their sanctioning power.

11 It is assumed that, as if by an "invisible hand", governance structures themselves will evolve in a way that minimizes inefficiencies, and which is "optimal for firms and investors" as well as "for society" (ibid., p. 7).

12 Mankiw claims that insurance or government guarantees should not be given at all, because these instruments are seen as distorting the incentive structure, inducing savings and loans to take excessive risks (Mankiw 1993, pp. 64–8).

References

Akerlof, G. A. and Romer, P. M., 'Looting: The Economic Underworld of Bankruptcy for Profit', *Brookings Papers on Economic Activity*, 2 (1993), 1–60.

Arrow, K. A., 'Economic Theory and the Hypothesis of Rationality', in J. Eatwell et al. (eds), *The New Palgrave: A Dictionary of Economics*, (New York: The Stockton Press, 1987), pp. 69–74

Arrow, K. A. and Debreu, G., 'Existence of an Equilibrium for a Competitive Economy', *Econometrica*, 22 (1954), 265–90.

BBC News, 'Enron at-a-glance', 22 August 2002 (http://news.bbc.co.uk/1/hi/business/1780075.stm).

Bebchuk, L. A. and Fried, J. M., 'Executive Compensation as an Agency Problem', *Journal of Economic Perspectives*, 17/3 (2003), 71–92.

Bebchuk, L. A. and Fried, J. M. and Walker, D. I., 'Managerial Power as Rent Extraction in the Design of Executive Compensation', *University of Chicago Law Review*, 69 (2002), 751–846.

Berenson, A., *The Number: How the Drive for Quarterly Earnings Corrupted Wall Street and Corporate America* (New York and Toronto: Random House, 2003).

Berle, A. A. and Means, C. G., *The Modern Corporation and Private Property* [1932], (New Brunswick and London: Transaction Publishers, 1991).

Campbell, D. E., *Incentives, Motivation and the Economics of Information* (Cambridge: Cambridge University Press, 1995).

Charness, G., 'Self-Serving Cheap Talk: A Test of Aumann's Conjecture', *Games and Economic Behavior*, 33/2 (2000), 177–94.

Coval, J., Hirshleifer, D., and Teoh, S. H., 'Self-Deception and Deception in Capital Markets' (ch. 6 in this book).

Crawford, V. P., 'Lying for Strategic Advantage: Rational and Boundedly Rational Misrepresentation of Intentions', *American Economic Review*, 93 (2003), 133–49.

Croson, R., 'Deception in Economics Experiments' (ch. 5 in this book).

Diamond, P., 'Political and Economic Evaluation of Social Effects and Externalities: Comment', in M. Intrilligator (ed.), *Frontiers of Quantitative Economics* (Amsterdam: North-Holland, 1971), pp. 30–2.

Easterbrook, F. H. and Fischel, D. R., *The Economic Structure of Corporate Law* (Cambridge: Harvard University Press, 1991).

Fehr, E. and Gächter, S., 'Fairness and Retaliation: The Economics of Reciprocity', *Journal of Economic Perspectives*, 14/3 (2000), 159–81.

Fehr, E. and Schmidt, K., 'A Theory of Fairness, Competition and Co-operation', *Quarterly Journal of Economics*, 114 (1999), 769–816.

Fox, L., *Enron: The Rise and Fall* (Hoboken, NJ: Wiley, 2003).

Hall, R. E., 'Comments and Discussion', *Brookings Papers on Economic Activity*, 2 (1993), 61–4.

Hamlin, A., 'Deception, Regulation and Politics' (ch. 8 in this book).

Hillier, B., *The Economics of Asymmetric Information* (Houndsmills: Macmillan, 1997).

Hirshleifer, J., 'The Expanding Domain of Economics', *American Economic Review*, 75/6 (1985), 53–68.

Jensen, M. C. and Meckling, W. H., 'Theory of the Firm, Agency Costs and Ownership Structure', *Journal of Financial Economics*, 3 (1976), 305–60.

Karni, E., 'Fraud', in J. Eatwell et al. (eds), *The New Palgrave: A Dictionary of Economics* (New York: The Stockton Press, 1987), pp. 416–17.

Krosnzner, R. S. and Strahan, P. E., 'Regulatory Incentives and the Thrift Crisis: Dividends, Mutual-to-Stock Conversions, and Financial Distress', *Journal of Finance*, 51 (1996), 1285–319.

Laffont, J.-J. and Martimort, D., *The Theory of Incentives: The Principal-Agent Model* (Princeton, NJ: Princeton University Press, 2002).

Mandeville, B., *The Fable of the Bees or Private Vices, Publick Benefits* [1714] (Indianapolis, IN: Liberty Fund, 1924).

Mankiw, G. N., 'Comments and Discussion', *Brookings Papers on Economic Activity*, 2 (1993), 64–8.

Rizvi, S. A. T., 'Deception and Game Theory' (ch. 1 in this book).

Simon, H. A., 'Rational Decision Making in Business Organizations' [1978]. Reprinted in W. L. Marr (ed.), *How Economists Explain: A Reader in Methodology* (Lanham, MD: University Press of America, 1982), pp. 281–315.

Smith, A., *The Wealth of Nations* [1776], ed. R. H. Campbell and A. S. Skinner (Oxford: Clarendon Press, 1976).

Stiglitz, J. E., *The Roaring Nineties* (New York: W. W. Norton, 2003).

Williamson, O. E., *The Economic Institutions of Capitalism: Firms, Markets, Relational Contracting* (London: The Free Press and Macmillan, 1985).

Williamson, O. E., 'The New Institutional Economics: Taking Stock, Looking Ahead', *Journal of Economic Literature*, 38 (2000), 595–613.

5

Deception in Economics Experiments

Rachel T. A. Croson

Abstract

Deception is ubiquitous in everyday life and economic exchanges. This chapter reviews the experimental literature on self-serving deception in coordination games, signaling games, and bargaining games and also describes the experimental consequences of deception. A final section suggests an organizing explanation for these findings – that humans are poor deception-detectors and yet are overconfident of their abilities to detect deception. Thus, individuals are insufficiently skeptical of statements they receive from others, consistent with the results observed in these experiments.

Introduction: theoretical considerations

Deception is ubiquitous in everyday life, both well-intentioned, such as telling your grandmother that you loved the (horrid) sweater she gave you for Christmas, and self-serving, for example, deceiving a bargaining opponent about the strength of your outside option. The first type of deception, well-intentioned deception, is an important part of human interaction and exchange. However, there is little or no research in economics addressing this question, thus it will not be covered in this chapter. Instead, this chapter reviews the experimental literature on self-serving deception, presents a description of its robust results, and suggests an organizing explanation for these findings.[1] Deception requires two conditions for its existence. First, the situation needs to allow for communication of some sort, the parties to deception need to observe something (possibly, something misleading) about the other, or communicate via natural language. Second, the situation must involve asymmetric information; something has to be known to one party and not to another about which the informed party can conceivably deceive the uninformed. This asymmetric information may be preferences (such as how much you liked the sweater), exogenous facts (such as what the outside option is), or intentions of what an individual will do in the upcoming interaction. Although the literature in game theory on asymmetric information is huge (Akerlof, Spence, and Stiglitz won the 2001 Nobel Prize for illustrating the importance of asymmetric information in various kinds of markets and situations), there is surprisingly little work in game theory or experiments on when individuals deceive.

In part, game theory's lack of focus on deception is caused by the fact that most game theory models are *equilibrium* models, where parties play "best responses" to the actions of others. Thus, while deception may be practiced, targets of deception are (in equilibrium) not fooled.[2] In these models, deception is often modeled by actions rather than words.

For example, the literature on signaling games involves some actors (unsuccessfully) deceiving other players. In Spence's classic model (1973), and those based on it, individuals have types – privately observable characteristics (for job candidates; intelligence). Players choose observable actions (going to college), which impose type-specific costs on them (inexpensive for smart candidates, expensive for less smart candidates). Other players (employers) observe these actions and make inferences about the type of player (their intelligence) who chooses these actions.

These models tend to have two classes of equilibria. In *separating* equilibria, different types take different actions; type is perfectly communicated via action and (thus) no deception is involved. In Spence's example, smart candidates pursue education and less smart candidates do not. Thus, employers can tell a candidate's intelligence by observing their educational choices. In pooling (and semi-pooling) equilibria, multiple types take the same action. In Spence's example, everyone goes to college. Thus individuals of one type are "deceiving" the other players (employers) into believing they are of some other type. However, in these equilibria, the other players (employers) are not fooled by this deception. Upon seeing a particular signal (a candidate who went to college), employers do *not* rely on that signal to convey information about the sender's (candidate's) type. Signaling models like these are used in many applications, including exchange situations, as in the labor market described by Spence, but in these theories, deception never works.

However, as noted by Farrell and Rabin (1996), "most information sharing is ... done through ordinary, informal talk" rather than through actions as in the signaling models described above (p. 104). A second area of game theory comes closer to our lay notions of deception by modeling it as *talk* rather than as action. In this literature, people playing games can communicate their preferences, private information, or intentions in the game. For example, in the Spence signaling game above, candidates might send a verbal message to employers (instead of, or in addition to their costly, observable educational choice). The employer can choose to rely on these messages or to ignore them.

It is relatively straightforward to show that, in equilibrium, receivers don't rely on these statements to make their decisions. If they did, everyone would claim to be the most attractive (intelligent) type. These statements are referred to as "cheap talk." Note that these statements are cheap *not* because they are valueless (although in this setting, they are), but because they cost nothing for the talker to produce. Contrast this with the signaling setting above, where the observable action (education) is costly to produce and, importantly, *differentially* costly for different types.

However, there are some settings where cheap talk can (theoretically) matter. In particular, games of *coordination,* where both parties want to choose the same action as each other, provide a role for cheap talk.[3] The more correlated the players' preferences are, the more cheap talk can matter in these games (Crawford and Sobel 1982).[4] That said, in these coordinative settings, the benefits from deception decrease severely. When parties' goals are simply to coordinate, there is no point in deceiving the other players in the game. So the condition which makes cheap talk effective (correlated preferences), also makes deception unattractive and unlikely. An excellent review of cheap-talk experiments in coordination games can be found in Crawford (1998).

This chapter will focus primarily on situations of competing interests (non-coordination games) where one party has an interest in deceiving another party. Although exchange situations clearly fall into this category, it is not limited to exchange situations. We restrict our attention to situations where there is communication, and will focus mainly on verbal deception rather than deception through actions. In particular, we will be most interested in experimental research in settings where deception should, theoretically, not be effective (where it truly is cheap talk and in equilibrium should be ignored), yet nonetheless seems to impact behavior and outcomes. We will propose an organizing explanation for this impact.

Economic models of exchange or economic models more generally, have very little scope for self-deception. In particular, individuals are assumed to have instatnt access to their own innermost thoughts, values, and feelings, which are assumed to be stationary over time. Thus, there is no asymmetric information, nor are there conflicting interests, or the opportunity or desire to deceive oneself. Some models (but no experiments) add limitations on these assumptions to generate game-theoretic models of behavior that include asymmetric information within an individual over time. Many of these models focus on self-control behavior rather than self-deception behavior. Since there are no experiments in this area, we will not review this literature here, but refer the interested reader to Elster (1986), Schelling (1984), and Gerschlager (2001).[5]

We begin by discussing two papers examining deception in coordination games. In coordination games, deception is rarely used, as predicted by equilibrium theory (there is no point in deceiving your counterpart if your goal is coordination). Next, we discuss three papers using signaling games such as the Spence labor market example above. In these experiments, deceptive statements should (in equilibrium) be made and ignored. However, the evidence suggests that these statements, while made, are believed more than is optimal for receivers, which is to their disadvantage. The third section discusses six papers on deception in bargaining. Theoretically, this setting is also one where deception should be attempted but should be unsuccessful. As in the second section, we observe individuals attempting deception and succeeding more than is predicted by equilibrium theory. Finally, we discuss three papers on consequences of deception (punishment). In these papers, individuals who have been deceived, and to whom the deception is revealed, are likely to punish their counterparts, even when this punishment is costly to them. A discussion section presents some robust results from this research and suggests an organizing explanation: that individuals are bad at detecting the deception of others (poor deception detectors) but believe they can tell when someone is lying to them, when in fact they cannot (they are overconfident of their abilities to detect deception. Thus individuals are insufficiently skeptical of statements they receive from others, consistent with the results observed in these experiments.

Deception in coordination games

Two papers examine deception in coordination games. Both find, consistent with neoclassical equilibrium theory, that in coordinative settings, little or no deception is observed. These results confirm the traditional assumptions that individuals will not deceive unless it is in their interest to do so. Crawford (1998) reviews the literature on cheap talk in coordination games, although the question of deceptive cheap talk is not mentioned.

Charness (2000) examines deception in a specific coordination game (the stag-hunt game). In these experiments, subjects could send a message about their intended action before playing, for example, as in endnote three; they could claim they would drive on the left. Traditional economic analysis predicts that parties will indeed communicate with each other (engage in cheap talk), but that there will be no deception about the intended action (parties will not lie to each other). The results from this experiment were exactly consistent with this prediction.

Palfrey and Rosenthal (1991) were concerned not with deception *per se* but with the impact of communication in large coordination games with many players (a threshold public goods game). In their experiment, players could send a message about their intentions. Like the results above, the authors find very little deception in their games, supporting their hypotheses and the prediction of traditional economic theory that players do not deceive others.

In these two papers the neoclassical equilibrium prediction of no deception is observed. However, this convergence between the equilibrium prediction and outcomes is not true in a more general situation, as seen below.

Deception in signaling games

Three papers experimentally examine deception in signaling games by adding communication as discussed in the introduction. All find that deception is used (senders lie about their type) but, contrary to equilibrium predictions (Spence 1973), it is often believed.

In Sopher and Zapater (1993), the authors implement a series of signaling games. One player (the sender) knows his "type" (type 1, 2, or, in some games, 3). The other player (the chooser) chooses actions (A, B, C, or, in some games, D). The payoffs from these actions to both players depend on the other players' type. Before the chooser moves, the sender can send a (free) message of the form "I am type X." Then the chooser chooses an action, and payoffs are earned. The results indicate that some players do indeed try to deceive their counterparts when it is in their interest to do so (for example, in their game 3, 18/32 players of type 3 claimed to be type 1).

However, contrary to game-theoretic predictions, receivers are likely to believe these false claims (in the same game, 64 percent of the time deceptive type 3's are believed by choosers). The authors conclude that choosers display a particular cognitive limitation. "In a game with two types, even if the players know that type 1 will always send the message

'I am type 1', they act as if they failed to understand that any other message must come from type 2" (p. 5). This experiment provides some evidence that deceptive messages are not ignored, as equilibrium concepts would assume.

In Forsythe, Lundholm and Reitz (1999) the authors use a traditional signaling game described as a market for product quality. Sellers know the quality of their good (their type), but buyers know only the distribution of qualities. In their cheap talk treatment, at no cost, sellers can announce a range of quality, which (they claim) includes the quality of their good. Buyers then decide whether or not to buy and at what price. Thus in this treatment of the experiment, sellers can deceive buyers about their good's quality, and many do (186 fraudulent claims out of a total 660 claims). Equilibrium analysis predicts that buyers will not be deceived, but in the experiment they are. In another antifraud condition, sellers are constrained to include their product's true quality in the quality range they quote to buyers. Here, deception is ruled out, yet buyers *still* sometimes overpay for the good "buyers are not always sufficiently skeptical of their [seller's] statements" (p. 484). In particular, the authors conclude, "Buyers are frequently taken in by the seller's overoptimistic statements and bid too much for the asset" (p. 483). This result is consistent with that of Sopher and Zapater who found that deception is more effective than equilibrium analysis would predict.

Interestingly, in this experiment the subjects switch roles – sometimes they play buyers and other times they play sellers. The authors find that "the same subjects who are quite willing to lie when acting as sellers are quite gullible when acting as buyers" (p. 483). This result suggests that it is not *ignorance* of the possibility of deception that causes players (in this experiment, buyers) to believe their partner's (the seller's) statements. The buyers who themselves deceived as sellers were *more* likely to be deceived, rather than less.

Finally, in Blume et al. (2001), subjects were assigned to the role of sender or receiver. The sender is informed about her own type, and can then send a message to the receiver. The receiver then takes some actions, which together with the sender's actual type, determine both players' payoffs. The paper reports on four different games, ranging from games of pure coordination (perfect common interest) as discussed in the previous section, to games of conflicting interest, addressed in this section.

As in the previous studies, the authors find "stable sucker behavior" (p. 82). That is, receivers blindly follow senders' messages even when it is not in their best interests. The authors note that "there were in fact some receivers who follow instructions ... without realizing the incentive implications. In that sense receivers prove gullible. It is interesting that even with ... considerable experience ... this sucker behavior does not vanish" (p. 101).

In these three papers, the neoclassical equilibrium makes two predictions. The first, that players will try to deceive their counterparts, is clearly supported. The second, that their counterparts will not be fooled, is not. We will find this pattern recurring in the next section which examines deception in bargaining.

Deception in bargaining

Five experimental papers have examined deception in bargaining. In bargaining situations, players interact in the context of a formal, game-theoretic structure (such as alternating offers) and equilibria are easily calculated. All of these equilibria require that deception not be believed. The papers in this section experimentally demonstrate, in contrast, situations where subjects are successfully deceived. A different literature from psychology examines deception in negotiations settings (see Schweitzer 2001 for an excellent review).[6] In these papers we see a similar pattern as in the previous section – participants in experiments deceive as predicted, but contrary to predictions, their deception is believed.

In an early experimental economics paper, Roth and Murnighan (1982) examine two-party free-form bargaining over lottery tickets. Each ticket represents a 1 percent chance of winning a prize, but the prizes are different for the two people (one prize is \$20 and the other, \$5). The authors note the existence of deception – "if it was common knowledge that the \$5 player did not know both prizes, the \$20 player often misrepresented his prize" (p. 1131), but do not analyze the amount of deception or its consequences.

Two papers examine deception in ultimatum bargaining (Boles, Croson and Murnighan 2000 and Croson, Boles and Murnighan 2003). In these games, one player (the proposer) makes an offer of how to divide a pot of money with their partner (the responder). The responder then accepts or rejects this offer. If the offer is accepted, the money is divided as proposed; if rejected, each party receives their outside option. These experiments allowed parties to communicate before beginning bargaining. These papers then compared behavior under three conditions; perfect information, informed proposer (the proposer knew the amount of money available to be divided, but the responder did not), and informed responder (the responder knew their outside option, but the proposer did not).

Consistent with findings from other studies, these experiments found deception was present and, often, believed. About 13.6 percent of messages sent by proposers and 13.9 percent of messages sent by responders contained deceptive statements about the pie size or outside option value. In the short term, proposers who deceived made significantly lower offers and were equally likely to have those offers accepted than those that did not. Responders who deceived received significantly higher offers (and were more likely to accept). In addition to these outcome impacts on deception, deception was correlated with the amount of communication. Dyads who exchanged more words were more likely to deceive.

Also, like Forsythe et al. reviewed above, participants in this study were insufficiently doubtful. The authors report finding no support for the hypothesis that "participants who themselves had an opportunity to lie would be more suspicious of their counterparts", and report that "deception was more frequent than doubt" (p. 254).

Valley, Moag and Bazerman (1998) examines the impact of communication in the "Acquire-a-Company" game of Samuelson and Bazerman (1985). In this game, the seller of a company, but not the buyer, knows its value (randomly drawn from a distribution between $0 and $100). The buyer of the company knows that the company is worth 1.5 times as much to him as it is to the seller. The buyer and seller bargain over the price. In the three treatments of the experiment (study 2), bargainers could communicate either face-to-face, via phone, or via written messages before engaging in bargaining.

The authors find that deception exists, but that it differs between different communication media. In particular, sellers deceive buyers about the value of the company 7 percent of the time when bargaining face-to-face, 55 percent of the time when bargaining by phone, and 33 percent of the time when bargaining via writing. Furthermore, these deceptions are believed. Buyers make offers consistent with the seller's statements in 79 percent of the dyads in the face-to-face condition, in 55 percent of dyads in the phone condition and in 33 percent of the dyads in the written condition. As expected, sellers earn less (and buyers earn more) in the phone condition than in any other treatment, where buyers deceive sellers about the value of the company and sellers act on these deceptive statements.

Valley, Thompson, Gibbons and Bazerman (forthcoming) run an experiment using the Myerson-Sattherwaite (1983) game. In this game, a buyer and a seller are each given a randomly (and independently) drawn valuation for a hypothetical good. The buyer and seller each name a price at which they are willing to transact. If the buyer's bid is greater than what the seller's ask for, the transaction occurs at the midpoint of their two prices. If not, no transaction occurs. This experiment uses this bargaining mechanism with no communication, written communication, and face-to-face communication.[7]

The authors find that, when they are able to do so, participants deceive their counterparts about their valuation. In the written treatment, 48 percent of sellers and 41 percent of buyers lie about their valuation. The frequency of deception decreases significantly in the face-to-face treatment, however, to 22 percent of sellers and 26 percent of buyers. These results reinforce those reviewed above, that when deception as a strategy is available, individuals will use it, but that the frequency of its use depends on the medium through which the communication occurs.

The bulk of the research on deception in game theory has occurred in bargaining games. As this section demonstrates (consistent with results from the previous section), two empirical regularities emerge. First, when they have an incentive to do so, individuals will attempt to deceive their bargaining counterparts. This regularity is consistent with neoclassical equilibrium theory and our notions of economic man. The second regularity, however, is that individuals are insufficiently skeptical of the messages they receive. This regularity is not consistent with neoclassical equilibrium and our notions of economic man. The next section addresses one consequence of this second regularity – the observed behavior when deception is revealed.

Consequences of deception

Finally, one reasonable question to ask involves the consequences of deception. Presumably, deception is used because it transfers resources from the deceiver to the target of deception. Three papers investigate the question of what happens when this deception is revealed.

Brandts and Charness (2003) construct a simultaneous game where one player (the sender) sends another (the receiver) a message about her intended actions. Both players then simultaneously choose an action. The payoffs are such that the sender has an incentive to deceive the receiver about her intentions. The receiver then has an (unanticipated) punishment option, costly to himself but more costly to the deceptive sender. The authors find that 33 percent of senders deceive receivers about their intentions, and that 28 percent of these are punished by receivers (as compared with a 12 percent punishment rate of non-deceivers). This experiment provides evidence, again, that deceptive messages are believed and, more importantly, when discovered, punished.[8]

Two papers discussed above, Boles, Croson and Murnighan (2000) and Croson, Boles and Murnighan (2003), also demonstrated the willingness of participants to punish deceivers. After playing two rounds of the ultimatum game, the private information was revealed and players continued with an additional two rounds. Both proposers and responders were less likely to deceive in the second two rounds than they had been in the first two (10 percent vs. 17 percent for proposers and 9.5 percent vs. 18.5 percent for responders). However, proposers who had previously lied and had been revealed were severely punished by responders in rounds three and four. In these rounds they made significantly higher offers to their responders (the authors refer to these as "apology offers"), yet these offers were also significantly more likely to be rejected. Thus responders were willing to punish their proposer counterparts for deceiving them; even though that punishment was personally costly (they earned their outside option rather than the large apology offer).

Schweitzer, Hershey and Bradlow (2004) examine the impact of deception in a repeated trust game. In the trust game, the sender sends money to the receiver, which is tripled in transit. The receiver can then distribute the money between the two players, dictator-fashion. Their subjects all played the role of the sender matched with a (simulated) receiver who kept all the money sent in the first two rounds, and then split it evenly thereafter. In some treatments, senders received messages (purportedly from receivers), promising to return money before rounds 1 and 2 (where they did) and before round 3 (where they did). The authors found that while trust could be rebuilt after receivers did not return money to senders (by an apology and a promise to do so in the future), recovering from actual deception (when receivers promised to send money back and then did not) was almost impossible.

These three papers demonstrate that individuals are willing to punish deception when it has been discovered. These results are consistent with those from experimental studies in other domains, which find that individuals are willing to punish unfair behavior such as low offers in ultimatum games (Croson 1996, Straub and Murnighan 1995, Blount 1995), low amounts sent in trust games (Fershtman and Gneezy 2001, Berg, Dickhaut and McCabe 1995, Buchan, Croson and Johnson 1998) and low contributions in public goods games (Fehr and Gächter 2000, Sefton, Shupp and Walker 2001, Croson 1999).

An organizing explanation

The studies reviewed here use varying situations and contexts to examine deception. However, from them come a number of results which are robustly and repeatedly observed in multiple settings. These are Individuals sometimes deceive when they have an incentive to do so (but rarely when they do not, as in the coordination game experiments).

Individuals are gullible – they believe deceptive statements when they should not.

This gullibility is not caused by lack of information about the possibility of deception – sellers who had themselves deceived buyers in the asset market experiment were more gullible than those who had not, and sellers with the opportunity to deceive in the ultimatum game experiments were no more doubtful of their counterparts' statements than those who did not.

The amount of deception and of gullibility varies across different communication media. Discovered deception is punished, even when it is costly to do so.

We propose an organizing explanation of *biased beliefs* and *norms of punishment* for these results. First, we suggest that individual's biased beliefs about their abilities to detect others' deception and their beliefs of others' abilities to tell when *they* are lying can generate many of these results. Second, we suggest that norms of punishment for discovered deception are used when the targets of deception discover they have been deceived.

Research has demonstrated that individuals are very bad at detecting deception (DePaulo, 1994) even among close and intimate friends (DePaulo and Kashy 1998). In addition, people are often overconfident of their ability to detect lies (Ekman and O'Sullivan 1991, DePaulo, Charlton, Cooper, Lindsay, Muhlenbruck 1997). Thus, individuals (falsely) believe that they will be able to tell when they are being deceived, particularly in face-to-face or phone interactions.[9]

This leads to gullibility as observed in these experiments. Individuals (falsely) believe they can detect others' lies, and are thus more likely to believe others' false statements. This explanation also explains why information about the possibility of deception (or deception of one's own) has no relationship to gullibility. Gullibility is not caused by individuals knowing that someone *may* lie, it is caused by their believing that they will be able to tell *when* someone lies.

Other research demonstrates that individuals falsely believe that *others* will be able to tell when *they* are lying, especially in face-to-face interactions (Gilovich, Savitsky and Medvec 1998). This biased belief explains the reduced number of lies told in face-to-face settings relative to other settings, even though the target of lies may be equally or less likely to detect a lie when told face-to-face, the deceiver's belief about the target's abilities are not correct, leading to reduced lying in face-to-face situations.

These two effects suggest a reexamination of the classical assumptions of rational expectations in game-theoretic settings. When actors can be fooled (expectations are not rational), individuals often experience regret caused by their decisions, which were based on incorrect expectations.

Finally, we suggest that when these biased beliefs of deception detection are demonstrated to be incorrect, individuals invoke norms of punishment. When one's ability to detect deception is called into question, the individual rationalizes by arguing that their counterpart is a particularly skilled or experienced liar. This rationalization induces the individual to severely punish their counterpart (even at high cost to themselves), in order to discourage this behavior. The counterpart's supposed skill with deception is used to justify this punishment.

These biases in individual's beliefs about their and others' abilities to detect deception are one possible explanation for the experimental results. Of course, there are many others, including social norms of behavior that are invoked by different settings, such as the misattribution of others' intentions (wanting to think the best of a friend or stranger). We hope this chapter will serve to spur further researchers to construct their own explanations for deceptive behavior.[10]

Summary and conclusion

This chapter has reviewed literature from experimental economics (in particular from experimental game theory), in which deception can happen. Results indicate that deception does occur exactly in those situations where equilibrium theory would predict that it does. However, contrary to equilibrium theory predictions, deception is believed by targets of deception. While many competing theories can be suggested to accord with these results, this chapter develops one in particular: individuals' beliefs about their abilities and the abilities of others to detect deception are biased. Further research formally modeling these biases, deriving new predictions from them, and testing these models is clearly needed to enhance our understanding of deception in economics.

Notes

1 An interesting literature in experimental economics on the appropriateness of researchers deceiving their subjects (a common practice in psychology but not accepted in economics) is outside the scope of this chapter. Interested readers should see Camerer 1997 and a debate in the Journal of Economic Psychology (Bonetti 1998a; 1998b; Hey 1998; McDaniel and Starmer 1998).

2 See the chapter by Rizvi in this book for a detailed discussion of deception in game theory.

3 For example, imagine pure coordination between two players. Each player can choose to drive on the right side or the left side of the road. Neither has a preference for which side of the road is used, but both strongly prefer to choose the same side as the other (otherwise, they risk an accident). Conversation can help the two parties coordinate on choosing the same outcome. Since there is no incentive for an individual to claim that they will drive on the right, and then actually drive on the left, this talk can be trusted by the other side and is effective in determining the outcome.

4 Dickhaut, McCabe and Mukherji (1995) experimentally test and support the conclusion that as interests diverge, individuals' signals become less informative (more pooling occurs). However, their experiment does not allow for communication between the parties, and is not reviewed in depth here.

5 Other types of deception such as game-playing are discussed in de Sales (2001, pp. 121–32).

6 Unlike bargaining settings, negotiation settings do not involve a formal structure but instead are free-form discussion and complex situations. Papers from this literature demonstrate that individuals deceive when they have incentives to do so. For example, O'Connor and Carnevale (1997) found that negotiators misrepresent common interest issues to gain concessions on other issues. In a similar negotiation study, Schweitzer & Croson (1999) found that the questions targets of deception asked influenced the type of deception negotiators used. Other work has identified a number of factors that influence the likelihood that negotiators will use deception. This work has found that the communication medium (Schweitzer, Brodt, and Croson 2000), incentives (Tenbrunsel 1998), and even goal setting (Schweitzer, Ordonez and Douma 2001) influence the use of deception. Recent work has also found that the uncertainty deceivers have about their information influences their use of deception (Schweitzer and Hsee, forthcoming). While these results are all

interesting and important, the settings used were relatively uncontrolled. The papers reviewed in this section, in contrast, all use formal bargaining settings with well-defined equilibria.

7 Radner and Schotter (1989) run a similar experiment comparing no communication and face-to-face communication in this setting. However, they do not report the frequency of deception observed in their experiment.

8 Anspach (2001) discusses a similar issue of how positive reciprocity can switch to vengeance or punishment.

9 This result is different than that discussed in Fiddick, Cosmides, and Tooby (2000) on *cheater detection.* Cheater detection involves capabilities in identifying an individual violating a rule. To identify cheaters, one observes the consequences of some actions and makes inferences about the previous actions that must have caused those consequences (such as, cheating). In contrast, this chapter presents evidence on our inabilities in identifying a particular individual speaking an untruth. To identify liars, one observes only a statement (not an action) and must determine if it is true or untrue.

10 For example, Rabin (1990) presents a formal model in which "agents have a propensity to speak the truth and to believe that others speak the truth" (p. 144). This propensity might be caused by the biased beliefs discussed above.

References

Anspach, M. R., 'Violence Deceived: Changing Reciprocities from Vengeance to Gift Exchange', in C. Gerschlager (ed.), *Expanding the Economic Concept of Exchange: Deception, Self-Deception and Illusions* (Boston, Dordrecht and London: Kluwer Academic Publishers, 2001), pp. 213–24.

Berg, J., Dickhaut, J. W. and McCabe, K. A., 'Trust, Reciprocity, and Social History', *Games and Economic Behavior,* 10 (1995), 122–42.

Blount, S., 'When Social Outcomes Aren't Fair: The Effect of Causal Attributions on Preference', *Organizational Behavior and Human Decision Processes*, 63/2 (1995), 131–44.

Blume, A., DeJong, D., Yong-Gwan Kim and Sprinkle, G., 'Evolution of Communication with Partial Common Interest', *Games and Economic Behavior*, 37 (2001), 79–120.

Boles, T. L., Croson, R. T. and Murnighan, J. K., 'Deception and Retribution in Repeated Ultimatum Bargaining', *Organizational Behavior & Human Decision Processes*, 83 (2000), 235–59.

Bonetti, S., 'Experimental Economics and Deception', *Journal of Economic Psychology*, 19 (1998a), 377–95.

Bonetti, S., 'Experimental Economics and Deception: Response', *Journal of Economic Psychology*, 19 (1998b), 411–14.

Brandts, J. and Charness, G., 'Truth or Consequences: An Experiment', *Management Science, 49 (2003), 116–30.*

Buchan, N., Croson, R. and Johnson, E., *Trust and Reciprocity: An International Experiment*, OPIM Working Paper 98-03-05 (Philadelphia: Wharton Business School, University of Pennsylvania, 1998).

Camerer, C., 'Rules for Experimenting in Psychology and Economics, and Why They Differ', in W. Albers et al. (eds), *Understanding Strategic Interaction: Essays in Honor of Reinhard Selten* (Heidelberg and New York: Springer, 1997), pp. 313–27.

Charness, G., 'Self-Serving Cheap Talk: A Test of Aumann's Conjecture', *Games and Economic Behavior*, 33/2 (2000), 177–94.

Crawford, V., 'A Survey of Experiments on Communication via Cheap Talk', *Journal of Economic Theory*, 78 (1998), 286–98.

Crawford, V. and Sobel, J., 'Strategic Information Transmission', *Econometrica*, 50 (1982), 1431–51.

Croson, R. T. A., 'Information in Ultimatum Games: An Experimental Study', *Journal of Economic Behavior and Organization*, 30/2 (1996), 197–213.

Croson, R. T. A., *Theories of Altruism and Reciprocity: Evidence from Linear Public Goods Games*, OPIM Working Paper 96-08-01 (Philadelphia: Wharton Business School, University of Pennsylvania, 1999).

Croson, R. T. A., Boles, T. and Murnighan, J. K., 'Cheap Talk in Bargaining Experiments: Lying and Threats in Ultimatum Games', *Journal of Economic Behavior and Organization*, 51/2 (2003), 143–59.

DePaulo, B. M., 'Spotting Lies: Can Humans Learn to Do Better?', *Current Directions in Psychological Science*, 3 (1994), 83–6.

DePaulo, B. M., Charlton, K., Cooper, H., Lindsay, J. and Muhlenbruck, L., 'The Accuracy-Confidence Correlation in the Detection of Deception', *Personality and Social Psychology Review*, 1 (1997), 346–57.

DePaulo, B. M. and Kashy, D. A., 'Everyday Lies in Close and Casual Relationships', *Journal of Personality and Social Psychology*, 74 (1998), 63–79.

Dickhaut, J. W., McCabe, K. A. and Mukherji, A., 'An Experimental Study of Strategic Information Transmission', *Economic Theory*, 6 (1995), 389–403.

Ekman, P., O'Sullivan, M., 'Who Can Catch a Liar', *American Psychologist*, 46 (1991), 913–20.

Elster, J. (ed.), 'The Multiple Self', *Studies in Rationality and Social Change Series* (Cambridge, New York and Sydney: Cambridge University Press in collaboration with Maison des Sciences de l'Homme, Paris, 1986).

Farrell, J. and Rabin, M., 'Cheap Talk', *Journal of Economic Perspectives*, 10/3 (1996), 103–18.

Fehr, E. and Gächter, S., 'Cooperation and Punishment in Public Goods Experiments', *American Economic Review*, 90 (2000), 980–94.

Fershtman, C. and Gneezy, U., 'Discrimination in a Segmented Society: An Experimental Approach', *Quarterly Journal of Economics*, 116 (2001), 351–77.

Fiddick, L., Cosmides, L. and Tooby, J., 'No Interpretation Without Representation: The Role of Domain-Specific Representations and Inferences in the Wason Selection Task', *Cognition*, 77 (2000), 1–79.

Forsythe, R., Lundholm, R. and Rietz, T., 'Cheap Talk, Fraud, and Adverse Selection in Financial Markets: Some Experimental Evidence', *Review of Financial Studies*, 12 (1999), 481–518.

Gerschlager, C., 'Is (Self-)Deception an Indispensable Quality of Exchange? A New Approach to Adam Smith Smith's Concept', in C. Gerschlager (ed.), *Expanding the Economic Concept of Exchange: Deception, Self-Deception and Illusions* (Boston, Dordrecht and London: Kluwer Academic Publishers, 2001), pp. 27–52.

Gilovich, T., Savitsky, K. and Medvec, V. H., 'The Illusion of Transparency: Biased Assessments of Others' Ability to Read One's Emotional States', *Journal of Personality and Social Psychology*, 75/2 (1998), 332–46.

Hey, J. D., 'Experimental Economics and Deception: A Comment', *Journal of Economic Psychology*, 19 (1998), 397–401.

McDaniel, T. and Starmer, C., 'Experimental Economics and Deception: A Comment', *Journal of Economic Psychology*, 19 (1998), 403–9.

Myerson, R. B. and Satterthwaite, M. A., 'Efficient Mechanisms for Bilateral Trading', *Journal of Economic Theory*, 29 (1983), 265–81.

O'Connor, K. M. and Carnevale, P. J., 'A Nasty but Effective Negotiation Strategy: Misrepresentation of a Common-Value Issue', *Personality and Social Psychology Bulletin*, 23 (1997), 504–15.

Palfrey, T. R. and Rosenthal, H., 'Testing for Effects of Cheap Talk in a Public Goods Game with Private Information', *Games and Economic Behavior*, 3/2 (1991), 183–220.

Rabin, M., 'Communication between Rational Agents', *Journal of Economic Theory*, 51/1 (1990), 144–70.

Radner, R. and Schotter, A., 'The Sealed-Bid Mechanism: An Experimental Study', *Journal of Economic Theory*, 48 (1989), 179–220.

Roth, A. E. and Murnighan, J. K., 'The Role of Information in Bargaining: An Experimental Study', *Econometrica*, 50 (1982), 1123–42.

De Sales, A., 'The Go-Between: Reflections on a Mechanism of Ritual Exchange', in C. Gerschlager (ed.), *Expanding the Economic Concept of Exchange: Deception, Self-Deception and Illusions* (Boston, Dordrecht and London: Kluwer Academic Publishers, 2001), pp. 121–32.

Samuelson, W. F. and Bazerman, M. H., 'The Winner's Curse in Bilateral Negotiations', in V. Smith (ed.), *Research in Experimental Economics 3* (Greenwich, CN: JAI Press, 1985), pp. 105–37.

Schelling, T. C., *Choice and Consequence* (Cambridge, MA and London: Harvard University Press, 1984).

Schweitzer, M. E., 'Deception in Negotiations', in S. Hoch and H. C. Kunreuther (eds), *Wharton on Making Decisions* (Hoboken, NJ: Wiley, 2001), pp. 187–200.

Schweitzer, M., Hershey, J. C. and Bradlow, E., *Promises and Lies: Restoring Violated Trust*, OPIM Working Paper (Philadelphia: Wharton School, University of Pennsylvania, 2004).

Schweitzer, M. E., Brodt, S. and Croson, R., *Visual Access and Context-Dependent Lies: The Use of Deception in Videoconference and Telephone Mediated Negotiations*, OPIM Working Paper 99-07-02 (Philadelphia: Wharton School, University of Pennsylvania, 2000).

Schweitzer, M. E. and Croson, R., 'Curtailing Deception: The Impact of Direct Questions on Lies and Omissions', *International Journal of Conflict Management*, 10/3 (1999), 225–48.

Schweitzer, M. E. and Hsee, C., 'Stretching the Truth: Elastic Justification and Motivated Communication of Uncertain Information', *Journal of Risk and Uncertainty* (forthcoming).

Schweitzer, M. E., Ordonez, L. and Douma, B., *The Dark Side of Goal Setting: The Role of Goals in Motivating Unethical Behavior*, OPIM Working Paper 01-05-02 (Philadelphia: Wharton School, University of Pennsylvania, 2001).

Sefton, M., Shupp, R. and Walker, J., *The Effect of Rewards and Sanctions in Provision of Public Goods*, Working Paper (Bloomington: University of Indiana, 2001).

Sopher, B. and Zapater, I., *Communication and Coordination in Signalling Games: An Experimental Study*, Working Paper 93-38 (Providence, RI: Department of Economics, Brown University, 1993).

Spence, A. M., 'Job Market Signaling', *Quarterly Journal of Economics*, 87 (1973), 355–74.

Straub, P. G. and Murnighan, J. K., 'An Experimental Investigation of Ultimatum Games: Information, Fairness, Expectations, and Lowest Acceptable Offers', *Journal of Economic Behavior and Organization*, 27 (1995), 345–64.

Tenbrunsel, A., 'Misrepresentation and Expectations of Misrepresentation in an Ethical Dilemma: The Role of Incentives and Temptation', *Academy of Management Journal*, 41 (1998), 330–9.

Valley, K. L., Moag, J. and Bazerman, M. H., '"A Matter of Trust": Effects of Communication on the Efficiency and Distribution of Outcomes', *Journal of Economic Behavior and Organization*, 34 (1998), 211–38.

Valley, K. L., Thompson, L., Gibbons, R. and Bazerman, M. H., 'How Communication Improves Efficiency in Bargaining Games', *Games and Economic Behavior* (forthcoming).

6

Self-Deception and Deception in Capital Markets*

Joshua Coval, David Hirshleifer and Siew Hong Teoh

Abstract

We argue that self-deception underlies various aspects of the behavior of investors and of prices in capital markets. We examine the implications of self-deception for investor overconfidence, and how firms and financial institutions can exploit the overconfidence of investors in a predatory fashion. These ideas link self-deception to deception by others. We also examine how investor self-deception and overconfidence can affect financial reporting and disclosure policy.

Introduction

In recent years, a body of evidence on security returns has presented a sharp challenge to the traditional view, known as the efficient markets hypothesis, that securities are rationally priced to reflect all publicly available information. Some of the more pervasive anomalies can be classified as follows:

1) Event-based return predictability (average stock returns on the days of publicly announced events are of the same sign as average subsequent long-run abnormal performance).
2) Short-term momentum (stocks that have done well/poorly over the past six to 18 months continue to do well/poorly over the next six to 18 months).
3) Long-term reversal (stocks that have done well/poorly in the past six to 18 months, "overreact" and perform poorly/well over the subsequent three to five years).
4) High volatility of asset prices relative to fundamentals.

5) Abnormal returns to stocks with a book value of assets that is large relative to the market value of their assets.
6) Short-run post-earnings announcement stock price "drift" in the direction indicated by the earnings surprise, but abnormal stock price performance in the opposite direction of long-term earnings changes.

There remains disagreement over the interpretation of the above evidence of predictability. One possibility is that these anomalies are chance deviations to be expected under market efficiency (Fama 1998). We believe the evidence does not accord with this viewpoint, because some of the return patterns are strong and regular. The book-to-market and momentum effects are present both internationally and in different time-periods. Also, the pattern mentioned in (1) above obtains for the great majority of event studies.

Alternatively, these patterns could represent the effects of variations in rational risk premia. That is, the abnormal returns may, in fact, be appropriate average compensation for the risks their investors are expected to bear. However, these patterns seem to imply that very high average stock returns can be achieved with simple trading strategies. Thus, for these patterns to be consistent with a frictionless, fully rational model of asset prices, individuals would have to perceive these strategies to be extremely risky.

A rational perception of high risk could arise if the payoffs from these strategies tended to be particularly poor exactly when some other important component of investors' wealth (such as the stock market as a whole) was also doing badly. Alternatively, investors could care about more than just the probability distribution of their possible wealth and consumption outcomes; they might care about the process by which uncertainty about these outcomes is resolved.

Either explanation for these patterns amounts to a claim that investors place very widely varying values on an additional dollar of investment payoff in different states of the world (MacKinlay 1995). Most research indicates that the outcome correlations required to deliver such variation in the value placed upon consumption are not apparent in the data; and that the investor preferences needed to achieve such variation are implausible.[1] Given this evidence, it seems reasonable to consider explanations for the observed return patterns based on imperfect rationality.

Moreover, there are important corporate financing and payout patterns that seem potentially related to misvaluation in the stock market. Firms tend to issue equity (rather than debt) after rises in market value, and when the firm or industry book/market ratio is low. In fact, firms seem to be able to engage in market-timing by issuing stock before the stock market as a whole is going to fall, and issuing debt instead prior to rises in the market (see Baker and Wurgler 2002). There are industry-specific financing and repurchase booms, perhaps designed to exploit industry-level mispricing. Transactions such as takeovers that often rely on securities financing are also prone to industry booms and quiet periods, and there is evidence that market misvaluation influences the volume and character of takeover activity (Dong, Hirshleifer, Richardson, and Teoh 2003), and the extent of investment activity more generally (Polk and Sapienza 2003).

Proponents of rational markets contend that the above anomalies either are linked to risks that are poorly captured in current asset pricing models or are simply the result of data-mining. To support their view, they point to the enormous body of evidence showing that the average active mutual fund manager cannot outperform the index.[2] Moreover, while some mutual funds do outperform the market, little if any evidence indicates this occurs any more frequently than would be expected by pure chance. Proponents of rational markets contend that if the above anomalies are pervasive, economically significant, and unrelated to risk, surely we should see evidence that professional money managers take advantage of them. The fact that we see scant evidence of outperformance indicates that they do not. As Rubinstein (2001) puts it, the evidence that the average mutual fund cannot beat the market is "a nuclear bomb against [the behavioralists'] puny sticks." On the other hand, Berk and Green (2003) (no behavioralists themselves) counter that even if managers have the ability to take advantage of such anomalies we should not necessarily expect to see this ability show up strongly in their performance. If new capital flows to managers who have strong track records and, due to declining economies of scale, restricts their ability to outperform going forward, little persistence will appear in manager return data.

In our view, the failure of the average mutual fund to beat the market is interesting but not particularly supportive of market efficiency. The efficient markets hypothesis does not say that the average investor cannot beat the market; it posits that no investor can beat the market (unless he or she possesses private information unavailable to other investors). And in fact, there is evidence that some investors do persistently beat the market, and that this abnormal performance is unlikely to derive from inside information (for perspectives on the persistence of mutual fund abnormal performance, see, for example, Grinblatt and Titman 1992, Carhart 1997, and Daniel, Grinblatt, Titman, and Wermers 1997; on the persistence of individual investor abnormal trading performance, see, for example, Coval, Hirshleifer, and Shumway 2003). From a psychological perspective, the evidence suggests that the funds that attract investors will be those that appeal to investors' emotions and beliefs, however biased. So there is no presumption that the average fund will do well. For example, if at some point investors are irrationally exuberant about the biotech sector, cash will flow to funds heavy in biotech firms. More rational portfolios that place lower weight upon biotech will, on average, earn high subsequent returns. However, such funds may not attract many investors – for the same reason that the mispricing is present in the first place.

The fact that vast amounts of wealth are invested in actively managed mutual funds that are unable to achieve superior performance does not support the view that investors are good at choosing funds. Nor does it support the view that funds make good choices on behalf of investors.[3] There is some dissonance between the views that investors trade foolishly in a fashion that creates market inefficiencies, and yet are smart enough to select those mutual funds that follow strategies designed to exploit these same inefficiencies.

Of course, one should not swing to the opposite extreme of dismissing the efficient markets hypothesis as a mere misconception. All serious students of financial markets agree that there are forces acting to make prices reflect information accurately. The question is what degree of efficiency is achieved. For example, investors' observation of historical performance should push them toward better mutual funds. This is just one instance of the general argument that when there is a profit opportunity, smart economic agents ought to exploit it. The general obstacle is that investors may be biased in their assessments. Such bias, in the context of mutual funds, can be hard to eliminate because of inattention, noise, sample size, post-selection/reporting biases, and fund manager turnover. Nevertheless, any intelligent critical judgment that investors bring to bear in evaluating investments will tend to make the market more efficient.

In any case, it is natural to consider whether failures of rationality explain the puzzling empirical patterns in securities markets. Starting in the 1980s, Richard Thaler and colleagues led the application of psychological evidence to problems in economics. Psychological ideas relating to overreaction stimulated the collection of a great deal of empirical evidence on stock price serial correlation and volatility. The publication of Fischer Black's (1986) presidential address to the American Financial Association on "Noise," and the 1987 stock market crash further increased academic interest in imperfectly rational trading. This set the stage for analytical modeling of the pricing effects of imperfectly rational trading.

Some pioneering models captured imperfect rationality in asset markets by including mechanistic traders who either make pure noise trades,[4] or positive feedback trades in which new purchases are an increasing function of past price moves.[5] This was an efficient way to illustrate some crucial insights about survival, arbitrage, and pricing. However, in full generality, the mechanistic modeling approach is very elastic. If noise trades can be arbitrarily correlated with other economic variables, *any* return pattern can be explained. It is not enough for behavioral finance to offer the model "everything else" as an alternative to rational finance. The economic content of mechanistic trader models comes from the choice of assumptions on trades to reflect facts about psychology or trading. In the hope of being more accurately predictive, recent research has explicitly modeled how decision-making occurs in a way that reflects psychological biases.

This paper discusses the potential role of a particular psychological bias – the tendency of individuals to deceive themselves – in explaining the above securities market phenomena. We speculate that self-deception is consistent with a variety of patterns in the experimental psychology literature (see, for example, Trivers 1985 and Arkes and Hirshleifer 2004). Individuals consistently convince themselves that their ability or judgment is above the population average. They talk themselves out of decision options that might call their past judgments into question. At times, they choose to disregard new information that is inconsistent with their priors. At other times, they are excessively quick to cast aside old evidence in favor of new.

In what follows, we discuss the evidence on self-deception in the psychology literature. We will then discuss a variety of models of securities market behavior that are based on self-deception. Finally, we assess the promise of self-deception in contributing to our understanding of securities market phenomena.

Self-deception in experimental psychology

Psychological evidence suggests that people are remarkably skillful at deceiving themselves. In our view, a wide variety of evidence from experimental psychology can be interpreted in terms of self-deception. Most people believe that their ability or judgment is better than it is (overconfidence), actively avoid decisions that risk calling their judgment into question (regret avoidance), and learn in ways that are inconsistent with Bayes's theorem (conservativeness and representativeness). Before examining these phenomena in greater detail, an important question to address is why self-deception exists in the first place.

Self-deception is a trait that some evolutionary theorists believe was actively selected for when humans were evolving. The argument is that sometimes it is easier for an individual to deceive others if he is genuinely fooled himself. Trivers (1985; 1991) discusses evidence that people cannot perfectly control indicators of their true internal states. This creates selection for the ability to read subtle cues to infer the mental states of other individuals. In Trivers's self-deception theory, individuals are designed to think they are better (smarter, stronger, better friends) than they really are. Truly believing this helps them fool others about these qualities. Thus, individuals may be able to posture more effectively to potential competitors, friends, and mates by genuinely believing that their abilities are greater than they are.

An alternative approach, suggested by Bernardo and Welch (2001), is that the presence of overconfident individuals confers an informational benefit upon the group. Overconfident individuals are more willing to make use of their own information rather than blindly follow the actions of predecessors in what has been called an informational cascade (see, for example, Bikhchandani, Hirshleifer, and Welch 1998). More generally, overconfident individuals may be more willing to generate new information or undertake untested activities that the group can learn about. These considerations suggest that natural selection (via kin selection or group selection) may sometimes favor self-deception and overconfidence.

We now proceed to discuss, in turn, several apparent manifestations of self-deception that may influence behavior in financial markets.

Overconfidence

Self-deception can explain overconfidence (a tendency to overestimate one's ability or judgment accuracy), and dynamic processes that support overconfidence such as biased self-attribution (a tendency to attribute successes to one's own ability and failure to bad luck or other factors), confirmatory bias (a tendency to interpret evidence as consistent with one's pre-existing beliefs), hindsight bias (a tendency to think you "knew it all along"), rationalization (straining to come up with arguments in favor of one's past judgments and choices), and action-induced attitude changes of the sort that motivate cognitive dissonance theory (becoming more strongly persuaded of the validity of an action or belief as a direct consequence of adopting that action or belief); see Cooper and Fazio (1984). Casual observation suggests that all these phenomena affect the decisions of both amateur and professional investors.

An extensive literature on calibration shows that people believe their knowledge is more accurate than it really is.[6] For example, their predictions of probabilities of events are too extreme (too high relative to the true frequency when they think the event probably will occur, too low when they think it will not). The confidence intervals they provide for quantities are too narrow, for example, 98 percent confidence intervals contain the true quantity only 60 percent of the time (Alpert and Raiffa 1982). Experts are well-calibrated in some contexts but not others (see Camerer 1995, pp. 592–3). Experts can be more prone to overconfidence than non-experts when predictability is low and evidence is ambiguous (Griffin and Tversky 1992). Overconfidence is greater for challenging judgment tasks, and individuals tend to be more overconfident when feedback on their information or decisions is deferred or inconclusive.[7]

Overconfidence is sometimes reversed for very easy items (Lichtenstein and Fischoff 1977).[8] Overconfidence implies *overoptimism* about individuals' ability to succeed in their endeavors. Such optimism has been found in a number of different settings (Miller and Ross 1975).

Dynamic processes that support overconfidence

Self-deception also explains why there are *action-induced attitude changes* related to overconfidence that motivate the theory of *cognitive dissonance*.[9] In one experiment, people who chose between two products downgraded their assessments of the one they did not pick. In another, women who had to exert greater effort to gain entry to a group subsequently liked the group more. In other experiments, people who were induced with mild incentives or by request to express opinions became more sympathetic to those opinions. A tendency to be excessively attached to activities for which one has expended resources, the *sunk cost effect*, has been confirmed in several contexts (Arkes and Blumer 1985). The self-deception theory suggests that a tendency to adjust attitudes to match past actions is a mechanism designed to persuade individuals that they are skillful decision makers (see also Nel, Helmreich, and Aronson 1969 and Steele and Liu 1983).

People tend to interpret ambiguous evidence in a fashion consistent with their own prior beliefs. They give careful scrutiny to inconsistent facts and explain them as due to luck or faulty data-gathering (see Gilovich 1991, chapter 4). This form of *confirmatory bias* can help maintain self-esteem, consistent with self-deception. Exposure to evidence should tend to cause rational Bayesians with differing beliefs to converge, whereas the attitudes of experimental subjects exposed to mixed evidence tend to become more polarized (for example, Isenberg 1986, Lord, Ross, and Lepper 1979). Forsythe et al. (1992) find that individuals more subject to this confirmation bias lose money in an experimental market to those who are less subject to it. Confirmatory bias may cause some investors to stick to unsuccessful trading strategies, causing mispricing to persist.

Overconfidence should cause people to fail more often than they expect to. But this suggests that rational learning over time would tend to eliminate overconfidence. So for self-deception to succeed, nature must provide mechanisms that bias the learning process. This is consistent with self-enhancing *biased self-attribution.* People tend to credit themselves for past success, and blame external factors for failure.[10] As Langer and Roth (1975) put it, "Heads I win, tails it's chance"; see also the discussion of DeLong, Shleifer, Summers, and Waldmann (1991). Overconfidence and biased self-attribution are static and dynamic counterparts; self-attribution causes individuals to learn to be overconfident rather than converging to an accurate self-assessment. Such a phenomenon may help explain the escalation by individuals of poor investments.[11] For example, in the disposition effect of Shefrin and Statman (1985), individuals are reluctant to sell stocks in which they have lost money relative to their winners; for supporting evidence, see, for example, Grinblatt and Han (2003).

In a financial market setting, this suggests that the confidence of an investor will tend to grow when public information is in agreement with his past investment choices, but does not fall commensurately when public information contradicts his private information. A possible sequence in the financial market setting is as follows: (1) If an investor is overconfident about his ability to dig up useful information, then he will sacrifice leisure to do more digging. (2) When he digs up a given piece of information, his ego is on the line (that is, overconfidence-inducing psychological mechanisms are triggered). (3) When an investor is in the habit of digging things out and trading actively on this basis, he becomes more overconfident (biased self-attribution is induced).

Anticipation and regret

Anticipation and regret represent additional dimensions along which individuals may be prone to self-deception. According to expected utility theory, instantaneous utility derives solely from current consumption resulting from current and past decisions. However, people also seem to derive instantaneous utility from anticipating future consumption and from regret or elation if current consumption differs from what was anticipated or experienced in the past, or what could have been obtained from alternative decisions (for example, Josephs et al. 1996, Ritov 1996). An individual enjoys their day at work more on a Friday than on a Monday (habit), on the Friday prior to a vacation than on other Fridays (anticipation), and on the Monday after a one-week vacation than on the

Monday after a two-week vacation that was accidentally cut short by a week (regret).

Chacko, Chowdhry, Cohen, and Coval (2002) model anticipation and regret in a time-consistent setting in which individuals rationally choose to deceive themselves. That is, after having deceived themselves and paid the consequences, if individuals are reminded of their self-deception, they "would not have done things differently." Individuals highly averse to regret will rationally convince themselves to be pessimistic. Individuals who derive utility from anticipation will rationally choose to be optimistic. Individuals will also optimally choose to learn in a conservative manner (see the discussion below on conservativeness), so that they smooth the effects of anticipation and regret through time.

An efficient heuristic method of comparing decision alternatives may be to line up and compare possible outcomes by the state of the world (rather than evaluating the expected utility of each alternative separately and then comparing). Thus, having feelings triggered by comparison of outcomes may be an effective mechanism for motivating good choices. Regret avoidance may also reflect a self-deception mechanism designed to protect self-esteem about decision-making ability (Josephs et al. 1996).

Regret theory (Bell 1982, Loomes and Sugden 1982) was developed to explain patterns of choices that violated expected utility theory. The idea is that the utility of an option depends not only upon the utility of its potential outcomes, but also on the disutility of not obtaining the outcomes associated with other options were they to prove to have been the correct choice. Research has demonstrated that anticipated regret increases regret-minimizing choices, changes attitudes about behavior, and changes future behavior (Josephs et al. 1996, Ritov 1996). Anticipation of regret about bad choices has been used to explain why consumers purchase higher priced but well-known brands and why they are reluctant to trade equivalent lottery tickets, even with an added cash incentive (Bar-Hillel and Neter 1996).

Another line of choice research has focused on regret for past actions. The general format of these studies is to describe two people who made choices that resulted in bad outcomes and ask, "Who feels worse (or more regret)?" Kahneman and Tversky (1982) presented the now classic stockholder problem in which two investors each lose $1200, but through different choices. Mr. Paul "loses" his $1200 by choosing to keep his stock in Company A, which remains unchanged in value, instead of availing himself of the opportunity to sell and buy stock in Company B, which increases in value by $1200. Mr. George loses his $1200 by choosing to sell his stock in Company B to buy stock in Company A. The majority of subjects state that Mr. George, who chose to act and lost, would feel more regret than Mr. Paul, who chose not to act but still lost. This result, that loss resulting from action is regretted more than loss resulting from inaction, has been called the "omission bias" (Spranca, Minsk, and Baron 1991, Ritov and Baron 1990).

Regret aversion can also explain the *endowment effect*, a preference for people to hold on to what they have rather than exchange for a better alternative, as with the refusal of individuals to swap a lottery ticket for an equivalent one plus cash.[12] The endowment effect has been confirmed in experimental securities markets.

Conservatism and representativeness

A final dimension to self-deception that relates to financial markets is the propensity of individuals to depart from Bayes's theorem in predictable ways. Edwards (1968) identified and later studies confirmed the phenomenon of conservatism; that under appropriate circumstances individuals do not change their beliefs as much as would a rational Bayesian in the face of new evidence. The more useful the evidence, the greater is the shortfall between actual updating and rational updating.

Edwards indicated that it takes approximately two to five observations to cause a subject to change his opinions as much as he ought based on a single observation. A tendency toward conservatism makes sense as a means of maintaining self-esteem. Individuals who change their beliefs are implicitly recognizing that their previous beliefs were not entirely correct. To put this differently, as Barberis, Shleifer, and Vishny (1998) mention (p. 315), such individuals can be viewed as overconfident about their prior information. Such overconfidence fits with self-deception: I believe I am very good at acquiring good information, so I stick with it.

Finance models designed to capture overconfidence often focus on confidence about a new signal, and therefore involve moving too far from the prior information toward the new information. This discussion of self-deception and the psychological evidence suggests that this is not necessarily the case. Individuals should hold too close to the prior if the prior is strongly associated with the individual's self-esteem, and move with the new information if the new information is more strongly linked to self-esteem. For example, Daniel, Hirshleifer, and Subrahmanyam (1998) argue that a private signal will tend to be tied closely to self-esteem, so that overconfidence should be about private but not public signals. Presumably the individual's prior belief reflects a combination of past private and public signals, so it should be more closely tied to self-esteem than a new public signal, and less tied to self-esteem than a new private signal.

The representativeness heuristic (Kahneman and Tversky 1973) involves decisions about whether a specific item belongs to a general class. The heuristic involves judging the item as probably belonging to the class if it shares some similarity to the class. This can be inaccurate because greater similarity is not always associated with higher probability. For example, the son of a man who is 6'7" tall is more likely to be 6'6" tall than 6'7" tall; big effects are not always the result of big causes; a fair coin is less likely to produce TTH than TT.

Since similarity often is associated with higher probability, this heuristic helps economize on limited cognitive capacity. This heuristic can help people detect patterns more quickly by looking for similarities. Furthermore, overconfidence should cause such a bias. The ability to discern meaningful patterns from complex inputs is an important ability. An overconfident individual who overestimates this ability should tend to treat identified patterns, which are actually coincidental, as meaningful. The financial industry of technical analysis is arguably based upon the excessive faith of individuals in their own abilities to detect meaningful patterns.

One explanation for conservatism is that processing new information and updating beliefs is costly. There is evidence that information presented in a cognitively costly form is weighted less: information that is abstract and statistical, such as sample size and probabilistic base-rate information. Furthermore, people may overreact to information that is easily processed, that is, scenarios and concrete examples.

The costly-processing argument can be extended to explain base rate underweighting. If an individual underweights new information received about population frequencies (base rates), then base rate underweighting is really a form of conservatism. Indeed, base rates are underweighted less when they are presented in more salient form or in a fashion which emphasizes their causal relation to the decision problem (see Koehler 1996). This costly-processing-of-new-information argument does not suggest that an individual will underweight his pre-existing internalized prior belief. On the other hand, if base rate underweighting is a consequence of the use of the representativeness heuristic, there *should* be underweighting of priors.

Griffin and Tversky (1992) suggest that base-rate underweighting and conservatism, interpreted as under- versus over-reaction to signals, can be understood as results of excessive reliance on the *strength* of information signals and under-reliance on the *weight* of information signals. The strength of an information realization is how "extreme" the evidence is (in some sense), and the weight of evidence is its reliability or precision. For example, a large sample of conditionally independent and identically distributed information signals has high weight. But if the preponderance of favorable over unfavorable signals is modest, it has low strength. Conservatism arises when people rely too little on high weight evidence such as a long sample, and base rate neglect when people rely too heavily on high-strength evidence such as a few signals all in one direction.

In reality, people try to recognize their own psychological failings and often take steps to adjust for them. For example, Shefrin and Statman (1984) suggested that individual investor demand for high-dividend-yield stocks is motivated by a desire for an external means of disciplining consumption. Such adjustment is imperfect for many reasons, but a notable one is overconfidence. An overconfident investor may be prone to deny his biases rather than recognize and compensate for them.

In summary, different experimental settings can lead to under-reliance or over-reliance on new signals; people seem to make judgments differently in different situations (see Grether 1992, Payne, Bettman, and Johnson 1992). Given the different possible effects, invoking the name of a bias does not provide compelling support for assuming underreaction or overreaction in a financial model. Further support can be provided by comparing the economic decision environment of the model with the specific experimental decision setting in which the bias was documented, and especially by running new experiments that match closely the decision environment in the financial model.

Self-deception in financial markets

We now discuss how the above notions of self-deception may help us understand the behavior of financial markets. Fama's famous early survey (Fama 1970) contrasted "semi-strong form efficiency," wherein market prices fully reflect all available public information, with "strong form efficiency," wherein market prices fully reflect even private information. It is well accepted that markets are not strong form efficient. But a bit of thought suggests that there is no absolute division between public and private information. Information in the newspaper is public, and information known only to an individual is private. But what if only a few people receive that newspaper? If only one person has the information, but she is happy to tell anyone who asks, is the information private? What if the individual shouts the information far and wide, but no one will listen? Is it very different for an individual to expend time and resources to read something in the newspaper (the contents of which are generally viewed as public information by financial economists) versus talking to another individual?

To consider such issues clearly we must take into account costs of conveying and processing information. Private information is just the extreme case of information that is hard to dig out. But the expense of digging it out may come not just from incentives for secrecy, but from the form in which it is presented (consider a pile of balance sheets versus a well-written analyst's report), the outlets at which the information has been certified, and so on. Information that is conveyed briefly and lucidly will have higher impact than information that is harder to make sense of. In other words, some forms of information are more salient than others. So far we have talked about some good reasons for differences in salience: brevity, clarity, and certification. However, an individual with limited information processing capacity will imperfectly optimize the decision of what information to process. Going beyond this, it is reasonable to think that there are some systematic biases in the way that irrelevant considerations affect salience – as with the use of sexually attractive models in product advertisements. Most studies of price forecasts find biases that are predictable using current observables. For example, forecasts are often found to be adaptive, that is, they respond partially to past forecast errors.[13] Such biases are potentially consistent either with Bayesian learning with an unknown distribution, or with overconfidence. Experimental studies involving a fixed distribution generally also yield biases, and forecasts are adaptive in most forecast experiments involving endogenously determined prices as well (see Camerer 1995). Consistent with overconfidence, forecasters seem to put too little weight on the known forecasts of other forecasters (Batchelor and Dua 1992).

Analyst forecasts of earnings are overoptimistic at long time horizons and pessimistic at short horizons (for example, Richardson, Teoh, and Wysocki 2004). Such biases may come from misperceptions or from agency incentives. However, we would normally expect rational agents to provide at least a positive incremental value in their forecasting activities. A large literature shows that real-world decision makers such as PhD admission committees or doctors do not predict outcomes as well as mechanical decision rules based on simple linear combinations of objective input measures (see Camerer 1991). This suggests that the rise of arbitrage based upon modern statistical analysis in securities markets will indeed reduce mispricing.

Overconfidence and asset prices

In a model with multiple securities, Daniel, Hirshleifer, and Subrahmanyam (2001) provide a model of the pricing of assets and securities (analogous to the traditional Capital Asset Pricing Model, or

CAPM, of financial theory) when investors are overconfident. In the traditional CAPM, a security's expected return is increasing in the security's risk. This reflects the notion that investors must be compensated for bearing high risk. The appropriate measure of risk in the model is the marginal contribution an extra unit of the security adds to the variability of a typical investor's portfolio. It turns out that this marginal contribution to risk is equal to the theoretical regression coefficient of the security's return on the "market portfolio," a portfolio consisting of all invested wealth in the asset market. This regression coefficient is generally referred to as the security's "beta."

In the overconfidence-based model, security terminal cash flows satisfy a linear factor model, and each investor observes signals about the factors and the idiosyncratic component of security payoffs. Risk-averse investors form what they perceive to be mean-variance efficient portfolios. Overconfident individuals trade with risk-averse arbitrageurs who form rational beliefs. A security's equilibrium expected return is linearly increasing in the security's beta with the market, and the security's current mispricing. Variables containing market price are proxies for the security's misvaluation. For example, a fundamental/price ratio such as book/market is driven down when favorable news drives a stock up. Since there is overreaction, this is when the stock is overvalued. Thus, a high fundamental/price ratio predicts high future returns. Aggregate value measures such as the market dividend yield or book/market positively predict future market returns.

Fundamental/price ratios mix two sources of predictive power. A fundamental/price ratio (for example, high book/market) tends to be high if either risk is high or if the market has overreacted to a highly adverse signal. In either case, on average, price rises. Since high book/market reflects both mispricing and risk, whereas beta reflects only risk, book/market tends to be a better predictor of returns. These two sources of predictive power are unequal. Beta helps disentangle these cases, so beta and book/market are joint predictors of future returns.

However, when overconfidence becomes very strong, and if the proxy for the unconditional expected value (for example, book value) is perfect, then the incremental ability of beta to predict future returns vanishes. The fundamental/price ratio dominates beta even though risk is priced. This is an extreme case, but it helps explain why empirical findings on the incremental effect of beta have been weak and inconsistent. The model also implies that in univariate regressions beta should predict future returns. The model further describes the tradeoffs in constructing optimal price-related proxies for misvaluation.

Another puzzling pattern for fully rational asset pricing theory is the forward discount puzzle. High bond yields in one country relative to another country should be an indicator that that country's currency is likely to have higher inflation, and therefore is expected by investors to depreciate relative to the other country's currency. The higher bond yield (in nominal terms) then provides investors with appropriate compensation for the greater expected real decline in the value of the first country's currency. This bond yield differential is called the "forward discount." The puzzle is that a higher-than-usual forward discount between two countries is associated on average with *appreciation* rather than *depreciation* in the first country's currency. In other words, investing in high interest-rate countries appears to be a "good deal" for investors.

Several authors have commented on the difficulties that fully rational models have in explaining this puzzle (see, for example, Engel 1996). A possible explanation for this puzzle is provided by investor overconfidence (see Hirshleifer and Wang 2001). A large forward discount may reflect an overreaction by overconfident investors to information (perhaps spurious) about likely high inflation. This overreaction drives down the value of the first country's currency too much relative to the other country's currency (that is, it drives up the exchange rate). Eventually, correction occurs as information arrives that forces investors to revise their beliefs. This correction leads to appreciation of the first country's currency.

Static models provide simple generalizations of the insights of the traditional Capital Asset Pricing Model that can encompass the effect of risk as well as mispricing. However, a static approach has no hope of capturing the distinction between short-term continuation and long-term reversals.

In both static and dynamic models, long-run reversal occurs when there is an overreaction to an impulse such as the arrival of good news. In a dynamic setting, short-run positive autocorrelation is consistent with long-run reversal so long as the process of overreaction and correction is sufficiently smooth. Such smoothness implies that when an impulse sets the price rising, it will probably rise some more; that on average the last up-move to the peak of the impulse response function is not followed by a precipitous drop; and when the price is falling, it tends to fall some more. In contrast, a long-lag autocorrelation tends to associate positive returns during the overreaction process with negative returns arising during the correction process.

The following describes the effects of *pure* (independent) noise trading, mechanistic models based on correlated trading (positive feedback), the effects of mistaken beliefs, and the effects of alternative preferences.

Pure noise trading

Pure noise trading and positive feedback trading cause overreaction, and hence negative autocorrelations in long-run returns. When a stock rises too high, it needs to correct back down. Equivalently, this overreaction causes excess volatility in returns. Furthermore, Campbell and Kyle (1993) showed that overreaction can cause aggregate stock market value measures such as dividend yield to predict future market returns, so that contrarian investment strategies are, on average, profitable.

DeLong, Shleifer, Summers, and Waldmann (1990a) model the consequences of unpredictable random trades. Two securities pay identical, riskless dividends. The price of one asset is exogenously fixed. The other asset is risky because pure noise trades cause stochastic mispricing. Rational arbitrageurs with exogenous short-time horizons limit their arbitrage trades for fear that the mispricing will get worse before it gets better. On average, the risky asset trades at a discount; the risk premium demanded by the rational investors.

The noise trading approach provides an explanation for the existence and behavior of closed-end fund discounts and their correlations with stock returns. According to DeLong, Shleifer, Summers, and Waldmann (1990a), noise traders buy and sell closed-end funds in a correlated fashion, causing discounts or premia relative to net asset value to fluctuate. The mispricing risk this creates makes these funds less attractive to rational investors, so on average there is a discount. This theory implies that fund discounts move together based on a systematic noise-trading factor; such co-movement exists (for example, Lee, Shleifer, and Thaler 1991). The theory also explains why such funds are created: to exploit optimistic noise traders.

Lee, Shleifer, and Thaler (1991) suggest that shifts in fund discounts reflect shifts in noise trader sentiment toward all small stocks. This is consistent with their evidence that narrowing of closed-end fund discounts is associated contemporaneously with high small stock returns. This implies that discounts predict small stock returns. If discounts were a consequence of *pure* noise trading, they would be uncorrelated with future fundamentals such as accounting performance. Swaminathan (1996) finds that at lags of greater than one year, high discounts predict both low future accounting profits and high future stock returns. This is consistent with fund investors overreacting to genuine information.

The co-movement in small stock returns documented in Fama and French (1993) may come from correlated imperfectly rational trades. The DeLong, Shleifer, Summers, and Waldmann (1990a) approach then suggests that small stocks, including closed-end fund shares, will earn high expected returns in compensation for their high mispricing risk.

Alternatively, low market-value stocks may earn high returns because a stock's low market value on average derives partly from its being undervalued (see, for example, Daniel, Hirshleifer, and Subrahmanyam 2001). The U.S. small firm effect has been weak or absent in the last 15 years, yet closed-end fund discounts remain.

Positive feedback trading

Positive feedback trading has several possible motivations, one being that investors form expectations of future prices by extrapolating trends, consistent with the representativeness heuristic. DeLong, Shleifer, Summers, and Waldmann (1990b) offer a model with a risky asset and risk-free cash, in which information arrives sequentially. The exogenous date 2 demand of the positive feedback traders is linearly increasing in the preceding price trend. Foreseeing this, rational speculators buy into price trends, exaggerating trends and overshooting. As a result there is excess volatility, and long-term negative autocorrelations in returns.

In Cutler, Poterba, and Summers (1990), there are two types of imperfectly rational traders (that is, traders overconfident in their understanding of the market), positive feedback traders, and fundamental traders who ignore price and trade based upon a signal about the security's payoff. Some fundamental traders observe this signal with a lag. This lag creates price trends that are profitably exploited by feedback traders. The gradual process of overshooting and correction induces both short-lag positive autocorrelation and long-lag negative autocorrelation. In the model of DeLong, Shleifer, Summers, and Waldmann (1990b), positive feedback trading loses money. In contrast, in Cutler et al., positive feedback traders can potentially make money from their activities. These potential profits come from being able to exploit underreaction.

More recent models with endogenous decisions have found things akin to pure noise trading – a limiting case of overconfidence, and positive feedback trading. But endogenously derived positive feedback is conditional and statistical, which seems more realistic than the older models. For reasons of both descriptiveness and predictiveness, explicit modeling of the psychology of investors is likely to supersede the mechanistic approach (except perhaps in otherwise-intractable applications).

Two recent papers provide models with a single risky security, which reflects the fact that people learn about their own abilities in a biased, self-promoting fashion. In these models, investors do not know the precision of their private information signals, which reflects their information-gathering ability. They learn about their precision through time by observing whether later public news confirms or disconfirms their previous signal. The analyses assume the dynamic complement of overconfidence; biased self-attribution. When investors receive confirming news, their confidence in their precision rises too much, and when there is disconfirming news their confidence declines too little.

In Daniel, Hirshleifer, and Subrahmanyam (1998), the impulse response function to a favorable initial shock, the private information signal, is hump-shaped. Price on average rises further as public information arrives, because confidence about the private signal, on average, grows. Eventually, however, accumulation evidence forces investors back to a more reasonable self-perception. This smooth hump-shaped impulse response implies positive short-lag and negative long-lag return autocorrelations. Daniel, Hirshleifer, and Subrahmanyam (1998) also numerically simulate the correlation of a public information surprise (such as favorable accounting performance) with future returns with self-attribution bias. At short lags this correlation is positive, but at long lags the correlation can be negative.

Gervais and Odean (2001) provide a model that accommodates an analytical solution for the learning process under biased self-attribution. As traders become overconfident, trading volume and market return volatility increase. Since equity is in positive net supply, the model also predicts that trading volume will be higher after market rises than market falls, consistent with Statman and Thorley (1998).[14]

Excessive trading

It has been argued that the volume of trade in speculative markets is too large, and overconfidence of traders has been advanced as an explanation (for example, DeBondt and Thaler 1995). Whether volume is too large is hard to establish without a benchmark rational level of volume. Rational dynamic hedging strategies, in principle, can generate enormous volume with moderate amounts of news.

However, as DeBondt and Thaler point out, support for overconfidence is provided by evidence suggesting that more active investors earn lower returns as a result of incurring higher transaction costs (Odean 1999, Barber and Odean 2000).[15] Also consistent with overconfidence, traders in experimental markets do not place enough weight on the information and actions of others (Bloomfield, Libby, and Nelson 1999). In experimental markets, investors also tend to overreact more to unreliable than to reliable information (Bloomfield, Libby, and Nelson 2000).

Barber and Odean (2002) find that investors who have experienced the greatest past success in trading are the most likely to switch to online trading, and will trade the most in the future. This evidence is consistent with self-attribution bias, meaning that the investors have most likely attributed their past success to skill rather than to luck. Also, there is some evidence that access to Internet trading appears to encourage more active trading (Choi, Laibson, and Metrick 2002). There is also evidence of overconfidence even by experienced dealers in an "opaque" experimental asset market, but not in a transparent one (Lamoureux and Schnitzlein 2001).

The dynamics of representativeness and conservatism in financial markets

Barberis, Shleifer, and Vishny (1998) offer an explanation for under- and overreactions based on a model in which actual earnings for a risky asset follow a random walk, but investors do not understand this. They mistakenly believe that the earnings process stochastically fluctuates between a regime with mean-reverting earnings, and a regime with expected earnings growth. Apart from misunderstanding the structure of the earnings process, the representative investor updates as a rational Bayesian. This structure is designed to capture the representativeness heuristic and conservatism bias.

If recent earnings changes reverse, investors erroneously believe the firm is in a mean-reverting state, and underreact to recent news, consistent with conservatism. If investors see a sequence of growing earnings, they tend to conclude (wrongly) that the firm is in a growth regime, and overextrapolate trends, which is arguably reminiscent of representativeness. Overreaction to a long enough trend implies subsequent low returns during the process of correction. Thus, there can be long-term overreaction and correction, implying negative long-lag return autocorrelation. Yet the average response to an initial impulse can be smooth, implying positive short lag autocorrelation. Similarly, the model can accommodate a positive short-term correlation between the asset return and an earnings change, and a negative long-term correlation. If sporadic events such as dividend initiations are viewed as isolated from earnings patterns, a single-event version of the model implies, under appropriate parameter values, underreaction.

Cross-sectional effects (such as a value effect) are simulated with earnings that are independently distributed across stocks. This implies a nearly risk-free arbitrage opportunity for a rational investor who buys and sells stocks based on return predictors. Such arbitrage would be risky in a setting where investors update their beliefs about systematic factors in earnings trends or reversals. The psychological literature on multiple cue learning may provide guidance for such a model.

Hong and Stein (1999) analyze a market in which, as in Cutler, Poterba, and Summers (1990), some traders react sluggishly, and others trade based on positive feedback. Each group of traders is risk averse, and is able to process only a subset of available information. Information about the liquidating dividend dribbles into the hands of different groups of news watchers. News watchers condition private signals on their own but ignore market prices, causing underreaction.

Momentum traders, in contrast, condition on the cumulative price change over the last *k* periods. Each trader takes a fixed position for a given number of periods. Momentum traders exploit the underreaction of news watchers by buying in response to price increases. This accelerates the reaction to news, but also causes overshooting. The smoothness of the overreaction process causes positive short-lag and negative long-lag autocorrelation. Slower information diffusion tends to launch a more powerful overreaction, leading to more negative long-lag autocorrelations.

Self-deception and deception

One might expect that the tendency to deceive oneself opens the door to deception by others. Both self-deception and the deception of others may be important in financial markets. For instance, the tendency to self-deception can make it easier for predators to deceive and exploit investors.[16] Overconfidence in one's ability to interpret signals can lead to excessive credulity in interpreting the signals transmitted by others. As a consequence, accounting and reporting policy can differ widely across firms and can influence actual firm valuation and performance.

In simple, fully rational settings, if disclosure is costless, all information is disclosed. Intuitively, in equilibrium investors are highly skeptical of a decision by a firm to withhold information.[17] There are some qualifications to this conclusion based upon proprietary costs, firms that do not receive information, and signaling incentives.[18] When there is a non-verifiable information signal as well as a verifiable one, it can be an equilibrium for the firm to withhold (fail to disclose) favorable verifiable information as a "macho" signal that it has favorable unverifiable information (Teoh and Hwang 1991).

Excessive credulity among investors further suggests the "unraveling" results of Grossman (1981) and Milgrom (1981) may no longer hold. Individuals who are overconfident may underestimate the importance of information they do not possess, thereby causing them to underweight the importance of non-disclosure. As Jonathan Swift put it, "The most positive men are the most credulous." (*Thoughts on Various Subjects*

1711) In this regard, it is interesting that experts in some experiments are more prone than non-experts to ignore decision tools that would be useful for both experts and non-experts alike for accurately performing an assigned task (Arkes, Dawes, and Christensen 1986).

A variety of evidence indicates that individuals are insufficiently skeptical about firms' motives for refraining from disclosing information. For example, Mathios (2000) examined the effect of the Nutrition Labeling and Education Act on purchases of salad dressing, which made mandatory the labeling of information about fat content. He found that even though there was voluntary labeling (mostly of low-fat brands) prior to the regulation, mandatory disclosure caused high-fat dressings to lose market share. Hanson and Kysar (1999) review a literature in consumer psychology and marketing on the ability of sellers to manipulate consumer perceptions of their products.

Investors also seem to be insufficiently skeptical of firms that refrain from disclosing information, or that disclose in a non-salient fashion. For example, there is evidence that firms tend to release good news early and bad news late,[19] the exception being that the possibility of litigation can induce disclosure of bad news (Skinner 1994). Such behavior is consistent with a fully rational equilibrium with proprietary disclosure costs (for example, Verrecchia 1990, Darrough and Stoughton 1990, Feltham and Xie 1992). However, this raises the question of whether such costs are high enough to explain this bias. Excessive investor credulity strengthens the incentive of firms to behave in such a fashion.

As a consequence of excessive credulity, it is plausible that a partial disclosure equilibrium analogous to that of the Verrecchia model will obtain – see Hirshleifer, Lim, and Teoh (2003). Firms with more favorable information disclose. But firms with sufficiently adverse information (below some cutoff) withhold information and delay revelation.

The combination of limited attention with overconfidence may be more potent in generating credulity than limited attention alone. If individuals are overconfident, they will fail to discount fully for the fact that they are ignoring some of the considerations relevant for their decisions. In consequence investors may be fooled by actions firms can take to manipulate perceptions.

The example of new equity issues and repurchases illustrates how limited attention and overconfidence may affect firms' incentives to take informative actions. A manager who has an incentive to maintain a high stock price will try to make profits in his firm's share trading. This encourages issuance of new shares when the stock is overvalued (owing either to information asymmetry or to market irrationality) and repurchase when the stock is undervalued. If the market is credulous and fails to discount fully for this incentive, then the manager will indeed get a good price for the shares it buys and sells through this procedure. The market may understand that new issues are an adverse indicator of value, consistent with a negative stock price reaction, but being insufficiently skeptical, the price does not fall enough. This leads to a long-run negative return. Similarly, consistent with the evidence, this story suggests a positive price reaction to repurchase and a long-run positive average abnormal post-event return.

Similarly, there is evidence that positive earnings adjustments of firms (accounting accruals) are associated with low subsequent abnormal stock returns (Sloan 1996). This suggests that firms are able to induce overvaluation through cosmetic accounting adjustments. Consistent with this hypothesis, this effect comes mainly from the discretionary component of accruals (Teoh, Welch, and Wong 1998a, Teoh, Welch, and Wong 1998b), and is particularly strong just before initial public offerings of equity as well as seasoned equity offerings (Teoh, Welch, and Wong 1998a, Teoh, Welch, and Wong 1998b, Teoh, Wong, and Rao 1998). Even the forecasts of earnings made by professional stock analysts are biased by an amount that depends on the level of the firm's accruals (Teoh and Wong 2002).

Managers generally like high stock prices, so stocks that are more subject to investor credulity should on the whole tend to be overvalued. The problem of credulity is likely to be greater for firms that are able to weave hard-to-refute stories to tell investors about future prospects. Thus, empirical findings of inferior performance of stocks with low book/market ratios, and the stronger relation of book/market to returns among high R&D firms (Chan, Lakonishok, and Sougiannis 2001), are consistent with credulity.[20]

Firms also seem to have a particular distaste for required disclosure of liabilities. Fully rational investor skepticism should force voluntary revelation of such information. Indeed, the fact that a firm or industry organization would campaign for secrecy would itself seem to reveal bad news. However, if investors are excessively credulous, rules forcing more disclosure can be helpful. This reasoning provides a motivation for mandatory disclosure rules.[21]

More broadly, Hirshleifer and Teoh (2003) provide a model in which investor interpretations of financial reports and market prices are influenced by limited attention. For example, limited attention causes credulity about so-called pro forma earnings disclosures (extra earnings disclosures outside of financial statements that do not have to satisfy Generally Accepted Accounting Principles). It also causes the market to overvalue firms that have high commitments of employee stock option compensation, as investors fail to take into account the dilution in stock value that would occur if these options are eventually exercised. Furthermore, the market misvalues diversified firms as it fails to properly disentangle the differing growth rates of the components of earnings derived from different business segments.

Finally, a recent study supports the widely-held view that analysts and investors may have been excessively credulous in interpreting information released by Enron prior to its 2001 collapse. Examining posts to Enron message boards on the Internet, Felton, and Kim (2002) found a variety of detailed warnings regarding Enron's off-balance sheet liabilities that turned out to be extremely prescient.[22] Of course, it is not obvious that even appropriately skeptical analysts should be able to have the foresight of the best-informed individual posting to an Internet message board.

Discussion

Although it is not obvious how the empirical securities market phenomena can be captured plausibly in a model based on perfect investor rationality, no psychological ("behavioral") theory for these phenomena has won general acceptance. Why is this the case? The criticisms of psychology-based theories can be classified into four major categories. First, the use of psychological theories in explaining securities market behavior is often viewed as an *ad hoc* exercise. Because of the wide array of evidence in the experimental psychology literature, skeptics feel that psychology-based researchers can easily "psycho-mine" the literature to find whatever evidence they need to account for the particular securities market phenomenon they are studying.

Second, although the array of experimental evidence in psychology is wide, it is not clear that the laboratory setting is sufficiently close to that of a financial market. For instance, little direct evidence exists as to whether psychological biases are important in influencing investor behavior when significant capital is on the line. On the other hand, the general finding from psychological studies has been that increased pecuniary incentives tend to moderate, but do not eliminate biases.

Third, even if psychological biases are important at the individual level, it is often argued that they should cancel out in aggregate. What is the mechanism that causes systematic patterns?

A final criticism of a psychology-based approach is that one would expect that, with time, psychological biases in financial markets disappear. What prevents individuals with psychological biases from either learning about and eliminating their biases or from losing so much money that they drop out of the market? We address each of these criticisms in turn.

A general criticism often leveled by economists against psychological theories is that, in a given economic setting, the universe of conceivable irrational behavior patterns is essentially unrestricted. Why overconfidence, why not underconfidence? What does this have to do with the representative heuristic, or cognitive dissonance? Does a summary of empirical patterns from psychology experiments deserve the name "theory"? Thus, it is sometimes claimed that allowing for irrationality opens a Pandora's box of *ad hoc* stories that will have little out-of-sample predictive power. In a specific investment setting, it can be hard to judge which documented psychological bias is relevant. This creates an extra degree of freedom for model-mining not present in the purely rational approach. However, DeBondt and Thaler (1995) argue that a good psychological finance theory will be grounded on psychological evidence about how people actually behave. We concur, and also believe that such a theory should allow for the rational side of investor decisions. To deserve consideration a theory should be parsimonious, explain a range of anomalous patterns in different contexts, and generate new empirical implications.

Financial economists are familiar with criticisms of psychological experiments: that the stakes are low, that subjects have little experience with the experimental setting, that there is weak incentive to pay attention or tell the truth, and that publication depends on finding an effect. What may not be as familiar is that there is data addressing these issues. On the whole, training and increasing rewards and number of repetitions often reduces, but does not eliminate biases. Lessons learned through repetition often do not carry over well across seemingly similar tasks. The well-known biases have been subjected to replication.[23] Many (though not all) of the cognitive biases are stronger for individuals with low cognitive ability or skills than for those with high ability or skills, consistent with biases being genuine errors (see Stanovich and West 2000).

Economists also argue that errors are independent across individuals, and therefore cancel out in equilibrium. Why should we expect any of these phenomena to matter in the aggregate? People share similar heuristics, those that worked well in our evolutionary past. So on the whole, we should be subject to similar biases. Systematic biases (common to most people, and predictable based upon the nature of the decision problem) have been confirmed in a vast literature in experimental psychology. The evidence simply does not support the idea that the errors people make are unrelated, or independent of the type of decision problems.

One of the reasons that financial economists have traditionally adhered to a fully rational framework is that it has a powerful motivation. People who behave this way will tend to do well, and so in an evolutionary sense should dominate the economy. More deeply, on a longer time scale the human mind evolved under pressure of natural selection, which should design a mind that works well. However, as was discussed previously, there are strong arguments for the survival of self-deception in the prehistoric environment in which humans evolved.

In the financial market setting, one might expect self-deception to be severely penalized and selected against. However, several papers argue the opposite: that self-deception can help individuals prosper in financial markets. Kyle and Wang (1997) argue that overconfident traders, by committing to trade aggressively on their information, can obtain an above-average share of informed-trading profits. Similarly, DeLong, Shleifer, Summers, and Waldmann (1990a) and Hirshleifer and Luo (2001) argue that overconfident traders, because they create mispricing risk and because they underestimate the level of risk that they assume, may earn greater expected returns than rational traders. Although they assume correspondingly high levels of risk, if survival in financial markets depends on terminal wealth levels, under appropriate conditions overconfident traders thrive relative to rational traders. Other papers that conclude that irrationality may persist in financial market settings include Blume and Easley (1990), Benos (1998), and Wang (2001).

Why don't people simply learn their way out of biased judgments? To some extent they do. One barrier is that learning is just too hard. Some of these biases are the side effects of heuristics that are necessary to cut the Gordian knot and come to a decision in the face of a complicated environment. The other barrier arises from self-deception itself. Individuals who think they are already competent may be slow to adjust their decision procedures (for example, see Einhorn and Hogarth 1978).

In general, psychology-based theories of securities market phenomenon are not necessarily direct substitutes for traditional finance theory. Much of traditional finance theory is compatible with psychological effects. Indeed, central to any robust psychology-based theory of financial markets will be the traditional analysis of how individual decisions aggregate, through market clearing, to determine equilibrium prices. It will be at the individual level, with the introduction of judgment and decision biases, where the traditional and psychological approaches depart.

While the degree of efficiency of securities prices remains a controversial issue, we have argued that self-deception holds promise as a basis for understanding capital market behavior. Self-deception unifies several regularities in psychology and finance in an appealing way, provides a variety of empirical predictions, and survives generic critiques of psychology-based financial theories. Biases consistent with self-deception have emerged in a range of experimental settings involving many subjects, which suggests that the effects of self-deception are unlikely to cancel out in the aggregate. There are plausible arguments for why self-deceiving beliefs and learning processes could have survived and proliferated in the prehistoric environment of human evolutionary adaptation. In consequence, it is reasonable to expect such beliefs will tend to persist in modern financial market settings. Several intriguing issues remain to be explored. These include the questions of when self-deception is most likely to operate unchecked (for example, when penalties are low and potential benefits are large), what other implications does self-deception have for financial behavior, and whether the further empirical predictions of theories based upon self-deception are borne out in the data.

Notes

* This paper was written for presentation at the December 2001 Austrian Ministry of Science Workshop on "Exchange, Deceptions and Self-Deceptions" in Paris, France. We thank Caroline Gerschlager and anonymous reviewers for very helpful comments.

1 See, for example, Chen (2003). Campbell and Cochrane (1999) find that a utility function with very strong "habit persistence" is required to explain the predictable variation in market returns. To be consistent with cross-sectional predictability findings (on size, book-to-market, and momentum, for example), a model would presumably require even more extreme variation across states of the world in the marginal value placed upon consumption (that is, in marginal utilities). Also, the model would require that marginal utilities co-vary strongly with the returns on portfolios formed based upon firm size, book-to-market ratios and past return momentum. No such correlation is obvious in examining the data.

2 The finding by Jensen (1968; 1969) that actively managed mutual funds do not outperform the market has been confirmed in dozens of subsequent empirical studies of mutual funds; see also Malkiel (1995).

3 Rubinstein (2001) offers overconfidence as an explanation for the empirical findings; it is somewhat surprising to see overconfidence playing a pivotal role in a brief in support of efficient markets. He

maintains that overconfidence causes managers and investors to work too hard to eliminate profit opportunities, making the market in a sense too efficient. It is plausible that overconfidence will cause individuals to generate more information. But Rubinstein's reasoning does not address the possibility that overconfident investors and portfolio managers may take actions that generate rather than correct mispricing. This is, however, a natural implication of overconfidence, as developed in several models (see, for example, Odean 1998 and Daniel, Hirshleifer, and Subrahmanyam 1998; 2001).

4 That is, they place trades that are purely random in size and direction; see Kyle (1985).

5 See Cutler, Poterba, and Summers (1990), DeLong et al. (1990a; 1990b), and Frankel and Froot (1986; 1990).

6 See, for example, Keren (1991), Lichtenstein, Fischoff, and Phillips (1982), McClelland and Bolger (1994), and Yates (1990).

7 Einhorn (1980), Fischoff, Slovic, and Lichtenstein (1977), Griffin and Tversky (1992), Lichtenstein, Fischoff, and Phillips (1982), Yates (1990).

8 This is not surprising on mechanical grounds, in the extreme case of perfect decision accuracy; it is possible to be underconfident but not overconfident about accuracy. It has been suggested that apparent overconfidence could be an artifact of the choice of questions that are not a "representative sample of the knowledge domain" (for example, Gigerenzer, Hoffrage, and Kleinbolting 1991), but overconfidence remains when questions are randomly selected from the knowledge domain, and has been documented in many practical choice settings (Griffin and Tversky 1992, Brenner et al. 1996, Soll 1996).

9 Festinger and Carlsmith (1959), Cooper and Fazio (1984), and Harmon-Jones and Mills (1999, chapter 1).

10 See Fischoff (1982), Langer and Roth (1975), Miller and Ross (1975), and Taylor and Brown (1988).

11 There are alternative explanations for sunk cost and escalation behavior; see, for example, Staw (1976), Arkes and Blumer (1985), Arkes (2002), and Hirshleifer and Welch (2002).

12 See Bar-Hillel and Neter (1996), Kahneman, Knetsch, and Thaler (1991), Knez, Smith, and Williams (1985).

13 See the discussions in Lovell (1986) and Williams (1987), but see also Keane and Runkle (1990). There is a similar finding for survey forecasts of macroeconomic variables (for example, Aggarwal, Mohanty, and Song 1995).

14 The implication of attribution/overconfidence models for whether there should be something akin to a disposition effect (holding

winners, selling losers) is not obvious. When a stock is first becoming a winner, rational arbitrageurs who foresee further price rises should drive the price up even higher than the overconfident think is justified. This encourages the overconfident to sell, consistent with the disposition effect. However, for a stock that has been a winner for some time, the arbitrageurs will sell to the overconfident as the price peaks. Other recent models of momentum and reversal have similar opposing effects.

15 Coval, Hirshleifer, and Shumway (2003), who find that a subset of active investors are able to consistently outperform the market, point out that "excessive" trading may be rational if it allows individuals to learn whether they have ability.

16 Coval, Hirshleifer, and Thakor (2004) analyze the incentives of financial advisers and intermediaries to exploit imperfectly rational investors. Stout (2003) argues that growing evidence that capital markets are not perfectly efficient is relevant for corporate law and public policy.

17 In the most basic possible setting, there is rationally extreme skepticism of failure to disclose – the "unraveling" results of Grossman (1981) and Milgrom (1981).

18 If there are costs of disclosure (for example, if the information that can be disclosed has value for competitors) the unraveling may be limited; there remains a pool of low-quality types that do not disclose (Verrecchia 1983). Similarly, if there is a probability that the firm does not possess information, then observers will not be completely skeptical about a firm that does not disclose any information (Dye 1985).

19 See Chambers and Penman (1984), McNichols (1989), Begley and Fischer (1998), and Haw, Qi, and Wu (2000).

20 Daniel, Hirshleifer, and Subrahmanyam (2001) provide an overconfidence-based explanation for such effects based upon overreaction to private information signals rather than credulity about managerial incentives. These accounts are reconcilable if management is able to manipulate not just public information sets but also information which investors perceive to be "private." For example, investors may trade upon information provided to them by analysts, even though this information is fed to analysts by management.

21 Coffee (1984, pp. 745–6) argues that critical adverse information was withheld from investors in municipal bond markets in which the Securities and Exchange Commission disclosure requirements do not apply, and that bond rating agencies were ineffective alternative

sources of information to investors, leading to such problems as the problems with New York City's bond offerings in the 1970s, and the Washington Public Power System's failure in the 1980s. Nevertheless, Palmiter (1999) argues that in private placement offerings (which are exempt from Securities Act of 1933 disclosure requirements) issuers generally disclose information similar to or going beyond what is required for registered offerings, and many foreign issuers voluntarily choose to list on the New York Stock Exchange and reconcile its financial reports with Generally Accepted Accounting Principles (GAAP). On the other hand, in many countries it is evident that the level of disclosure voluntarily achieved is much less than that provided in the United States.

22 For example, one post from March 2000 warned, "Dig deep behind the Enron financials and you'll see a growing mountain of off-balance sheet debt which will eventually swallow this company."

23 See, for example, Camerer (1995), Rabin (1998) and Hertwig and Ortmann (2001).

References

Aggarwal, R., Mohanty, S. and Song, F., 'Are Survey Forecasts of Macroeconomic Variables Rational?', *Journal of Business*, 68 (1995), 99–119.

Alpert, M. and Raiffa, H., 'A Progress Report on the Training of Probability Assessors', in D. Kahneman, P. Slovic and A. Tversky (eds), *Judgement under Uncertainty: Heuristics and Biases* (Cambridge: Cambridge University Press, 1982).

Arkes, H. R., *Incremental Investment Decisions and the Diagnosticity f Feedback*, Working Paper (Columbus: Ohio State University, 2002).

Arkes, H. R. and Blumer, C., 'The Psychology of Sunk Costs', *Organizational Behavior and Human Decision Processes*, 35 (1985), 124–40.

Arkes, H. R., Dawes, R. M. and Christensen, C., 'Factors Influencing the Use of a Decision Rule in a Probabilistic Task', *Organizational Behavior and Human Decision Processes*, 37 (1986), 93–110.

Arkes, H. and Hirshleifer, D., 'Integrating Heuristics and Biases: An Evolutionary Approach' (Columbus: Ohio State University, in progress, 2004).

Baker, M. P. and Wurgler, J., 'Market Timing and Capital Structure', *Journal of Finance*, 57 (2002), 1–32.

Barber, B. and Odean, T., 'Trading is Hazardous to your Wealth: The Common Stock Investment Performance of Individual Investors', *Journal of Finance*, 55 (2000), 773– 806.

Barber, B. and Odean, T., 'Online Investors: Do the Slow Die First?', *Review of Financial Studies*, 15 (2002), 455–88.

Barberis, N., Shleifer, A. and Vishny, R., 'A Model of Investor Sentiment', *Journal of Financial Economics*, 49 (1998), 307–43.

Bar-Hillel, M. and Neter, E., 'Why Are People Reluctant to Exchange Lottery Tickets?', *Journal of Personality and Social Psychology*, 70 (1996), 17–27.

Batchelor, R. and Dua, P., 'Conservatism and Consensus-seeking Among Economic Forecasters', *Journal of Forecasting*, 11 (1992), 169–81.

Begley, J. and Fischer, P. E., 'Is There Information in an Earnings Announcement Delay?', *Review of Accounting Studies*, 3 (1998), 347–63.

Bell, D. E., 'Regret in Decision Making Under Uncertainty', *Operations Research*, 30 (1982), 961–81.

Benos, A., 'Aggressiveness and Survival of Overconfident Traders', *Journal of Financial Markets*, 1 (1998), 353–83.

Berk, J. and Green, R. C., *Mutual Fund Flows and Performance in Rational Markets*, NBER Working Paper No. W9275 (Cambridge, MA: NBER, 2003).

Bernardo, A. and Welch, I., 'On the Evolution of Overconfidence and Entrepreneurs', *Journal of Economics and Management Strategy*, 10 (2001), 301–30.

Bikhchandani, S., Hirshleifer, D. and Welch, I., 'Learning from the Behavior of Others: Conformity, Fads, and Informational Cascades', *Journal of Economic Perspectives*, 12 (1998), 151–70.

Black, F., 'Noise', *Journal of Finance*, 41 (1986), 529–43.

Bloomfield, R., Libby, R. and Nelson, M., 'Confidence and the Welfare of Less-informed Investors', *Accounting, Organization and Society*, 24 (1999), 623–47.

Bloomfield, R., Libby, R. and Nelson, M., 'Underreactions, Overreactions and Moderated Confidence', *Journal of Financial Markets*, 3 (2000), 113–37.

Blume, L. and Easley, D., 'Evolution and Market Behavior', *Journal of Economic Theory*, 58 (1990), 9–40.

Brenner, L. A., Koehler, D. J., Liberman, V. and Tversky, A., 'Overconfidence in Probability and Frequency Judgments: A Critical Examination', *Organizational Behavior and Human Decision Processes*, 65 (1996), 212–19.

Camerer, C. F., 'The Process-Performance Paradox in Expert Judgment: How Can Experts Know So Much and Predict So Badly?', in K. A. Ericsson and J. Smith (eds), *Towards a General Theory of Expertise: Prospects and Limits* (New York: Cambridge University Press, 1991), pp. 195–217.

Camerer, C., 'Individual Decision Making', in J. H. Kagel and A. E. Roth (eds), *The Handbook of Experimental Economics* (Princeton, NJ: Princeton University Press, 1995), pp. 587–703.

Campbell, J. Y. and Cochrane, J. H., 'By Force of Habit: A Consumption Based Explanation of Aggregate Stock Market Behavior', *Journal of Political Economy*, 107 (1999), 205–51.

Campbell, J. Y. and Kyle, A. S., 'Smart Money, Noise Trading, and Stock Price Behaviour', *Review of Economic Studies*, 60 (1993), 1–34.

Carhart, M. M., 'On Persistence in Mutual Fund Performance', *Journal of Finance*, 52 (1997), 57–82.

Chacko, G., Chowdhry, B., Cohen, R. and Coval, J., *Rational Exuberance*, HBS Working Paper (Boston, MA: Harvard Business School, 2002).

Chambers, A. E. and Penman, S. H., 'Timeliness of Reporting and the Stock Price Reaction to Earnings Announcements', *Journal of Accounting Research*, 22 (1984), 21–47.

Chan, L. K., Lakonishok, J. and Sougiannis, T., 'The Stock Market Valuation of Research and Development Expenditures', *Journal of Finance*, 56 (2001), 2431–56.

Chen, J., *Intertemporal CAPM and the Cross-section of Stock Returns*, EFA 2002 Berlin Meetings Discussion Paper, Working Paper (Los Angeles: Marshall School of Business, University of Southern California, 2003).

Choi, J. J., Laibson, D. and Metrick, A., 'How Does the Internet Affect Trading? Evidence from Investor Behavior in 401(k) Plans', *Journal of Financial Economics*, 64 (2002), 397–421.

Coffee, Jr., J. C., 'Market Failure and the Economic Case for a Mandatory Disclosure System', *Virginia Law Review*, 70 (1984), 717–53.

Cooper, J. and Fazio, R. H., 'A New Look at Dissonance Theory', in L. Berkowitz (ed.), *Advances in Experimental Social Psychology*, 17, (Orlando, FL: Academic Press, 1984), pp. 229–64.

Coval, J. D., Hirshleifer, D. and Shumway, T., *Can Individual Investors Beat the Market?*, Harvard NOM Working Paper No. 02-45 (Boston, MA: Harvard Business School, 2003).

Coval, J., Hirshleifer, D. and Thakor, A., 'Exploitative Intermediaries', in progress (Harvard Business School, University of Michigan and Ohio State University, 2004).

Cutler, D. M., Poterba, J. M. and Summers, L. H., 'Speculative Dynamics and the Role of Feedback Traders', *American Economic Review*, 80 (1990), 63–8.

Daniel, K. D., Grinblatt, M., Titman, S. and Wermers, R., 'Measuring Mutual Fund Performance with Characteristic-Based Benchmarks', *Journal of Finance*, 52 (1997), 1035–58.

Daniel, K. D., Hirshleifer, D. and Subrahmanyam, A., 'Investor Psychology and Security Market Under- and Over-Reactions', *Journal of Finance*, 53 (1998), 1839–86.

Daniel, K. D., Hirshleifer, D. and Subrahmanyam, A., 'Overconfidence, Arbitrage, and Equilibrium Asset Pricing', *Journal of Finance*, 56 (2001), 921–65.

Darrough, M. and Stoughton, N., 'Financial Disclosure Policy in an Entry Game', *Journal of Accounting and Economics*, 12 (1990), 219–44.

DeBondt, W. F. M. and Thaler, R. H., 'Financial Decision-Making in Markets and Firms: A Behavioral Perspective', in R. A. Jarrow, V. Maksimovic and W. T. Ziemba (eds), *Finance, Handbooks in Operations Research and Management Science*, 9 (Amsterdam: North Holland, 1995), pp. 385–410.

DeLong, J. B., Shleifer, A., Summers, L. and Waldmann, R. J., 'Noise Trader Risk in Financial Markets', *Journal of Political Economy*, 98 (1990a), 703–38.

DeLong, J. B., Shleifer, A., Summers, L. and Waldmann, R. J., 'Positive Feed-Back Investment Strategies and Destabilizing Rational Speculation', *Journal of Finance*, 45 (1990b), 375–95.

DeLong, J. B., Shleifer, A., Summers, L. and Waldmann, R. J., 'The Survival of Noise Traders in Financial Markets', *Journal of Business*, 64 (1991), 1–20.

Dong, M., Hirshleifer, D., Richardson, S. and Teoh, S. H., *Does Investor Misvaluation Drive the Takeover Market?* Working paper (Ohio State University, York University and Wharton School, 2003).

Dye, R. A., 'Disclosure of Nonproprietary Information', *Journal of Accounting Research*, 23 (1985), 123–45.

Edwards, W., 'Conservatism in Human Information Processing', in B. Kleinmutz (ed.), *Formal Representation of Human Judgment* (New York: Wiley, 1968), pp. 17–52.

Einhorn, H. J. and Hogarth, R., 'Confidence in Judgment: Persistence in the Illusion of Validity', *Psychological Review*, 85 (1978), 395–416.

Einhorn, H. J., 'Overconfidence in Judgment', *New Directions for Methodology of Social and Behavioral Science*, 4 (1980), 1–16.

Engel, C., 'The Forward Discount Anomaly and the Risk Premium: A Survey of Recent Evidence', *Journal of Empirical Finance*, 3 (1996), 123–92.

Fama, E. F., 'Efficient Capital Markets: A Review of Theory and Empirical Work', *Journal of Finance*, 25 (1970), 383–417.

Fama, E. F., 'Market Efficiency, Long-Term Returns and Behavioral Finance', *Journal of Financial Economics*, 49 (1998), 283–306.

Fama, E. F. and French, K. R., 'Common Risk Factors in the Returns on Stocks and Bonds', *Journal of Financial Economics*, 33 (1993), 3–56.

Feltham, G. A. and Xie, J., 'Voluntary Financial Disclosure in an Entry Game with Continua of Types', *Contemporary Accounting Research*, 9 (1992), 46–80.

Felton, J. and Kim, J., 'Warnings from the Enron Message Board', *Journal of Investing*, 11 (2002), 29–52.

Festinger, L. and Carlsmith, J. M., 'Cognitive Consequences of Forced Compliance', *Journal of Abnormal and Social Psychology*, 58 (1959), 203–11.

Fischoff, B., Slovic, P. and Lichtenstein, S., 'Knowing with Certainty: The Appropriateness of Extreme Confidence', *Journal of Experimental Psychology*, 3 (1977), 552–64.

Fischoff, B., 'For those Condemned to Study the Past: Heuristics and Biases in Hindsight', in D. Kahneman, P. Slovic and A. Tversky (eds), *Judgement under Uncertainty: Heuristics and Biases* (Cambridge: Cambridge University Press, 1982).

Forsythe, R., Nelson, F., Neumann, G. and Wright, J., 'Anatomy of an Experimental Political Stock Market', *American Economic Review*, 82 (1992), 1142–61.

Frankel, J. A. and Froot, K. A., 'Understanding the US Dollar in the Eighties: The Expectations of Chartists and Fundamentalists', *Economic Record, Supp*., 62 (1986), 24–38.

Frankel, J. A. and Froot, K. A., 'Chartists, Fundamentalists, and Trading in the Foreign Exchange Market', *American Economic Review*, 80 (1990), 181–5.

Gervais, S. and Odean, T., 'Learning to be Overconfident', *Review of Financial Studies*, 14 (2001), 1–27.

Gigerenzer, G., Hoffrage, U. and Kleinbolting, H., 'Probabilistic Mental Models: A Brunswickian Theory of Confidence', *Psychological Review*, 98 (1991), 506–28.

Gilovich, T. R., *How We Know What Isn't So: The Fallibility of Human Reason in Everyday Life* (New York: The Free Press, 1991).

Grether, D. M., 'Testing Bayes' Rule and the Representativeness Heuristic: Some Experimental Evidence', *Journal of Economic Behavior and Organization*, 17 (1992), 31–57.

Griffin, D. and Tversky, A., 'The Weighing of Evidence and the Determinants of Overconfidence', *Cognitive Psychology*, 24 (1992), 411–35.

Grinblatt, M. and Han, B., *Disposition Effect and Momentum Profit*, Working Paper (UCLA and Ohio State University, 2003).

Grinblatt, M. and Titman, S., 'The Persistence of Mutual Fund Performance', *Journal of Finance*, 47 (1992), 1977–84.

Grossman, S. J., 'The Informational Role of Warranties and Private Disclosure about Product Quality', *Journal of Law and Economics*, 24 (1981), 461–83.

Hanson, J. D. and Kysar, D. A., 'Taking Behavioralism Seriously: Some Evidence of Market Manipulation', *Harvard Law Review*, 112 (1999), 1420–572.

Harmon-Jones, E. and Mills, J., 'An Introduction to Cognitive Dissonance Theory and an Overview of Current Perspectives on the Theory', in E. Harmon-Jones and J. Mills (eds), *Cognitive Dissonance: Progress on a Pivotal Theory in Social Psychology* (Washington, DC: American Psychological Association, 1999).

Haw, I., Qi, D. and Wu, W., 'Timeliness of Annual Report Releases and Market Reaction to Earnings Announcements in an Emerging Capital Market: The Case of China', *Journal of International Financial Management and Accounting*, 11 (2000), 108–31.

Hertwig, R. and Ortmann, A., 'Experimental Practices in Economics: A Challenge For Psychologists?', *Behavioral and Brain Sciences*, 24 (2001), 383–403.

Hirshleifer, D., Lim, S. S. and Teoh, S. H., *Disclosure to a Credulous Audience: The Role of Limited Attention*, Working Paper (Columbus: Fisher College of Business, Ohio State University, 2003).

Hirshleifer, D. and Luo, G. Y., 'On the Survival of Overconfident Traders in a Competitive Security Market', *Journal of Financial Markets*, 4 (2001), 73–84.

Hirshleifer, D. and Teoh, S. H., 'Herd Behavior and Cascading in Capital Markets: A Review and Synthesis', *European Financial Management*, 9 (2003), 25–66.

Hirshleifer, D. and Wang, Y., *Investor Overconfidence and the Forward Discount Puzzle* (Columbus: Fisher College of Business, Ohio State University, 2001).

Hirshleifer, D. and Welch, I., 'An Economic Approach to the Psychology of Change: Amnesia, Inertia, and Impulsiveness', *Journal of Economics and Management Strategy*, 11 (2002), 379–421.

Hong, H. and Stein, J. C., 'A Unified Theory of Underreaction, Momentum Trading and Overreaction in Asset Markets', *Journal of Finance*, 54 (1999), 2143–84.

Isenberg, D. J., 'Group Polarization: A Critical Review and Meta-Analysis', *Journal of Personality and Social Psychology*, 50 (1986), 1141–51.

Jensen, M. C., 'The Performance of Mutual Funds in the Period 1945–1964', *Journal of Finance*, 23 (1968), 389–416.

Jensen, M. C., 'Risk, the Pricing of Capital Assets, and the Evaluation of Investment Portfolios', *Journal of Business*, 42 (1969), 167–247.

Josephs, R., Larrick, R. P., Steele, C. M. and Nisbett, R. E., 'Protecting the Self from the Negative Consequences of Risky Decisions', *Journal of Personality and Social Psychology*, 62 (1996), 26–37.

Kahneman, D., Knetsch, J. L. and Thaler, R. H., 'The Endowment Effect, Loss Aversion, and Status Quo Bias: Anomalies', *Journal of Economic Perspectives*, 5 (1991), 193–206.

Kahneman, D. and Tversky, A., 'On the Psychology of Prediction', *Psychological Review*, 80 (1973), 237–5l.

Kahneman, D. and Tversky, A., 'The Psychology of Preferences', *Scientific American*, 246 (1982), 160–73.

Keane, M. P. and Runkle, D. E., 'Testing the Rationality of Price Forecasts: New Evidence from Panel Data', *American Economic Review*, 80 (1990), 714–35.

Keren, G., 'Calibration and Probability Judgments: Conceptual and Methodological Issues', *Acta Psychologica*, 77 (1991), 217–73.

Knez, P., Smith, V. L. and Williams, A., 'Individual Rationality, Market Rationality, and Value Estimation', *American Economic Review Papers and Proceedings*, 52 (1985), 397–402.

Koehler, J. J., 'The Base Rate Fallacy Reconsidered: Normative, Descriptive and Methodological Challenges', *Behavioral and Brain Sciences*, 19 (1996), 1–53.

Kyle, A. S., 'Continuous Auctions and Insider Trading', *Econometrica*, 53 (1985), 1315–35.

Kyle, A. and Wang, F. A., 'Speculation Duopoly with Agreement to Disagree: Can Overconfidence Survive the Market Test?', *Journal of Finance*, 52 (1997), 2073–90.

Lamoureux, C. and Schnitzlein, C., *Mechanism-Dependent Behavior: Overconfidence in Experimental Asset Markets*, Working Paper (Tucson: College of Business, University of Arizona, 2001).

Langer, E. J. and Roth, J., 'Heads I Win Tails It's Chance: The Illusion of Control as a Function of the Sequence of Outcomes in a Purely Chance Task', *Journal of Personality and Social Psychology*, 32 (1975), 951–5.

Lee, C., Shleifer, A. and Thaler, R., 'Investor Sentiment and the Closed-End Fund Puzzle', *Journal of Finance*, 46 (1991), 75–109.

Lichtenstein, S. and Fischoff, B., 'Do Those Who Know More Also Know More About How Much They Know?', *Organizational Behavior and Human Performance*, 20 (1977), 159–83.

Lichtenstein, S., Fischoff, B. and Phillips, L., 'Calibration of Probabilities: The State of the Art to 1980', in D. Kahneman, P. Slovic and A. Tversky (eds), *Judgement under Uncertainty: Heuristics and Biases* (Cambridge: Cambridge University Press, 1982), pp. 306–34.

Loomes, G. and Sugden, R., 'Regret Theory: An Alternative Theory of Rational Choice under Uncertainty', *Economic Journal*, 92 (1982), 805–24.

Lord, C. G., Ross, L. and Lepper, M. R., 'Biased Assimilation and Attitude Polarization: The Effects of Prior Theories on Subsequently Considered Evidence', *Journal of Personality and Social Psychology*, 37 (1979), 2098–109.

Lovell, M. C., 'Tests of the Rational Expectations Hypothesis', *American Economic Review*, 76 (1986), 110–24.

MacKinlay, A. C., 'Multifactor Models Do Not Explain Deviations from the CAPM', *Journal of Financial Economics*, 38 (1995), 3–28.

Malkiel, B. G., 'Returns from Investing in Equity Mutual Funds 1971 to 1991', *Journal of Finance*, 50 (1995), 549–72.

Mathios, A. D., 'The Impact of Mandatory Disclosure Laws on Product Choices: An Analysis of the Salad Dressing Market', *Journal of Law and Economics*, 43 (2000), 651–77.

McClelland, A. G. and Bolger, F., 'The Calibration of Subjective Probabilities: Theories and Models 1980–1993', in G. Wright and P. Ayton (eds), *Subjective Probability* (New York: Wiley, 1994), pp. 453–82.

McNichols, M., 'Evidence of Informational Asymmetry from Management Earnings', *The Accounting Review*, 64 (1989), 1–27.

Milgrom, P. R., 'Good News and Bad News: Representation Theorems and Applications', *Bell Journal of Economics*, 12 (1981), 380–91.

Miller, D. T. and Ross, M., 'Self-Serving Bias in Attribution of Causality: Fact or Fiction?', *Psychological Bulletin*, 82 (1975), 213–25.

Nel, E., Helmreich, R. and Aronson, E., 'Opinion Change in the Advocate as a Function of the Persuasibility of his Audience: A Clarification of the Meaning of Dissonance', *Journal of Personality and Social Psychology*, 12 (1969), 117–24.

Odean, T., 'Volume, Volatility, Price and Profit When All Traders are Above Average', *Journal of Finance*, 53 (1998), 1887–934.

Odean, T., 'Do Investors Trade Too Much?', *American Economic Review*, 89 (1999), 1279–98.

Palmiter, A. R., 'Toward Disclosure Choice in Securities Offerings', *Columbia Business Law Review*, 1 (1999), 1–135.

Payne, J. W., Bettman, J. R. and Johnson, E. J., 'Behavioral Decision Research: A Constructive Processing Perspective', *Annual Review of Psychology*, 43 (1992), 87–131.

Polk, C. and Sapienza, P., *The Real Effects of Investor Sentiment*, Working Paper (Evanston, IL: Northwestern University, 2003).

Rabin, M., 'Psychology and Economics', *Journal of Economic Literature*, 36 (1998), 11–46.

Richardson, S., Teoh, S. H. and Wysocki, P. D., 'The Walkdown to Beatable Analysts' Forecasts: The Roles of Equity Issuance and Insider Trading Incentives', *Contemporary Accounting Research* (forthcoming 2004).

Ritov, I. and Baron, J., 'Reluctance to Vaccinate: Omission Bias and Ambiguity', *Journal of Behavioral Decision Making*, 3 (1990), 263–77.

Ritov, I., 'Probability of Regret: Anticipation of Uncertainty Resolution in Choice', *Organizational Behavior and Human Decision Processes*, 66 (1996), 228–36.

Rubinstein, M., 'Rational Markets: Yes or No? The Affirmative Case', *Financial Analysts Journal*, 57 (2001), 15–29.

Shefrin, H. and Statman, M., 'Explaining Investor Preference for Cash Dividends', *Journal of Financial Economics*, 13 (1984), 253–82.

Shefrin, H. and Statman, M., 'The Disposition to Sell Winners Too Early and Ride Losers Too Long: Theory and Evidence', *Journal of Finance*, 40 (1985), 777–90.

Skinner, D., 'Why Firms Voluntarily Disclose Bad News', *Journal of Accounting Research*, 32 (1994), 38–60.

Sloan, R., 'Do Stock Prices Fully Reflect Information in Accruals and Cash Flows About Future Earnings?', *Accounting Review*, 71 (1996), 289–315.

Soll, J. B., 'Determinants of Overconfidence and Miscalibration: The Roles of Random Error and Ecological Structure', *Organizational Behavior and Human Decision Processes*, 65 (1996), 117–37.

Spranca, M., Minsk, E. and Baron, J., 'Omission and Commission in Judgment and Choice', *Journal of Experimental Social Psychology*, 27 (1991), 76–105.

Stanovich, K. E. and West, R. F., 'Individual Differences in Reasoning: Implications for the Rationality Debate?', *Brain and Behavioral Sciences*, 22 (2000), 645–65.

Statman, M. and Thorley, S., *Overconfidence and Trading Volume* (Santa Clara, CA: Santa Clara University, 1998).

Staw, B. M., 'Knee-deep in the Big Muddy: A Study of Escalating Commitment to a Chosen Course of Action', *Organizational Behavior and Human Performance*, 16 (1976), 27–44.

Steele, C. and Liu, T., 'Dissonance Processes as Self-Affirmation', *Journal of Personality and Social Psychology*, 45 (1983), 393–7.

Stout, L. A., 'The Mechanisms of Market Inefficiency', *Journal of Corporation Law*, 28 (2003), 635–69.

Swaminathan, B., 'Time-varying Expected Small Firm Returns and Closed-End Fund Discounts', *Review of Financial Studies*, 9 (1996), 845–88.

Taylor, S. E. and Brown, J. D., 'Illusion and Well-Being: A Social Psychological Perspective on Mental Health', *Psychological Bulletin*, 103 (1988), 193–210.

Teoh, S. H. and Hwang, C.-Y., 'Non-Disclosure and Adverse Disclosure as Signals of Firm Value', *Review of Financial Studies*, 4 (1991), 283–313.

Teoh, S. H., Welch, I. and Wong, T. J., 'Earnings Management and the Long-Term Market Performance of Initial Public Offerings', *Journal of Finance*, 53 (1998a), 1935–74.

Teoh, S. H., Welch, I. and Wong, T. J., 'Earnings Management and the Underperformance of Seasoned Equity Offerings', *Journal of Financial Economics*, 50 (1998b), 63–99.

Teoh, S. H. and Wong, T., 'Why Do New Issues and High Accrual Firms Underperform? The Role of Analysts' Credulity', *Review of Financial Studies*, 15 (2002), 869–900.

Teoh, S. H., Wong, T. J. and Rao, G., 'Are Accruals During an Initial Public Offering Opportunistic?', *Review of Accounting Studies*, 3 (1998), 175–208.

Trivers, R., *Social Evolution* (Menlo Park, CA: Benjamin/Cummings, 1985).

Trivers, R., 'Deceit and Self-Deception', in R. Robinson and L. Tiger (eds), *Man and Beast Revisited* (Washington DC: Smithsonian Press, 1991).

Verrecchia, R. E., 'Discretionary Disclosure', *Journal of Accounting and Economics*, 5 (1983), 179–94.

Verrecchia, R. E., 'Endogenous Proprietary Costs through Firm Interdependence', *Journal of Accounting and Economics*, 12 (1990), 245–50.

Wang, F. A., 'Overconfidence, Investor Sentiment, and Evolution', *Journal of Financial Intermediation*, 10 (2001), 138–70.

Williams, A. W., 'The Formation of Price Forecasts in Experimental Markets', *Journal of Money, Credit, and Banking*, 19 (1987), 1–18.

Yates, J. F., *Judgement and Decision Making* (Englewood Cliffs, NJ: Prentice Hall, 1990).

Part III

Subjectivism and Deceptive Behavior in Markets

7

Price Theory and the Study of Deception in the Exchange Process

Laurence S. Moss

Abstract

The general equilibrium approach in orthodox economics largely abstracted from the passing of time. In a timeless world, strategy and deception are difficult to define. The mainstream analysis of the second half of the twentieth century was mostly about establishing the limits within which price ratios might profitably vary in a world where people keep promises and are honest. Curiously, another group of milestones (some of which date back to the 1920s and 1930s) exist that, when taken together, may spark a renewed interest in the economics of fraud and deception.

Introduction

It is elementary to point out that in a voluntary exchange the parties to that exchange expect to gain, and that is what motivates the exchange activity in the first place. I shall refer to this as the "fundamental theorem" of economic exchange. The modern Austrian school has made much of this insight and claims that this appreciation of voluntary exchange has given rise to a most elaborate body of knowledge about market exchange and the institutions that surround it (Rothbard 1962, p. 72). Price theory, as it has evolved in modern economics, cannot afford to stop with this insight.

Consider the beaver-deer example that Adam Smith provides in the sixth chapter of the first book of his remarkable *Wealth of Nations* (Smith 1976 [1776], p. 65). The setting is that of an ancient village of hunters who have not yet divided the land and settled down to farming (Smith's "nation of hunters"). There is no private property in land and the capital accumulation process has yet to emerge. Smith asks whether, in such primitive surroundings, there is any "rule" for exchanging objects so that a mutually assented-to rate of exchange can be determined. Without an agreed rate of exchange, no exchange will take place. Also, the magnitude of the exchange rate will determine the division of the gains from trade between and among the traders; that is, which trader gains the most and which trader gains the least.

Smith suggests that in these primitive circumstances the traders would initially take notice of the conditions of production surrounding the trapping of a beaver and those associated with hunting and capturing a deer. Based on this technical information, the traders might conclude that the hunter (let's call him Ike) should offer to exchange two deer for the other trader (let's call him Mike)'s single beaver. Why two deer and not three or four? I shall explain Smith's reasoning more precisely below, when I return to the broader pattern of reasoning that Smith inaugurated in his work. Here, I simply wish to point out that in addition to recognizing the mutual gains associated with trade – what I have called the fundamental theorem – there is a long tradition in economics concerned with deciding what it is that determines the precise *ratio of exchange* between objects in the market. In this case, the objective conditions surrounding the production of the objects about to be traded have played a major role in the explanation.

Still, it is clear that regardless of the rate of exchange at which the trade takes place, the individuals who act today may come to regret their decisions later on. The passing of time permits preferences to change and, with them, the reassessment of historical or past behavior. It is therefore necessary to qualify the fundamental theorem with the caveat that it is only at "the moment" of exchange that both parties expect to gain, because the passing of time may lead to revisions, reevaluations, and regrets (Rothbard 1962, p. 72). It may also lead to outrage when one trading partner realizes that the other has tricked him or deceived him. More likely than not, it is the expectation by one trader that their counterpart is planning to deceive them that may discourage the exchange from taking place altogether. It is with both the passing of time and the perception that time is passing that I am mostly concerned in this essay.

The passing of time

The concept of exchange includes not only goods and services. It includes the exchange of promises as well, and here, the passing of time and expectations about the future are essential components of the exchange situation that cannot be overlooked. As early as 1651, the English philosopher Thomas Hobbes reasoned that in his "state of nature," where government does not exist, only barter trades involving easily identifiable tangibles would take place. Contracts involving the exchange of promises would not exist because they would be perceived as much "too risky." Let us summarize Hobbes's reasoning.

In an exchange where one party performs "now" and another party performs "later," what assurance does the promisee (the party that receives the promise) have that the promisor (the party that makes the promise) will keep that promise? Hobbes's primitive version of the *homo economicus* assumption is what generates this uncertainty. If, to return to Smith's example, Ike were asked to trade two deer now and Mike were to promise to deliver the beaver but not until next week on Tuesday evening at 9 p.m., Ike might become deeply suspicious. What is to prevent Mike from keeping the two deer and skipping town, thereby reneging on his promise to deliver the beaver? And Mike can be suspected of more scurrilous behavior still. What if Mike, all the time he was negotiating with Ike, had the wicked thought never to deliver the beaver at all? What if, from the start, Mike had made a false promise, all the time only pretending to be honest? Here we have gone beyond the world of simple breach of contract into the more sinister world of false promises and business fraud. Mike might be a *homo economicus* conman, acting not simply to further his wealth but also using the machinations of someone willing to use guile and deceit to steal wealth from others (Williamson 1975, p. 26).

The advocates of the fundamental theorem of economics seemed to have ignored what Hobbes understood happens with some regularity in his model. There is a tendency among modern Austrian school writers to advance the doctrine of mutual gain by ruling out the problem of Hobbes's false pretender conman. This is done by (1) relegating the problem of credible promise-making to another discipline such as sociology or political science and stating that in "pure" economics we assume a preexisting rule of law to which all actors adhere (Rothbard 1962, p. 702; Mises 1998 [1949], p. 720), or (2) invoking a variant of the reciprocity idea that cheaters, rogues, and conmen will be eventually exposed, their reputations for honest dealing destroyed and their presence in the market system marginalized as punishment for their nefarious deeds (Shearmur and Klein 1997, pp. 29–45). In other words, the dissemblers in our midst will be eliminated by the workings of the competitive market, their treacheries exposed and their reputations lost. According to some market optimists, the liars, deceivers, and scam artists will "inherit the wind" (Frank 2000, p. 213).

But even if there are strict penalties for conning behavior, it still may be subjectively profitable for individuals to engage in offensive behavior (Becker 1976 [1968], pp. 39–85). The present value of the "con" or the time preference of the dissembler may be great enough to encourage this risky behavior that so many others find offensive and destructive of market value (Darby and Karni 1973, pp. 67–86). To pass over deceptive behavior in the market as if it were an aberration or minor canker on the polity is a conclusion that can be reached after argument and analysis, but this conclusion is not something one should affirm prior to the study of the market process and its actual workings. In my view, the analysis of deceptive behavior is an important part of any thorough-going analysis of market behavior.

Orthodox price theory abstracts from the passing of time

As I shall explain, the main lines of analysis in economic theory from the last quarter of the twentieth century seemed to have abstracted completely from the problem of deception. But why should any systematic approach to economics ignore or rule out the economics of deception? It is a fact about market behavior that among the "costs of using the price system" is the need to negotiate, monitor and enforce contracts (Coase 1988 [1937]). All contracts by definition involve the exchange of at least one promise. Resources and entrepreneurial perspectives need to be directed to the problem of default, precisely because the intentional misrepresentations of significant "facts" about the object of the trading activity can result in disproportionate gains to one of the traders and horrendous losses to the other. Indeed, the market system has developed and continues to develop a variety of "security-enhancing devices," from locks and security alarms, to collateral, pledges, and hostages, to those specialized "experts" who proclaim the authenticity of documents and by ritual and speech acts confer and affirm valuable relationships of trust in the marketplace (Kronman 1985, Searle 1995). To ignore or marginalize such a vastly important part of the national economic activity seems in retrospect to have been both irresponsible and unscientific. Let us be more specific still.

Suppose Mike represents to Ike that his beavers are perfectly healthy and robust animals. However, Mike has purloined health certificates and forged affidavits from veterinarians to bolster his deceitful claims. In reality, his beavers may be missing teeth and be pathetically weak and losing fur all over. Ike naïvely relies on Mike's false representations and parts with his deer for that sickly beaver. Moments later, after Mike has quickly departed, Ike realizes that the trade he agreed to was an unfortunate one for him and regrets having made it. The beaver that Ike received was non-conforming. Ike lost out, not because his tastes changed and not because he behaved recklessly. Ike lost out because Mike swindled him.

Indeed, subsequent investigation may reveal that Mike invested heavily in certain security-enhancing rituals or customs that evoke trust in others, with the hidden intention of swindling Ike. Ike was the target of Mike's dissembling behavior, and the payoff to Mike might be great enough to outweigh the consequences of having his scheme revealed later and his reputation damaged. Incredibly, Mike may rise up in the hierarchy of social life by behaving in this and other strikingly shocking ways.

The fifteenth-century writer Nicolai Machiavelli may have had individuals like Mike in mind when he declared that scurrilous behavior was the source of much upward mobility in society. In his *Discourses*, Machiavelli claims to have learned from his study of the careers of men who achieved political greatness that "it seldom happens that men rise from low condition to high rank without employing either force or fraud, unless that rank should be obtained ... by gift or inheritance..." (Machiavelli 1950 [1513], p. 318).

Summarizing what is ahead

In the following, I offer a simplified account of the internal development of price theory. Price theory became the core of mainstream microeconomics in the twentieth century and the heart of general equilibrium economics (GEE). It is necessary to set forth the context within which several milestones on the road to the development of GEE took place. In mainstream economics, the emphasis is on how specific facts about the circumstances of production (such as the technological coefficients of production) interact with established consumer preferences and scarce supplies of inputs to establish limits within which the rates of exchange between all products and services can profitably vary. This technological focus and the concern with GEE do not rule out the role that subjective preferences play in the price-determining process. I do think that the emphasis on equilibrium prices in several markets coexisting simultaneously diverts attention from the socially perceived perception of certain facts about the product, the product's characteristics and the machinations of the suppliers that lie at the heart of any sustained subjective analysis of exchange and the problem of how the potential gain from trade gets divided.

In the middle section, I shall identify another group of milestones, some of them as early as the 1920s, that have gradually contributed to a renewed interest in the economics of fraud and deception. Here the emphasis is on how subjective preferences, strategies, and information and the assessment of information with the passing of time (rather than technological coefficients) give shape to market prices. In what follows, I only touch on the problem of lying and bluffing and the idea of "mixed strategies" as a solution concept for the problem of rational decision making within a strategic game. I suggest that lying and bluffing also play a role in price formation. In the final section, I offer a short conclusion.

On the determination of price(s)

Adam Smith's rule

The fourth-century philosopher Aristotle left us with a stimulating but mostly normative analysis of exchange. I use the word "analysis" because by classifying the several types of exchange that he knew and understood and then speculating about the impact these sorts of exchange had on the moral development of citizens, Aristotle contributed to social science. He distinguished barter and money exchange and then showed how the introduction of the money commodity permitted the exchange process to evolve in what he believed to be unnatural directions (Meikle 1991 [1979]). Aristotle bequeathed to generations of scholars a compelling intellectual problem that stimulated discussion over the centuries that followed (Langholm 1979). In one place Aristotle asserted that a natural exchange is based on an "exchange of equivalents," but he was not clear at all about how, say, houses and shoes, or certainly deer and beaver could be made commensurate with each other (Meikle 1991 [1979], p. 158). The fact that the problem may indeed be unsolvable has not been a barrier to discussion and analysis, and the discussion of this problem has given rise to centuries of scholastic scholarly commentary and debate (Langholm 1979).

Smith was not the first to suggest that Ike and Mike would consider the comparative "quantities of labor" that are expended in acquiring the objects of exchange as providing initial guidelines as to what the final barter rate of exchange should look like. We have seen that since "it usually costs twice the labor to kill a beaver which it does to kill a deer [therefore] one beaver should naturally exchange for or be worth two deer" (Smith 1976 [1776], p. 65).

But Smith warned that the proposed terms of trade is often only a starting point for negotiation. The deer-beaver traders will "naturally" make allowances for the different degrees of (subjective) hardship represented by the expended labor and the fact that some types of labor require more ingenuity and dexterity than others. It is clear from Smith's discussion that he believed that at least at one time in the history of modern civilization, certain ascertainable and even measurable brute facts about the conditions of production of the commodities about to be bartered set a benchmark for subsequent negotiation. Initially, two deer are exchanged for one beaver because beaver are harder to find and more difficult to capture. Smith went on to explain, how, in modern society and with the adoption of money, it is the cost of production of the commodities that plays an important role in establishing relative commodity prices and, by implication, the underlying (barter) terms of exchange. Subsequent generations of classical school writers did not follow Smith in abandoning the labor theory of relative values and instead adhered to the labor theory of relative prices as a rough and ready rule of thumb to estimate rates of exchange in market settings (Stigler 1965 [1958]).

The classical theory of comparative advantage

Indeed, the classical school of thought of the nineteenth century harkened back to Smith's work for inspiration and doctrinal support. Although most agreed that outside a nation of hunters, relative labor-time inputs would not determine the relative exchange ratios that existed in the market, still the labor theory was a good first approximation for establishing basic economic principles. This was certainly the position of David Ricardo (Ricardo 1966 [1817]).

In his *On the Principles of Political Economy and Taxation*, Ricardo presented the theory of comparative advantage as part of his chapter "On Foreign Trade" (Ricardo, pp. 128–49). According to Ricardo, while foreign trade cannot increase the amount of "value" in a country, it "will very powerfully contribute to increase the mass of commodities" (Ricardo, p. 128). To illustrate what he had in mind, Ricardo provided a numerical example. We are to assume throughout the example that labor cannot emigrate from one region to the other. Let us lay out Ricardo's numbers in a table as shown below (cf., Thweatt 1987, p. 34; and Ricardo, p. 135).

England	Portugal
(costs in man-years of labor)	(costs in man-years of labor)
CLOTH 100.	CLOTH 90.
WINE 120.	WINE 80.

Now, we are to imagine a situation BEFORE international trade between these nations has begun. In this world of two isolated regions, the relative price of wine in England will be 6/5. We are following

Smith's rule. A unit of wine will trade for one whole unit of cloth plus an additional fifth of a unit of cloth. Only in that way will the traded goods balance the (English) labor-time expended on their respective constructions. Similarly, in Portugal and before international trade begins, the relative price of wine in Portugal compared to the price of cloth will be 8/9. This means that prior to the opening of (international) trade a unit of cloth will command in Portugal one whole unit of wine plus an additional fraction of a unit of wine. Again, it is the Portuguese labor-time that is being balanced in the marketplace.

This implies that when trade begins, an English trader would prefer to purchase his wine in Portugal for only 8/9 of a unit of cloth rather than pay (in England) one and one-fifth (6/5) units of cloth for a single measure of wine.

Similarly, the Portuguese wine trader will make their way to England, where they hope to get a better price for the wine. Eventually, a single rate of exchange will prevail. As long as they each trade wine for cloth or cloth for wine following a rate of exchange between the limits set by the comparative labor inputs in the two trading areas, both traders can expect to gain by trade. (The gain is measured in the "labor saved," which indirectly expands consumer satisfaction by increasing the abundance of consumer goods in the region.)

The English specialize in the production and export of cloth and the Portuguese in the production and export of wine. These nations gain because the "mass of commodities" in both areas increases as a result of specialization and exchange. In Ricardo's words, "foreign trade [is] highly beneficial to a country, as it increases the amount and variety of the objects on which revenue may be expended, and affords, by the abundance and cheapness of commodities, incentives to saving, and to the accumulation of capital..." (Ricardo 1966 [1817], p. 133).

Ricardo emphasized how surprising this result might seem at first. After all, when the Portuguese import a unit of English cloth, they are importing something that absorbed more (English) labor than they themselves would have expended (in Portuguese labor) had they produced it themselves (in England cloth takes more labor to produce [100] than in Portugal [90]). But it is the search for bargains that motivated trade in the first place, not the balancing of labor time. Despite the higher labor costs vis-à-vis their own economy, the Portuguese were able to obtain any given measure of imported cloth for fewer units of wine exports than they would otherwise have expended had they given up some domestic wine production in order to transfer the formerly employed wine-growers into the Portuguese cloth factories. In other words, they obtained more cloth for that amount of labor than they would have obtained had they relied on domestic production methods alone. Their productivity gain came from specializing in the production of the product in which they were comparatively most productive and then trading part of the output for imported products.

In England, the situation was quite similar. The English, by exporting cloth, were giving up the "labour of 100 men, [possibly] for the produce of the labor of 80 [men]" (Ricardo 1966 [1817], p. 135). Had the English relied on their own homeland production opportunities, they would have had to transfer 120 men out of cloth production for each measure of wine that they were now importing. As long as the English give less than the labor of 120 men, they gain from trade. The "saved" labor can be re-employed elsewhere in the economy to produce other commodities, adding to the general opulence of the region. As Ricardo explains, the exchange is profitable for the English because it makes the "sum of enjoyments" larger in the nation.

This theory of comparative advantage has been used by generations of economists to explain the pattern of trade between nations. It is still a staple in most college economics courses. So long as the traded goods are traded at an exchange ratio somewhere between the limits set by the comparative labor ratios in the domestic economies, that is, as long as the exchange ratio of cloth and wine is larger than 8/9 and smaller than 6/5, both countries gain from trade and the "sum of enjoyments" expands. But where would the final equilibrium terms of trade lie between the two labor ratios?

John Stuart Mill had arrived at the solution to this problem sometime after 1828, and only after struggling with the fundamentals of the problem (Thweatt 1987, p. 39). According to Mill (who was reasoning within the restrictions of two-country/two-commodity trade), the exchange rate between the Portuguese wine and the English cloth would have to be such that the total exchange value of the Portuguese wine exports and the total exchange value of English cloth exports would be equal. While comparative labor quantities set the limits within which the final terms of trade could profitably vary, it would be the reciprocal demands in each country for the products of the other country that would lock in the final terms of trade between the limits established by comparative labor expenses of production (Mill 1965 [1848] II, pp. 598–99). The equilibrium terms of trade would be kept in check by the marvelous flows of international specie that are capable of altering the nominal price levels in the two trading areas until the balance finally settles down without the need for any additional specie flows. These mechanisms of monetary adjustment had already been examined in the writings of David Hume and David Ricardo (Viner 1964 [1937]).

This classical trade theory was expanded to the many-commodity case by Mountifort Longfield and others, and Alfred Marshall made fundamental contributions to its graphical exposition with his famous "offer curve" analysis (Marshall 1974 [1930]). What is now the orthodox theory of international trade is noteworthy for its emphasis on the role that comparative labor productivities play in setting the limits or range by which the final terms of trade can vary without eliminating the profitability and mutual advantage brought about by free commercial exchange itself.

The neoclassical or the orthodox synthesis circa 1950

The theoretical problem remains that of explaining market prices. To repeat, why is it that two deer ordinarily exchange for one beaver? What is it that constitutes an adequate explanation of relative prices in the market?

As I have remarked, at least one thread of analysis connects several generations of writers. That is: the labor-time expended in producing the goods themselves. It is as if the measure of labor-time captures some brute facts about production itself, namely, what is more commonly called the technological coefficients of production. Indeed, if it takes 120 English man-years to produce a unit of wine in England, then that tells us something definite about the physical productivity of both English soil and labor used in conjunction with English technological knowledge. Something also must be said about transportation costs and the supporting infrastructure, such as the existing roads and harbors in England. I might elaborate for several pages about the factors that work together to give shape to the factual results about labor productivity in England, but I suspect that I would not have very much to say about the subjective strategies and expectational rivalries that surround the trading process itself. By focusing on technology and geography and ignoring the strategic strategies and rivalries inherent in the trading process itself, we also ignore the role that deception and fraud play in the overall market process.

The cause of these omissions is that the orthodox theory of price seriously ignores the process of price formation in markets. It is especially ironic that the centerpiece of orthodox economics, which is the theory of competitive price, describes a situation in which each seller "supposes itself to be unable to alter the price of its product by changing the weekly ... quantity it puts on the market" (Shackle 1972, p. 258; see also Weintraub 1985). When the analyst "is called upon to explain how an equilibrium market price is arrived at, [the analyst typically] refers to the mutual confrontation of a south-eastward sloping demand curve and a north-eastward sloping supply curve: the price, it [is supposed], must be lower in order that a larger weekly or annual quantity may be sold" (Shackle 1972, p. 258). Shackle calls this competitive model "contradictory." Either the supply decisions of the sellers really do have an influence on price, or they do not. The muddle is created by skipping over any description of how the sellers come to obtain knowledge about the market structure in which they compete. The orthodox model of perfect competition is based "unquestioningly on inferences which depend on the exact and formal fulfilment of mathematical conditions by the economic subject matter" (Shackle 1972, p. 260). But real-world people in actual markets do not set out each day to fulfill mathematical conditions – they act to render their conditions more favorable (Mises 1998 [1949], p. 97). It is therefore quite puzzling as to how human action in market settings produces the formalisms implied by the supply and demand mathematical apparatus. This problem remains unresolved today despite the enormous mathematical apparatus that supports economics (Walker 1997, pp. 55–91).

Subjective ideas about language, promises, and alleged product characteristics are really not at the center of mainstream price theory. Orthodox theory is most comfortable with the study of the final equilibrium results, and those results are often tightly circumscribed by the technological characteristics of the production process. Indeed, this seems to be the unfortunate legacy from Smith's simple beaver-deer example.

General equilibrium prices

Consider the crowning achievement of neoclassical analysis in the twentieth century and the core of most applied economic specialties, the general equilibrium model of a competitive exchange system (Weintraub 1985). The logic of the market process was set out in a rigorous fashion by Kenneth Arrow, Gerard Debreu, and Lionel McKenzie (Ingrao and Israel 1990, Weintraub 1985). In 1957, Francis M. Bator summarized the model and its implications for the study of the "new welfare economics" (Bator 1957).

In order to explain the "new welfare economics" by using the simple geometric diagrams with which economists were largely familiar, Bator imagined a two-person, two-industry, two-commodity, two-factor-of-production world in which the two agents had well-behaved and stable preference orderings and the production functions were also stable and well-behaved. Economies of scale in production were ruled out. When factors of production are paid their competitive wages, each factor is paid a distributive share that just absorbs the entire national dividend. Bator demonstrated that in such a world, a benevolent monarch could institute three rules that would guarantee a Pareto-efficient allocation of resources and national dividend among the citizens. The rules were as follows:

First, resources would be allocated between the two industries such that the marginal rates of factor substitution were the same in both industries. This means that the trading industries reshuffled resources between them, so that the most that one industry might give up (or "pay") for another unit of one of the resources was just a fraction of a cent shy of *the least amount* the other would accept to give up another unit of that resource. For this reason, no additional exchanges of this resource take place. An equilibrium resource allocation is in place.

Unless this condition were satisfied among the industries, it would be possible, by reshuffling the factors of production between the two applications, to increase output in one industry without lowering it in the other industry. When the equality is satisfied, then we would have a Pareto-efficient allocation of resources. This means that increasing output in one industry will necessarily cause output to fall in the other industry.

There are an infinite number of such resource allocations that satisfy this first equilibrium condition, and they correspond to the infinite array of points along something economics students know to be a "production possibilities curve."

Second, for all consumers (there are only two in Bator's simple presentation), the marginal rate of substitution must be the same. The marginal rate of substitution records the largest amount of one commodity a particular consumer is willing to give up in order to obtain another unit of the other commodity.

If these substitution rates were not equal, then it would be possible to reshuffle the existing national product between the consumers, making at least one trader better off and leaving all the others at their original satisfaction levels. Again, in the technical language of orthodox economics, along the "efficiency locus" in the famous Edgeworth-Bowley box, it is impossible to make one individual's utility level increase without decreasing the utility level of the other individual. Along this efficiency locus we have an infinite number of Pareto-efficient allocations of produced national output among the individual members of the society.

Finally, in general equilibrium the slope of the production-possibilities schedule (something called the "marginal rate of transformation") must exactly equal the marginal rate of substitution for any consumer. Again, without this equality, it would be possible, by reshuffling resources between industries and increasing output in one sector and decreasing output in the other and then redistributing the new final output among the traders, to increase the utility level of at least one individual trader without decreasing the utility levels of the others.

The "new" welfare economics of the 1950s showed that there are still a myriad of possible allocations of resources and distributions of the national product that are compatible with Bator's three equilibrium conditions. Under some of these distributions, Mike is fabulously rich and Ike poor and under other distributions their situations are reversed. The achievement of Pareto efficiency by the benevolent dictator who meticulously attends to the establishment of the mathematical conditions set out above will not solve the problem of social welfare. Something else is needed.

Bator concluded that a "social welfare function" is needed to help decide which individual deserves better treatment than the other individual. In the absence of such a social welfare function, the Pareto efficiency criteria alone are inadequate to solve the broader problem of social justice. Hence, the new welfare economics that was developed during the second part of the twentieth century is about supplementing the Pareto efficiency criteria with something else. A theory of justice is needed to complement neoclassical economics.

But this was not all Bator demonstrated. Summarizing the well-traveled paths of GEE, Bator showed that the *homo economicus* model of mainstream economics, in which individuals maximize objective utility functions subject to budget constraints and owners of firms adjust their output levels to given observed competitive prices that themselves adjust by a mysterious process to clear all markets of shortages and surpluses, was sufficient to generate this Pareto-efficient result. Bator (following a long-established tradition in economics) dropped his benevolent monarch for the abstractions of the purely competitive model. He suggested that the formal institutions of modern capitalism (the idea of perfectly competitive markets) were themselves adequate to give rise to the Pareto-efficient economy as expressed by the three mathematical conditions listed above. The moral of the story is that competitive free markets do not solve the problem of social justice, but they can be used to supplement and clarify the problem.

Bator's world of general equilibrium is a world that resembled the "laissez-faire model," where the technical conditions of production combined with the well-defined unchanging preferences of the agents working and consuming in this world interact to establish a consistent set of factors and product prices in which there is no unemployment and no other market disequilibrium whatsoever.

Some commentators have argued that this formal representation of a trading economy has captured Adam Smith's vision of an exchange economy as expressed in *Wealth of Nations*. But this forever will be a matter for speculation and interpretation since Adam Smith did not write down equations nor try to solve them simultaneously. Instead, he used historical examples and drew on what he thought were common sense observations. The world of general equilibrium flounders also on the problem of pure competition. According to Frank Hahn, "classical general equilibrium theory assumes that every agent knows all prices and that every agent has all the information that is needed about every good" (Hahn 1984, p. 83). But what kind of human being could possibly possess and process so much information!

It is clear that the world of general equilibrium as it was expressed in the 1950s and 1960s also abstracted from the passing of time. Arrow suggests that by assuming markets in which claims are exchanged to commodities for delivery at different points of time and (also) depending on certain contingencies, the abstract model of a myriad of competitive markets – the general equilibrium model – could escape the passing of time since the traders could anticipate all future contingencies and provide for them by entering into contracts that were made contingent based on certain future events (Arrow 1963/64). All planned future transactions are mysteriously collapsed into the present moment. According to Shackle, the general equilibrium model of the economy is about a system of "simultaneous" equations in which the notion of simultaneity has absolutely nothing to do with the passing of time. The equations "pre-reconcile the choices of several individuals [and] make these choices dependent on each other, as a unity. ... All choices, therefore, must be simultaneous and the system of actions which they represent must be strictly *timeless*. In a pre-reconciled system there can be no earlier and later. The system of actions must be looked on as *exempt from time*. In the notion of general equilibrium the rejection of time imposes itself inexorably" (Shackle 1972, pp. 250 and 253–4).

The world of the GEE has also been described as a world of "evenly rotating" change. There are no surprises at all and the future is like the past. By abstracting from the passing of time in any meaningful sense, general equilibrium abstracts from the problem of deception in markets. There is no reason to worry in Hobbesian fashion that Mike's promises made today will not be kept tomorrow. Ike can allay his fears and eliminate his mistrust by purchasing an insurance policy, insuring him against the event that Mike might cheat him.

However, general equilibrium modeling did not evolve without provoking some critical and important commentary along the way, both from within neoclassical economics and from certain dissenters outside the central core of the discipline. In what follows, I shall survey several milestones along the way that helped bring us back full circle to the problem of price formation in a world in which individuals interact sometimes with stratagem and guile.

On the formation of price rather than the determination of price

The Austrian contribution

The early Austrian school writers, especially Carl Menger, wrote about the "formation" of the market price and how the traders in the market expected to gain utility as a result of the trades that were to occur. In the 1880s, Eugen von Boehm-Bawerk went even further and explained how the final equilibrium price that balanced the demand and supply for some traded commodity would have to be smaller than the maximum offer price of the marginal buyers and larger than the minimum acceptance prices of the marginal sellers. For the early Austrians, the limits within which the final equilibrium price would vary were set by the subjective preferences of the buyers and sellers. Among Austrians there was a strong discomfort about following Ricardo and later John Stuart Mill and about attributing any dominating role to labor productivity considerations in setting the limits within which the final exchange rate could profitably vary.

Austrians prided their approach to price formation as an alternative to the "cost of production theory" of price that foolishly tried to explain final goods prices in terms of other prices (Mises 1960 [1933]). They also disagreed with some implications of the supply and demand model insofar as it suggested that both "objective" (that is, productivity) and "subjective" (that is, preferences) mutually interacted to determine market prices, much like the twin blades on a scissors mutually work together to slice paper. Mainstream economics in the twentieth century did not follow the Austrian school on this point. It became canonical in the study of economic theory that it is the forces behind both supply and demand that interact to "simultaneously" establish money prices and, by implication, relative prices as well.

It is noteworthy that at one place in Boehm-Bawerk's seminal analysis of the formation of the market rate of interest, he admits that technical substitution, in the form of the ability to substitute present goods for larger amounts of future goods, did place a limit on the market rate of interest that would otherwise be formed through the interaction of subjective preferences in the market (Boehm-Bawerk 1959 [1889] II, p. 273). Boehm-Bawerk's admission that productivity (reflecting technology) could play an independent role in the formation of the interest rate may have infuriated the elderly Carl Menger. Menger rudely dismissed Boehm-Bawerk's analytic system as one of the "greatest errors" ever made in economics (Schumpeter 1994 [1954], p. 847 n).

Modern Austrians hark back to Carl Menger's teachings when they admire a remark by Friedrich von Hayek, who stated that "it is probably no exaggeration to say that every important advance in economic theory during the last hundred years was a further step in the consistent application of subjectivism" (Hayek 1955 [1941], p. 31). Even though Hayek's many contributions admitted the important role that technology plays in shaping economic events, his search for a consistent subjectivism inspired the American wing of the modern Austrian school to declare displeasure with mainstream economics and especially GEE (Vaughn 1994).

Friedrich A. Hayek

Hayek is a wonderful subject for our study of the equilibrium approach. In his early writings, Hayek saw merit in GEE (Caldwell 2001). Indeed, he was heavily influenced by his teacher Friedrich von Wieser, whose early presentations of economic theory set the contours for the orthodox or neoclassical approach toward modeling the GEE. Hayek's *Pure Theory of Capital* made use of several Wieserian distinctions that he came to reject in his later years as misleading and responsible for distorting knowledge of what was the essential economic problem that society had to solve (Hayek 1962 [1941]).

Toward the end of the nineteenth century, von Wieser modeled the whole economy as under the exercise and control of a benevolent monarch and all resource owners as honest, never cheating, not exercising power over one another and acceding to the wishes of the benevolent dictator without back-talk or argument (von Wieser 1967 [1927]). In such an ideal world, land would have to be allocated a certain way so that the "sum of enjoyments" would be at a maximum and collective utility also at a maximum. Saving would be carried up to a point and then no further, in line with the subjective time preferences of the entire population. Von Wieser's benevolent monarch model set the tone for much general equilibrium reasoning during the first part of the twentieth century. Incidentally, as we have already seen in our summary of Bator's model, the benevolent monarch could implement three important mathematical conditions so as to provide a Pareto-efficient resource allocation.

This thought experiment established the setting for and appreciation of the role that money prices play in a world in which there is no benevolent monarch present at all and market prices are established in accordance with the model of perfect competition. If all markets were characterized by perfect competition, information would flow freely, no seller or group of sellers could exert monopoly power and production techniques would be well behaved. In that case, market-formed prices would generally guide the allocation of resources along lines that were similar to ones that the benevolent monarch would have done to produce a Pareto-efficient allocation of resources.

For von Wieser, the appreciation of the price system involved understanding how it resembled the wisdom of a benevolent omniscient dictator writ large over hundreds of thousands of citizen households over a huge geographic area. Of course, the conditions of monopoly and the presence of hierarchy, power grabbing, corruption, fraud, and so on, prevented the actual markets of the world from adequately simulating the conditions that a rational benevolent dictator would bring about. Von Wieser suggested that government intervention was needed to achieve the conditions that Bator outlined above. Unlike Bator, von Wieser wanted the ideal blueprint to emerge so society could get closer to what he thought would be social justice.

During the economic calculation debate of the 1930s, Hayek began a long struggle to escape from the household management model of economic life and move toward something else (Moss 2002). The "something else" was imperfectly spelled out at the time of his death in 1992. Basically, Hayek rejected the idea that markets are all about maximizing some objective function such as societal utility or social welfare. Hayek dismissed Bator's search for a welfare function as largely a chimera (Hayek 1975, p. 75). Instead, markets provide for the creation and replication of certain broad customs, norms and rules that allow individuals the greatest chances of completing their private projects. According to Hayek, the market order produced certain rules of fair dealing and basic honesty, and the market prices that emerged performed a remarkable "coordination" function more effectively than when political organizations might try to "improve" on the market outcomes.

According to Hayek, deceptive acts are important to the study of public policy, especially the mismanagement of money and credit by the banking system. In some versions of the Mises-Hayek-Rothbard theory of the trade cycle, an economic boom is launched when the banking system expands credit-based lending without first waiting for the real saving in the economy to increase (Rothbard 1962, p. 763). The boom cannot continue indefinitely and, if it does not end for some other reason, must end in a business depression or worse. During the business crisis, investors learn that they have been deceived about the compatibility of their business projects and the supply of real saving available to help them complete those projects.

In another context, Hayek explained why and how socialist central planners used deception to carry out their plans. The practices include schemes to divert "[market] demand into socially desirable directions while preserving the subjective impression [*sic*] of free choice" (Hayek citing H. D. Dickinson 1952 [1935], p. 205). Most tragically, totalitarian despots would unite the otherwise diverse preference orderings of their throngs of followers by ganging up against minorities, as the Nazi Party did in its war against the Jews and Stalin did in his war against the kulaks (Hayek 1952 [1935], pp. 206–7). The impression one gets from a study of Hayek's published writings is that deception is something that is itself imposed on the market order, but not something that naturally arises as part of the market process of price formation itself. Why Hayek was so complacent about the problem of fraud and deception is not explained in his writings.

Oskar Morgenstern and conjectural expectations

In 1937, Hayek tackled the difficult issue of what type of knowledge about future market conditions a nation of rational agents would have to hold for the economy to be "in equilibrium." Basically, their expectations about their ex ante plans would have to line up in some essential way. Following in the footsteps of another pioneer Austrian, Oskar Morgenstern, Hayek concluded that "correct foresight is then not, as it has sometimes been understood, a precondition which must exist in order that equilibrium may be arrived at. It is rather the defining characteristic of a state of equilibrium" (Hayek 1952 [1937], p. 42).

Morgenstern had already demonstrated during the 1920s and again in 1935 that perfect foresight was virtually impossible to comprehend. His claim was stronger than what is found in Hayek's 1937 essay. According to Morgenstern, "unlimited foresight and economic equilibrium are ... irreconcilable with one another" (Morgenstern 1976 [1935], p. 174). In order to support his claim, Morgenstern recalled the story of the legendary detective Sherlock Holmes who was pursued by his opponent, the cunning Moriarity. Holmes leaves on a local train that will make all stops from London to Dover, but fortunately spots Moriarity at the train station. He quickly reasons that Moriarity will board an express train and be at Dover ahead of Holmes in order to catch him as Holmes disembarks. This assumption is correct, and Holmes cleverly avoids disaster by boarding a local train and getting off at an in-between stop.

Now, Morgenstern asks, what if Moriarity "had been still more clever [and] had estimated Holmes' mental abilities better..." (Morgenstern 1976

[1935], p. 174). Then he would have traveled to an intermediate station, knowing that this was what Holmes would have decided to do in order to avoid capture. But what if Holmes was even cleverer than Moriarity and knew that that was exactly what Moriarity was going to do? With such foresight, Holmes would have remained on the train all the way to Dover, (therefore) avoiding capture by Moriarity. An endless chain of "reciprocally conjectural reactions and counter-reactions" is now in motion (Morgenstern 1976 [1935], p. 174). The moral of this story is that there is no such thing as perfect foresight, and if there were, it might make general equilibrium impossible (cf. Koppl and Rosser 2002).

In my view, Hayek never went as far as Morgenstern in rejecting the general equilibrium construct. Hayek must be credited, not as an opponent of equilibrium economics, but as someone who delved deeply into the knowledge difficulties such a conception generates and who would have genuinely welcomed a solution.

In 1945, Hayek published "The Use of Knowledge in Society" (Hayek 1952b [1945], pp. 77–91). Starting from the premise that the knowledge available to an economy is never in one central location but is spread throughout the families, farms, and households in basically multi-varied forms and formats, he defined the problem of the division of knowledge in social organization. The role of the price system is no longer to reconcile all choices and ensure that markets clear without surplus or shortage. Prices are seen as generating incentives for self-interested agents to utilize information in valuable ways. Changes in prices signal expectations about the future availability of resources and encourage substitutions and conservations. In later essays, Hayek would place greater emphasis on the discovery along with the utilization of information by the price system (Hayek 1978 [1968], pp. 179–90). These discussions were absolutely brilliant departures from the stultifying ground rules of GEE and its vague claims that knowledge of all production techniques and agent preference orderings were freely available without cost to all.

Surprisingly, Hayek does not consider the fact that agents may invest heavily in misinformation and deceptions. In his early writings it is the decentralization of information that interests him and not the problem of the diffusion of misinformation that we have identified in this essay as an important phenomenon.

Hayek's work proceeded independently of the pioneering work of one of his contemporaries, Ronald Coase, who had broken ground on a related question as early as 1937.

The Coasian point of departure

Ronald Coase's biography does not include a stint at the University of Vienna, and by all accounts he never considered himself a member of the Austrian school of economics or a crusader in support of the Menger vision of a purely subjectivist economics. Still, he contributed greatly to the articulation and clarification of ideas that are indeed further steps in the consistent application of subjectivism, as I shall now emphasize.

In his 1937 paper, "The Nature of the Firm," Coase reminded his readers that there were costs to using the pricing system (Coase 1988 [1937]). Contracts had to be negotiated and then executed between traders. As time passed, these same contracts had to be monitored and sometimes their terms and conditions enforced in a courts of law. Indeed, the costs of using the price system could be economized by substituting hierarchical organization in the form of principal and agents or, more directly, employers and employees. Here we have one important rationale for the modern business firm: namely, that it substitutes hierarchy for the price system when the price system is too costly to use. Whereas Hayek had emphasized the quick and accurate diffusion of information via the price system, Coase laid the foundations for explaining the role that hierarchy can play in sometimes retarding the diffusion of information, especially in the presence of trade secrets and proprietary information (see Moss 1991).

The Coasian contribution was like a bomb with a slow fuse. Decades later, the emergence of comparative institutional analysis in the writing of Oliver E. Williamson and others brought the tools of economic analysis directly to an important business problem (Williamson 1975). Williamson reminded his readers that economic man often calculated with guile and deceit and that this creates problems that might be best mitigated by certain formerly unappreciated institutional arrangements. Let us examine the familiar problem of "hold-up" between trading firms.

Consider two firms along an existing supply chain. Mike Industries (MI) manufactures a new communication device that uses a special custom chip. Ike Circuits (IC) supplies chips to a variety of buyers, including Mike Industries. One day, Mike's CEO visits Ike's CEO and explains that his company needs a certain custom chip manufactured within a few months and will pay $40 for each unit. IC is encouraged to make a huge multi-million dollar investment (a sunk cost) in the machinery that will be needed to service MI's orders. IC makes the multi-million dollar investment, relying on MI's promises and representations, and now incurs extra business expenses, both fixed and variable.

MI finds out (from a loose-lipped IC engineer) that the marginal cost of one of these custom chips is a mere $5. No sooner is this found out then

MI's CEO writes a letter to IC's, explaining that starting next quarter it will pay $5 a chip rather than the $40 discussed earlier. (It is a well-established principle in managerial economics that in the short run, a firm need only cover its variable costs in order to remain interested in maintaining its rate of production.) MI's CEO has "held up" IC's CEO. This is a classic business drama. It is also borderline theft.

Now had IC been smarter, they never would have bothered to invest in the new chip facility. IC's CEO should not rely on MI's verbal promise. This is one sure way to avoid "hold up." But then a mutually advantageous exchange would not have taken place, and that would have been a loss for the economy as a whole. One way to avoid such a disaster (and by no means the only way) might have been for IC to merge with MI. The rationale for this "vertical integration" is to avoid deceptive scamming that, if expected by the potential victim, would make a profitable business deal impossible. With the comparative institutional approach, institutions such as vertical integration are presented as strategic tools for avoiding deception and swindling. The transaction costs of using the price system are too high and hierarchy is more appropriate. Williamson builds on Coase's initial insights by realizing that the costs of using the price system include the costs of avoiding fraud and flushing out dissembling behavior in the workplace.

The problem that Coase articulated appeared in other contexts as well. Whenever organizations were established to carry out various missions, there was a real possibility that the goals and interests of the real parties in interest might not be faithfully reflected and cared for in the decisions of the agents of these principals. Monitoring the behavior of the various agents and establishing proper incentives so as to scientifically align the interests of the agents with the interests of their principals has blossomed into a veritable and important subdiscipline in financial economics (Laffont and Martimort 2002).

The Akerlof point of departure

In Hayek's work during the 1930s, we have the clear recognition that knowledge is not freely available for the taking and that it is located in the nooks and crannies of the market order, with its relevance often circumscribed by details of time and place. In 1970, Akerlof raised a problem, not of the availability of information, but of the allocation of information in simple exchange situations and what difference that makes toward the achievement of the mutual economic gains from trade (Akerlof 1970). It often happens that the seller knows something that the buyer does not know about a particular product or service. If the buyer asks the seller what it is that the seller knows, the seller might lie or exaggerate. So how can the buyer know what is true?

For example, the seller of a used automobile typically knows whether or not it is a lemon. When asked by the buyer whether it is indeed a lemon, the seller might lie and represent that the defective car is in "good condition." The buyer knows that the seller faces these incentives and therefore (other things equal) will not trust the seller's answers. The buyer will lower his (maximum) offer price for the used car so that there will be "room" for any unfortunate future repairs and extra maintenance expenses associated with buying a lemon. But the car might be a perfectly good car and not a lemon at all. The seller might reject the buyer's insulting offer and withdraw this car from the market completely rather than sell it at such an unfairly discounted price. Other buyers and sellers will reason and behave the same way, and the probability of actually buying a lemon will go up as the non-lemons are withdrawn from the used car market. The asymmetrical distribution of this sort of information might make a series of perfectly viable exchange opportunities impossible. Akerlof speculated further that it might make resale markets altogether impossible, which would be an unfortunate economic result. Indeed, as we stated at the beginning of this essay, the fundamental theorem of modern economics is the importance of mutual gains from trade. Asymmetrical information has worked to make the capturing of those gains difficult if not all but impossible.

Consider a different business situation also discussed by Akerlof (Akerlof 1970, pp. 492–3). A buyer of life insurance knows whether or not he smokes cigarettes and is thus a strong candidate for high blood pressure or cardiovascular disease. This buyer might lie to the insurance company, hoping to capture a lower premium by not disclosing the fact that he is a smoker. The insurance company knows that their insureds know whether or not they are smokers, but the insurance companies have no reliable way of deciding whether their insureds are lying or not. As a result, premiums remain higher and over time the worst insurance candidates line up to purchase the insurance. A whole group of willing buyers choose to assume the risk and not to buy insurance at all because the price is too high. Again we have a series of mutually advantageous market exchanges not taking place all because information is not freely available or not at all.

Now Akerlof's main point is that we do see used car markets and we do see life insurance policies being sold by the millions. How is this possible? What makes it possible are the roles that certain institutions play in making markets possible. Akerlof's institutions include reputation in the form of trademarks, logos and symbols. In addition, used car dealers give warranties and earn a solid reputation for making good on their promises, and insurance companies require of their insureds that they sign legal affidavits that will deny their beneficiaries benefits if it turned out that they lied at the time they purchased the insurance. In the writings of Douglass North (1990), Robert C. Ellickson (1991) and others, we learn how repetition and reputation can work together and give rise to institutions that help to overcome the negative economic implications of information asymmetry.

Implications of these developments for the study of deception

The 1970 publication of Akerlof's article is something of a milestone event. It is no longer a question of the existence of information or the utilization of information that already exists. With Akerlof, we are concerned with which party to the trade has access to information and how that makes a difference in an ongoing bargaining process in which prices are being formed. The emphasis has firmly shifted from the mathematically focused "determination of price" to the older Austrian school problem emphasized by the early Austrian school writers, namely the "formation of price" – how price is formed in a market system when the buyers and sellers have access to different bodies of information and the traders might indeed choose to lie about what it is that they know.

Price formation and deception

Lying and bluffing

Lying about one's plans and intentions is a common component of military strategy and battle. The topic has crept into the study of economic organization at a number of places over the centuries. I have argued elsewhere that a tradition of "Platonic deception" exists in Western intellectual thought, in which governments are advised to lie to their own citizens so that a more far-reaching social order will result (Moss 1996). In this section, I direct my attention to a different problem – the problem of price formation. We are not interested in the technologically determined limits within which the market price might profitably vary; rather, we are interested in the subtle creation and utilization of information that in a bargaining situation might lead to a different division of the gains from trade or even induce the buyer to change his or her "maximum offer price" or perhaps the seller's "reservation price." The natural place to start this discussion is with the problem of "bluffing" in games of chance.

Suppose Ike and Mike are playing the game of "five-card-draw poker." Mike has drawn an ordinary pair of spot cards in his five-card hand and was not able to improve that hand under the rules of the game. Ike does not have any specific knowledge of what cards Mike has been dealt. Nor does Mike have any idea that Ike's hand contains a "flush" (five cards of the same suit) and is therefore the higher hand. Mike decides to "bluff," that is, he bids high amounts of money and exudes a deceptive air of confidence about his concealed hand. Ike accepts Mike's accelerating bets and raises the stakes still higher.

Now, this sequence can end in two different ways. Ike might "call" and both players reveal their hands. It is now established that Mike was "bluffing" because his hand is ordinary and in fact a losing hand. Ike will remember this event, and Mike's reputation for truth-telling during the card game of poker has been damaged (but not necessarily to his disadvantage). The next time Mike has a losing hand, his bluff will not be believed, but then again, Mike might wait until he has a high winning hand before repeating his exuberant betting. Ike might raise the stakes and call his bluff, thinking Mike has a poor hand, and this time lose quite badly.

Alternatively, Ike might have backed away from matching Mike's bids and the round might end without either player revealing his hand. Mike's bluff might have gone undetected by Ike. Clearly, in the case of poker and other card games, deceptive behavior is what elevates the game from one of mere chance to one of stratagem and legend. Deceptive behavior can be socially acceptable and most desirable, especially in card games.

The central lesson from our study of the poker game is that, by mixing his strategies, Mike can make five-card poker a much more profitable game. If Mike bluffs 2/3 of the time when he has a poor hand and he drops out the other third of the time, Ike might be fooled as to whether Mike has a good hand or a poor hand and be deftly relieved of his cash balances by Mike's dissembling behavior. The idea that "randomization" of strategy can be profitable becomes in the writings of Borel and later von Neumann the central idea of modern game theory (von Neumann and Morgenstern 1967 [1944]). Von Neumann proved that "every two-person zero-sum game has an equilibrium point when randomized strategies are permitted" and this result opened the door to modern game theory (Luce and Raiffa 1957, p. 72).

Lying and bluffing in the formation of price

Let's consider still another variation of the problem of deception in the marketplace. Mike has a used Ford to sell that he believes is worth no less than $4000. Ike has offered $3500 but is now reluctant to increase his offer price. Mike acts secretly to extract a higher offer from Ike and successfully closes the deal at $4200. Mike has a friend phone him up during the meeting with Ike. Mike simulates a conversation with the caller in which he states that the Ford remains unsold and that he is delighted that the caller is so keenly interested in this particular model. Ike hears the one-way conversation and believes that it is a real conversation and that the Ford is in imminent danger of being sold to a different buyer. Ike raises his offer price to $4200 and Mike agrees to sell.

What has Mike done? Mike has invested resources in a scam or fraudulent event designed to misrepresent facts that the potential buyer considers to be both relevant and important. What fact specifically has Mike misrepresented? Mike has made the car seem a bit more desirable than it really is. Mike misrepresents the potential future "liquidity" of this Ford model by making the market situation seem more dynamically competitive than it really is. Ike may never come to regret his "buy" decision and may never regret the price that he finally offered to pay, but Mike has engaged in a "deceptive act" in order to help form the final "equilibrium" price. The final price at which the transaction took place was not "determined" but was formed by the intentional misrepresentation of important information.

Of course, we do not have to end the story of Mike's machinations with Ike always as the victim. Why couldn't Ike go on the offensive, hiring a "shill" to dress up as an automobile repair expert and walk past Mike, explaining what a heap of rust the car really is and why a rational buyer should not pay more than $3500 for it? Now Mike will lower his reservation price in light of the new "credible" information, thereby benefiting Ike. If the amount Ike saves on the purchase price is greater than what it cost him to arrange for the imposter to pass by, then he will have earned a positive return on his investment in dissembling behavior. Deception has been used in this case to alter the division of the gains from trade. It did not prevent the actual trade from taking place.

Conclusion

The phenomenon of deception becomes especially obvious when we allow time to pass. The passing of time is essential to all negotiation, and negotiation is often a part of contract formation. If we imagine a market situation in which all trades occur at a simultaneous moment as long as the set of market prices causes all markets to clear, then we necessarily obscure the possibility of detecting deception in human action. One damaging legacy of GEE is how it obscures the strategies and concerns raised by the passing of time. Its focus on simultaneous market clearing obscures problems of exchange involving the credibility of promises. In a simultaneous moment, all parties consenting to the exchanges expect to gain. There is no following moment for regret, disappointment, or even outrage. How important is the pursuit of deceptive activity to our understanding of the market process?

I think that it is quite important indeed. The end of the twentieth century was one in which a larger portion of the gross national product of the advanced economies consisted of service industry outputs. A significant share of service products involves the authentication of one party's claim for the benefit of the counter party (compare McCloskey 1994, p. 78). Accountants, for example, authenticate the financial statements of corporations for the benefit of investors who rely on that information when trading shares. When accountants intentionally misrepresent selected transactions to help their clients fool the shareholders and enrich themselves, a fundamental pillar of the market system is demolished. The consequences include a rapid retreat from the web of impersonal financial trading as investors discount the value of traded shares and other financial contracts. The market system as a whole loses its efficiency as distrust and precaution become the order of the day, raising transaction costs.

Deceptive behavior ranges from glamorous Las Vegas magic shows in which the "marks" are the paying customers who delight in being fooled and pay generously for the experience, to the culturally charged nuances of harmless "puffery" in advertising and sales in which the customers might take notice of the ease with which they were tricked into buying the product. When deception winds its way to the worthless receipts that Charles Ponzi gave to his "investors" in his bankrupt company before the pyramid scheme finally collapsed in 1920, we have a form of deceptive behavior that is offensive to many. The investigations following the collapse of the Enron Corporation has generated evidence of "intentional misrepresentations" aimed at the duped shareholders. All deceptive behavior involves the intentional misrepresentation of what the targets consider to be "significant information," and the targets rely on those representations, only later (subsequently) to be surprised and in some cases disappointed. I make no clarion call for government regulation of industry, of advertising, or of investment securities or anything whatsoever, since instances of deceptive behavior can be found in government administration as well (Moss 1996). My purpose in this paper is purely conceptual and analytic.

I claim that the study of deception in the exchange process is a subject worth pursuing. I claim that it has been overlooked by the long history of price theory in economics in which relative prices are shown to be "determined" in whole or in part by technological coefficients that limit the range of values over which negotiated prices can profitably vary. The equilibrium model as it was perfected in the work of Arrow, Debreu, and McKenzie has contributed to the obfuscation of the deception problem by its emphasis on the single moment and the requirement that all choices be perfectly reconciled by a process that involves perfect foresight about the behavior of others. As we move away from the "single moment" to the passing of time and sequence of plan making and plan evaluation, we gain a stadium view of the important role that deceptive activity plays in economic life in general and in the formation of market prices in particular. If Hayek's statement that every great discovery in economics is due to the consistent advance of subjectivism in economics is true, then it is time that we reemphasized the importance of subjectively held fragments of knowledge (both information and misinformation) in the ordinary functioning of the market process (Hayek 1955, p. 31). It is just as silly to claim that information is perfectly distributed and freely available as it is to claim that the information possessed is accurate and without the stain of intentional error, deceit, or guile.

References

Akerlof, G. A., 'The Market for "Lemons": Quality Uncertainty and the Market Mechanism', *Quarterly Journal of Economics*, 84 (1970), 488–500.

Arrow, K. J., 'The Role of Securities in the Optimal Allocation of Risk Bearing', *Review of Economic Studies*, 31 (1963/64), 91–6.

Bator, F. M., 'The Simple Analytics of Welfare Maximization', *American Economic Review*, 17 (1957), 22–59.

Becker, G. S., 'Crime and Punishment: An Economic Approach', in G. S. Becker, *The Economic Approach to Human Behavior* [1968] (Chicago, IL: University of Chicago Press, 1976), pp. 39–85.

Boehm-Bawerk, E. von, *Capital and Interest* [1889], 3 vols (South Holland, IL: Libertarian Press, 1959)

Caldwell, B., '(HES Presidential Address), Hayek: Right for the Wrong Reasons?', *Journal of the History of Economic Thought*, 23 (2001), 141–51.

Coase, R., 'The Nature of the Firm' [1937], in R. Coase, *The Firm, the Market and the Law* (Chicago, IL: University of Chicago Press, 1988), pp. 33–55.

Darby, M. R. and Karni, E., 'Free Competition and the Optimal Amount of Fraud', *Journal of Law and Economics*, 16 (1973), 67–86.

Ellickson, R. C., *Order without Law: How Neighbors Settle Disputes* (Cambridge, MA: Harvard University Press, 1991).
Frank, R. H., *Microeconomics and Behavior*, 4th edn (New York: McGraw Hill, 2000).
Hahn, F., *Equilibrium and Macroeconomics* (Oxford: Blackwell, 1984).
Hayek, F., 'Socialist Calculation III: The Competitive "Solution"' [1935], in F. Hayek, *Individualism and Economic Order* (London: Routledge, 1952), pp. 181–208.
Hayek, F., 'The Use of Knowledge in Society' [1945], in F. Hayek, *Individualism and Economic Order* (London: Routledge, 1952b), pp. 77–91.
Hayek, F., *The Counter-Revolution of Science: Studies on the Abuse of Reason* (New York: The Free Press, 1955).
Hayek, F., *The Pure Theory of Capital* [1941] (London: Routledge, 1962).
Hayek, F., *Law, Legislation and Liberty: The Mirage of Social Justice*, (Chicago, IL: University of Chicago Press, 1975).
Hayek, F., 'Competition as a Discovery Procedure' [1968], in F. Hayek, *New Studies in Philosophy, Politics, Economics and the History of Ideas* (Chicago, IL: University of Chicago, 1978), pp. 179–90.
Ingrao, B. and Israel, G., *The Invisible Hand: Economic Equilibrium in History of Science* (Cambridge, MA: MIT Press, 1990).
Koppl, R. and Rosser, Jr, J. B., 'All That I Have to Say Has Already Crossed Your Mind', unpublished manuscript (2002).
Kronman, A., 'Contract Law and the State of Nature', *Journal of Law, Economics and Organization*, 1 (1985), 5–32.
Laffont, J.-J. and Martimort, D., *The Theory of Incentives: The Principal-Agent Model* (Princeton, NJ: Princeton University Press, 2002).
Langholm, O. I., *Price and Value in the Aristotelian Tradition: A Study in Scholastic Economic Sources* (Bergen: Universitetsforlaget, 1979).
Luce, R. D. and Raiffa, H., *Games and Decisions: Introduction and Critical Survey* (New York: Wiley, 1957).
Machiavelli, N., *The Prince and the Discourses* [1513] (New York: Random House, 1950).
Marshall, A., *The Pure Theory of Foreign Trade [and] The Pure Theory of Domestic Values* [1930] (Clifton, NJ: Augustus M. Kelley, 1974).
McCloskey, D. N., *Knowledge and Persuasion in Economics* (Cambridge: Cambridge University Press, 1994).
Meikle, S., 'Aristotle and Exchange Value', in D. Keyt and F. D. Miller, Jr (eds), *A Companion to Aristotle's Politics* (Oxford: Blackwell, 1991), pp. 156–81. (This is a revised version of a paper that appeared under the

title 'Aristotle and the Political Economy of the Polis', *Journal of Hellenic Studies*, 99 [1979]).

Mill, J. S., *Principles of Political Economy with Some of Their Applications to Social Philosophy* [1848], 2 vols., in J. M. Robson (ed.), *Collected Works of John Stuart Mill*, 2–3 (Toronto: University of Toronto, 1965).

Morgenstern, O., 'Perfect Foresight and Economic Equilibrium' [1935], in A. Schotter (ed.), *Selected Economic Writings of Oskar Morgenstern* (New York: New York University Press, 1976), pp. 169–83.

Moss, L., 'The Chicago Intellectual Property Rights Tradition and the Reconciliation of Coase and Hayek', *Eastern Economic Journal*, 17 (1991), 145–56.

Moss, L., 'Robber Barons and Entrepreneur-Promoters', in P. Boettke and M. J. Rizzo (eds), *Advances in Austrian Economics*, 2A (Greenwich, CT: JAI Press, 1995), pp. 95–107.

Moss, L., 'Platonic Deception as a Theme in the History of Economic Thought', *History of Political Economy*, 28 (1996), 533–57.

Moss, L., 'Hayek's Borderless Economy: His Escape from the Household Model', in J. Birner, P. Garrouste and T. Aimar (eds), *F. A. Hayek as a Political Economist: Economic Analysis and Values* (London: Routledge, 2002), pp. 97–112.

North, D. C., *Institutions, Institutional Change and Economic Performance* (Cambridge: Cambridge University Press, 1990).

Ricardo, D., *On the Principles of Political Economy and Taxation* [1817], in P. Sraffa and M. Dobb (eds), *The Works and Correspondence of David Ricardo*, 11 vols (Cambridge: Cambridge University Press, 1966).

Rothbard, M. N., *Man, Economy, and State: A Treatise on Economic Principles*, 2 vols (New York: D. Van Nostrand, 1962).

Schumpeter, J. A., *A History of Economic Analysis* [1954] (London: Routledge, 1994).

Searle, J., *The Construction of Social Reality* (New York: The Free Press, 1995).

Shackle, G. L. S., *Epistemics and Economics: A Critique of Economic Doctrines* (Cambridge: Cambridge University Press, 1972).

Shearmur, J. and. Klein, D. B, 'Good Conduct in the Great Society: Adam Smith and the Role of Reputation', in D. B. Klein (ed.), *Reputation: Studies in the Voluntary Elicitation of the Public Good* (Ann Arbor: University of Michigan Press, 1997), pp. 29–45.

Smith, A., 'Report of his Lectures [on Jurisprudence] 1766', in R. Meek (ed.), *Lectures on Jurisprudence* (Indianapolis, IN: Liberty Classics, 1982).

Smith, A., *An Inquiry into the Nature and Causes of the Wealth of Nations* [1776], in R. H. Campbell, A. S. Skinner and W. B. Todd (eds), *The Glasgow Edition of the Works and Correspondence of Adam Smith* (Indianapolis, IN: Liberty Classics, 1976).

Stigler, G., 'Ricardo and the 93 Per Cent Labor Theory of Value' [1958], in G. Stigler, *Essays in the History of Economic Thought* (Chicago, IL: University of Chicago Press, 1965), pp. 326–42.

Thweatt, W. O., 'James and John Mill on Comparative Advantage: Sraffa's Account Corrected', in H. Visser and E. Schoorl (eds), *Trade in Transit: World Trade and World Economy, Past, Present and Future* (Dordrecht: Kluwer, 1987).

Vaughn, K., *Austrian Economics in America: The Migration of a Tradition* (Cambridge: Cambridge University Press, 1994).

Viner, J., *Studies in the Theory of International Trade* [1937] (London: George Unwin, 1964).

Von Mises, L., *Human Action: A Treatise on Economics* [1949] (Auburn, Alabama: Ludwig von Mises Institute, 1998).

Von Mises, L., *Epistemological Problems of Economics* [1933] (Princeton, NJ: D. Van Nostrand, 1960).

Von Neumann, J. and Morgenstern, O., *Theory of Games and Economic Behavior* [1944] (New York: Wiley, 1967).

Von Wieser, F., *Social Economics* [1927], trans. A. F. Hinrichs (New York: Kelley Publishers, 1967).

Walker, D. A., *Advances in General Equilibrium Theory* (Cheltenham: Edward Elgar, 1997).

Weintraub, E. R., *General Equilibrium Analysis: Studies in Appraisal* (New York: Cambridge University Press, 1985).

Williamson, O. E., *Markets and Hierarchies: Analysis and Antitrust Implications: A Study in the Economics of Internal Organization* (London: Macmillan, 1975).

Part IV

Social Institutions and Regulation: How to Control Deception

8

Deception, Regulation and Politics*

Alan Hamlin

Abstract

In traditional economic models of regulation and politics, individuals are modeled as opportunistically self-interested; they use whatever information is available to them to their own advantage regardless of notions of honesty or deception. The possibility of deception arises under conditions of asymmetric information, but actual deception is not seen as a significant property of equilibria. The structures of the principal-agent and mechanism design problems are reviewed to illustrate these approaches and to discuss some of the issues arising. The possibility of reconsidering the specification of individual motivations so that norms of honesty may play some motivational role is discussed, in order to provide an alternative account of trust, honesty, and deception within a broadly economic framework.

Introduction

Deception may be conceived and defined in many ways, and I shall make no attempt at a full discussion or definition here; rather I will simply stipulate that deception occurs whenever an individual deliberately uses or reveals false information, or omits using or revealing true information, in an attempt to influence beliefs or behavior to the advantage of the deceiver. Four points may be noted immediately from this sketch of a definition:

- That it makes no explicit reference to the identity of the deceived, leaving open the possibility that this may be another individual, a collective agent (for example, government), or the deceiver (self-deception). However, in what follows I will focus on the deception of others.[1]

- That it makes explicit reference to a particular motivation. Deception is, on this account, both deliberate – so that errors or mistakes do not count as deception – and motivated by reference to the deceiver's own interests and advantages. This is to limit the idea of deception as discussed here to exclude so-called white lies, which might be argued to be motivated by reference to the interests of the deceived, and other "fictions" where the motivation may be more complex.[2]
- The use of deception is linked to the more general idea of power. Following Dahl and others,[3] power maybe defined as the ability to get another to act in a particular way when, uninfluenced, they would have acted in another way. Clearly, then, deception is one way, but by no means the only way, in which power may be deployed.
- There is a deliberate vagueness about the phrase "uses or reveals false information." Clearly the paradigm case of deception is one in which the deceiver simply communicates false information directly to the deceived. But, equally clearly, communication may also be indirect; information may be "signaled" in a variety of ways. The definition offered here is intended to encompass all forms of direct and indirect signaling.

The most obvious requirement for the possibility of deception is asymmetric information. In a world in which all individuals are fully informed and know this to be true – so that there is both full information and common knowledge of that fact – there can be no deception. Moreover, even where information is incomplete, so that there is genuine uncertainty, deception cannot occur if all individuals face the world with identical informational resources and know that this is the case. So, by definition, there can be no deception unless information is, or is believed to be, distributed across individuals asymmetrically. And this immediately tells us why deception is absent from many traditional textbook economic models. These models are designed to focus on the market process itself and to interrogate issues such as the impact of market structure, or the existence of externalities; and so these simple models are often cast in a world of full (or at least symmetric) information and common knowledge. It is not that such traditional economic models take deception to be irrational, or that they yield the result that deception does not occur, it is simply that they operate in an environment in which deception is ruled out by construction – so that this class of models is simply silent on the matter of deception. Only when we move to consider models that admit of private (that is, asymmetric) information does the question of deception arise.

Perhaps the most obvious starting point for the modern, systematic analysis of private information in economics is Hayek (1945) where the key argument is that a major distinguishing feature of the market mechanism is its ability to aggregate private information efficiently. This point, in reverse, is also an important part of the early discussion of the public goods problem (Samuelson 1954 onwards), where the free rider issue is recognized as crucially based in private information and the incentives that individuals' may face to deceive – to fail to report their true willingness to pay, for example. More recently, the "economics of information" has become a standard part of the repertoire of economists, with several basic paradigms employed to capture the essence of the problems posed by asymmetric information.[4]

It is also clear that the areas of the economics of regulation and of the economic analysis of politics are areas where issues of deception – of honesty, trust, commitment, and so on – are likely to be particularly important. In both areas, a key issue is the delegation of power – by the regulator to the firm, or by citizens to politicians – and the delegation of power naturally raises the prospect of the abuse of power, and the means of abusing power often involve deception of one kind or another. Although I will not spend much time in this essay dealing explicitly with models of regulation or politics, the discussion will be motivated by the general concerns that such models raise, and by the general structure of these models; in the terminology of economics – the principal-agent structure and the mechanism design structure.

One key theme of what follows will be the normative status of the idea of deception. The definition outline offered above takes a purely descriptive view of deception, and this is not accidental. This is the view that is most consistent with mainstream economic analysis. But terms such as deception, honesty, and trust might also be considered as intrinsically normative. The simple idea being that deception is a "bad" thing in itself, regardless of its impact on outcomes such as the allocation of resources.[5] Such a normative conception of deception is somewhat alien to mainstream economic analysis. Later in this essay I will attempt to make some progress with such a conception, starting from the recognition that if deception, honesty, and trust are to be of real normative concern, they should be of real normative concern to at least some of the individuals within the model, and that this should carry implications for their motivations and their behavior. Thus, I shall consider some of the implications of admitting into our models individuals who are at least somewhat "virtuous" or "honest" in terms of their private motivations.

The remainder of this essay will be presented in five further sections, first I will provide a brief outline of the principal-agent and mechanism design paradigms that provide the basis for the economic analysis of asymmetric information and, therefore, the possibility of deception. I will provide two simple examples: one in the context of regulation, the other in the context of the provision of public goods – both of which clearly carry over into the area of politics. Following that, I will discuss in more detail the motivation of agents that might be described as somewhat "virtuous," and the implications of recognizing such individuals in terms of the design of economic or political institutions. I then develop an extended account of the modeling of trust and honesty that draws on the idea of somewhat virtuous motivations. Finally, I offer some concluding remarks.

Principal-agent models and mechanism design

The now-standard economic approach to asymmetric information may be divided, for our purposes, into two: the principal-agent framework and the mechanism design framework. I will discuss each in turn. The purpose of this section is simply to introduce the structure of the issues, and to establish links to the idea of deception.

The principal-agent framework studies the relationship between a relatively well-informed agent, and a relatively poorly informed principal, so that the agent has an informational advantage over the principal. There must also be some difference between the interests of the agent and those of the principal; so that the agent could, if unconstrained, use her informational advantage to further her own interests, at the expense of those of the principal. The central question in this context is then, how the principal can design the nature of the relationship governing the relationship (the "contract") so as to maximize the benefits to the principal? This requires the principal to design a contract from a perspective that recognizes that the agent will seek to optimize from her own perspective, taking the contract as a constraint, and utilizing the private information available to her. This framework provides a workhorse model for many situations – the relationship between shareholders and managers, the relationship between employers and employees, the relationship between regulators and regulated firms, the relationship between citizens and elected politicians, and so on. More detailed examples will be mentioned in the next section.

The general presumption in this class of models is that agents will use their informational advantage to further their own ends without reference to any external notions of "honesty" or "deception." Information is simply seen as a "resource" or "commodity," and all individuals can be expected to utilize the resources at their command in whatever way is most profitable. In Williamson's terminology, individuals are seen as entirely opportunistic.[6] Here, opportunism implies that agents will be unconstrained by any normative concerns in seeking out opportunities to advance toward their goals. The opportunistic pursuit of self-interest then generates a strong view of *homo economicus* as the completely unscrupulous egoist.

The literature distinguishes two cases: the moral hazard problem and the adverse selection problem. The moral hazard problem[7] arises when the well-informed agent can take actions that are hidden from the principal. For example, in the context of an insurance market, imagine the case in which the risk associated with any insured individual depends upon that individual's actions – their effort to avoid the insured-against outcome, for example – but that these actions are unobservable by the principal – the insurance company. Each individual, once insured, will face an incentive to undersupply effort, so raising the risk. This problem will result in inefficiency and, in extreme cases, the non-existence of markets.

The adverse selection problem[8] arises when the informed agents' actions depend on information that is fixed, but not observable by the principal. For example, in the insurance context again, imagine the case in which each individual has private information on their own risk, but that this information is not observable by the insurance company. If the company offers a standard insurance contract at a fixed price, set in relation to the average risk, only those customers who believe that the insurance represents good value *given their private information on their own risk* will buy the insurance. The set of customers will, therefore, be adversely selected and, knowing that this might occur, the insurance company might prefer not to offer the insurance rather than suffer the losses associated with an adversely selected market. In this way, the adverse selection problem also causes inefficiency and, in extreme cases, may cause some markets to fail to exist.

Note that a key difference between the two cases relates to the nature of the information that is unobservable by the principal. In the adverse selection case the only unobservable is a variable associated with agents; we may refer to this variable as identifying each agent's "type." Each agent is of a particular, and fixed, type, but only the agent knows her own type. All actions made by agents are observable. By contrast, in the moral hazard case there are unobservable or hidden actions that are endogenous in the sense that agents choose the action only after the contractual details of the relationship between principal and agents are fixed. In this case, there is no necessity for the set of agents to be divided into "types," and indeed, all agents may be identical.

The mechanism design framework operates at a rather different level. A "mechanism" is a specification of how some set of resources will be allocated, or some economic decisions made, as a function of data concerning the individual agents in the system. This "data" may include such things as preferences or other information, which may be asymmetrically distributed. The focus of the mechanism design literature is then the question of identifying the optimal mechanism for any given situation. Of course, this depends upon some particular specification of the normative criterion against which optimality is to be judged. Clearly then, one "mechanism" of considerable interest is the market mechanism, and one might consider the fundamental welfare theorems of standard welfare economics to be examples of the mechanism design approach, addressing the question of the optimality of a particular mechanism (that associated with a full set of perfectly competitive markets). Thus, while the principal-agent framework focuses attention on specific relationships within an economic structure and analyzes the significance of contractual forms in serving the interests of principals, the mechanism design framework looks more broadly at the set of economic institutions and analyzes their impact on social outcomes.

We may now briefly consider the results of these literatures at a simple and general level. A key idea to understand in the context of both the principal-agent model and the mechanism design approach is incentive compatibility and the associated revelation principle.[9] The fundamental idea here is that the search for the optimal contract or mechanism can be limited to the class of arrangements in which all agents truthfully reveal their types, or truthfully reveal their actions. It is important to stress that the revelation principle does not assert that all arrangements that emerge in equilibrium will, as a matter of fact, be such that honest revelation of types and/or actions will arise, but only that for any equilibrium that does emerge there is an essentially identical equilibrium that involves full revelation, so that the set of possible equilibrium outcomes can be fully captured within the set of fully revealing equilibria.

How, then, does the revelation principle bear on the idea of deception? In one sense, it tells us that it is the possibility of deception, rather than the actuality of deception that is significant. To explain this interpretation, consider two alternative versions of a principal-agent situation. In case 1, the contract between the principal and the agent has not been optimally designed with incentive compatibility in mind, and so, in equilibrium, the agent uses some form of deception to increase her payoff. In case 2, which is in every other respect identical to case 1, the contract is optimally designed with incentive compatibility in mind, and so the agent now faces a positive incentive to reveal honestly her private information; but the final payoffs to both agent and principal are identical to those in Case 1. The benefit derived from deception in case 1, is re-defined as an incentive payment to induce honesty in case 2, so that the differences between cases 1 and 2 might be seen as more terminological than real. And this is, in essence, the message of the revelation principle: any equilibrium that involves deception can be transformed into an equilibrium that involves no deception without affecting the basic structure of the payoffs. The *possibility* of deception says something important about the nature of the strategic interaction between the individuals, but the *actuality* of deception in equilibrium is inessential and adds nothing to the story.

In this view, then, actual deception is not the real issue. Private or asymmetric information, and hence the possibility or threat of deception, is the real issue. The holder of private information is normally the owner of a valuable asset, and this asset can be used to generate improved payoffs, an informational rent. The precise details of how the improved payoff is achieved, whether or not it involves deception, or incentive payments, are less important than the fact that it is achieved. Note also that there is no presumption that deception is less efficient than other means of realizing informational rents. Again, the revelation principle tells us that any equilibrium involving deception is fully equivalent to another equilibrium with no deception – and this full equivalence includes an equivalent inefficiency. Just as deception may be said to reduce efficiency relative to the ideal case of full, symmetric information, so does the need to impose incentive compatibility in order to ensure the provision of incentives to reveal private information.

Examples

A simple example of the application of the principal-agent framework, and the idea of revelation principle of the "incentive compatibility constraint" can be provide in the form of a simplified version of the Baron and Myerson (1982) model of the optimal regulation of a monopoly:
Assume that the monopoly firm maximizes its profit Π, and that the regulator aims to maximize welfare W, as indicated by:

$$\text{Max } W = S + \alpha\Pi$$

where W = welfare, S = consumer surplus, Π = profits and $\alpha \leq 1$

($\alpha = 1$ would give the case of pure efficiency motivation, $\alpha < 1$ would give a distributional preference in favor of consumers and away from profits/shareholders).

In terms of information, assume that the firm is fully informed, while the regulator has no accurate information on the firm's costs. The firm then has to report its marginal cost θ to the regulator knowing that this cost figure will be used by the regulator to fix an output level Q and a transfer payment T (from the regulator to the firm) as functions of the announced cost. So,

$$Q = q(\theta)$$
$$T = t(\theta)$$

These functions are chosen by the regulator to maximize W, given the reported θ, which lies in the known range from the low of θ_1 to the high of θ_2.

If the regulator directly and accurately observed marginal costs, at say, C, so that there was no asymmetry of information, and if $\alpha = 1$, the regulator could always choose such that:

$$P(Q(C)) = C$$

and $$T(C) = 0$$

That is, the regulator could choose the first-best efficient equilibrium in which price is equal to marginal cost and there is no transfer payment.

But if the regulator does not observe costs, and has to rely on reported costs, it will need to provide an incentive for the firm to report costs accurately (since without such an incentive the firm would be able to manipulate or deceive the regulator by announcing false costs). That is, given the regulator's policy, it must be the firm's profit-maximizing strategy to tell the truth, by announcing the true θ. This, then, is the incentive compatibility issue in this case. More formally, if $\Pi(A,B)$ indicates the profits made when announcing a cost of A when the true cost is B, then profit associated with announcing the truth $\Pi(\theta^*, \theta^*)$ must be greater than the profit available from any lie $\Pi(\theta, \theta^*)$ for all θ not equal to θ^*.

The introduction of this additional constraint leads to the basic results that:

$$P(Q(\theta)) = \theta + (1-\alpha)(\theta - \theta 1)$$
$$\Pi(\theta) \geq 0$$
$$T(\theta) \geq 0$$

The interpretation of these results is relatively straightforward.

Prices are above marginal cost unless either

$$\alpha = 1 \text{ (no concern for distribution)}$$

or $$\theta = \theta_1 \text{ (announced costs are at the minimum)}$$

Profits are, therefore, almost always greater than zero.

Transfers are also almost always greater than zero.

Profits are essentially being used by the regulator as the incentive to ensure that the firm reports costs accurately, and the transfer payment is effectively subsidizing the firm to produce a greater quantity than it would otherwise do.

This type of model can be developed and extended in a number of ways, for example, to consider the case where the firm may be able to reduce costs by expending some managerial effort, which is not directly observable by the regulator. However, the basic point remains: the regulator has to provide appropriate incentives to the firm to engage in the desired behavior (truthful reporting, the provision of effort, and so on) and these incentives will constrain the regulator's ability to maximize W. At the same time, the incentives will show up as increased levels of profit under regulation, and increased transfer payments.

It should be clear that an essentially similar model can be structured to apply in the context of politics, and particularly the relationship between the citizens and their elected government.[10] Of course, additional issues are raised by the fact that, in this setting, there are many principals (voters) rather than one, but the essential logic applies. Well-informed politicians can exploit their informational advantage unless the citizens provide costly incentives for them to reveal the truth. In the second-best equilibrium that arises as a result of the optimal degree of control by the principal, agents are better off than they would have been in the first-best, fully efficient state that might arise in the full information case, since they can earn an informational rent.

A second example relates to the classic public goods problem mentioned in the introduction. Here the issue can be seen as one that falls within the mechanism design paradigm. Essentially, the requirement is for a mechanism that will ensure that the optimal amount of a pure Samuelsonian public good will be provided. The first-best optimal arrangement is one in which the quantity of the public good is set so as to equate the sum of all individuals' marginal valuations of the good with the marginal social cost of supplying the good, and this may be financed by charging each individual a tax equal to their own marginal valuation. The difficulty is that the information required to calculate the optimal quantity is not directly available to the decision-maker/government. Furthermore, any simple attempt to elicit the information is unlikely to be successful since each individual may expect that the information will be used to set taxes and so face an incentive to understate her own valuation in order to avoid payment while free-riding on the public good financed by others.

The revelation principle in this case points to the possibility of designing a mechanism such that each individual will accurately reveal her own private valuation – but this must be bought at a price – and the price is that the mechanism will not generally raise sufficient revenue to finance the provision of the optimal quantity of the public good, so that finance will have to be raised by other (inefficient) means. The relevant mechanism, known as a Clarke-Groves-Vickrey mechanism,[11] is fairly simple. Essentially, it asks everyone to announce his or her valuation in the context of a two-part rule. The first part of the rule simply says that the quantity of the good to be provided will be set by equating the sum of the announced valuations equal to the marginal supply cost. Taken by itself, this would imply that everyone faces an incentive to announce a valuation greater than the truth, since this will add to the total supply of the good, at no cost to themselves. The second part of the rule is then to present each individual with a potential cost. An individual will pay if and only if that individual's announcement is critical or marginal in determining the quantity. More precisely, individual J will pay if and only if the sum of the valuations of all individuals excluding J would imply a different quantity to that implied by the sum of all individuals including J. And the amount that J will pay will simply be the difference between the total cost and the sum of all individuals' evaluations excluding J's. This design exactly balances an incentive to overstate valuations with an incentive to understate valuations, so that each individual will rationally announce their true valuation. In the case that you are critical or marginal to the decision (the only case that matters either in terms of your impact on the overall decision or in terms of making a payment) you will not wish to overstate your true valuation since that will lead to your paying more than the good is worth to you; on the other hand you will not wish to understate your preferences since this will lead to the provision of less of the good. These two incentives combine to make it rational to announce precisely your true valuation.

However, as already noted, the mechanism is not fully efficient; it cannot be since it has to overcome the problem of the private information. While it can deliver information on the optimum quantity of the public good, it will not deliver the relevant finance. Indeed, in some cases (where no individual is critical/marginal in the relevant sense) it may deliver no finance at all. And it is important to stress that one could not use the information gathered by the mechanism to set taxes, since that would be to undermine the whole exercise by re-introducing an incentive to deceive. Taxes would have to be raised by some unrelated means (an income tax, say) which generates inefficiency.

As with the principal-agent framework, the applicability of the mechanism design framework to regulation and politics is immediate. In the political context, an obvious key question is how to design a democratic political system (voting rules, rules of representation, the separation of powers and so on) so as to generate the best available social outcomes – and this is clearly a mechanism design problem. Of course, to say that the applicability of the framework is immediate is not to say that the application is easy. Modeling a political system is complex, and capturing the key features in a model that is tractable is a demanding task.[12]

These two simple examples illustrate the operation of the revelation principle/incentive compatibility constraint in situations of asymmetric information where deception is a potential feature of behavior. They also illustrate the general point, made in the previous section, that actual deception can be avoided by appropriate design of contracts and mechanisms, so that actual deception is not a deep feature of economic equilibria in models of asymmetric information. Of course, the possibility or threat of deception is a deep feature of these models, but their essential argument is that, at least in principle, we can always design our economic and social contracts and institutions in such a way that recognizes this threat and delivers equilibrium behavior that involves no deception. Nevertheless, there are a number of papers that specifically address issues of deception in political settings by focusing on the processing of information in political communication. For example, Banerjee and Somanathan (2001), drawing on earlier work by Austen-Smith (1990; 1992), model the idea of political communication or "voice" by allowing individuals to report a signal to a politician who has to make a policy decision under uncertainty. The receipt of the signal may influence the politician's decision, and so individuals may face an incentive to "speak" whenever they believe that the policy impact of "speech" will favor them regardless of the truth of what they say. One of the conclusions of the analysis is that in situations where individuals may lie – that is, report a signal falsely – politicians will place little or no value in political speech, and so will not change their policy choices in response to reports received. Only where individuals are constrained to report truthfully, perhaps by an appropriate mechanism design, will political voice be effective in influencing political outcomes. This result is an example of another key idea in recent economic thought in the area: the idea of "cheap talk."[13] Here, the basic idea is that when talk, communication, or information transmission is "cheap" in the sense that it involves no real cost or commitment on the part of the speaker, it will have no real impact on the behavior of others, or on economic or social outcomes. Of course, there are exceptions – most obviously when the situation at hand is a pure coordination game, so that the speakers face no incentive to deceive – but one can easily see this idea as being a further illustration of the role of the threat (rather than the actuality) of deception.

Motivations

So far, I have taken the standard economist's approach that emphasizes the asymmetry of information, and maintains the economist's standard assumption that all individuals in the model, whether principal or agent, or playing any other role, are of the *homo economicus* type in the standard sense of pursuing their own interests opportunistically. The question I want to explore here, and in what follows, relates to the introduction of a further aspect of motivation – the possibility that at least some individuals might recognize some normative rules of behavior – such as a norm of honesty or promise keeping and so not conform to the simple model of opportunistic economic rationality. In this way, we might seek to incorporate into models the idea of deception as a normatively charged phenomenon.

I should say immediately that there is no conceptual difficulty in incorporating the idea of, say, honesty into a more-or-less standard account of economic rationality. If honesty is something I value, I can simply include it in my "utility function" and, once it is included, I will once again be a consistent and "opportunistic" utility maximizer in the sense that I will be honest if and only if the payoff in terms of honesty at least compensates for any losses that might arise from foregoing opportunities to be dishonest. Opportunism is not defeated by the introduction of honesty as an argument in the agent's utility function; rather, the margin at which opportunism operates is simply shifted. This approach runs the risk of confusing formalism with interpretation. The questions that I wish to address revolve around particular interpretations of what rationality requires and, in particular, the possibility that there may be significant heterogeneity of motivation within any population. In short that there may be different "types" of individuals – differentiated by their motivational make-up or disposition – so that, for example, some may be dispositionally honest in the sense that they are committed to the general strategy of honesty, rather than simply valuing honesty as an argument in their utility function. Of course, the use of this terminology of "types" immediately brings to mind the selection and possibly adverse selection issue in which different types may be distinguished, and this is entirely deliberate.

Start from a simple assumption – that some (but not all) individuals are dispositionally honest, while others are dispositionally opportunistic. I will take this to mean that the honest will reliably tell the truth, reveal information, keep promises, and so on, even when it is not in their own narrowly conceived interest to do so, while the opportunistic will do whatever is in their interests regardless of its honesty/dishonesty. This assumption is clearly very different from that which forms the basis of the models discussed above, where it is essentially assumed that all individuals are opportunistic. How would such an assumption of motivational heterogeneity matter? What difference would it make?

These questions may be approached by considering the standard strategy of normative economic reasoning that might be summarized under the heading of the "invisible hand" strategy. The core idea in this strategy (most clearly drawn out in the mechanism design literature) is that the economist attempts to structure the external environment – the relative prices of alternative actions, and hence the various incentives facing decision makers – in such a way that the self-interest of the individual agents is channeled into actions that promote outcomes that satisfy some specific normative criterion. This strategy may be thought of as a strategy that attempts to "economize on virtue" in the sense that it avoids relying on the virtue of individuals in aiming to reach socially desirable outcomes – it substitutes external mechanisms and devices for internal virtue.[14] Of course, in the limiting case where individuals are conceived as entirely without virtue – that is, entirely selfish in their private motivations – there is no alternative to this strategy of economizing on virtue. And even when we admit the possibility of individual virtue, it may still be the appropriate strategy in at least some cases – but the introduction of individual virtue does at least raise the question of whether alternative strategies may be better in at least some circumstances.

In particular, I would suggest three strategies that are available in a world which admits of the possibility of individual virtues such as honesty, and of the possibility of motivational heterogeneity, which are simply ruled out in models which assume that all agents are entirely opportunistically selfish. These may be termed the strategies of "screening for virtue," "virtue production," and "virtue enhancement." I will say a little about each in turn, although I should stress that they should not be seen as substitutes – in at least some cases, these strategies may work together as complements.

Screening for virtue simply employs the basic economic idea of comparative advantage at the level of motivational dispositions. If individuals differ by motivational type, and different social roles make differential use of the motivations of the individuals that take on those roles, there is clearly a potential social gain from allocating individuals to those roles that are particularly suited to their type. In crude terms – if some roles involve more discretionary power than others do, there will be a social gain from allocating those roles to individuals of the more virtuous type. Of course, simply to say this is by no means enough. We need to be clear that we have to design institutional structures that can be expected to screen individuals in the required manner, since there will always be an incentive for the "wrong" type of individuals to seek appointment to the roles that offer power.[15] But I am not concerned with such detailed analysis of particular institutional devices here; my aim is merely to identify the strategy.

Producing virtue is equally straightforward as a strategy, and equally difficult in terms of institutional design. The idea here is simply that motivations are not exogenous, but are rather endogenous to the institutional structure. In short, some institutional structures are more likely to encourage and support virtues such as honesty, while other structures may undermine virtue. To the extent that increasing the proportion of individuals who are virtuous may be expected to improve social outcomes, the strategy of investing in social institutions that contribute to the production of virtue may be justified. Notice that they **may** be justified, not that they **will** be justified. This strategy, like all strategies, will carry costs as well as benefits. Institutions that encourage virtue may also introduce inefficiencies, so that there may be a trade-off between these two desirable features. I make no claim that such a strategy is necessarily a good one, or that it dominates any other strategy (in general some mix of strategies might be appropriate). I simply suggest that this strategy and the other strategies involving virtue are worthy of some consideration.

These two strategies of screening for virtue and virtue production are relatively obvious. One involves increasing the extent of virtue in society; the other attempting to allocate whatever virtue exists most effectively. The third strategy is slightly less obvious, and involves the idea of enhancing or amplifying the impact of whatever virtue may exist in society. A more detailed example of this strategy will be provided in what follows, but for the moment I simply note the general idea that specific institutions may operate very differently in the presence of (even a very limited number of) virtuous individuals, so that the recognition of virtue even as a rare characteristic may allow certain social outcomes to be feasible, which are beyond the reach of a society that completely lacks individual virtue.

Each of these three strategies presents an alternative basis for institutional or mechanism design – whether we are concerned with the institutions of regulation, or the institutions of politics. They share the characteristic that they deliberately rely on virtue, rather than attempting to economize on virtue. But they also open up lines of criticism that may apply to more traditional economic models. If the world actually includes some individual virtue, of the general type treated here, but if we design the institutions of the world as if this were not so, guided by the standard economist's strategy of economizing on virtue, we run several risks. The first risk is that we adversely select for virtue; that is, we screen into those roles that are granted most power precisely the individuals who are least virtuous. The second risk is that we destroy virtue; just as virtue can be encouraged and supported by some institutional structures, so can it be discouraged and damaged by others. The third risk is that we dampen or decrease the impact of whatever virtue may be present.

Trust and honesty

I now turn explicitly to the case of trust and honesty in an attempt to pull together some of the issues raised. The issue of trust and honesty may be seen as strongly (inversely) related to the issue of deception and central to many problems in regulation and politics. I focus on the positive virtues of trust and honesty here, rather than the negative act of deception (which can be thought of as arising in the absence of trust and honesty), just because it is possible to put the issues more simply.[16]

I will first lay out the basic nature of the reliance predicament, in which trust and honesty are the key issues, and then canvass three complementary approaches to that predicament, including one that draws on the idea of heterogeneous motivational dispositions and illustrates the possibility of the strategy of virtue enhancement – in this case, the enhancement of the virtue of honesty – so as to address a problem that arises from the overwhelming threat of deception.

The reliance predicament

Consider the predicament set out as an extensive form game in Fig. 1. There are two players: **A**, who moves first, has a choice as to whether to rely (**R**) on the second player (**B**), or not to rely (**N**). If **A** chooses **N**, the interaction ends and each player receives a pay-off of zero. If **A** chooses **R**, however, player **B** is brought into play and faces a choice between exploiting (**E**), in which case **A** receives a pay-off of -1 and **B** receives a pay-off of 3; and cooperating (**C**), in which case each player receives a payoff of 2. We should think of action **E** as involving deception, while action **C** involves honesty – for example we could interpret the model in terms of promise keeping where the initial choice faced by **A** is a decision of whether or not to rely on a promise that was previously given by **B**. **B**'s decision is then whether to honestly keep the promise, or renege on the promise, in order to deceive **A**.

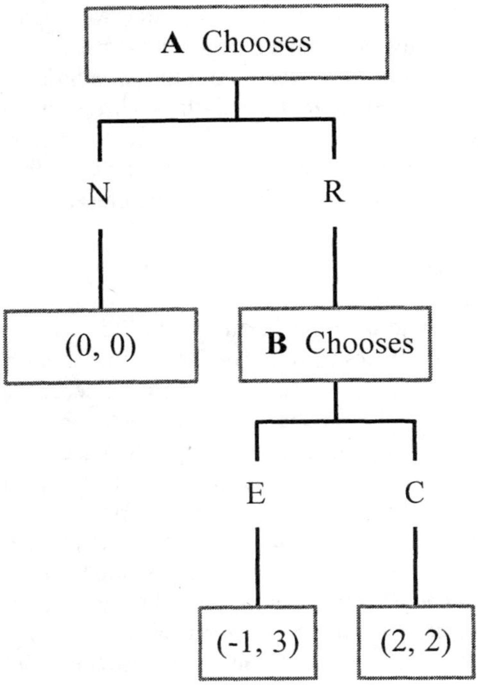

Figure 1: The reliance predicament.

This reliance game is similar in some respects to the prisoner's dilemma, although it differs most obviously in the fact that the players move in sequence, so that there is no question of symmetry between the players. One clear similarity is that the unique equilibrium under fully rational and opportunistic motivations is sub-optimal. That is, in the case of the reliance predicament, if both **A** and **B** are rational in the standard economic sense, and this fact is common knowledge, then **A** will argue that if she chooses **R**, **B** will certainly choose **E,** giving **A** the payoff of -1. With this in mind, **A** will certainly choose **N**. **A** will not "rely" on **B**, since it is clearly opportunistically rational for **B** to exploit reliance. Yet both **A** and **B** would be better off if they chose **R** and **C** respectively. The threat of deception undermines the possible Pareto improvement that is simply inaccessible to simple rational *homo economicus* players. In particular, **B** cannot credibly commit to choosing **C**, since **A** knows that such a promise will carry no weight in **B**'s decision making – it is simply "cheap talk." I should perhaps emphasize that the "problem" here is *not* that **A** is actually exploited. In fact, no exploitation occurs in equilibrium (as usual, it is not actual exploitation/deception that is the problem, but the credible possibility of exploitation/deception). The problem is rather a lack of trust or honesty. **B** is not trusted because she is not trustworthy, and this fact restricts the pay-offs to both players.

Within the grammar of argument that rational actor analysis admits, any resolution of the reliance predicament must be based on some change to the nature of the game being analyzed. The logic of the analysis of choice *within* the original game – defined by the nature of the players, their information, and the strategies available to them and the pay-off structure – is not in doubt. I distinguish between three types of change to the underlying game, which correspond to three distinct approaches to the reliance predicament.[17]

Approaches to the reliance predicament – repetition

One standard move in the analysis of games such as the reliance predicament is the move from the one-shot game to an indefinitely repeated game. If the interaction between **A** and **B** is to be repeated, and this fact is common knowledge, **B** may have an incentive to build a reputation for choosing **C**, and this possibility will be known to **A**. And if the repetition is indefinite, **B**'s incentive will not unravel under backwards induction. Under certain circumstances, this can lead **A** to choose **R** and **B** to choose **C,** so that the Pareto optimal outcome is realized.

All of this is both true and important in many cases, but it does not represent a response to what may be seen as the basic difficulty. The fundamental logic of the reliance predicament is untouched by this type of argument. Even in the presence of reputational considerations, there can still arise cases in which the opportunistic rationality and therefore dishonesty of *homo economicus* will be a barrier to trust, and a sufficient barrier to prevent the realization of mutual benefits. What is at stake is the ability of agents to *be* honest, rather than simply acting honestly when it is in their interests to do so. It is the opportunistic, forward-looking expediency of rational *homo economicus* that makes him/her untrustworthy. Arguments such as the argument of the indefinite repetition of the game will certainly reduce the number of cases to which the predicament applies. It is an empirical question as to whether the cases that remain are sufficiently numerous, or sufficiently important, to merit concern. I believe that numerous important cases remain, and that they are particularly likely to arise in the arenas of regulation and politics.

Approaches to the reliance predicament – enforcement

A second possible resolution of the reliance predicament involves varying the objective pay-offs associated with the different strategy choices. This possibility is uninteresting in itself, since it is obvious that by arbitrarily changing the pay-off structure we can transform the reliance predicament into a wide variety of different games. However, there is a more specific and interesting interpretation. In the face of a social predicament, we might seek to employ social institutions to provide solutions that are not accessible to individually rational action. In particular, institutions might be put in place that impose penalties on players taking certain actions, or provide rewards to other actions. Fines can be imposed, subsidies paid, and so on. However, although such social institutions are conceivable, they must pass at least two tests of feasibility. First, they should be institutions that work within resource limits. If an institution is to offer additional rewards to certain actions, the resources required to finance those rewards must come from somewhere, and from somewhere within the model. And second, they should be institutions that could be designed and operated by people of the type that populate the model – in this case by *homo economicus*.

The most obvious type of institution that might resolve a reliance predicament is an institution that penalizes player **B** if she takes action **E** – punishing deception. If this penalty is large enough (in our example, if it is greater than 1), **B**'s rational response to **A** choosing **R** will be to choose **C**. Knowing this, it will be rational for **A** to choose **R** and the Pareto optimal outcome will be realized. Such an institution does not require major resources since it offers no rewards (indeed, in equilibrium, penalties are never paid either), but the credible threat of penalties is sufficient to change behavior (the threat of penalty is sufficient to offset the threat of deception). Moreover, if the institution is somewhat costly to maintain, it is likely that these costs could be financed out of the real gains enjoyed by the players. Furthermore, this type of institution would also seem to be capable of being designed by *homo economicus*; since the institution offers a Pareto improvement, it would be approved by all potential players of the game *ex ante* – even if they did not know which of the two roles they would be playing.

But can such an institution be operated by *homo economicus*? As "public choice" critics of traditional economic models have rightly insisted that to simply assume that there exist public institutions that are themselves reliable is to assume the real problem away. The difficulty here is that we are introducing a third "player" into the game – the enforcer – without explicitly modeling her choices. Obviously, if the enforcer is a "benevolent dictator" in the sense that they are benevolent enough to act in the public interest, and powerful enough to take whatever action is required, the institution of enforcement will be effective. But if, as would seem more consistent with the standard economic approach, the enforcer is herself opportunistically rational, the simple fact that the act of enforcement benefits the two original players will not provide the enforcer with a reason to act in that way. If the enforcer is granted powers sufficient to ensure honesty by **B**, she must be assumed to use those powers to maximize her own pay-off, regardless of the impacts on **A** and **B**. In these circumstances, it is by no means obvious that the introduction of enforcement will yield the desired result.

I shall return to the issue of enforcement below. I do not believe, as some public choice scholars seem to, that this problem is necessarily insoluble, but I do believe that it imposes a strict limitation on the range of institutions that can be sustained in a world of opportunistically rational individuals. In short, all institutions must ultimately be self-enforcing. That is, while some enforcement may be possible *within* an institution, the institution as a whole must be self-enforcing in the sense that it operates only by channeling the self-interest of the individuals who act within it. Invisible hands are the only kinds of hands that are allowable in this world of unrelieved egoism. While I would certainly not wish to deny the importance of invisible hand mechanisms, they clearly have their limits. To insist that only invisible hand mechanisms are available is extremely restrictive.

Approaches to the reliance predicament – dispositions

We come now to the third and, for present purposes, most significant way in which we might modify the reliance game in order to resolve the underlying predicament – that is, by modifying the assumed nature of the players to allow them access to dispositions other than opportunistically rational egoism. There are two issues involved here. The first relates to the distinction between choice of actions and choice of dispositions. The second relates to the distinction between virtuous and non-virtuous motivations of the choosing agent. I wish to involve both issues, but will begin with an extreme case in which only the first is relevant, so that all agents are conceived as rational egoists in the sense that all of their basic desires are essentially self-interested.

Suppose that anyone can have a surgical operation performed on the brain which will ensure that the individual will be honest – faithfully keeping promises and refusing all opportunities to deceive. Suppose further that the possibility of this operation is common knowledge. Suppose also that the operation is irreversible and leaves the person with a distinctive scar on the forehead – a scar that is impossible to fake. The operation has no other effects or risks and is costless to perform. It seems clear that it would be rational for egoists to undergo such an operation to the extent that they expect to be involved in the reliance game in the player **B** role.[18] Player **A** will have rational grounds to trust a scarred player **B**, and so the Pareto optimal outcome will be realized, leaving **B**, in particular, better off. Furthermore, if there is any element of choice in the formation of partnerships, potential **A**'s will seek out scarred players as partners, so that profitable interactions will be more plentiful for the scarred than the unscarred. The scarred will then do better than the unscarred in terms of lifetime payoffs.

Note that, just as the common knowledge of rationality is important in standard game theoretic analysis, so the common knowledge of the operation and the observable signal of the scar is important here. **A**'s have good reason to trust scarred players on rational grounds – that is, they trust them because they are identified as trustworthy. Common knowledge of the possibility of the operation, plus the scar, together constitute a perfect signal: the operation makes honesty both credible and transparent. If we change the details of the story, we will get different results. If there is common knowledge of the possibility of the operation but no scar; and everyone knows only that a proportion (p) of individuals have undergone surgery, without knowing who the honest types are, all **A**'s will then face a gamble. With probability p strategy **R** will carry a pay-off of 2, and with probability (1-p) strategy **R** will carry a pay-off of -1. If **A** is risk neutral and must choose a pure strategy (that is, she cannot randomize between **N** and **R**) she will choose **R** if and only if p is greater than 0.33. But notice that in this case, individuals will have no reason for undergoing the operation. Whether *you* will be trusted is completely unrelated to whether *you* have had the operation. You will do best where p is relatively high, so that **A**'s will be more likely to "trust" their partners, but where you yourself have not had the operation so that you are free to deceive these trusting **A**'s. This is a classic free-rider problem: everyone would like p to be high (that is, they want others to have the operation), but will not have the operation himself or herself.

While the case of brain surgery illustrates the possibility of purely egoistic commitment, it lacks any element that bears on virtue. It might be that a purely egoistic commitment gives rise to behavior that is apparently virtuous, as with honesty in the brain surgery example, but it would be just as plausible to construct an example in which there are good egoistic reasons to adopt a commitment that generated behavior that was apparently immoral. There can be no general presumption that commitments adopted on egoistic grounds lead to morally appropriate behavior.

The brain surgery example uses the device of surgery as a means of commitment and represents the limiting case of a disposition where the commitment is hard-wired, transparent, and irreversible. Despite the extreme nature of the example, the surgery example does point to the necessary requirements for any disposition to work. A disposition must be credible, translucent, and long-lived. That is, it must not be private information; so that we see a link here to the standard accounts that stress asymmetry of information. Brain surgery was assumed to carry all three of these properties to the limit, but a workable disposition does not need limiting values.

I will now take the second step in our discussion of the dispositional approach to the reliance predicament and introduce the idea of a virtuous disposition. Consider the possibility that there are at least some agents in the community who perceive honesty to be a morally charged matter. They feel, we might suppose, moral guilt and shame if they deceive others.[19] Whatever the details, honesty/deception is an issue that triggers their desire to act as morality requires – independently of the impact of honesty/deception on their other interests. Such agents may wish to adopt a disposition to be honest by direct reference to this moral desire. I term such a disposition a virtuous or moral disposition. The disposition is moral in the simple sense that it is morally grounded: it involves an essential appeal to moral categories relating to the goodness or badness of acts. Two obvious questions arise in connection with such moral dispositions: how do moral dispositions operate in relation to interests, and how can they be acquired?

To begin, let us simply suppose that a moral disposition to be honest exists. If so, then it operates just like any other disposition. All dispositions operate to reconfigure decision-making over actions. A moral disposition differs from an egoistic disposition in its grounding, not in its mode of operation. But we would point to one particular aspect of the relationship between moral dispositions and interests. In the case of the reliance predicament, a moral commitment to honesty has an important, though contingent, property: namely that life may go better in terms of her own interests for an agent with such a moral disposition, than it would in the absence of such a disposition. In this case, then, a moral disposition carries no cost in terms of the sacrifice of interests. Indeed, on the contrary, the moral disposition actually promotes the agent's interests in a manner that is inaccessible to a disposition of narrow self-interest. To put the point in other words, the moral disposition of honesty is behaviorally equivalent to the disposition that would be chosen by the rational egoist if only there existed a credible and translucent means of commitment (as in the case of brain surgery). I do not claim that all moral dispositions have this property. Clearly, in other contexts, moral considerations might pick out dispositions that would carry costs in terms of the sacrifice of interests, and differ from the disposition that would be chosen by the rational egoist. The point is simply that there can be no general presumption that moral dispositions are always costly in terms of other interests.

I now turn to the question of the acquisition of moral dispositions. Again, the general point here is that the acquisition of a moral disposition is broadly comparable to the acquisition of any other disposition: A disposition is rationally acquired in light of the agent's full range of underlying desires and beliefs. The key difference is simply that a moral disposition depends crucially on the desire to act as morality requires, and on beliefs about the specific content of morality. An agent will have a reason to acquire a moral disposition to the extent that she believes that morality requires action of the particular type picked out by that disposition, and to the extent that the strength of her desire to act as morality requires is sufficient to overcome other pressures. This last point links to the discussion of the relationship between moral dispositions and interests. Where moral dispositions actually promote interests, we might expect such dispositions to be relatively widely chosen, since they require little moral strength; the simple belief that morality requires actions of the relevant type will be almost sufficient. In cases where moral dispositions carry costs in terms of interests, we might expect such dispositions to be less widespread, since they require greater moral strength: that is, a stronger desire to act than morality requires. In this way we might expect to observe heterogeneity in the dispositional make-up of the population, with some agents being "more moral" than others.

I take our discussion of trust and honesty to suggest support for three broad conclusions. First, that trustworthiness/honesty as a disposition may be privately profitable to those who possess it and are identifiable as such. In itself, this provides the basis for the prediction that trustworthiness/honesty is likely to emerge, although its scope may be limited and its foundations relatively fragile. Second, that honesty is best understood as a moral disposition that gains further support from broadly egoistic considerations. And third, that the moral dimension of honesty will have genuine behavioral consequences.

We would also suggest that everything we have said about the example of trust and honesty would apply with only detailed modification in other relevant examples. Honesty is by no means the only moral disposition that is relevant to issues of regulation and politics. I suggest that other such dispositions may be rationally accessible to agents with a basic desire to act morally. However, the extent to which such dispositions are realized in practice will depend not only on the strength of the underlying moral commitments, but also on other factors such as the presence of relevant institutional support.

Enforcement again

I now return to the issue of enforcement in order to illustrate the possibility that a type of mechanism may be identified which enhances or amplifies the social effect of whatever stock of virtue – in this case honesty – there may be in society. The mere existence of some dispositionally honest individuals – at least beyond some critical number – may be enough to allow such mechanisms to operate.

As already noted, the ancient challenge "Who shall guard the guardians?" has often been taken, in public choice circles and elsewhere, to demonstrate that appeal to external enforcement procedures as a means of resolving social dilemmas is question-begging: relying on enforcers seems no solution to the problem of the general unreliability of agents. But the question-begging nature of external enforcement depends on the background assumptions concerning motivation. The presence of just *some* reliably honest individuals in society may change our view of enforcement – not only because of the prospect of screening honest individuals into the role of enforcer, but simply as a result of the possibility that any enforcer selected at random will be honest.

To be more specific, we will reconsider the reliance predicament introduced above. Begin with the standard case in which everyone is an opportunistically rational egoist. As we said earlier, to be effective in such a world, enforcement must punish player **B** if she takes action **E**. If the punishment is large enough (greater than 1 in our example) it will be rational for **B** to choose **C**, and so it will be rational for **A** to choose **R**. If sufficient punishment can be relied upon, the threat of punishment will substitute for trust/honesty so that agents will act *as if* they are honest and thereby induce trusting behavior. Of course, if all act in this way under the threat of punishment, the punishment will never be invoked in equilibrium.

How might such an effective punishment regime be designed? The problem is how to limit and direct the powers of the enforcer. The obvious way to provide the enforcer with an incentive to punish would seem to be to allow the enforcer to retain (a share of) the "fine" imposed. But the enforcer then has an incentive to "fine" agents regardless of their actions. One step seems obvious: the enforcer should be brought into play only when requested by the injured party – enforcement should be "reactive" rather than "proactive" in this sense. Let us assume that this idea can be institutionalized. Figure 2 illustrates a modified version of the game. **A** now has an additional choice. If **A** chooses **R** and **B** chooses **E**, **A** now faces a second decision – whether or not to call in the enforcer. If called in, the enforcer will exercise her power to "fine" the agents by taking an amount x from **A** and an amount y from **B**.

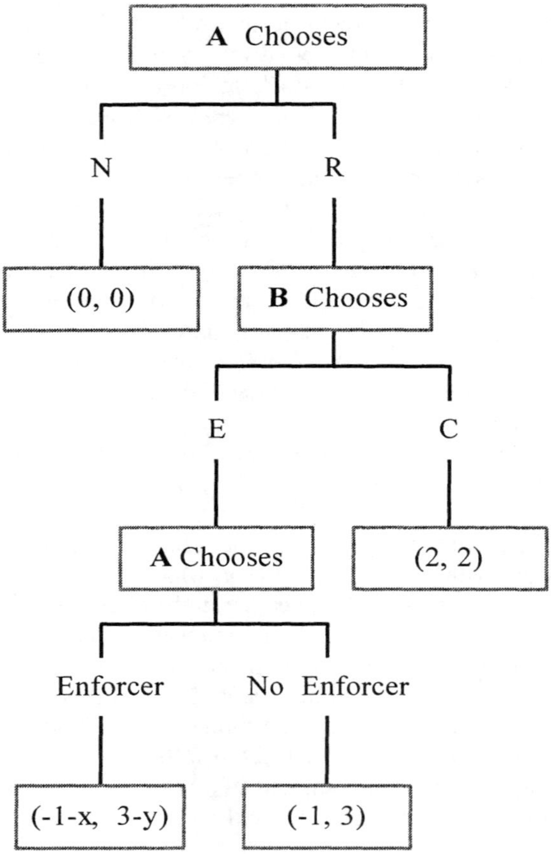

Figure 2: The reliance predicament with purely egoistic enforcement.

A will call in the enforcer only if enforcement is beneficial to her (that is, if $x < 0$). If enforcement is at all costly to **A**, it would be irrational for her to call in the enforcer even if this would punish **B** sufficiently to ensure that **B** would not choose **E** (that is, $y > 1$). In short, the threat of calling in the enforcer would not be credible unless $x < 0$, yet it will be impossible for an opportunistically rational enforcer to commit to setting $x < 0$ for exactly the same reasons that made it impossible for **B** to commit to **C.** If the threat of enforcement is not credible, the mere logical possibility of enforcement will not affect the way the game is played, so that it will still be rational for **A** to choose **N**. We conclude that while purely egoistic enforcement can help to realize the Pareto efficient outcome, it will only do so in very specific and somewhat limited conditions.[20]

How is this discussion of the reliance predicament and enforcement altered if we admit the existence of some dispositionally honest individuals? Assume that a non-zero proportion **p** of the population is honest in this sense, but that dispositions are totally opaque so that we cannot select for honesty. In the role of **B,** an honest individual would always choose **C.** In the role of enforcer, an honest individual will always act to compensate **A** in the event that **B** chooses **E,** and fine **B** to finance this compensation and, perhaps, to cover costs (z).

Even if no institution of enforcement is available, clearly the presence of honest individuals may allow the Pareto efficient outcome to be attained. As we noted earlier, the basic example of Figure 1 is such that a risk-neutral **A** will choose **R** if **p** > 0.33, and the Pareto efficient outcome will then be achieved if **B** is honest. Thus, provided that **p** > 0.33, the Pareto efficient outcome will be reached in a proportion **p** of cases. If **p** < 0.33 the Pareto efficient outcome will never be reached.

Now, if reactive enforcement is available, there is a probability **p** that the enforcer, if called into play, will turn out to be honest. This case is illustrated in Figure 3. The expected benefit to **A** from calling in the enforcer if **B** proves unreliable is now (2**p**+(1-**p**)(-1-x)), and this will be greater than the -1 payoff to not calling in the enforcer if x < 3**p**/(1-**p**). This, then, is the condition for the threat of enforcement to be credible. Assuming, as before, that y > 1, an egoistic **B** will choose **C** if the threat of enforcement is credible. Thus, whenever the threat of enforcement is credible, the Pareto efficient outcome will be realized.

So, in the case of partially virtuous enforcement, where some enforcers are dispositionally honest, the Pareto efficient outcome can be achieved in **all** cases provided that x < 3**p**/(1-**p**). This condition ties together critical values of the damage that can be done to the innocent party by a self-interested enforcer (x) and the probability that an individual chosen at random will be honest (**p**). Recall that in the purely egoistic case, enforcement improved the outcome of the predicament only if x < 0. In the case of some honest individuals but no enforcement, Pareto efficiency could be reached with probability **p**, when **p** > 0.33. But with some honest individuals and "reactive" enforcement, the Pareto efficient outcome can be reached in every case even if x > 0, or **p** < 0.33, provided that x < 3**p**/(1-**p**). For example, even if x = 1, the requirement is only that **p** > 0.25, so that any proportion of virtuous individuals above one quarter would be sufficient to realize the Pareto efficient outcome universally.

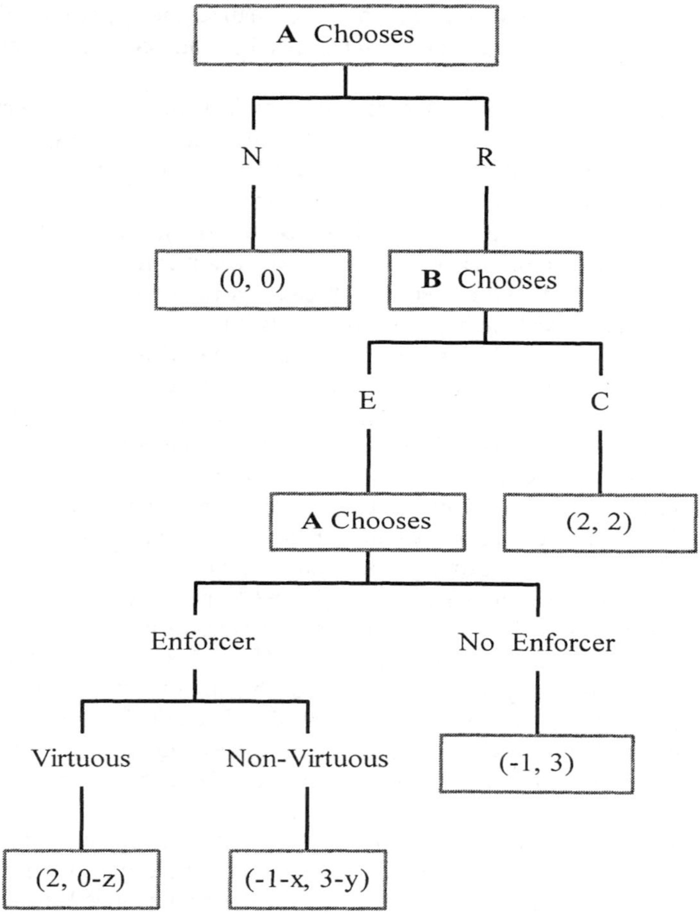

Figure 3: The reliance predicament with possibly virtuous enforcement.

The point I wish to emphasize here is that the recognition of the *existence* of even a minority of honest individuals can help to cut through the problem of "guarding the guardians." Of course, there are still issues to resolve in the design of enforcement mechanisms. There is a need to limit the harm that opportunistic enforcers can inflict on "innocent" parties (x), and the need to ensure that enforcement is reactive. But the mere existence of some honest individuals renders the institution of enforcement much more viable – even when there is no possibility of selecting for honesty and no attempt to increase the stock of honesty.

Enforcement can be a virtue-enhancing (in this case honesty-enhancing) mechanism: that is, hierarchical institutions of enforcement can serve to magnify the impact of the limited virtue that is available in society and make everyone act *as if* they were virtuous. In the earlier discussion of the standard economic approaches to deception, I stressed that it is always the threat of deception, rather than the actual practice of deception, that is the real problem. Standard economic models show that actual deception can be avoided in equilibrium, but the damage has already been done. One way to think about the approach outlined in this section is that the recognition of heterogeneous motivation directly addresses the issue of the assumed threat of deception, and so tackles the issue at its source. Indeed, I have indicated that even if the threat of deception is still strong (in the sense that the proportion of dispositionally honest individuals is relatively small), the explicit recognition of motivational heterogeneity can allow institutional strategies that may radically improve social outcomes.

Concluding remarks

Standard economic models barely touch on the issue of deception; in full or symmetric information models, deception is ruled out by assumption, and in asymmetric information models actual deception (as contrasted with the possibility or threat of deception) is not seen as a central issue. This is partly because these models do not admit of essentially normative concepts such as "deception," "honesty," or "trust," and focus almost entirely on each individual's optimal use of the resources (including informational resources) under her control. This does not imply that these models are uninteresting; indeed, they provide deep insights into a wide range of issues. They even provide a key initial insight into the idea of deception, via the idea of incentive compatibility and the revelation principle. The point here is that it is normally possible to avoid the occurrence of actual deception by the relatively simple means of structuring incentives to reward honesty – and that this can be done without any additional loss of efficiency. In a very loose sense, asymmetric information implies that the first-best equilibrium will not generally be available and that those individuals who have access to valuable private information will be able to extract a rent. But once this is recognized, whether we select an equilibrium in which the informed individuals achieve their rent via deception, or an equilibrium in which these individuals achieve their rent via the receipt of incentive payments that ensure that they honestly reveal the information, is largely immaterial.

All of this would be fine if deception were not itself a normatively charged concept. If we wish to consider the possibility that deception, honesty, trust, and so on, are normatively charged concepts, we must do so in an environment in which at least some of the individuals in our models recognize and are influenced by these normative concerns. The second half of this essay has therefore been concerned to sketch out an alternative approach to issues such as deception, honesty and trust that operates within a broadly economic (rational choice) framework, but which allows at least some of the individuals within the framework to be somewhat "virtuous" in that they recognize the "intrinsic" value of honesty or trust. In principle, such models might be applied to any subject matter, but the subject matter of the economic analysis of regulation and, particularly, politics, seems to provide especially important contexts, since in these areas appeal to normative considerations might be expected to be particularly relevant.

Notes

* An earlier draft of this paper benefited from discussion at a workshop on "Exchange, Deceptions and Self-Deceptions," held at the Maison de la Science de lHommes, Paris, 7-8th December 2001. I am grateful to the participants, and particularly Caroline Gerschlager, for their comments. Some parts of this paper draw on Brennan and Hamlin (2000) and I am happy to acknowledge Geoff Brennans contribution. As always, all errors remain my own.

1 For the beginning of an economic account of at least one form of self-deception see Akerlof (1989); for more general discussion see McLaughlin and Rorty (1988).

2 This aspect of the definition rules out not only any positive, other-regarding motivation, but also any motivation that hinges on conventions or social norms that govern communication within a group.

3 See Dahl (1963), Bell et al. (1969).

4 By serendipity, while this essay was in preparation, the 2001 Nobel Prize for economics was awarded (jointly to Akerlof, Spence and Stiglitz) for path-breaking work on the economics of asymmetric information in the 1970s. This follows the 1996 Nobel award to Mirrlees and Vickrey for related work. Riley (2001) provides a survey of the field, a text-book account is provided by Macho-Stadler and Perez-Castrillo (1997).

5 This simple idea relates only to the simple concept of deception defined above, if more positive or social forms of "deception" are

included in the definition, the normative status of deception may not be so clear.

6 See Williamson (1975; 1996). Williamson (1996, page 6) defines opportunism as "self interest seeking with guile" and refers to the asymmetric information setting as key.

7 See, for example, Holmstrom (1979; 1982).

8 The classic reference is Akerlof (1970).

9 A voluminous literature has developed, significant early papers include: Hurwitz (1972), Groves and Ledyard (1977), Myerson (1978), and Dasgupta, Hammond, and Maskin (1979).

10 For two relatively straightforward and early examples see Barro (1973) and Weingast (1984). For more general and modern discussions see Persson and Tabellini (2000), especially chapter 4.

11 See Clarke (1971), Groves and Ledyard (1977), Vickrey (1961).

12 For various attempts see Persson and Tabellini (2000), Brennan and Hamlin (2000) and references therein.

13 For a discussion and survey of the relevant literature, see Farrell and Rabin (1996).

14 See Brennan and Hamlin (1995; 2000), Frey (1997a; 1997b).

15 For an argument that political representation may act as a device for screening for virtue, see Brennan and Hamlin (1999).

16 An extensive literature on trust has developed in recent years; see, for example, Gambetta (1988), Hardin (1996), and Hollis (1998). The discussion here draws on Brennan and Hamlin (2000).

17 These three approaches are not mutually exclusive, so that emphasizing any one of them does not involve arguing against the other two.

18 Of course, an irreversible commitment to promise keeping may be costly in situations other than the reliance predicament, and the rational egoist contemplating the operation would balance expected costs and expected benefits.

19 I do not mean here to commit to a moral psychology in which it is an anxiety about bad feelings due to a bad action that induces the agent to act morally. It may just be that the agent feels that exploiting reliance is wrong: that view would in itself count against acting in that way. Guilt and shame are simply convenient heuristics to employ in depicting the agent's rationality.

20 In the setting of a repeated game an enforcer has an incentive to build a reputation for "fair" enforcement and so may credibly deliver a zero (or even negative) x. But this type of resolution of the dilemma by recourse to repetition is also available to the players directly, so that, again, the impact of the self-interested enforcer may be small.

References

Akerlof, G., 'The Market for "Lemons": Quality Uncertainty and the Market Mechanism', *Quarterly Journal of Economics*, 84 (1970), 488–500.

Akerlof, G., 'The Economics of Illusion', *Economics and Politics*, 1/1 (1989), 1–15.

Austen-Smith, D., 'Information Transmission in Debate', *American Journal of Political Science*, 34 (1990), 124–52.

Austen-Smith, D., 'Strategic Models of Talk in Political Decision Making', *International Political Science Review*, 13 (1992), 45–58.

Banerjee, A. and Somanathan, R., 'A Simple Model of Voice', *Quarterly Journal of Economics*, 116 (2001), 189–228.

Baron, D. and Myerson, R., 'Regulating a Monopoly with Unknown Costs', *Econometrica*, 50 (1982), 911–30.

Barro, R., 'The Control of Politicians: An Economic Model', *Public Choice*, 14 (1973), 19–42.

Bell, R., Edwards, D. V. and Wagner, R. H. (eds), *Political Power: A Reader in Theory and Research* (London: Macmillan, 1969).

Brennan, G. and Hamlin, A., 'Economizing on Virtue', *Constitutional Political Economy*, 6 (1995), 35–56.

Brennan, G. and Hamlin, A., 'On Political Representation', *British Journal of Political Science*, 29 (1999), 109–27.

Brennan, G. and Hamlin, A., *Democratic Devices and Desires* (Cambridge: Cambridge University Press, 2000).

Clarke, E., 'Multipart Pricing of Public Goods', *Public Choice*, 8 (1971), 19–33.

Dahl, R.A., *Modern Political Analysis* (Englewood Cliffs, NJ: Prentice-Hall, 1963).

Dasgupta, P., Hammond, P. and Maskin, E., 'The Implementation of Social Choice Rules: Some General Results on Incentive Compatibility', *Review of Economic Studies*, 46 (1979), 185–216.

Farrell, J. and Rabin, M., 'Cheap Talk', *Journal of Economic Perspectives*, 10/3 (1996), 103–18.

Frey, B., 'A Constitution for Knaves Crowds Out Civic Virtues', *Economic Journal*, 107 (1997a), 1043–53.

Frey, B., *Not Just for the Money* (Cheltenham: Edward Elgar, 1997b).

Gambetta, D., *Trust* (Oxford: Blackwell, 1988).

Grossman, S. and Hart, O., 'An Analysis of the Principal-Agent Problem', *Econometrica*, 51 (1983), 7–45.

Groves, T. and Ledyard, J., 'Optimal Allocation of Public Goods', *Econometrica*, 45 (1977), 783–809.

Hardin, R., 'Trustworthiness', *Ethics*, 107 (1996), 26–42.

Hayek, F. von, 'The Use of Knowledge within Society', *American Economic Review*, 35 (1945), 519–30.

Hollis, M., *Trust within Reason* (Cambridge: Cambridge University Press, 1998).

Holmstrom, B., 'Moral Hazard and Observability', *Bell Journal of Economics*, 10 (1979), 74–91.

Holmstrom, B., 'Moral Hazard in Teams', *Bell Journal of Economics*, 13 (1982), 324–40.

Hurwitz, L., 'On Informationally Decentralized Systems', in C. B. McGuire and R. Radner (eds), *Decision and Organization* (Amsterdam: North Holland, 1972).

Macho-Stadler, I. and Perez-Castrillo, J. D., *An Introduction to the Economics of Information: Incentives and Contracts* (Oxford: Oxford University Press, 1997).

McLaughlin, B. P. and Rorty, A. O. (eds), *Perspectives on Self-Deception* (Berkeley: University of California Press, 1988).

Mirrlees, J., 'An Exploration of the Theory of Optimum Income Taxation', *Review of Economic Studies*, 38 (1971), 175–208.

Mirrlees, J., 'The Optimal Structure of Incentives and Authority within an Organisation', *Bell Journal of Economics*, 7 (1976), 105–31.

Myerson, R., 'Incentive Compatibility and the Bargaining Problem', *Econometrica*, 47 (1978), 61–73.

Persson, T. and Tabellini, G., *Political Economics* (Cambridge, MA: MIT Press, 2000)

Riley, J., 'Silver Signals, Twenty-Five Years of Screening and Signalling', *Journal of Economic Literature*, 39 (2001), 432–78.

Samuelson, P. A., 'The Pure Theory of Public Expenditure', *Review of Economics and Statistics*, 36 (1954), 387–9.

Spence, M., *Market Signalling* (Cambridge MA: Harvard University Press, 1974).

Vickrey, W., 'Counterspeculation, Auctions and Competitive Sealed Tenders', *Journal of Finance*, 16 (1961), 8–37.

Weingast, B., 'The Congressional-Bureaucratic System: A Principal-Agent Perspective', *Public Choice*, 44 (1984), 147–92.

Williamson, O. E., *Markets and Hierarchies* (New York: The Free Press, 1975).

Williamson, O. E., *The Mechanisms of Governance* (Oxford: Oxford University Press, 1996).

9

Deception, Self-Deception and New Institutional Economics

Gisela Kubon-Gilke

Abstract

In the neoclassical model of general equilibrium, there is analytically no room for concepts of deception or self-deception. In New Institutional Economics this view changes. The threat of deception is important as exchange is characterized by asymmetric information or incomplete contracts. The main question of this paper deals with self-deception. It will be shown that it is of analytical importance to consider the relationships between cognitive laws of perception, emotions, motivations, and behavior of individuals. A context which favors suitable motives may lead to competitive advantages for the corresponding institutions. However, it is to some extent misleading to characterize these psychological effects as irrational or anomalous. As will be made clear, these considerations are of special importance for New Institutional Economics and for questions concerning the labor market. Further research is needed to analyze the relevance of psychological considerations for the effects of political measures. This concerns, for example, environmental policy, family policy, tax reforms, and implementing new forms of social security.

Introduction

Although deception and self-deception are relevant categories in the classical works of economics (see Gerschlager 2001), they lose this role with the development of neo-classical theory (see Moss in this volume). This paper aims to show that this is due for one part to the fact that neo-classical theories try to circumvent psychological foundations of human behavior by a rationality concept assuming that human beings behave *as if* they followed rational calculations. This "as if" assumption is based on competition and evolution concepts in its turn and does not allow any statements on "real" human behavior. Apart from this, it will be shown that there is no relevant form of deception under conditions of anonymous exchange, symmetrical and complete information, and verifiable contracts.

The situation changes if we leave the model world of general equilibrium. In New Institutional Economics (NIE), the institutional consequences of asymmetrical information are studied, among other things. While the neo-classical reference model may disregard any form of deception, as it is either not possible or not relevant, NIE approaches consider the threat of deception as an essential problem. They raise the question of which institutions or forms of contract will develop in order to make the compliance with mutual obligations credible, if the compliance with the contract is not in the genuine interest of the parties (that is, if there is not purely a problem of coordination). If a mutually advantageous exchange can only be realized by credible commitments, then the question is raised: which rules and institutions can guarantee them?

In this paper, I will present some very basic remarks on the concept of rationality and its relation to deception, and outline in short the basic arguments of New Institutional Economics with regard to the threat of deception. The problem of self-deception will be discussed under two aspects. First, there is the question in how far self-deception is compatible with the concept of bounded rationality, which is of considerable importance for institutional analysis. Second, there is the even more important question of whether self-deception or illusions in the sense of cognitive psychology are a foundation for credible commitments.

It is indeed possible, as will be demonstrated, to find explanations for credible commitments on these psychological foundations, but it seems to be inappropriate to refer to these laws of cognition simply with the term self-deception. Just as it can be criticized that the behavioral consequences of these effects are termed "anomalies" (see, for example, Frey 1997, who refers to the phenomenon that using rewards might lead to a loss of intrinsic motivation and, accordingly, to a reduction of effort or commitment),[1] it is misleading to consider the rules of perception as sources for self-deception, even if some examples of visual perception show that the structuring of single elements in a whole can lead to illusions (interpreted as misrepresentations of the transphenomenal world). These rules are in many cases very functional and mostly result in "reasonable" behavior. The relation between perception and emotions, cognition and behavior, is used as an example to demonstrate that a psychological foundation of institutional economics makes analytical sense. It will be shown that this leads to a quite different understanding of the term deception. In addition, it will be demonstrated that the term self-deception should be used with extreme care, so as not to put behavior as a whole, wrongly, under suspicion of irrationality, anomaly, and manipulation.

Rationality and deception

There are a number of reasons given for the use of the rationality assumption in economic analysis. Some economists are of the opinion that *homo economicus* indeed can be interpreted as a mirror of real behavior. Others claim that the rationality assumption models "worst case behavior." One of the most important justifications, however, uses an analogy to evolutionary theory.[2] Alchian (1950) argues that maximizing behavior by economic agents does not have to be justified in terms of their true objectives but rather by the results of competitive, or rather, evolutionary processes. Using an analogy to biology, he argues: "Consider ... the simplest type of biological evolution. Plants 'grow' on the sunny side of buildings not because they 'want to' in awareness of the fact that optimum or better conditions prevail there but rather because those leaves that happen to have more sunlight grow faster and their feeding systems become stronger" (Alchian 1950, p. 214). Even though the growing of the plants and the formation of the leaves is due to biological mechanisms, it is, according to Alchian, possible to model this process by assuming that "rational" leaves choose their individual positions accordingly. Alchian further argues that the same applies, for example, to firms and the profit maximization assumption or to households and the utility maximization hypothesis. He adds that it does not require the *motivation* to maximize utility. In his view, it is "an alternative method which treats the decisions and criteria dictated by the economic system as more important than those made by the individuals in it" (Alchian 1950, p. 213). He illustrates his idea concerning the dominance of the *system* as follows: "Assume that thousands of travelers set out from Chicago, selecting their roads completely at random and without foresight. Only our 'economist' knows that on but one road are there any gasoline stations. He can state categorically that travelers will *continue* to travel only on that road; those on other roads will soon run out of gas. Even though each has selected their route at random, we might have called those travelers who were so fortunate as to have picked the right road wise, efficient, foresighted, and so on" (Alchian 1950, p. 214).

This kind of justification for utility maximization is presented in a similar fashion – although without reference to evolutionary arguments – in the revealed preferences approach. The thesis says that real behavior, which is channeled by budget constraints, shows certain characteristics, which can be suitably described by the assumption of a utility function to be maximized. Indifference curves could be derived from real choices and budget restrictions. On this basis, experiments are made to find out whether real behavior corresponds to the axioms of the revealed preferences hypothesis. There are a number of studies in which even the revealed behavior of small children and animals leads to the conclusion that it could be described as utility-maximizing behavior, even though it is not based on explicit calculations (see, for example; Harbaugh, Krause, and Berry 2001).

These forms of justifying the utility maximization hypothesis, however, should be regarded with some reservations. In particular, the analytical approach is problematic if the preferences are endogenous and vary according to context. Holländer (2001), for example, shows that the statements of the revealed preferences model are no longer fully valid if utilities are interdependent in the sense of Duesenberry's approach. In other contexts, similar problems show up as well. In every case in which the preferences change with the context – for example, with the *kind* of restrictions – psychological considerations should be taken into account at least for the change of preferences; they can explain under which circumstances and in which way the context systematically influences the formation preferences (see Kubon-Gilke 1999).

These relationships could give rise to fundamental doubts with respect to the universal applicability of a rationality assumption without reference to psychological insights, but nevertheless, the rationality assumption is prevalent in mainstream economics. It should be noted that it is not possible to draw conclusions from this concept of rationality with respect to specific forms and consequences of deception or self-deception in the sense of psychological insights into human behavior. Remaining open are the motives people have and the cognitive laws that control their interpretations and actions.

This is also why in models applying as-if assumptions, the use of the term deception only makes sense in a very wide, evolutionary understanding of the term.[3] Accordingly, the term deception is not discussed solely in the context of competition in economic theory. It is also used in evolutionary models in biology. Biologists, too, usually do not interpret deception as *conscious* behavior. If, for example, certain species of animals mimic the appearance of other, poisonous species, one can hardly speak of a rational decision to deceive. Instead, the term deception is used for the effect of a behavior or of certain characteristics which are *functionally* equivalent to deception (see Dawkins 1978). At least in the choice of words, an as-if concept is implied, as evolved behavior is described as if the creatures in question or their genes acted consciously in that way. If one can refer to as-if rational behavior as deception at all, one could do it only in this kind of evolutionary context, for without a psychological background, we are not able to apply any concept of the intention to deceive or of purely deceptive effects of certain behavior.

In the economic model of general equilibrium, there is another reason why phenomena of deception do not enter the theoretical discussion. In this model, we are in a world without any transaction costs. It is directly assumed that exchange takes place without any friction. This also precludes deception, as far as it could affect the exchange negatively. Some economists are of the opinion that the model of general equilibrium only opens up a frame of reference, to which real economic phenomena are compared – in particular, combined with the question of how close the results of real economic behavior and competition come to those predicted by the general equilibrium. However, it is debatable whether, in view of real transaction costs, this model is a suitable point of reference in the sense of hypothetical isolation (see Schlicht 1985) or not. If a world without transaction costs is assumed, the constraints of the model must include that potential problems with regard to deception are solved, be it in a system of informal norms, by a perfect system of formal laws, under which every exchange agreement can be verified and put through, or by the individuals renouncing deception for other reasons.

New institutional economics and the threat of deception

Assuming that no advantageous exchange can be agreed upon and put through at no cost, the approaches of the NIE come into the focus of analysis. In NIE, the term exchange refers to the organization of an economy characterized by division of labor. Up to some limits specialization is perceived to be beneficial. However, the question arises of how to coordinate all the diverse economic activities carried out by the individuals so that the members of the society can make the best of it. Different coordination systems might perform this task. The economy can be coordinated using market exchange, a command system, a system of traditions, or a mix of different systems. NIE deals with the question of the evolution of institutions as means to make the coordination of economic activities easier and less costly.

According to North (1991, p. 97), institutions serve as restrictions for individuals, among other things preventing deception and the exchange problems resulting from it. He writes:

"Institutions are humanly devised constraints that structure political, economic, and social interaction. They consist of both informal constraints (sanctions, taboos, customs, traditions, and codes of conduct) and formal rules (constitutions, laws, property rights). Throughout history, institutions have been devised by human beings to create order and reduce uncertainty in exchange."

Uncertainty refers not only to uncertain states of the world, but also to whether individuals will keep their promises in relation to an exchange contract, and under which circumstances. Institutional Economics addresses the questions of how these rules of providing credible commitments are made, how they are stabilized, and how they channel economic transactions. This regards those rules which are necessary so that an exchange on the market can take place (for example, moral rules, property rights) as well as institutions which arise for economic activities on the market or instead of the market. If the use of the market system generates considerable transaction costs, there might evolve institutions instead of the market or structuring the market (for example, company size and structure, endogenous market regulations such as quality premiums).

In NIE, the term deception refers to two problems. In a narrow sense, it can be understood as not keeping promises or not performing what is agreed upon in contracts. In a wider sense, the term refers to hidden violations of social norms and laws.

An essential problem tackled in NIE is that rational individuals should be able and willing to exploit their position strategically in case of information advantages. This means that one cannot rely on simple promises because there are no incentives to keep the promises. If, for example, an employee promises to work with considerable effort, but the employer cannot observe this effort, then it is assumed that specific contractual clauses or other means are needed in order to make the employee keep his promise.

Partly, this possibility is referred to as "worst case" behavior, which can, however, not be excluded totally and thus must be prevented by suitable means. Another justification refers to the rationality assumption of the evolutionary justification described above. In principal-agent models, the threat of deception plays a role in so far as, because of asymmetrical information, a constraint of incentive compatibility, also referred to as truth-telling or self-selection constraint (see, for example, Mas-Colell, Whinston, and Green 1995, ch. 14),[4] is introduced into the profit maximization calculations of the principals who try to make an agent act according to their wishes. For the general problem of hidden information between owner and manager, reference is made to the revelation principle, which is valid for many incentive problems:

"A contract that asks the manager to announce the state θ and associates outcomes with the various announcements is known as a *revelation principle.* The revelation principle tells us that the owner can restrict himself to using a revelation mechanism for which the manager always responds truthfully; revelation mechanisms with this truthfulness property are known as incentive compatible (or truthful) revelation mechanisms" (Mas-Colell, Whinston, and Green 1995, p. 493).

In the case of incentive compatibility, it must be the best interest of the agent to reveal the state of the world truthfully and/or to fulfill the requirements of the contract. In equilibrium, there is no form of deception, but the threat of deception determines the forms of contracts or institutions which regulate the economic behavior of principals and agents. This is not only true in bilateral relationships, but also in complex situations with asymmetrical information. Tirole (1992), for example, shows that for the problem of side payments between controllers and employees in a company, there is a *grand contract*, which prevents the workers from shirking as well as causing the controllers to control the work results properly. Tirole draws the conclusion that side payments (as a kind of deception) will hardly arise. However, they still are a relevant problem but will not occur in equilibrium just because of suitable contracts. The same holds true, for instance, with regard to efficiency wages. The problem of costly monitoring and of workers who might shirk has to be considered by firms. The solution of paying efficiency wages or using other feasible and appropriate incentive systems prevents shirking. The problem of asymmetric information gives rise to specific institutional structures, but in equilibrium the shirking problem itself disappears and is not visible because all workers have incentives to choose high effort.

Also in other institutional economic approaches, the ultimate problem is to identify incentive structures which cause such behavior in individuals, so that the total surplus is as high as possible. Not only problems of asymmetric information arise. Phenomena, such as not being able to specify contracts completely or to verify information before third parties, lead to similar problems (for an overview, see Kubon-Gilke 1997, ch. 3).

In the theory of the firm, it is argued, with respect to specific investments, that in the case of incomplete contracts, those who invest specifically can be exploited, so that the way of negotiation and/or the distribution of property rights must be defined in a way that no exploitation is possible and the investors choose an efficient investment amount ex ante. The threat of deception – for example, the danger of exploiting specific investors – is once more a reason why institutions are regarded as a solution for making mutually credible commitments. Thus, one can state, in a very wide understanding, that the danger of promises not being kept is finally responsible for the institutional structure of economies. The distribution of property rights is interpreted as a *credible rule* when it comes to distributing a surplus and to exercising control rights. The rules can, among others, define the specific process of negotiation between the parties or the distribution of a surplus. As the results of the distribution are anticipated, they determine the ex-ante incentives and thus the amount of the surplus to be distributed later.

In the case in question, however, such rules must not necessarily be coupled to a certain distribution of property rights. Some kinds of contracts (for example, where one party is allowed to fix quantities and prices and the other party has to decide whether to accept or to reject the conditions) may generate identical incentives compared to a specific distribution of property rights. In the theory of the firm, however, not all contracts are regarded as admissible solutions. Instead, the analysis restricts itself to analyze the advantages of, for example, vertical integration as a specific distribution of property rights and the incentives carried out by property right structure. This may be because of the implicit assumption that, in the stage *before* the search of mechanisms for the distribution of property rights, some strategic problems – such as the premature exclusion of communication opportunities, the strategic division of the negotiations into sub-games, and so on – are not seen as relevant, as compared to other, contractual solutions, and that therefore certain opportunities of deception are not taken. This is, however, questionable, as the strategic possibilities when agreeing on negotiation mechanisms can be of such importance that a cooperative solution is prevented. If it is assumed that, given certain mechanisms or institutional arrangements, individuals would act in this context less strategically than under other circumstances, this implies that there must be effects on a psychological level that do not conform to the rationality assumption used otherwise and which must have decisive influence on the result of the analysis (for a more detailed discussion of these problems, see Kubon-Gilke 1997, ch. 3). At least, the reason for analyzing a certain subset of institutional solutions and disregarding analytically equivalent contractual solutions should be discussed.

The traditional approach of NIE using different forms of the rationality assumption reveals a specific concept based problem with regard to the threat of deception. It is attempted to explain all phenomena by a utility maximization hypothesis with preferences given exogenously. Thus decisive (psychological) mechanisms are implicitly driven into the constraints, which is hinted at in the ad-hoc formulation of the potential set of solutions in New Institutional Economics. The most prominent example refers to the theory of the firm. As mentioned above, most models do not consider equivalent contractual solutions of the problems discussed (for example, unverifiable forms of contracts and specificity of investments or effort). The same holds true for pre-selected solution sets regarding problems of asymmetric information or of implicitly assuming that some strategic problems are solved despite the fact that these solutions can hardly be explained by using the rationality assumption.

Some approaches in NIE part with the strict rationality assumption and introduce instead the concept of bounded rationality. The strict rationality assumption is loosened only in so far as cognitive restrictions are assumed which prevent the formulation of complete contracts, taking into account all potential circumstances for the future. The basic possibility of deception is discussed in the same way as in the strict rationality concept. Bounded rationality with its focus comes much closer to reality in certain aspects, but even this concept can be criticized. It is not sufficiently clear whether there is a basic turn in the direction of psychologically founded assumptions on behavior or whether it is just a modified as-if assumption for the case of transaction costs (see Schlicht 1990). Bounded rationality will not be discussed here in further detail, as the problem of behavioral assumptions is taken up again at a later stage.

Besides the already mentioned questions of institutional economics, in particular of the theory of the firm, there are other areas of economic theory where the arguments related to the threat of deception follow the same lines, but where, for example in the economics of crime, the cost of fighting perception is considered. The economics of crime is a prime example for the way in which economic theory treats the problems of deception.[5] Even this theoretical approach does not base the rationality assumption solely on the real behavior of individuals:

"...criminals respond to changes in opportunity costs, in the probability of apprehension, in the severity of punishment and in other relevant variables as if they were indeed the rational calculators of the economic model – and this regardless of whether the crime is committed for pecuniary gain or out of passion, or by well educated or poorly educated people" (Posner 1986, p. 206).

In the analysis of Becker (1968), the marginal damage caused by a criminal act is compared to the marginal cost of preventing the crime and thus a socially optimal measure of crime is derived. Even in this case, deception can only be understood in the evolutionary sense described above. The term denotes behavior which fulfils the function of deception, but in the behavioral assumption no supposition is implied with respect to the intentionality of a crime. To be exact, it is not even possible to discriminate between criminal and non-criminal behavior, as in all cases it is assumed that behavior results from utility maximization taking into account certain restrictions. The approach of the economics of crime can be characterized by saying that by a variation of some constraints – structure and amount of prices (sanctions) as well as intensity of control – the behavior of those individuals can be influenced who consider an action accompanied by externalities which, in common usage, is referred to as a crime.

Behavioral assumptions and NIE

Whereas economics of crime is concerned with the fact that the government causes individuals, by means of imposing sanctions (which could be interpreted as a kind of tax), to take into account the external effects of their (criminal) acts in their private calculations, the NIE arguments run differently, as they are looking for the endogenous emergence of institutions. The mechanism which controls institutional change is seen as similar to the market process of competition. Nevertheless, there are very different opinions on how this competition controls the emergence and stabilization of institutions. In the simplest cases, the purely functional argument uses the concept that the "useful" institutions are bound to arise in any case.

Behavioral assumptions and models of evolution

Demsetz (1988, p. 107) presents a prime example in his theory on the development of property rights. He argues that private property rights will arise if they are a means of internalizing external effects and if the advantages of internalization are greater than their cost. The argument of the economics of crime for the fight against crime is very similar, with the sole difference that Demsetz does not address the government with exogenous rules as a body creating suitable rules, but assumes that in any case exactly those rules will arise which will support the optimal internalization of external effects. The main difficulty of these concepts is that the mechanism which safeguards the evolution of socially useful rules is not named. In particular, it is to be taken into account that the costs of establishing private property rights depend essentially on whether individuals in general will spontaneously accept private property, or whether property rights have to be forced on them by external sanctioning mechanisms. Informal norms and the behavior of individuals must safeguard the mutual acceptance of these rights; otherwise, the cost of internalization of external effects by private property will be prohibitively high. Eggertson regards this as essential for the effectiveness of economic institutions, not just in the context of property rights:

"All societies ... depend vitally on self-enforcement, customary law, and value systems for preventing general conditions of open access and destructive wealth-seeking..." (Eggertsson 1990, p. 284).

While traditional market analysis regards all prerequisites for the functioning of the market as exogenous and places the rationality assumption within this framework, this is no longer possible on the level of competition between the institutions, simply because many institutions, like property rights, are reflected in norms and traditions. Thus, there is no simple way of transferring the competition argument to the level of institutions and to a model which explains property rights themselves as endogenous, and the adherence to norms of respecting property as exogenous. If Demsetz's purely functionalist argument is true, an honest society without any form of deception should evolve, with regard to norms and the adherence to norms, together with suitable forms of property. Apart from bringing differing opinions about the state of the world into accordance, an honest society would not need any courts because all promises would be kept and it would not be necessary to use third parties to enforce contracts. Therefore, the honest society is able to concentrate on productive activities and on (honest) exchange and does not have to battle transaction costs regarding threats of deception. This not only contradicts reality, it is furthermore not compatible with the rationality assumption in its strictest form, which is otherwise used. A rational member of an honest society would have strong incentives not to keep promises in every respect. For example, deviations must be expected in all cases of situations characterized by prisoners' dilemmas. Therefore, it does not seem possible to stabilize honesty in the long run.

As soon as an explanation is needed for informal norms, habits, and traditions, which are, firstly, institutions themselves and which, secondly, affect the costs of establishing other institutions, the as-if rationality argument is no longer suitable. This is due to the fact that the evolution of norms is guided by mechanisms other than competition on markets. Considering the different evolutionary systems, it is not possible to apply as-if rationality in general. Some of the models discussed in its stead are very problematic as well. If an argument of group evolution is used, as by Hayek (1969), which says that social rules arise spontaneously for the best of society *because* they serve the best interest of the group, it is overlooked that this leaves the usually individualistic frame of economic analysis as well as the fact that the group approach to evolution is very much debated (for criticism of group evolution, see Dawkins 1980, for a defense of this approach, see Sartorius 2002).

Besides the individual and the group the gene and/or relations are considered as suitable units of evolution of social behavior. The question of which behavior emerges as an evolutionarily (and culturally) stable strategy is posed on the genetic as well as on the tradigenetic level. Also in this approach, the possibility of deception is to be seen in an evolutionary sense. There are many examples from the animal world supporting arguments why no purely altruistic or "honest" behavior will emerge as evolutionary stable strategies. Dawkins (1980, pp. 333ff.) discusses the example of tern populations, in which it was possible to discern different behavior in individual birds. The majority of the terns catch fish for themselves ("honest fishers"). A minority of terns ("pirates") behaves as clepto-parasites and steals fish from other birds. Now the question is raised, in an as-if sense, of which strategy is best if there is only the choice of being either pirate or honest fisher. In the first instance, the answer depends on the proportion of pirates within the total population. Now assume that all terns are honest fishers, but one turns pirate:

"Since there are many honest fishers bringing fish back to the colony, the single pirate makes a good living, better than any honest fisher, who has to spend time and energy catching fish. So, if there is a genetic component to the difference between the two strategies (a big 'if'), we might predict that pirates, being favored by natural selection, would become more numerous in future generations. But now suppose pirates come to form the majority. To go to the extreme, suppose there were almost no honest fishers in the population at all. Why then, obviously everyone would starve, since no fish would be caught. Under these conditions a single honest fisher would do better than a typical pirate. Admittedly he would run a grave risk of losing most of the fish he caught, but so would any pirate losing the few fish that he succeeded in stealing. So, if there were many pirates and few fishers we would expect natural selection to favor the fisher strategy" (Dawkins 1980, p. 333).

With respect to human behavior, the assumption of complete rationality is abandoned sometimes in favor of the assumption of purely programmed behavior, and the question of stable behavior in an evolutionary context is raised which may contain elements of deception. As there are elements of learning besides the genetic way of passing on information, at least in the context of humans, the evolutionary argument is broadened by passing on information through learning processes in other approaches (see, for example, Boyd and Richerson 1994, p. 74).[6]

For all models which are closely related to evolutionary concepts, there is the problem that the selection process is described in detail, but the aspect of variation is considered only rudimentarily. Some implicit assumptions are made, which considerably influence the result and should thus receive more attention in analysis. One essential problem is, for example, that only a restricted set of potential behavior is assumed. When transferring the competition argument to the institutional level, a set of rules is pre-selected, and one of them emerges as superior in the context of evolution. Such assumptions lead to a disregard for certain forms of the threat of deception. In particular, different rules (mostly very simple behavioral rules) are considered, but it is not discussed that there might be different interpretations of what the rules imply, that rules might erode due to strategic behavior, and that there always is a kind of "fuzziness" with regard to behavior guided by social rules. It remains unclear why individuals, who are otherwise assumed to be totally or partly rational, should renounce certain options to create an advantage for themselves within the given framework of norms. In the following, this problem will be discussed in greater detail.

The problem of mutual understanding

Many informal rules leave considerable room for interpretation whether the norm was adhered to or not. If there is, for example, a norm to give a tip for certain kinds of services, then there is usually a certain range of acceptable amounts to be given. If all individuals chose the option of rounding off to the lower unit, the norm would change and erode in the course of time. But not only these informal norms show that, without a common understanding of what is meant by an agreement, there must be, after all, an overwhelming number of possibilities of deception, and even the most comprehensive contracts could hardly exclude that a person looking for his advantage finds an unusual interpretation of the agreement that frees him of his obligations. Here is an anecdotic example showing that, besides the literal meaning of an agreement, the common interpretation plays a very important role, with respect to the parties to the contract as well as with respect to an external body to be called in for the realization of the contract (see Cooter and Ulen 1988, p. 212 for the example): An American farmer replied to an advertisement in a small local newspaper, in which a seller promised, against a payment of $25, to describe a sure method of killing locusts and to send the necessary means to carry it out. The farmer sent in the money and received a small parcel with two wooden blocks. An attachment contained an instruction according to which a locust was to be placed on block A and then to be squashed with block B. The seller had fulfilled his promise in a literal sense, but nevertheless, all parties concerned, even the courts, which had to decide in this case, were fully aware that the way it was fulfilled did not correspond to the general understanding of what a buyer would expect from such a deal.

To keep the transaction costs of an exchange at an acceptable level, buyers and sellers need to have a similar understanding of the meaning of their agreement, and they must, in most cases, adhere spontaneously to the promises made. Without these prerequisites, one could not imagine how commerce via the Internet – be it simple sales at fixed prices or auctions – with its asynchronous payments and transfers of goods could be employed in the long term. All this leads to the question of how such supra-individual understandings arise and why people adhere to the corresponding rules of behavior if they, on the one hand, have room for deviation, and on the other, can anticipate how other people will act on the basis of these rules.

The strict rationality assumption does not contribute to the explanation of such phenomena. Bounded rationality with its focus on cognitive limitations at least refers to cognitive laws which could explain how rules arise, and why, in spite of a large number of different interpretations of a contract, all those concerned finally *know* which meaning is behind it. This implies that all individuals have a common understanding under which circumstances individuals behave in accordance to a contract or deceive individuals by inappropriate interpretations of contracts, agreements, or rules.

Cognition and rule formation

Cognition and self-deception

Self-deception has been a much-debated term in philosophy for a long time, as it seems to imply that somebody has knowledge of something, but at the same time deceives himself and does not have – or not accept for himself – knowledge of the thing in question. The philosophical traditions of the discussion on self deception will not be presented here in detail. The discussion could, however, be of interest also for economic theory because cognitive phenomena associated with self-perception show in which way human perception is organized, how rules form, and why it is possible that different individuals often spontaneously gain a common understanding of the transphenomenal world. This common understanding accompanied by obligations to act according to the perceived structures is an important source with regard to psychologically credible commitments.

In the frame of NIE, self-deception is usually associated with the fact that individuals do not make use of all strategic options or that an implicit pre-selection of institutions and rules can be defined, as other institutions are not compatible with the cognitive "restrictions." If cognitive laws are referred to, it is often said that, for example, visual perception would demonstrate how much influence context has on the structuring of impressions. A standard example is the following optical illusion in which one estimates the length of both lines differently.

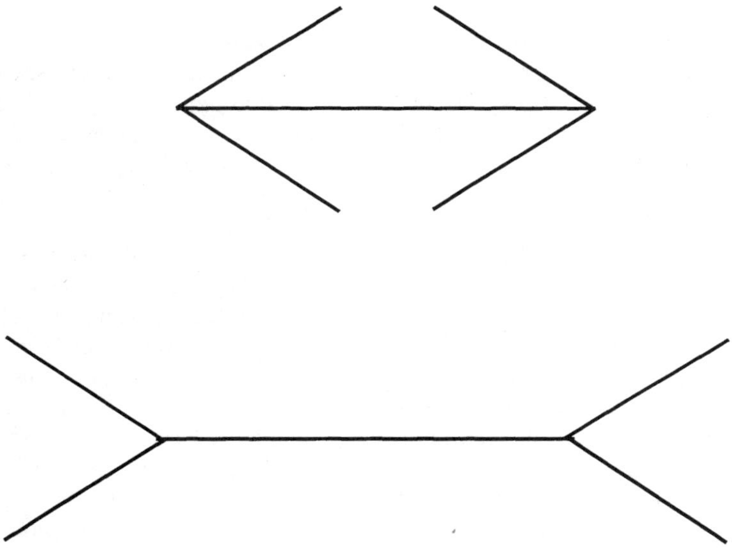

Figure 1: Müller-Lyer-Illusion (Metzger 1986)

The length of both lines is identical, but nevertheless it is hardly possible to escape the illusion that the lower one is longer. There are a number of examples of this kind. As the structuring of perception is supra-individual, visual perception is used as an example of why such rules and interpretations evolve which safeguard a common understanding of the parties concerned.

The use of the term "self deception" in this context is, however, highly problematic. Optical illusions merely give memorable examples of the rules at work in structuring perception. Without these rules, no appropriate and quick reaction to many events in the surroundings would be possible. In addition, these rules make it possible for people to communicate because they all perceive the transphenomenal world similarly. In most cases, the laws of perception and their impact on motivations and emotions may well lead to meaningful behavior. Furthermore, the use of the word self-deception raises the problem that emotions and motivations, which are inseparably linked to perception, could then be described inadequately as irrational or anomalous because this description misses the essential theoretical point, their importance for institutional analysis. This will be discussed below using some examples of theoretically relevant cognitive and motivational relevant effects

Cognition and behavior

In labor market theory, for instance, it is meanwhile of some importance to give more consideration to the concept of intrinsic motivation (see Deci 1975). It is pointed out that the institutional design in which work takes place is important for the individuals to perceive work contexts in such a way as to feel intrinsically motivated and to act accordingly. In general, it is agreed that the context of work determines how individuals motivate their own actions and how they behave. Frey (1997) argues that the motivational and behavioral effects due to changes of the perceived context are theoretically relevant and that they should be taken into account. He presents a vast range of examples to demonstrate that intrinsic motivation can be destroyed by specific incentives and regulations. In this respect, the restructuring of wage systems and hierarchies is considered to be of particular importance. However, in the case, for example, of environmental regulations, he argues that similar effects on perceived obligations might appear. This should be considered with regard to environmental measures. Frey introduces the concept of *homo economicus* maturus as an extension of the traditional model of *homo economicus*. All behavioral changes due to motivational changes he calls anomalies. The term anomaly refers to the phenomenon that destroying intrinsic motivation by incentives seems to contradict the traditional *homo economicus* assumption. In this sense he interprets the phenomena as an analytical anomaly. However, this might be problematic. In the following, it will be shown that this should not be considered as self-deception or anomalous, otherwise the real significance of these contexts is too quickly brushed aside.

The discussion of intrinsic and extrinsic motivation hints at the fact that motives and ways of behavior depend on the *reasons* – "enjoyment" of the activity or rewards – which are ascribed to one's own behavior and the behavior of others. Attribution theory (Kelley 1973, Heider 1977) analyzes the rules according to which these reasons are perceived and how this perception has a durable influence on the attitude to certain activities and on preferences. The laws of perception responsible for attributing our behavior to external incentives or, for example, to our own interest in the activity, are based, in their turn, on gestalt theoretical considerations on the structuring of perception and the associated emotional and motivational consequences.

In particular, works on visual perception have shown that the contents of perception are determined by characteristics such as simplicity, clarity, symmetry, and so on (gestalt laws), and that the elements are arranged in such a way that a concise and clear structure emerges, which cannot be characterized correctly by simply calling it an illusion. This is true for any kind of perception; it is not limited to optical vision. Just one example of these structuring phenomena: If people, within the frame of a memory experiment, are told a story which really consists of two stories; and the stories alternate with each other sentence by sentence, the test subjects can usually retell both stories without any difficulty. But it seems completely impossible to retell the mixed story.

Clarity, cognitive patterns, and attribution

Without presenting the basis of gestalt theory in detail (see Kubon-Gilke 1997, pp. 348ff.), some essential elements will be described in the following. The general organization principle of perception is particularly apparent in the use of *patterns*. Complex phenomena are associated with patterns, which show in their turn concise structuring. In visual perception, circles, squares, and regular triangles are concise geometrical figures. An individual figure, such as a very "angular" trapezium, is not memorized as that particular figure, but as a modification of a simple standard figure, in this case as a modified triangle. Perception of natural and social environments is organized on the same principles. In this case, the forming of patterns is called categorization. Specific social phenomena are associated with social patterns in the same way an angular trapezium is associated with a triangular pattern in visual perception. These social patterns are strongly connected with expectations of role behavior. Such roles are defined by certain interactions and are themselves abstract patterns. In the following, this will be discussed mainly with regard to motivational effects.

For questions of motivation it is of particular relevance that one's own behavior and that of others is judged according to simple patterns. *Prominent* reasons for behavior are required. According to Kelley (1973, p. 114), cause-effect relations are perceived via related causal patterns. In attribution theory it becomes particularly apparent that the development of individual motives is very closely related to the perception of such causal patterns. One's own behavior may be attributed to different causes. Teaching, for instance, might be attributed to different prominent causes such as focusing on the wage, the authority situation of an employee, the contribution to a common goal, or to be intrinsically interested in teaching itself. When structuring perceptive impressions, the causes which are considered as decisive receive more emphasis, other potential reasons are discounted. Kelley described this as the *discounting principle*.

In the context of the discussion on the destruction of intrinsic motivation by external incentives, it is furthermore of importance that the perception of certain facts can change. What happens when an individual receives new information? If this conforms to the clarity tendency, it can be associated with the current pattern of perception, accompanied by systematical structuring effects. However, if the "exceptions" become more and more obvious and the information in total fits the pattern less and less, then phenomena which are prone to slow changes can change abruptly and permanently in perception, which leads to corresponding changes in motivation. Precisely this phenomenon is discussed regarding the destruction of intrinsic motivation. In the above mentioned experiment, tested were the consequences which arise if – in case of a given internal attribution, which considers the subject's own interest in an activity as the *decisive* cause for its performance – an additional potential cause for the activity is introduced, which in principle contradicts this attribution. For instance, in experiments, initially intrinsically motivated individuals perform specific tasks such as completing puzzles. Introducing rewards systematically destroys the intrinsic motivation. If new prominent causes lead to a massive deviation from the currently given pattern, for example, if rewards are given for the activity that do not correspond to the internal attribution, then it may result in a different cause-effect relationship being attributed to the subject's own behavior. This implies corresponding changes in motivation and behavior. Deci (1975, p. 139), who uses a wide, but not very precise definition of intrinsic motivation and emphasizes not only the aspect of "enjoyment," gives an attribution theoretical explanation for his experimental results:

"Initially, subjects were intrinsically motivated and the perceived locus of causality was internal. They engaged in behavior because it provided them with internal rewards, that is, they did it in order to feel competent and self-determining. Then, when they were performing the activity in order to make money, so the perceived locus of causality became external, leaving them with less intrinsic motivation."

With respect to the question of how these insights can be integrated into economic models, just two specific problems will be mentioned here. First, the laws of perception show that pattern changes are abrupt and that additional incentives do not destroy intrinsic motivation step by step. Furthermore, the change of an attribution pattern can be characterized by strong hysteresis effects. If, given intrinsic motivation of employees, more and more performance-oriented wage components are introduced into the firm's wage system, which make the internal attribution less and less concise and finally lead to a sudden change in perception toward external attribution, then successively abolishing the performance-oriented components will not necessarily result in causing intrinsic motivation again at the same point of change. The structuring effects in the context of the new attribution pattern can lead to the phenomenon that only very massive changes of the wage system will cause the justification of one's own behavior to return to its original state.

Second, it is to be considered in economic modeling that the different patterns are not independent from each other, as they must make up a meaningful, concise structure in a kind of equilibrium process. This could mean that the change of perception on a certain level affects a number of other patterns, as the equilibrium of patterns was destroyed by the change, and a new, consistent whole emerges. An example for these relationships is given by an experiment by Bem and McConnell (1970).

"Bem and McConnell ... asked students who believed in increased student control over their university's curriculum to write an essay advocating precisely the opposite. The typical result occurred: students shifted their opinion toward the attitude in the essay" (Arkes and Garske 1982, p. 312).

Up to here, the findings correspond with many phenomena of the reduction of cognitive dissonance. If subjects are persuaded or caused by minimal incentives to write down a point of view totally contrary to their former attitude, individual problems of justification arise. This behavior usually cannot be attributed to external incentives, thus the dissonance is reduced by adjusting one's attitude to the point of view which is written down. In addition, the experiment gives a clear indication of the interdependence of the patterns. The students were asked after the experiment, which opinion they had supported *originally*. It is noteworthy that they had already given that in writing, named, to the researchers before the experiment started.

"Nevertheless, students falsely recalled that they had been initially much more in favor of decreased student control than they really were! Students misremembered their initial opinion by claiming that they really remained consistent with their present opinion all along" (Arkes and Garske 1982, p. 313).

The sudden change in a causal category can lead to a restructuring of the overall picture, in the case of the experiment described including the memory of previous attitudes. Frey (1997, pp. 41ff.) discusses similar phenomena under the heading "transfer effect," referring to the fact that the changes in intrinsic motivation as a consequence of changes in the incentive system in one area can also affect other areas as well, where the economic incentives did not change.

Deception in this context can be understood as a particular misunderstanding. In addition to intentional deception, it may occur, because of different experiences and contexts, that individuals associate identical information with different rules or patterns. In this sense it is at least possible that agreements can lead to misunderstandings and that the parties accuse each other of deception, while it is not possible to relate that to intentional deception.

After a short explanation of the psychological foundations of attribution theory to clarify the systematic relationship between intrinsic and extrinsic motivation, the question is relevant whether the distinction between intrinsic and extrinsic motivation is sufficient and useful for economic analysis, in particular for the theory of the firm.

Categories of motivation

The concept that intrinsic motivation is related to enjoyment of the activity does not fit many activities. Saving somebody's life or taking part in a civil war as a volunteer has nothing to do with "enjoyment." The distinction between extrinsic and intrinsic motivation seems extremely unsuitable in the case of behavior in a context of authority. The subjects in the famous experiment named for Milgram, who, apparently in an experiment on teaching methods, administered electric shocks to their so-called students (that was the perception of the subjects), did so not because of monetary incentives, as the participants in many series of experiments received little or no money. Sadistic enjoyment is not a good explanation either, as many of the subjects suffered from sleep disorders and other problems for a long time after the experiment and were deeply irritated about their own behavior (see Milgram 1974). In order to criticize the categorization of these phenomena either as intrinsic or as extrinsic motivation it is not sufficient to refer to the fact that there are more than just these two forms of motivation. Furthermore, the question must be raised whether it is not, after all, a useful simplification to include all motives which cannot be attributed to external controls or incentives into a second group of motivations, whatever the name of this group may be.

The problems of such a definition become most apparent in specific models based on this distinction. Frey (1997) states very clearly that not only monetary incentives, but also certain governmental rules and regulations can destroy intrinsic motivation. This thesis is supported by psychological knowledge, although in each case a very careful discussion is necessary about which kind of intervention influences attribution patterns and thus individual motivation in which way. The distinction between both kinds of motivation becomes particularly difficult if the potential *consequences* of the destruction of intrinsic motivation are no longer discussed, as there is only the category "extrinsic motivation" left, which leaves no room for further meaningful distinctions. If the cause of one's own behavior is not attributed internally, this is not the same as the attribution of one's own behavior to a typical wage and exchange pattern. This is made clear by the Milgram experiment.

In the discussion of gestalt theoretical foundations, it was argued that one's own behavior and the behavior of others is perceived on the basis of concise causal patterns. These are characterized by prominent, clearly differentiated structures, but there are typically more than *two* potential causal patterns for one's own behavior. Internal attributions and justification by remuneration are only two variations. Behavior can just as well be perceived as a contribution to a common goal or as submission in a hierarchical relationship. This leads to very different motivational and behavioral consequences as compared with the other two justifications of one's own behavior. Theory must not be too economical with categories, for otherwise essential relationships in the forming of motivation will be overlooked.

The question arises, however, whether it makes sense to use simply *more* categories of motivation, to define simply *different* categories, or whether the theoretical basis should start out from a different level than the specific causal patterns. The inflation of motivation categories without psychological foundation will soon appear to be arbitrary and therefore does not offer many perspectives. An alternative approach proposes to differentiate between *ego-centered and task-centered behavior* (Asch 1987, pp. 303ff.) Asch points out that the ego is not the entire control center of perceptions, emotions, motivation, and behavior. The starting point of motivational processes often lies in the perceived structures of the environment and their imperfection. Frequently, exemptions, differences, and inconsistencies in the categories perceived by individuals in great unanimity give reason to act – be it only to set a picture on the wall straight. In gestalt psychology, the concept of requiredness was formulated in this context (see Wertheimer 1991, pp. 50ff.) It refers to the fact that preferences and motives are *caused* or at least *influenced* by the context as perceived by individuals according to the laws of perception. From this theoretical background, a different picture of the nature of human behavior arises than from the as-if rationality assumption. The threat of deception plays a different role in analysis as well. Deception is thus no constant factor in human behavior. Whether promises are kept or not, how much effort is put into work, in how far a person supports colleagues in their tasks is not independent of the institutional context. Social psychologist Asch (1987, p. 24) writes on the consequences of requiredness:

"People have a need not to exploit others, but also to enter in productive relations with them. To share and play a part in the life of the group can become a matter of supreme interest. We should go further to say that they have a need to live with others truthfully, to establish relations of trust, good faith, and cooperation not based solely on the calculations of profit. They need to act according to what they perceive as inherently fitting, not only to follow arbitrary custom. It is perhaps not true that external suggestion, imitation, and prestige are *the* essential factors in the formation of attitudes and convictions. The grasping of the objective character of a social situation – of its structure, of the requirements it sets out for action – frequently plays a role."

Framing effects and credible commitment

In this context it is important to note that this description not only uses psychological knowledge in order to describe the ways in which individuals perceive their own behavior and their motivations. These relationships are also analytically relevant for NIE, as the context in firms, for instance, is essential for the motivation and behavior of employees, who cannot be simply "deceived" or manipulated by the context of the company, but whose behavior, because of institutional structures, influences the success of a firm. This view does not conform to principal-agent models. Principal-agent theory reduces motivational effects and mentions pure incentive effects. In contrast, in this paper it is argued that psychological effects of forming and changing motivations and obligations are of even more importance in order to understand the mechanisms of making commitments credible. Common understandings and perceived obligations make it possible to communicate and to make credible promises. The psychological basis of rule formation is important for the understanding of the structure of formal institutions such as laws or firms as well as for the analyses of informal rules and norms. The perception of obligations as a behavioral impact of the perceived context might be of special interest with regard to the analyses of trust (see Hamlin in this volume for modeling trust phenomena) because trust seems to be a very prominent example of mutually credible commitments beyond rationality. In the meanwhile, there are many examples of incorporating psychological effects into the *homo economicus* model (see, for example, Kubon-Gilke 1999 and 2001 for a discussion of some of those models). This might be possible by conscientiously formulating utility functions. However, it is necessary to discuss whether it is useful to refer to utility maximization or to directly applying the psychological theories to explain psychologically credible commitments. In any case, psychological theory has to be considered in detail. Without psychological theories "real" utility function cannot be derived; in addition, it is not possible to justify simple as-if assumptions or to base economic analysis directly on psychological mechanisms.

Even the distinction between ego-centered and task-centered behavior and the corresponding motives only make sense if the psychological foundation of the laws of perception, the forming of patterns, the possible sudden change and the interdependence of these patterns are taken into account. It must also be made clear that individuals attempt to behave consistent with the perceived patterns. On this theoretical basis, intrinsic and extrinsic motivation (in the sense of a wage system) are recognized as special cases of the general principle according to which individuals justify their own behavior via concise, prominent causes and strive for consistency with regard to the perceived cause-effect relationships. This theoretical basis is, as already mentioned, relevant for the theory of the firm, for the institutional design of companies can support various attribution patterns, which leads to very different behavior, depending on whether individuals act within a perceived authority, group, or performance wage context, or whether they attribute the cause of their behavior internally and really perceive "enjoyment" of their activity. All forms of motivation in this context are, neither in reality nor in analysis, an anomaly, nor are they expressions of self-deception, if this psychological basis is taken into account in economic analysis. This does not exclude the fact that, in certain cases, it may make sense to limit the analysis to one or two forms of motivation for reasons of simplification.

Conclusion

This paper has shown that there is no room for deception in the model of general equilibrium, first, because of the as-if rationality assumption, which does not allow statements on the motives of individuals, and second, because of the assumption that exchange takes place without friction. In New Institutional Economics this view changes, as the exchange analyzed is characterized by transaction costs. In the case of asymmetric information or incomplete contracts, the threat of deception is essential; the question is raised of which institutions allow individuals to make credible commitments with respect to their behavior. One criticism of NIE addresses the fact that under the prevailing rationality assumption, the threat of deception should be even more important. In some NIE models it is implicitly suggested that in some institutional contexts deception is less relevant than in others, because some contractual or institutional solutions are not considered as part of the feasible set of solutions. Such considerations could give rise to an interpretation that there is a relationship between deception and self-deception. However, this would be a very problematic interpretation. Psychological laws for the formation of rules can also show the analytically relevant importance of context for perception, motivation, emotions, and behavior of individuals. A context which favors suitable motives can lead to a competitive advantage for the corresponding institutions. However, it does not make sense to characterize the behavior of individuals influenced in this way as an expression of self-deception or as manipulated behavior. This may lead to regarding the functionality of laws of perception and the resulting behavior, which is in most cases meaningful and reasonable, as irrational or anomalous. The psychological effects are, in their turn, of analytical importance, as they may show, among other things, that there is no exogenous predisposition of individuals for deception and that this should not be assumed in an as-if sense either. The concept of requiredness makes it clear that individuals receive impulses for behavior from perceived structures and can establish genuine interest in cooperative social relationships in which the incentive for deception is not dominant.

Notes

1 The discussion of these effects does not focus solely on labor contracts but shows generally that behavior is due to the perceived context.
2 For the following arguments see Kubon-Gilke (1996).
3 For an instructive analysis of the problems involved in the as-if approach see Arni (1989).
4 Profit maximization by the principal, taking into account the agent's individual rationality constraint (who must at least be granted the reservation utility so that he accepts a contract) has no direct distribution implication. Instead, the only question raised is in how far principal and agent succeed in reaching the utility possibilities frontier.

5 It should be noted that crime does not necessarily imply intended or not intended deception. This depends on the definition of deception. Murder, theft, and fraud might be treated differently if deception is understood as not keeping promises. If deception is defined as hidden violation of social norms and laws, this broad definition incorporates all kinds of crime into the concept of deception.

6 Nevertheless, very simple learning models are used for deriving culturally stable strategies. These recur in particular on conditioning models, and there are a number of arguments as to why essential aspects of learning cannot be comprehensively described by these learning models (see Kubon-Gilke 2001).

References

Alchian, A. A., 'Uncertainty, Evolution, and Economic Theory', *Journal of Political Economy*, 58 (1950), 211–21.

Arkes, H. R. and Garske, J. P., *Psychological Theories of Motivation* (Monterey, CA: Brooks/Cole 1982).

Arni, J. L., *Die Kontroverse um die Realitätsnähe der Annahmen in der Ökonomie* (Grüsch: Rüegger 1989).

Asch, S. E., *Social Psychology* (Oxford and New York: Oxford University Press, 1987).

Becker, G. S., 'Crime and Punishment: An Economic Approach', *Journal of Political Economy*, 76 (1968), 169–217.

Bem, D. J. and McConnell, H. K., 'Testing the Self-Perception Explanation of the Dissonance Phenomenon: On the Salience of Premanipulation Attitudes', *Journal of Personality and Social Psychology*, 14 (1970), 23–31.

Boyd, R. and Richerson, P. J., 'The Evolution of Norms', *Journal of Institutional and Theoretical Economics*, 150/1 (1994), 72–87.

Cooter, R. and Ulen, T., *Law and Economics* (Glenview and London: Scott and Foresman, 1988)

Dawkins, R., *Das egoistische Gen* (Heidelberg: Springer, 1978).

Dawkins, R., 'Good Strategy or Evolutionarily Stable Strategy', in G. W. Barlow and J. Silverberg (eds), *Sociobiology: Beyond Nature/Nurture? Reports, Definitions, and Debate* (Boulder, CO: Westview Press, 1980), pp. 331–67.

Deci, E. L., *Intrinsic Motivation* (New York and London: Plenum Press, 1975).

Demsetz, H., *Ownership, Control, and the Firm: The Organization of Economic Activity*, I (Cambridge, MA and Oxford: Blackwell, 1988).

Eggertsson, T., *Economic Behavior and Institutions* (Cambridge: Cambridge University Press, 1990).

Festinger, L., *A Theory of Cognitive Dissonance* (Stanford, CA: Stanford University Press, 1957).

Frey, B. S., *Markt und Motivation. Wie ökonomische Anreize die (Arbeits-)Moral verdrängen* (Munich: Vahlen, 1997).

Gerschlager, C., 'Is (Self-)Deception an Indispensable Quality of Exchange? A New Approach to Adam Smith's Concept', in C. Gerschlager (ed.), *Expanding the Economic Concept of Exchange. Deception, Self-Deception and Illusions* (Boston, Dordrecht and London: Kluwer Academic Publishers, 2001), pp. 27–52.

Harbough, W. T., Krause, K. and Berry, T. R., 'GARP for Kids: On the Development of Rational Choice Behavior', *American Economic Review*, 91 (2001), 1539–45.

Hayek, F., *Freiburger Studien – Gesammelte Aufsätze* (Tübingen: Mohr [Siebeck], 1969).

Heider, F., *Psychologie der interpersonalen Beziehungen* (Stuttgart: Klett, 1977).

Holländer, H., 'On the Validity of Utility Statements: Standard Theory versus Duesenberry's', *Journal of Economic Behavior and Organization*, 45 (2001), 227–49.

Kelley, H. H., 'The Process of Causal Attribution', *American Psychologist*, 28 (1973), 107–28.

Kubon-Gilke, G., *Motivation und Beschäftigung* (Frankfurt and New York: Campus, 1990).

Kubon-Gilke, G., 'Institutional Economics and the Evolutionary Metaphor', *Journal of Institutional and Theoretical Economics*, 152 (1996), 723–38.

Kubon-Gilke, G., *Verhaltensbindung und die Evolution ökonomischer Institutionen* (Marburg: Metropolis, 1997).

Kubon-Gilke, G., 'Intrinsisch motiviertes Verhalten – nicht Anomalie sondern Normalfall?', in M. Held and H. G. Nutzinger (eds), *Institutionen prägen Menschen. Bausteine zu einer allgemeinen Institutionenökonomik* (Frankfurt and New York: Campus, 1999), pp. 44–64.

Kubon-Gilke, G., 'Verständnis und Einsicht. Kategorien psychologischer Lerntheorien und ihre Relevanz für ökonomische Fragen', *Ökonomie und Gesellschaft*, 17 (2001), 343–67.

Kubon-Gilke, G. and Schlicht, E., 'Gefordertheit und institutionelle Analyse am Beispiel des Eigentums', *Gestalt Theory*, 15 (1993), 257–73.

Mas-Colell, A., Whinston, M. D. and Green, J. R., *Microeconomic Theory* (New York and Oxford: Oxford University Press, 1995).

Metzger, W., 'Über optisch-haptische Maßtäuschungen an dreidimensionalen Gegenständen', in W. Metzger, *Gestaltpsychologie, Ausgewählte Werke aus den Jahren 1950 bis 1982*, ed. Michael Stadler and Heinrich Crabus (Frankfurt: Waldemar Kramer, 1986), pp. 291–321.

Milgram, S., *Das Milgram-Experiment* (Reinbek: Rowohlt, 1974).

North, D. C., 'Institutions', *Journal of Economic Perspectives,* 5/1 (1991), 97–112.

Posner, R., *Economic Analysis of Law*, 3rd edn (Boston and Toronto: Little, Brown & Co., 1986).

Sartorius, Chr., 'Die Evolution von Verteilungsgerechtigkeit', in M. Held, G. Kubon-Gilke and R. Sturn (eds), *Normative und institutionelle Grundfragen der Ökonomik, Jahrbuch 1: Gerechtigkeit als Voraussetzung für effizientes Wirtschaften* (Marburg: Metropolis, 2002), pp. 231–56.

Schlicht, E., *Isolation and Aggregation in Economics* (Heidelberg and New York: Springer, 1985)

Schlicht, E., 'Rationality, Bounded or not, and Institutional Analysis', *Journal of Institutional and Theoretical Economics*, 146 (1990), 703–19.

Schlicht, E., *On Custom in the Economy* (Oxford and New York: Oxford University Press, 1998).

Schlicht, E., 'Institutionen prägen Menschen', in M. Held and H. G. Nutzinger (eds), *Institutionen prägen Menschen* (Frankfurt and New York: Campus, 1999), pp. 30–43.

Schlicht, E., *Arbeitsmarkttheorie* (forthcoming 2004).

Smith, A., *Der Wohlstand der Nationen* [The Wealth of Nations, 1776] (Munich: DTV, 1983).

Tirole, J., 'Collusion and the Theory of Organizations', in J.-J. Laffont (ed.), *Advances in Economic Theory, Sixth World Congress*, II, Econometric Society Monographs No. 21 (Cambridge: Cambridge University Press, 1992), pp. 151–206.

Wertheimer, M., *Zur Gestaltpsychologie menschlicher Werte, Aufsätze 1934 – 1940*, ed. H. J. Walter (Opladen: Westdeutscher Verlag, 1991).

Part V

Preconditions of Markets and Deception: Anthropological Perspective

10

Deception and Its Preconditions: Issues Raised by Financial Markets*

Vincent-Antonin Lépinay and Ellen Hertz

Abstract

In this article, we attempt to debunk a classical view of deception in financial markets. Contrary to many popular accounts, deception is not a pervasive activity in these markets, or at least market participants do not act and speak as if it were. We therefore try to understand the precise conditions under which the feeling of being deceived takes form. We explore the reasons for this relatively infrequent feeling of deception and argue that the answer must be sought in the organization of financial exchanges themselves. We emphasize the complex web of elements (material, regulatory, moral) that contributes to these exchanges and we show how all of these elements must be aligned for the imputation of deception to make sense. One of the results of this article is to orient the investigation of deception increasingly toward an examination of the products or commodities exchanged (bonds, equities, more complex services), with the implication that too much attention has been paid to human motivations in research on the question of deception to date.

Introduction

Interdisciplinary efforts are always complicated, and especially so when they tackle a subject matter as rich and complex as the notion of deception. It seems to us that the first question one should raise when asked to join such an interdisciplinary project is: why? More specifically, we have been asked to join this project as "anthropologists of finance," we therefore ask what anthropology might provide that other disciplines cannot, and why finance has been selected as a particularly important area for exploration. In our opinion, what is asked of us is to provide insights into "the native point of view" within financial markets, to flesh out the descriptions of economic actors with empirical insights into their culture and values, beliefs and superstitions, social networks and class backgrounds. The choice of financial markets for an empirical contribution to this collective effort is justified by the fact that financial markets appear to be a particularly rich terrain for mining the question of deception: they involve large stakes, high volatility of prices, uncertain returns, competing modelizations of risk, a second-degree relation to what is termed the "real economy," the large influence on price formation of rumor, fads, and other phenomena considered to be purely social in nature, and the consequent emphasis on human factors in what is classified as the distortion of value.[1]

If this is a correct assessment of what is expected of us, our first task is then to clarify in what ways we can and cannot meet these expectations. This we do in the initial section of the text, first by discussing two issues – speculation and size – loosely related to deception in financial markets, which we nonetheless believe should be distinguished from it, and second by providing our working definition of deception. In the second section of the text, we outline the theoretical framework that we use to approach our material, and point to the ways in which this framework has shaped our empirical observations and the use we make of them. This section seeks to make clear the ways in which our approach differs from much of the literature in economic anthropology, and why we believe these differences are important. In the third section we present a number of vignettes, financial situations observed by Lépinay during his fieldwork in the dealing room of a leading Parisian bank. Through these vignettes, we seek to demonstrate that imputing causality for loss of value in financial markets is, both sociologically and technologically, a very complex business that rarely results in accusations of deception. Our presentation is thus based on the belief that, contrary to what one might expect, deception in financial markets is a relatively rare event.[2] We stress the fact that, as anthropologists, we are interested in the social preconditions, not the psychological likelihood, of deception. Thus, we arrive at the question of deception through the backdoor, as it were, by examining the conditions of the possibility of deception and what actors do in the absence of such conditions, as we believe this provides the most instructive manner for tackling the question of deception from an empirical point of view. Finally, in our conclusion we suggest a number of ways in which the social science of financial markets requires economic anthropology to rethink some of its key terms and premises.

Deception and the order of causes

Deception versus speculation

As we have said above, certain specific characteristics of financial markets are thought to make them particularly profitable arenas for deceptive practices. The large amounts of money at stake attract the greedy and unscrupulous. The reality of risk and uncertainty on many of these markets suggests that investors accept the possibility of losing money as part of the game and will be less likely to grumble or blame their loss on others. Likewise, the "irrationality" of financial markets, buffeted by rumors, fads, and bubbles, makes it impossible for actors to formulate objectively verifiable predictions about price movements, and thus makes it more difficult for them to identify empirically when they may have been deceived.

It is important to emphasize that while these features and others may indeed render certain forms of deception more likely in financial markets, they also make it more difficult to carry out deceptive schemes successfully. An unscrupulous fund wishing to rid itself of a poorly performing product may spread false rumors of coming profits in an attempt to raise share prices long enough to sell off its shares in a rising market, but it cannot predict the strength or duration of the market's reaction, and may find itself hoisted by its own petard. Price volatility creates the conditions for "unjustified" movement in the value of financial instruments, but this volatility can work against a would-be deceiver as well as for her. Likewise, the difficulty in distinguishing false information from true confronts all actors in the market, irrespective of the innocence or malice of their intentions.

In our view, one of the sources of the belief that financial markets are particularly prone to deceptive practices lies in the association that is made between speculation and deception. The notion of speculation is notoriously hard to pin down, and the features that distinguish it from its moral counterpart, investment, are vague and ideologically motivated.[3] Nonetheless, Keynes's classic discussion in *The General Theory of Employment, Interest and Money* will serve our purposes here. Keynes likens speculation:

"...to those newspaper competitions in which the competitors have to pick out the six prettiest faces from a hundred photographs, the prize being awarded to the competitor whose choice most nearly corresponds to the average preferences of the competitors as a whole; so that each competitor has to pick, not those faces which he himself finds prettiest, but those which he thinks likeliest to catch the fancy of the other competitors; all of whom are looking at the problem from the same point of view" (1936, p. 158).

What bothers Keynes in this passage is the boot-strapping or circular form that the determination of value takes in speculative markets. Value is disconnected from the "underlying" or "real" economy, and determined in relation not to the object of exchange but to estimations about others' estimations of that object, or worse still, to estimates about others' estimations of how still others will evaluate this same object, such that the "real" qualities of the object being evaluated cease to have any direct relevance for the determination of price.

The speculative quality of financial markets is a necessary feature of their organization, but it is often mistaken for a form of deception in and of itself. Like speculation, deception can involve a discrepancy between the "real" or "underlying" value of a financial instrument and the market value or price paid by a particular investor at a particular moment. In the case of speculation, the source of this discrepancy is collective and generalized; it resides in the particular way in which the mass of investors react to information and create price movements. In the case of deception, the source of this discrepancy is individual and localized – the result of an intention to deprive someone of value that she could have possessed. While these distinctions may appear clear in theory, they frequently collapse in practice, as the moral ambiguity associated with speculation is used as a narrative resource for imaging scenes of deception, and the anxiety provoked by the move away from the notion of "real" or "underlying" value spills over into fantasies of manipulation and control.

Deception and size

Many of these fantasies of manipulation and control revolve around the second misconception that we wish to draw attention to: the presumption, widespread in popular discussions of financial markets, that small is definitely not beautiful. This disdain for smallness generally takes the form of a fear that small investors are manipulated by large ones and more generally, by the market as a whole.[4] Contrary to this ideologically constructed picture, our analysis focuses on particulars. We believe that whether and when the difference between large and small, or professional traders and amateurs is important, is an empirical question.

There are two distinct aspects at work here. First, professionals are surrounded by equipment that allows for direct interventions in the markets. They are constantly fed by many sources of information, and nothing (or nearly nothing) can happen on the market that is not available for them to notice. Their ability to make this connection with the market is one of their greatest powers: the flows of information are literally plugged into their desks. In an economy mainly driven by news, this gives them an immense advantage over "unconnected" traders.

From this angle of comparison, individual traders are rarely able to compete with professionals. This difference, however, is shrinking, and more and more small investors are connected to real time sources of market information. At another level of operation, however, small traders are still systematically penalized. They are obliged to use the services of intermediaries and there is necessarily a lag between the moment they send their orders and their implementation by the intermediaries. Nonetheless, as we shall see, deception does not necessarily transpire through the manipulation of very small units of time. Time matters but not always on a first-come-first-serve basis. As in all strategic games, it is sometimes better not to strike first.

A second and more interesting element also requires us to distinguish small from big players. Small traders do not "weigh" as much as big, and this is a crucial drawback for the formulation of deceptive strategies. Individual traders are not able to bet much with their limited financial resources, whereas professionals have much greater capacities and can flood, or at least attempt to flood, the market when they want to manipulate prices. However, once again this distinction does not always hold. Professional traders are increasingly scrutinized by the risk management divisions of large institutional investors. The golden years when traders were free to develop their own strategies without any obligation to account for them are long gone. Today, their ability to move in any direction and to play the market according to "gut feelings" is highly circumscribed, and correlatively the surplus value of bigness that professionals could enjoy is limited. More troubling still, there is no such thing as a size sufficient to guarantee dominance on the market today. Even big players can be out-signaled when a great number of small players gather to make them err.

There is thus an interesting inversion of the disdain for smallness, which takes the form of the recent claim by professional traders on various U.S. financial markets that the day traders and amateur traders that flourished during the 1990s "distorted" the market; they made work difficult for the professionals. These professionals argued that small investors cannot search for accurate information, in part because they lack the most recent information technologies, in part because they lack the economic and social sophistication necessary to distinguish false rumors from reliable hints. These failings would not be a problem if they were limited to a small set of investors in the market. In such a case, the "noise" caused by these ill-informed exchangers would be filtered by better informed investors, to wit, the professionals. But in large enough proportions, "noise" becomes rumors and rumors beget "information." It is the last stage of this trend, of course, that is of primary concern for professional traders: false and true blend together in a way that prevents the traders from sorting out which one is to be followed and which can be overlooked. Of course, this search for purity by the "well informed" relies on a very questionable model of "information" on markets. Professionals portray themselves as the gate keepers of market efficiency. They found their critique on a very strong assumption that there exist fundamentals in the economy, and by resorting to this "real economy," they implicitly pave the way for a moral discourse about who is fit to play the market.

In our view, it is unproductive to start from the view that "small" players are positioned at a disadvantage with respect to deceptive practices, or, more generally, to divide the trading community into two (or more if one goes into more refined categories) groups and label them as potential victims or perpetrators, respectively, of deception. Such a starting point, often implicit in discourses surrounding financial markets, bypasses most of the interesting features specific to these markets and closes the investigation at the moment it should be opened. In this paper, we favor another perspective which consists in taking as a starting point for our analysis the precise ways in which market agents label themselves and other agents (big, small, "noisy," "follower," and so on).

Working definition of deception and the question of the "empirical"

In this paper, we define deception narrowly – too narrowly some would certainly say; but we will argue for the merits of this narrow definition in what follows. In our analysis, deception involves three elements: (i) the intention to deceive, (ii) an explicit or implicit measure of real value with reference to which the deception can take place, and (iii) a loss of value, whether or not this loss is perceived by the deceived party. The combination of these three elements eliminates certain practices from the purview of our study while including others. First and foremost, an obvious fact with interesting implications: loss of value on a financial market is necessary for deception to occur. The wisest scheme to deprive a gullible investor of her money by selling her shares in a company that is intentionally misrepresented does not amount to deception unless the investor actually loses money. If, by some set of circumstances, the shares take off and our gullible investor profits, the intention to deceive her amounts to naught. As already mentioned, the possibilities for failed deception of this sort are real.

If loss of value is a necessary but not a sufficient feature of deception, it is because this loss must be directly related to an identifiable cause, that is, as the effect (loss of value) of a cause (intention to deceive) on the part of the deceiving actor. Here, a methodological caveat is necessary: despite long-term fieldwork and intensive interviewing, the intentions of economic actors are scarcely more accessible to the anthropologist than to any other observer, for actors have very little interest in revealing their strategic behavior to this degree. The empirical question then becomes, under what conditions do financial actors *impute* their losses to the intentionality of other financial actors, and when can this imputation rise to the status of an accusation of deception. As social scientists, our object of study is not the intention to deceive itself, but the imputation by others of an intention to deceive. It is not necessary that the person thought to be deceived actually perceive the deception, but it is necessary that the imputation of deception be accompanied by an attempt to prove the intention to deceive from the discussions, records, communications, or actions surrounding the allegedly deceptive act.

Finally, and still less intuitively, deception is only present when an outside observer can identify with some certainty a "real" value out of which the deceiving party is cheating the deceived. Thus, a person who buys shares in a Silicon Valley start-up that fails is not a victim of deception, no matter how insistent and hyperbolic the salesperson, unless this sales person was in the position to know with some certainty something about the value of this company that she did not reveal to her client. Wishful thinking, eagerness to receive a commission on sales, impatience to be rid of a product about which one knows little, and a general tendency toward exaggeration and hype are all insufficient, not because they lack intentionality but because the measure of "real" value against which they are operating does not have sufficient consistency.

It is on the basis of this working definition of deception that we argue in this paper that, contrary to expectations and stereotypes, the conditions for successful deception in financial markets are not frequently met. We have already mentioned some of the generic reasons for this infrequency: all market actors are faced with the difficulties of sorting out useful information from "noise." Market volatility and "irrationality" affect would-be deceivers and victims alike. If we look at various financial contexts in more detail, as we will do in the third section of the text, we discover that the uncertain and mediated nature of financial markets has a great number of aspects, all of which condition the possibilities for successful deception. Financial markets depend on extremely complex instruments of all kinds: hardware, software, legal conventions, regulatory rules, time zones, and the Internet, to name just a few. They are exceedingly innovative, with new products invented and circulated before their inventors have fully understood their characteristics. They are, as we have said, extraordinarily information-sensitive, while at the same time producing enormous quantities of bad information. As a result, the occasions on which actors can allow themselves to think that they *have identified* values or intentions (others' or their own) with enough stability so as to manipulate them are rather few, and the occasions on which these manipulations work to produce the desired effect even fewer. Without clear and pre-defined ideas as to what is being exchanged on which terms by whom, it becomes much more difficult to formulate the intention to deceive and to know in relation to which standard of non-deception this deception is taking place. Both the nature and value of the products exchanged emerge only after complex processes of definition, modelization, portfoliation and valuation, performed separately or in concert by financial actors, some of whom are machines. This starting point leads us to our theoretical section in which we outline, as clearly as possible in the limited space available, the nature and specificities of our approach to the socio-anthropology of financial markets.

Theoretical framework

Anti-social social theory

Markets, particularly financial markets, are thoroughly mediated. They are loaded down with instruments and tools, settings and rules, models and algorithms, conventions and contracts, all mobilized for the completion of deals. This equipment is not "instrumental" but central to the functioning of these markets; without it, trades would quite simply not be possible. Prices would not be available on a regular basis, information would not flow from place to place, no one would be responsible for market-making or other forms of public service necessary to maintain liquidity, techniques for evaluating value would be so rudimentary as to prevent reasoned action, in short, markets would not be markets. All of this "machinery" literally makes the market: it is not the context and support for exchange that would take place some other way in its absence, but rather, constitutive of the exchange itself, necessary mediations that allow for the circulation of goods and services.[5]

If we insist rather heavily on this point, it is because it has been resisted with such force by much of orthodox economic analysis. Standard economic analysis has tended to categorize such instruments and rules as extraneous to what is purely "economic" about the exchange. In this paper, we mobilize an alternative way of defining the economy that refuses to take for granted the very contingent boundaries used by mainstream economics.[6] However, if our analysis cuts against the grain of standard economic approaches, it also rejects that division of intellectual labor whereby anthropologists come along after the context that allows for exchange has been thoroughly occulted and point out with a wag of the finger that human beings are not mere rational automatons, that they also "have culture." Thus, contrary to a large body of literature in economic anthropology, we do not claim that everything is culture (or any other analytical category), because this claim reduces to a magma of representations and value-oriented practices the different and specific institutional-technological systems that allow for different forms of exchange behavior and thus different forms of markets. Like institutional economists, we share an interest in the market effects of institutions and the ways price and value come into being variously in different settings. However, we are less at ease when it comes to tracing boundaries around economies as most institutional economists do, or even around institutions. Thus, for example, when examining a regulatory rule in financial markets, we would be inclined to treat this rule not as an institutional element *influencing* the formation of value that pre-exists it, but rather, as a part of the very possibility of determining certain forms of value for exchange in specific situations.

Our starting point is thus resolutely empirical, but in a way that might strike our readers as new. The idea is to describe as concretely as possible precisely what must happen, and who and what must be in place in all domains of the social field for a market to come into existence and function in the particular way it does. A lovely example of the kind of analysis we have in mind can be found in William Cronon's *Nature's Metropolis.*[7] Cronon describes with extraordinary care the changes that took place in the Chicago grain market during the latter half of the nineteenth century, ranging open-mindedly over the social horizon from new transportation technologies to changing patterns of rural-to-urban migration to new agricultural techniques, populist political movements, and evolving notions of urban planning. The author makes a refined social-theoretical argument that we wish to pursue in this research: where economists would treat a good part of this discussion of the Chicago markets (its infrastructures, rules, equipment, social movements) as involving non-economic features ancillary to the functioning of efficient markets, Cronon takes great care to inscribe the contingent coming-into-existence of different types of markets as a process embedded in the natural and cultural contexts of precise historical moments. Each combination of these elements makes up a different market but there is never a "real" market against which one could judge its empirical instantiations.

More generally, our focus on all forms of agents and not exclusively on persons comes from the Actor Network perspective in sociology.[8] Building on a large volume of studies in technology, science, and culture (sometimes referred to as "STS"), this perspective has developed a new and fruitful framework of analysis that attempts to assimilate the long neglected material conditions of the production of science and technology within an analysis of "culture" and "society" as traditionally understood. In so doing, Actor Network studies paradoxically rid social theory both of Actors, conceived as individuals equipped with will and autonomy, and of Networks, conceived as stable social formations. The greatest achievement of Actor Network Theory (ANT) for our purposes here is its focus on the negotiation of what it terms "commonalties" through the aggregation of agents of different natures. As a highly equipped arena, finance is a perfect domain for this approach.

This has some important implications for recent trends in economic anthropology. Instead of starting with a set of anthropological or sociological[9] categories that are meant to explain the economy better than economics, ANT's approach is to credit the thesis that what economists say about the economy deserves special treatment and cannot be simply dismissed. Thus, we seek to understand how the very technical nature of financial markets (how rules form, how values are computed, how investment decisions are made) has a bearing on the particular forms of deception one can find there. Deceptive behaviors do not spring out of thin air: they are grounded in very particular settings that need be described in order to understand how the financial milieu makes certain practices possible while excluding others.

Deception in equipped contexts

The material nature of markets, marketplaces, and exchange has some very important consequences for the analysis of deception. Specifically, the search for *responsibility* or *causality* cannot be limited to the realm of humans doing deals or trading in a neutral environment. Instead, it is now entangled in the complex workings of the equipped environment in which deals are being made. The exchange is no longer – but was it ever? – a face-to-face moment when people meet other people *over* deals. The intercourse is a completely different one, one that cannot be understood through the kinds of thought experiments philosophy produces when it tries to simulate these situations. Let us try to approach the specific features of this equipped exchange.

Deception arises in the context of actions that unfold in a technical arena. While aimed at someone or something through someone, the exchange is necessarily layered. The feelings that are triggered by events (for example, the slowdown of returns, the collapse of prices...) are not as simple as one might expect. One of the reasons for the relatively mild reactions to these events that one frequently observes when doing empirical research lies, we believe, in their interconnection. Price changes are related to the whole set of agents that can effectively shift them. A typology of situations can be identified, structured by the two extremes of the spectrum. On the one hand, the exchange partner can be pinpointed, as in classic accusations of bad faith: trader X blames trader Y for not disclosing information relevant to the real value of a stock traded over the counter. On the other hand, the assignment of responsibility can take more technical forms, involving not only traders but the machines used to send orders and the rules traders have to comply with to take part in the market: in such cases, trader X can blame no one but machines and/or rules for her failure to make a successful trade. To put it simply, we might say that because the deception is linked to bigger *beings,* it takes on different forms. While it was possible to locate the origin of the deceptive behavior in the first case, it is no longer possible when more heterogeneous elements drift into the picture. And this lack of human imputability can go as far as locating responsibility within the "market" as a whole, thus building a meta-entity that aggregates several layers of actors.

Thus, our research question: when in the chain of events and communications that leads to loss of value in the market does one actor impute this loss to another's deceptive intentions? In the following we will examine some of the elements specific to particular forms of financial exchange that block such a clear attribution of human responsibility – the ambivalence of preferences, the shifting nature of products, the mediated access to value, the possibilities for experimentation and exploration on the market – before coming to our discussion of the few examples of real-live deception we have been able to witness.

Conditions of the possibility of deception

Preferences and the possibility of deception

One of Lépinay's first assignments in the Paris bank for which he was conducting research allowed him to inquire into the day-to-day business of salespersons, traders, and engineers in the main trading room. Let us briefly describe the sales process that is usual for over-the-counter (OTC) financial products traded here. OTC products are tailor-made, usually for sale to company treasurers or wealthy individuals. In both cases, the clients are in search of a special product that can boost their portfolio or hedge risks against market fluctuations. The salesmen advertise the products customized by the bank and try to attract customers. The latter can compare the prices and products of different providers, either through a formal request for a proposal or through looser procedures involving trust-based relationships on the market.

This first negotiation – casting the qualities of the service, defining the market from which the product will take its value – is of paramount importance. The first step of such a trade often takes place in the dealing room. The clients are introduced to the world of finance in a very concrete manner: the salesman, who is trying to convince them to buy the bank's services, gives them a guided tour. Various signs are emitted to provide evidence for the rigor and solidity of the institution that proposes managing the client's capital.[10] Furthermore, the salesman appeals to the client's sense of self-importance by making clear the degree to which this is a service available only to the lucky few. The trust that the salesperson is trying to establish between them is nourished with many different ingredients, but this visit is one of the crucial and delicate steps in the process. Presence counts. But what are the potential clients provided with during this tour?

The visit quickly moves into a presentation in which the clients are shown the features of the services sold by the bank. Most of the time, the prospectuses are not very detailed. They lay out the conditions for the exchange and sometimes supply back tests that display the results of the products over the past years.[11] At this stage, the products are still very "soft" and malleable.[12] Lépinay, working with a salesperson, witnessed the following negotiation that involved the choice of a stock to be included in the client's basket:

> "Stockholm is a very good stock, but if you want, we can swap it with another one, we can put something less aggressive ... if you look at the span, it never collapsed and the volume is low ... you have to consider the market, who offers this kind of product? ... (a request from the client) ... but you have to tell me quickly so that I can negotiate with the engineers."

As this example demonstrates, many of the dimensions of the "product" being sold here – a basket of investment instruments taken as a whole – will remain unspecified for several weeks or even several months if the client hesitates. The bank, through its salesman and engineers, tries to shape the products with a view to turning them into something likely to become a "good" or a "service." This long period of framing, discussion, and assessment by the client sometimes terminates in a trade. Sometimes it dissolves and the salesman sets himself to the task of attracting the client with another product or attracting another client altogether.

As we have said above, without relatively clear and stable preferences, no deception can take place. And the conditions that allow for preferences to surface bring us back to the same material, collective, and mediated qualities of financial markets that we discussed above. Needless-to-say, there is a whole spectrum of possibilities accounting for the slow framing (or lack thereof) of preferences in an exchange. The framing of preferences can be hampered by an inability on one or the other side of the negotiation to determine the agent to whom the preference should be attributed. A representative from one of the companies that Lépinay studied acknowledged the lack of real cooperation with the bank salesmen and engineers: "they weren't driving us as we expected ... they weren't present when they should have been, at the crucial moments..." Thus, one of the greatest difficulties encountered in formalizing the notion of an exchange in finance lies in the irrelevance, under observed empirical conditions, of the notion of agent. This point extends far beyond the examples of the companies studied in this paper. Institutional economics has long shown how the agent-principal structure of firms jeopardizes a pure concept of company preferences.

Fuzzy financial service

Economics has already relaxed the strong assumption of neo-classical models wherein goods are defined, known, and understood in one and only one way.[13] In these models, goods do not make difficulties: they are available to common sense and they are not likely to deceive or even to trigger surprise in the consumer. But uncertainty is only one way to tackle the question of the definition of goods and services. Furthermore, it is not the way people in financial markets grasp the goods they buy and sell.

From the first interactions (meetings between salespersons and clients) to the moment when the product-service is incorporated within a portfolio and displays its performance on the market to be assessed by the buyer, "the" product constantly changes shape. As strange as this may seem, this reshaping challenges the possibility of deception. It further highlights another misconception in the common sense approach to financial services. At first glance, the fungible quality of financial products – the fact that, without distinct "use values" financial products seem to consist uniquely in a bottom line "exchange value" – would suggest that formulating decisions about what products "are" is easier than it is in the case of goods and services encumbered with other social uses. However, as it turns out, the bottom line is only one dimension of the complex possession of financial products we are trying to understand; other qualities such as "aggressiveness," relation to risk, relative newness, and market venue, are far more important in the initial probing toward the formulation of the product-service. Furthermore, the "bottom line" itself is constantly displaced by investors who can, through the articulation of new preferences, radically extend or shrink the timeframe within which this "bottom line" is supposed to hold.

This constant shifting challenges the possibility of deception by people involved in the exchange. More specifically, it is at one and the same time a resource for and a limit on the assignment of responsibility. As a resource, it is always possible for the client to demonstrate the shift in the nature of the product and to ask for compensation. This happens, for example, when clients expected a high return from a security and experienced a loss. It functions, to the contrary, as a limit when the reshaping of the product detaches it from its originator. The link that justified the claim of liability slowly dissolves, finishing as a vague imputation. These modifications do not necessarily take clear forms; sometimes they are even quite imperceptible, and because they take place in contexts of overall change, they do not lend themselves to easy identification.

Furthermore, when the trade is done, the story is not over. The client can and does take advantage of the service provided by the bank throughout the life of the product. For example, when he wants it redesigned to adjust to his new needs or when he asks for a new mode of settlement from the bank, he slightly modifies the service for which he has contracted. The service takes on successive contents over the time of the contract, from its first steps to its closing (at term, and even sometimes after term when the term ceases to function, as when still other events happen to the contract). Each step of this long chain of events is handled by different persons in the bank but also in the investing company.

Another series of interviews that Lépinay conducted with treasurers dealing in similar products (OTC customized contracts for complex treasury bonds) highlights the problem of the formation of preferences. The slow process of the exchange described from the perspective of the dealing room had its equivalent in the companies.[14] The same hesitation was at work among the treasurers, and more importantly, the same proliferation of people contributing to the deal. Each case displayed its own formula but the common element was the fracturing of the decision-making process. Given the amounts of money involved, it was not only the treasurer but also the chief financial officer and sometimes even the board of directors who made these decisions. This should not come as a surprise: in big companies, decisions, like property, are collective. But the outcome of a fractured decision often turned out to be a decision that fits with none of the expectations of any of the participants

Product definition and agent preferences are intimately connected here. In this example, because the product remained inchoate, the *preference* of the company experienced the most severe difficulties in coming to light and when it did it was no longer a *preference* but rather the pallid result of a complex procedure.[15] Furthermore, the *instability* of company preferences was even more striking than the difficulty they had coming into existence. Sometimes, decisions were simply postponed for months for lack of a clear *need* articulated by the accounting department. No decision was possible because too many criteria were available and possibly relevant for a judgment to be made. The treasurer did not know on which grounds he was being asked to choose among possibilities, and the companies had too many different goals to pursue, scattered across too many different options, to allow for a decision to be made.

This continual renegotiation of the form of the service following the shifting nature of the client's preferences raises the broader question of how the parties to the exchange recognize the products with the passing of time? Which features do they hang onto in order to construe it as one and the same product and not as a series of different products? When preferences and products obtain this degree of dynamism, the question of deception must be examined by taking into account not so much the intentions of the economic actors, but all of those moments when they are swaying *between* intentions, responding to the shifting nature of a product which itself is in a constantly shifting relation to economic value.

From this point of view, financial exchanges are not different from any other arena of exchange. It turns out that their fabric (flows of money) is not what it seems, a one-dimensional space easily grasped and translatable into calculative terms. To the contrary, though money is at stake in these exchanges, this can be said only *a posteriori.*

Distributed imputation: dealing with machines, dealing with people

Once the nature of the client's preferences and the service or good she is purchasing have been determined, however temporarily, the product is placed in the hands of traders. However, the kinds of responsibility that these traders exercise vary enormously, as does the nature of their interactions with the market. During his fieldwork, Lépinay was given the opportunity to spend time with traders, a couple of weeks in all. We draw from this period two descriptions of the everyday work of two traders, which serve to illustrate the very different frameworks of human-machine responsibility under which traders in the same firm operate.

The first of these traders – for simplicity's sake we call him the simple product trader (SP) – trades listed CAC Index options.[16] He acts as a market maker and a proprietary trader simultaneously, a strange feature of financial markets that has been under scrutiny by financial economics and financial microstructure analysts. As a market maker, he *regulates* the listed CAC Index options market for which he has been assigned responsibility by the regulatory body of the Parisian financial markets; his job is to assure liquidity for these options. As a proprietary trader, he reactivates his greed and seeks out profitable strategies for the portfolio he is managing on his own (or rather, the bank's) accounts.

Our second trader manages more complex products, built from common stock or options – we call him the complex product (CP) trader. Once sold by the bank salesmen, the trader is in charge of hedging the bank's commitment. He is mostly occupied with understanding how his portfolio behaves. For this purpose, he is assisted by a series of tools: software providing him with great quantities of information about the swift changes occurring on the market and, more central to his concerns, changes in the value of his own portfolio.

We use this comparison to illustrate the phenomenon of what we call distributed imputation. Distributed imputation is a concept that allows us to formulate the great variety of scenarios involved in the assignment of causality or responsibility in financial markets and elsewhere.[17] Sometimes, macro-entities may be at issue, the burden of the responsibility for loss of value being carried entirely by non-humans. The shifting of this burden from one individual to another, from individuals to commonalities, from commonalities to techniques and so on involves a constant reshuffling of ideational categories by social actors. The work of decoding these hierarchies of imputation is the everyday occupation of people involved in exchanges. It amounts to ranking, distributing, and sharing chains of causation and responsibility among a highly heterogeneous network of beings. In the two examples that follow, we see two very different chains of imputation at work, as well as the ambivalences and uncertainties that surround these chains for the traders involved.

The everyday work of an SP trader

The day begins just before 9 a.m. The various machines that will be used during the day are switched on. Some of them were not switched off the day before because of back-ups in the information to be processed by the information technology department. His telephone is located in the middle of the desk, just under the computer screen. The phone turret[18] is small, with digital keys and pre-dialed number keys for the more frequent calls. It will be the more important tool in his daily work. The microphone is at the tip of a flexible handle and the trader will move it several times a day in accordance with his feelings for his interlocutor. He will use it as a singer would, grasping the tip forcefully when he wants to show (or at least convey through audio waves) anger. When he wants to send an order to his broker, he comes closer to the microphone and whispers as if to protect his order from the "market." When he settles a special joint product through joint orders, he increases the secrecy of his intervention, speaking even lower and articulating his sentences like a minister. The trader is seated on a very comfortable rolling chair, but unlike most of the other office chairs, his actually slides on the floor of the trading room. He spends most of his time on his rolling chair, in various positions depending on his decision in relation to the market.[19] Gracefully, he glides around his desk on flat, smooth ground, from one instrument to the other, back and forth from his chief's desk to his assistant trader's workstation. These bodily dispositions are important, for they display the nature of the work he is performing; clearly, there are many theatrical features to this job.

At 9 a.m., the market opens and the first contacts with the brokers take place. Lépinay's trader's telephone is programmed with a dozen pre-dialed brokers' numbers, but he deals mostly with only three. With these happy few, the discussion is lively, playful and sometimes very childish. They come back to the deals that were not concluded the day before, the remaining offers of other traders. The broker indicates the trend of the market as he sees it emerging, the bid-offer spread for each maturity already filled with prices by other traders. Whenever another trader sends an offer or a bid to a broker, the trader who gets the information takes it into account and fills what he calls his "volatility table." This is nearly the only tool he uses to get a grip on the market apart from prices. And this is also the most time consuming activity for the trader: staring at the table for hours to spot inconsistencies in the market and discussing them with his brokers to find out where the market is going.

From one perspective, the material infrastructure necessary for this activity is very crude and rough. From another, it could be said that it is simply light. As we have seen, he fills his volatility table with the prices other traders offer on the market. Each intersection of a column (maturity) and a row (strike price) is filled with a price and the software yields the volatility magnitude for this product. A couple of months before we studied this trader, he had designed his own software, a simple macro on EXCEL, at a time when he was fed up with calculating volatility on a pocket calculator. In addition to the current volatility table, every day at noon his assistant hands him the volatility table and prices from the previous day's transactions. The two of them along with the chief of the desk then comment on the changes that occurred during the day.

Taking care of one's books

The trader uses the knowledge he gains from these calculative practices both to act as a market maker and to take care of his own books. This often amounts to building financial "montages" to fill gaps in current supplies of derivative products. By simultaneously buying and selling different simple products, one can coin a new being, with new properties, a brand new "meta product" to hedge as yet unanticipated risks. These "montages" require complete commitment from the broker and the hard work of scanning the market to find the right dealers. Specifically, if the trader seeking to hedge this new risk wants, for example, to buy one and sell two SP of different maturities, he needs these transactions to be completed simultaneously without any delays that could leave him with an incomplete "meta-product," that is a larger risk exposure than that which he faced initially. Under these conditions, the broker has to make the whole deal for the trader, going back to the traders on both sides to barter. Finally, when he reaches an agreement with the parties, he coordinates the sending of the orders so that the Paris stock exchange can match them.

The greatest tensions that Lépinay witnessed during his fieldwork stemmed from this kind of transaction. One of the reasons is that the trader has to unveil his "interests," his weakness, and his strength. He is compelled to offer a lot of information to the broker if he wants him to cooperate. Without the broker, it is difficult for the trader to get a grip on and an understanding of the market. Because product prices are also reflected in the trader's own volatility table, he is not forced into relying entirely on his brokers for information. However, much of the information the trader retrieves from the market is filtered by his brokers and these can do much harm to a blindly trusting trader. More importantly, he has to go through his broker and use him to arrange the deals (not only but mostly the "montages"). From this point of view, the broker really *is* the deal for the trader. Lépinay's trader did not hesitate to tell him of "shifty brokers" who had betrayed him and with whom he no longer wants to have dealings.

The trader that Lépinay followed had a lot of stories to tell about cheating and mistrust on the market. However, he was also dependent on his equipment in a way that his stories did not always reflect. One day, as Lépinay was observing his activities, an SP trader turned down an offer to trade. When asked why he refused to trade with this person, the unexpected reply was:

> "On too short terms, I don't have a pricer subtle enough to yield precise pricing; I usually don't trade on these terms, I would rather trade on longer term securities. Previously, I would, but I got stuck into a bad valuation and I lost money because of the pricer. We don't develop very refined pricers here [at the bank]."

The question that came to mind immediately was: how can he so easily express doubt about his pricer in this case, whereas in other cases he makes so little mention of his tools (pricers, volatility table...). So far, these tools had remained hidden behind the personal nature of the market. The market was essentially a human affair between brokers and traders *about* prices. But with an order appearing on a different set of trades – options with close terms – the market took on quite a different look. Its human nature did not suddenly disappear. Instead, it shifted to the background, superseded by the equipped nature of this sub-market. This new configuration of "the market" features faulty equipment rather than deceptive human traders. The reason why these other traders and brokers, once feared, move to the back of the new landscape is quite simple: without a precise pricer giving him the value of his options, fearing the traders is not yet an issue.[20] He cannot even make use of these valuables. But neither can his opponents on the market, unless they are equipped with a more *refined pricer*. Thus, even if the person is brought back into the framework of this potential moment of deception, he comes back equipped. It is no longer a subject that is held responsible, it is an equipped subject and this difference is enormous when studying the question of deception.

When we move to the other part of the tale of two traders, we discover a case that takes us one step further toward the erasure of human activity on the market.

The everyday work of a complex products trader

The Complex Products (CP) traders usually manage the books for over 500 products, not for the bank's own accounts but for the clients'. The bank sells contracts to the clients, either institutional or individual. They invest money in products and get a reward, following a formula that mixes different types of financial instruments.[21] The traders must make sure the bank will be able to pay off what it owes its clients at the term of the contract. Basically, he is only in charge of the "insurance," hedging the bank's commitments; he does not have to make the most of it or to take risks; the bank has already recuperated the market price of this product through its commercial margin. This hedging activity occupies him all day long, for as these product formulae blend securities from all over the world, the trader must turn from one market to another, following their closing times. During the time Lépinay did his field research with these traders, they were preoccupied by a new class of products, named "correlation" or "worst of" products. They were part of a growing class of product; capital guarantee securities.

A simplified example will help the reader form an idea of the nature of this beast. Twenty stocks from major European companies are gathered in a product. The client does not get an average of this mix; the formula is much trickier. What he gets, in addition to his initial investment, is a percentage (usually greater than 100) of the worst performing stock's return. Hedging such a product requires buying everyday the least performing stock and selling others – bought the day before when they were the least performing. This reshuffling of his portfolio is roughly all the trader does, and can do, in a day's work.

When the trader arrives at his desk before 9 a.m., he launches the pricers that have not run during the night. Pricers are software, very complex and expensive, devised by the information technology department devoted to Structured Products Computer Support. They are supposed to supply the trader with the value of these products at any time of the day and night. However, these products are so complex that the pricers require several hours to run and give a decent approximation of product value. If the trader wants to have the whole book's value, he has to launch several pricers, frequently triggering the first pricer at the closing of the previous day. Complex products such as the one dealt in this dealing room need Monte Carlo simulation processing, a very slow program but the only secure solution found so far. The result of this slow treatment is striking when compared with our previous trader. Most of the time, the traders cannot say whether their bottom line is positive or negative at any given moment. Whereas the SP traders can know their position instantly if they know the price, the CP traders spend hours in this very strange waiting attitude. He is compelled to wait and to rely on his slow equipment, all the while attempting to anticipate what the market shifts will have done to his portfolio.

A first comparison with the SP traders reveals two very different temporalities. CP traders sometimes say they are paid to *watch over* the machines, and taking a nap is not ill-considered; it is out of the question for SP traders. Another difference in the temporalities of these products can be found in the modes of hedging. The products with multiple underlying instruments usually require hedging on different market places with different opening hours. Tokyo, New York (NYSE and the NASDAQ), Chicago, and all the main European markets need to be scrutinized. The scattered geography of hedging is very confusing.

Because the prices of one market influence those of the others and the value of the products are dependent on the correlations between them and the underlying products, the traders cannot settle their operations on the markets in a simple fashion. The pricers run on very different prices, some dating back to the day before, some from only a couple of hours ago, and the value is always changing, reshuffled by different moves hundreds or thousands of kilometers from each other.

Bypassing the pricers: doing calculus with a pen

The processing of information by the pricers usually comes to an end toward 3 p.m. and the French market closes at 5:30 p.m. Nonetheless, it is common that the pricers do not complete their task by the end of the day. They can fail to make enough "tries," to simulate enough possible paths or they can break down during processing. In these cases, the trader must take over the responsibility for valuation and an even more striking configuration occurs. Lépinay had the occasion to witness this several times, mainly because he carried out his fieldwork during a very choppy period. When the equipment surrenders, the trader tries to mimic the computer and software with cognitive abilities much less powerful and wide-ranging than that of the computer. He has to resort to an intuitive treatment of the product dynamics. Instead of carrying out simulation procedures, he considers the curves of the stocks (or a bunch of stocks) he wants to analyze and applies classical tools of analysis. From the prices he observes, he builds an implicit function and derives its first derivative. From this, he can define the number of stocks he needs to buy to hedge his position. One has to keep in mind the roughness of this treatment. The pricers and the risk analysis software generally use the first, second, and crossed derivatives to assess products. The traders cannot go that far, not only because they do not have the time but because they are neither trained nor equipped to do so.[22] The desk is so packed with keyboards, telephones, and other things that they literally quite simply have no place to do their calculus. It was during such a day (a "manual day") that Lépinay understood why pocket calculators are such a precious resource (and why each trader writes his name on his).

Whereas, in the case of the SP traders, the difficulties came from their relations with brokers and other traders, in the case of CP traders, clearly the difficulties shift toward interactions with the equipment supporting the understanding of products on the market. Complex Products are not sleek market items; they depend too much on complex tools to be valued in a continuous way and their chaotic temporality runs against their commodity features. The question of the fairness of the moves is hampered, distorted, and even blocked by the complexity of the products.

He cannot disaggregate the market down to a unit small enough to make sense of the accusation of deception. The other individual who would be the cause of his loss is beyond his reach, blurred by the complexity of the product at hand. For the CP trader, neither deceiving nor being deceived is a technical possibility. True, their portfolios may be affected by the deceptive activities of various actors on various markets: the revelation that a Tokyo bank has been concealing its bankrupt state, for example, may send all manner of shockwaves through the markets and these may be reflected in the valuation of her portfolio, but the individuation necessary for a successful act of deception is quite simply unavailable within the chain of imputation.

Trading as experiments and exploration

In the previous sections, we have tried to illustrate the various ways in which expectations about products on financial markets can be too vague or mediated to allow for either the practice or the experience of deception. In this section, we would like to highlight another approach to the market, in which the entire purpose of traders' activities changes nature. For both amateur and professional traders, there are moments when the market is viewed not as a source of potential wealth but as a source of pure information. These moments of exploration or experimentation involve approaching the market with a set of intentions quite distinct from those deployed in more stereotypical market scenarios. They are instructive because they demonstrate the fragility of the assumption that everything that goes on in financial markets can be understood as a form of applied greed. To the contrary, traders often act just to "see what happens," and while this may be in the service of profit-making in the long run, their behavior requires different explanatory tools.

Learning by losing: Alice in Internet

Our first example of trading as experimentation comes from a study of amateur on-line traders that Lépinay and his colleague Fabrice Rousseau launched in November 1999.[23] They were amazed by the growing success of financial services provided on line in a country where managing one's own assets was not common and was often even looked down upon. The very slow rise in individual investor activity seemed to take on a different speed when the Internet allowed for direct access to the market. Thus far, individual investors had asked the advice of bank specialists and the products put forth by these intermediaries were often *balanced products,*[24] mixes of bonds, currencies, and common stocks. The French legislation fostered long-term investment in these products by exempting them from taxes when individuals held on to them for more than four years. But the financial market was not considered a place for small individual investors. The only people who would set foot in this arena were wealthy individuals with long expertise in financial affairs.

The euphoric period of the "Internet bubble" brought to the market a completely different population. While the daily trades on the Paris Stock Exchange were still in the hands of professional investors, the proportion of trades made by individuals grew substantially. More importantly for our purposes, the population of small investors changed even more markedly. The rationales that brought them into the market were far from simple. During our first month of interviews, we met a young woman[25] who had been trading for less than a year. We decided to follow her during her trading sessions.

Alice's trading practices are highly enlightening for our analysis of deception, as they allow us to highlight a regime of economic activity different from that of economists' accounts. Financial exchanges are about making money, but they require their participants to affront the omnipresent need to map markets in order to take valuable positions in them. Alice conceived of her trading activity as a test, a way (among others at her disposal) to retrieve pieces of information about the New Economy. She consistently refused to take positions on "Old Economy" common stocks as well as on blue chips of the New Economy.

> "I trade with a view to understand the way the NASDAQ moves ... the lighter the noise and the less rational, the more I invest. No way, I am not going to spend money on AOL or any other SSII. ... If I don't like a company, if there is nothing it can teach me or if everybody buys it, I am definitely not going to buy it. ... The companies [on which she bet] have to thrill me, as symbols of market strategies or because they have interesting business models. I don't care about financial mechanisms. ... I use my deals as means to exercise intuition. It is really an intuition practice. There is only CISCO where I didn't exercise my intuition. I knew it was in the heart of INTERNET."

The amount of money that she invested in this trading was not significant from a professional standpoint. Nonetheless, from her point of view it was something. It meant something and she did not act foolishly when it came to changing her positions. Making *experiments* was not exactly like playing a game. There was some importance to it but it is precisely the quality of this importance that we must try to understand.

An interesting connection with the notion of deception is to be found in her approach to the economy. Alice never imputed the high volatility of her stocks to the other traders or, more globally, to financial operators.

When she learned that she had been let down by a bet, she always linked her disappointment not to the financial arena through the usual figures of manipulation, bad assessment, bubble driven positions and the like, but to people operating in the *real economy*. This bypassing of finance was formulated at several levels of the economy: the company as a whole (which had failed to convince investors of its own solidity or that of its products, or to establish the right marketing campaign); more specifically still, the public relations department of the company (it had hired the wrong publicist);[26] more generally, customers (not up to the innovation put forth by the company), etc. She regularly asserted that most Internet company failures were due to a lack of *ripe markets*, once again providing a very "non financial" account of financial distress. When we discussed the failure of a new company that sold a combo TV-computer, she went on: "the TV system is stupid and dumb ... people are getting more and more intelligent and they are willing to get more and more intelligent facilities ... all intelligent facilities trigger intelligent usage" and she concluded her point with the strange, nearly naïve, statement, "People are not ripe for this technology yet."

None of these causal chains takes into account the layering of price determination in financial markets. Instead, the ductility of this market opened up for Alice the possibility of a link to the real economy, as she downplayed the role of financial intermediaries and brought other actors to the foreground. Alice set aside finance as an explanatory category. Instead, she related her feelings (judgments) about the value of her investment to the analysis of what she took to be underlying them. Our focus on Alice is thus meant to shed light on a neglected sequence of market practices. Our point is not that the experience of deception among this type of financial operator is impossible. Our point is to highlight the fact that trading on the market can be viewed as not a game to win or lose but rather as an educational or experimental process, interesting in its own right. Furthermore, the pedagogy that Alice applies here is not limited to this kind of trader (amateurs, small amounts of capital, women, etc.). Instead, testing the market for signs and moods is one of the main activities of professional traders as well, at certain rather well defined moments in their day.

Bouncing the market back and forth

Professional traders, while following very different patterns of action and justification than those displayed by Alice, also conduct experiments on and with the market. Indeed, the very heaviness of their equipment, their professional networks, and the information they must process requires that they dispose of certain exploratory regimes and practices designed to help them qualify the "feel" of the market. This is well demonstrated in a recent study of the construction of derivatives markets in the U.S. in the 1970s. Donald MacKenzie had the opportunity to interview traders who had experienced two different organizations of the markets over the course of their careers: "human" markets, where pricing was "man-made," determined by open outcry in the trading pits, and "scientific" markets in which pricers delivered the prices through automatic matching of bids and offers. 27 One of these traders employed a telling metaphor to describe his daily morning activities: "I bounce the market back and forth," he said, to describe how he would emit small signals (small orders to buy or sell at experimental prices) and analyze the feedback in order to evaluate the market.

Like the ping pong player that bounces his ball before serving, the trader exercises a series of tests on the market, seeking relevant information before committing himself. He cannot just ask for information from the market, he has to dive into it, observing how his presence modifies the very waters in which he is swimming, in order to resurface with an accurate sounding. For our purposes here, the important thing to note is that during this experimental phase, the feeling and practice of deception are impossible. The trader tests a series of hypothesis and all of the information he receives, whether "positive" (his hypothesis proves correct and he makes money) or "negative" (his hypothesis appears incorrect and he loses money), is equally useful.

This first phase is followed by a second, non-experimental phase, in which the market is approached as if stabilized; the trader simply decides, or rather the normal trading routines decide for him, that the market is to be treated as stable after a certain number of experimental moves. The market may be acting in a very choppy and volatile fashion, but as long as the trader does not suffer "unduly" from this volatility, the trader can stick to his morning mapping. In this phase, the market has been differentiated enough to allow for an imputation of intentionality or at least of articulation. It is thus only during this second period, where the market has been mapped and interpreted, no matter how rapidly, that feelings of deception become possible.

Of course, these "phases" are intertwined and it would be a simplification (one that traders themselves apparently indulge in) to say that mapping out necessarily takes place in the morning, quickly followed by trading in a stable environment. We need not insist on a clear distinction between exploratory and "real" trading regimes to make the point we wish to emphasize here. The importance of exploration for the question of deception lies in the interpretive premises on which it is based. Exploration involves interacting with what is taken to be an unknown object. Alice and the professional trader take different manifestations of the unknown as the object of these interactions. Alice, much less equipped than our professional trader, is engaged in a long process of knowledge acquisition about not only financial markets but also what she takes to be a "real economy" from which financial mediations are absent. The professional trader has temporally circumscribed the unknown, through well-defined trading routines. For both of them, however, these are moments when they are interacting with the market as matter, not as the human actors which seem, at other moments, to comprise it.

What we are emphasizing, then, is the ways in which, particularly for the professional trader, the market can appear as purified "object" at one moment, and purified "subject" at another. It is in its purified subject incarnation that the market is capable of producing the feelings of real-live deception, to which we now turn.

Purified deception

Reading the market

In some rare cases, markets allow for the clear imputation of a loss of value to the intentional acts of another economic agent. Lépinay was given the chance to witness one of these moments during his fieldwork. The bank he was studying had served as underwriter for a company on the primary market for corporate bonds. Its sales department was in charge of finding clients for these bonds. One afternoon as the salesmen were experiencing considerable difficulties selling these instruments, the head of sales stood up all of a sudden and exclaimed with a little smile of understanding: "That's Merrill Lynch. Merrill Lynch is flooding the market!" He had "seen behind" the market, reduced it to an identifiable unit, its general opaqueness giving way to momentary transparency. For this brief instant, the head of sales could pinpoint the motives and identity of the agent that was troubling his new issue.

As should be clear by now, this case comes at the end of a long and slow process of market "decantation"; the series of conditions we have been examining were finally met. First of all, products and preferences were specified: this particular bond issue from this particular corporate client had taken shape. Their issuing price on the primary market had been determined through negotiation between the various underwriters and the underlying corporation. The attribution of motives was also clear: the sales team now had to sell as many of these bonds as possible for their client. The head of sales knew perfectly well that his bonus depended quite directly on the results of the success of this particular underwriting effort. Furthermore, his income and prestige depended indirectly on this success as well, for if the issue went well, other companies would ask for the bank's services.

A second element was in place as well. The transparency of market information was not clouded in this case by the alternative temporality and agency of calculative equipment. Unlike the traders trying to evaluate the worth of their stocks, the head of sales can *ignore* the medium through which he retrieves his information from the market. He reads value directly off the Bloomberg screen that displays the bid for this class of bonds, and no computation of complex interactions among prices and products is necessary.

As a third element, the "real economy" and financial markets could, in this case, be clearly distinguished. If we focus on the first steps of "the career" of this bond, we see that the issuing price is not even a *market magnitude* since, like all primary issues, it has been evaluated on an accounting basis. The "real economy" – the economic state of the company, the worth of its business, the current state of the market for competing products, etc. – has been factored into the issuing price by economists in the banks rating the new issue, and the number of bonds issued is then determined in relation to these criteria. Thus, at the moment of issue the market is not yet reacting in relation to changes in the "real economy," and the Head of Sales need not consider the possibility of this sort of influence if he notices a rapid change in price. Instead, he can presume that price will vary only in relation to supply and demand of this or like bonds.

Last but not least, the Head of Sales can identify a motive for the deceptive behavior: Merrill Lynch is a competitor, has not underwritten this bond, and wants its sales to go as poorly as possible. Furthermore, the Head of Sales happened to know that Merrill Lynch was underwriting another company's bonds on the primary market. The two companies were very much alike and the clients willing to buy one company's securities would probably not buy the other company's as well. The Head of Sales considered this simultaneity as an intentional attack, basing his judgment on the low price Merrill Lynch had set for its offer. His verdict was that Merrill Lynch was dumping its supply on the market with the intention to bring down prices.

Finally, all of the conditions are met and it is possible to talk of deception as a form of human behavior meant to deprive another human on a market of something to which it has a certain right (the right to a fair market price for a corporate bond). Everything is in place for a real experience of deception, but a very strange experience it turns out to be. A strange combination of frustration and amusement, a sense of injustice at the manipulation to which he has been exposed, combined with the sense of triumph and near delight that comes with experiencing a second's worth of market legibility.

Noise and information

There is one category of deception that we have set aside so far – no doubt the one that first springs to mind when one thinks of deception in financial markets – and that is insider trading. When inside traders take advantage of privately held information to enter a deal, they instantiate a kind of deception that seems to cut directly against our current argument. Insider trading looks like a clear-cut case of information asymmetry and unequal network extension. If we have left this phenomenon for last it is because it represents a most interesting test case for the very concept of deception in financial markets.

The puzzle of insider trading resides in the fact that such practices hinge on a very special kind of event, with its own particular temporality. Whereas the traders studied so far, like the vast majority of traders on financial markets, were struggling to distill information from various forms of noise, insider traders are in possession of information that depends on the very existence of this noise for its extra value. The trader who sheds his shares in a company because of inside knowledge that it will soon release a poor mid-term report is able to profit from his inside knowledge not only because it is private but also because it is about to become public. Thus, it is not so much the "inside-ness" of this information that counts but rather the necessary evolution from private to public that produces the conditions for this form of deception.

The becoming-public of private information is one of the most perilous moments in finance – and incidentally, one very well monitored by national regulatory bodies – but it is not the most frequent. Private information is very quickly swallowed up by the market. Examining the conditions that must be met in order for this particular kind of deception to happen, we find that not only must the information be private and soon to become public, but other traders must respond mechanically to its release: they must be stable enough to allow for their correct manipulation by the insider. Of course, nothing can guarantee that these deceptive strategies will hold. Other events can and do occur to transform the state of the world on which the insider based his plans.

The necessary and necessarily rapid transformation of private information into public knowledge is structured by the particular temporality of financial markets. It is the periodicity of performance reports, earnings anticipation, and other kinds of business activity disclosures that punctuates the noise of daily market transactions. Our

Head of Sales who managed momentarily to see through Merrill Lynch's deceptive strategy also benefited from one of these moments in finance. He could interpret the rival bank's intentions as deceptive precisely because he knows, as does his rival, that primary market certainties (the momentary fixedness of price and ownership) lead necessarily to secondary market uncertainties. The fixedness of information must give way to the fluidity of noise if this fixedness is to allow for profitable deception. Thus, as others have pointed out before us, any instance of successful insider trading necessarily destroys the conditions of its own possibility.

Our point here may appear to resemble that of economists who argue that financial markets are generally efficient because it is to everyone's advantage to have as much information circulate as freely as possible. This is not our point – we leave these measurements to economists – nor do we make the behaviorist argument that insider trading is necessarily infrequent. For better or for worse, we do not have statistical or empirical observations to offer on the *frequency* of deceptive practices of this nature. What we are offering in this section is the socio-anthropological argument that the *presence* of deception in financial markets depends on a great number of conditions (micro-sociological, technological, legal, and informational), one of which is an *absence* of deceptive behavior sufficient that deceptive strategies can be successfully formulated and executed.

Conclusion: imputation in an entangled world

Deception can only be contemplated when responsibility can be imputed. The field of this imputation needs to be clarified for a claim to be raised. When tracking the chain of causation up to the guilty party is not possible, deception is simply not available as a narrative resource. As we have shown, complex markets often put agents in a position such that no assignment of responsibility is possible. In a sense, here we assert nothing more than that old motto of economic philosophy: markets transform and transcend the boundaries of individual morality. Aggregated actions and unintended consequences do not lend themselves to easy moral judgments.

However, behind the problem of aggregation lies another, more original interrogation. Rather than asking which economic actors engage in deception and how, we can now reverse the inquiry and ask what products could claim such simplicity that an observer could easily pinpoint deceptive behavior and from there, the author of the deception? In other words, what products are stabilized enough to allow for an *experience* of the exchange as a person-to-person relationship (about a product) instead of a person-to-product relationship (involving another person or set of people)?

The exploratory research outlined in this paper allows us to reverse the traditional way in which economic anthropologists pose the question of the relation between persons and things within markets. Most studies in this field have followed, more or less consciously, the Marxist path, construing exchanges as person-to-person relationships.[28] In this perspective, to talk of a person-to-thing relationship is to engage in commodity fetishism; the critical anthropological gesture is thought to consist in seeing the persons behind the commodities.

This illustrates research on deception the fact that deception depends on the presence of persons and things as equal partners in the transaction. People faced with financial exchanges are faced with a complex set of elements (contracts that define rights over time, rules that define practices, calculations that define values, machines that define possible interventions) that materialize socio-cultural strategies for individuating, qualifying, segregating, and agglomerating the millions of discrete exchanges that make up financial markets. Without these distinctions, circulation in meaningful terms is not possible. The relevance of finance to the question of deception lies precisely in the demonstration that the bias toward human actors and configurations of intention has led us to neglect the product. It is as much the multi-dimensionality of these products and instruments that conditions the possibilities of fair or dishonest trading as the multi-dimensionality of human motives and cognitive maps.

Notes

* This paper was written as part of a cross-disciplinary inquiry into Exchange, Deceptions and Self-Deceptions, directed by Caroline Gerschlager of the Vienna University of Economics and Business Administration and financed by the Austrian Federal Ministry of Education, Science and Culture with additional support from the Maison des Sciences de l'Homme (Paris). We would like to extend our warm thanks to Caroline Gerschlager, Nicolas Yazgi and to an anonymous peer reviewer for their very helpful comments and criticism.

1 Both authors have conducted long-term participant observation in financial markets. In 2000 and 2001, Vincent-Antonin Lépinay spent

twelve months in a dealing room in one of the leading Parisian banks on the international financial scene – in a dealing room with the biggest market returns. Ellen Hertz also spent twelve months observing professional and amateur investors during the opening year of the Shanghai stock market in 1991. In this paper, we will draw our empirical material principally from Lépinay's fieldwork.

2 The scandals originating in the United States that shook world financial markets in 2001/2 (Enron, WorldCom, Tyco, and so on) would seem to imply otherwise, but we remind our readers that these events represent a miniscule proportion of the total number of financial transactions in the world, even during a period of crisis. We will discuss the necessary preconditions for these forms of deceptive practice below.

3 See Hertz, E. (2000).

4 See, for example, Labarde, Ph. and Maris, B. (2000). For a highly politicized version of the narrative of small vs. large that accompanied the creation of China's first post-socialist stock exchange in Shanghai, see Hertz, E. (1998).

5 Let it also be noted that in treating instruments and rules together we are combining two elements that would be treated separately in an orthodox economic approach: the former is considered irrelevant because excessively "interior" to the market itself, the latter irrelevant because excessively "exterior." In our analysis, regulatory rules and equipment might deserve separate analysis to the extent that they stand independently as possible candidates to account for deception or because they constrain market activities in very different ways. However, we would insist on the fact that excluding these elements from our analysis as economists might by, for example, qualifying the difference between them with the concepts of endogenous vs. exogenous constraints, is not possible within our framework.

6 Recent endeavors to take the economy seriously as a topic and not as a resource can be found in Callon, M. (1998).

7 See Cronon, W. (1992).

8 For an overview of this theoretical trend, see Callon, M. (1986), Latour, B. (1996), Law, J. and Hassard, J. (1999).

9 One of the main achievements of ANT is its ability to operationalize an interdisciplinary approach. Once again, this is not a battle against disciplines as such, but rather the recognition of the shift in disciplinary boundaries necessary to let in new objects of study. It is

not surprising that this move came from technology studies, where cultural and social categories seemed less obvious resources.

10 Even if the relationship that is on the verge of forming is not one of fund management, the client is interested in probing the seriousness of the bank. If fund management is an option, this display of solidity is even more important. The visit and the "tour" in the trading room are used to display this solidity.

11 Exchange conditions are controlled by the COB, the French regulatory body in charge of the fairness of financial market exchanges and investor protection.

12 The engineers who create the products, along with the traders and salesmen, usually propose different sets of modifications to the clients: different stocks that will constitute the product, arranged formulas to take into account the client's needs

13 See the famous lemons case: Akerlof, G. (1970).

14 Robert Eccles' study bears evidence of the same problems in investment banking. Preferences of the companies are as under-defined when it comes to modifying their industrial structure as they are for market deals. See Eccles, R. G. and Crane, D. B. (1988).

15 Lépinay remembers the astonishment of traders when they discovered the tickets and the confirmation of a deal were signed by the municipal legislature and not by finance specialists.

16 Buying a CAC Index Option, an investor can hedge against the fall of the Index: if he buys a put – a right to sell – the Index at a given date and at a given value, he can balance a portfolio composed of CAC 40 stocks.

17 We use this term by analogy with the classical analysis of distributed cognition in Hutchins, E. (1996). Hutchins demonstrates how the knowledge and information processing necessary to maneuver large boats in a harbor is distributed among many different actors, some of which are machines.

18 In this room, it was an ETRALI turret, a telephone set with a screen displaying pre dialed telephone numbers.

19 He usually slouches when he has entered into a deal, whereas when he turns down an offer from a broker, he reclines the back and pushes his back to the bottom of the seat, leaning toward the bottom of the seat as if he was looking for a fix point in the market.

20 The option nature of these securities explains why the pricer is so necessary. These products change prices very quickly and in magnitudes disproportionate to the changes of the underlying

instrument; as they come closer to maturity, the shifts in prices are enormous.

21 One simple formula holds that a client lends one million today to Hertz & Lépinay, and in ten years this honorable bank will return the one million plus a sum that is a function of the formula. The trader has to invest this one million and make it yield at least what the formula requires that his employer give back to the client.

22 There are more and more traders with backgrounds in mathematics or physics but as they become familiar with the markets they forget much of their scientific know-how and stop calling upon their basics in math.

23 See Lépinay, V.-A. and Rousseau, F. (2001).

24 These products were built by banks with an express purpose: engaging the investors in the different forms of the economy (diversification) but through a single, easily calculated product.

25 Alice is her real name, and after she gave us her agreement, we decided to keep it in our publication: she shares so many features with Lewis Caroll's character we could not imagine a better fictional name for her.

26 Alice worked in a public relation group at that period and she scrutinized the websites of her prospects.

27 For recent studies, see MacKenzie, D. (2001), MacKenzie, D. and Millo, Y. (2003).

28 For a helpful overview, see the "Introduction," in: Parry, J. and Bloch, M. (1989); for a first step toward a reversal of this trend, see Appadurai, A. (1988).

References

Akerlof, G., 'The Market for "Lemons": Quality Uncertainty and the Market Mechanism', *Quarterly Journal of Economics*, 84 (1970), 488–500.

Appadurai, A. (ed.), *The Social Life of Things* (Cambridge and New York: Cambridge University Press, 1988).

Callon, M., 'Some Elements for a Sociology of Translation: Domestication of the Scallops and the Fishermen of St-Brieuc Bay', in J. Law (ed.), *Power, Action and Belief: A New Sociology of Knowledge?*, Sociological Review Monographs (London: Routledge and Kegan Paul, 1986).

Callon, M. (ed.), *The Laws of the Markets* (London: Blackwell, 1998).

Cronon, W., *Nature's Metropolis: Chicago and the Great West* (New York: W. W. Norton, 1992).

Eccles, R. G. and Crane, D. B., *Doing Deals: Investment Banks at Work* (Boston, MA: Harvard Business School, 1988).

Hertz, E., 'Stocks Markets as "Simulacra"', *Tsantsa*, 5 (2000), 40–50.

Hertz, E., *The Trading Crowd: An Ethnography of the Shanghai Stock Market* (Cambridge: Cambridge University Press, 1998).

Hutchins, E., *Cognition in the Wild* (Cambridge, MA: MIT Press, 1996).

Keynes, J. M., *The General Theory of Employment, Interest and Money* (London: Macmillan, 1936).

Labarde, Ph. and Maris, B., *La Bourse ou la vie. La grande manipulation des petits actionnaires* (Paris: Albin Michel, 2000).

Law, J. and Hassard, J., *Actor Network Theory and After*, Sociological Review Monographs (London: Blackwell, 1999).

Latour, B., 'On Interobjectivity', *Mind, Culture, and Activity*, 3 (1996), 266–70.

Lépinay, V.-A. and Rousseau, F., 'Les Trolls sont-ils incompétents? Enquêtes sur les financiers amateurs', *Politix*, 52 (2001), 121–54.

MacKenzie, D., 'Physics and Finance: S-Terms and Modern Finance as a Topic for Science Studies', *Science, Technology and Human Value*, 26 (2001), 115–44.

MacKenzie, D. and Millo, Y., 'Constructing a Market, Performing Theory: The Historical Sociology of a Financial Derivatives Exchange', *American Journal of Sociology*, 109 (2003), 107–45.

Parry, J. and Bloch, M. (eds), *Money and the Morality of Exchange* (Cambridge and New York: Cambridge University Press, 1989).

11

Deception in Economic Anthropology

Paul van der Grijp

Abstract

Social reality is full of deception and self-deception. Although economic anthropology, with its particular research methods and inductive approach, is well equipped to identify and analyze ethnographic examples of this kind, deception is not yet a current notion. The concepts of asymmetrical ideology linked with asymmetrical exchange are proposed as analytical equivalents to deception. These concepts are applied in five ethnographic case studies of both non-Western (Polynesian) and Western (North-American and European) societies. In order to be able to do so, we must leave behind a relativistic stance, well anchored within the discipline of anthropology.

Relativism and asymmetrical ideology

In economic anthropology, deception may hardly be called a current concept. This is not because anthropologists see deception as a *failure* in market efficiency or as an *irrationality*, similar to the way it appears to be seen within the core approach in economics (see Gerschlager 2001), but probably due to culture relativism. The central idea of culture relativism is that different societies/cultures have different cultural codes, a tautological thesis, which is still shared by *almost all* anthropologists and may be known as descriptive relativism (Wilson 1970). There is, however, no *communis opinio* concerning the related thesis that there is no universal criterion elevated above all particular cultures to know whether the values and norms of one culture are better than those of another (epistemological relativism). A third form of relativism emphasizes that cultures should tolerate each other and each other's cultural expressions, whatever they may disagree on, on the basis of their own culturally anchored values and norms (ethical relativism). Although epistemological and ethical relativism are past stations for most contemporary anthropologists – with the exception of postmodernists (for a critical review, see Gellner 1995, Godelier 2000, Spiro 1996) – descriptive relativism is still a strong, underlying value within the discipline.

Deception is a normative concept derived from the Latin word *deceptio*, which shares with the English word "deception" the meanings of deceit and fraud and has, moreover, the meaning of mistake. It derives from the past participle *decipere* (= to mislead, to deceive) which, in turn, is derived from *de-capere*, to take away.[1] In all cases, also when we speak about (economic) self-deception and illusion, we are dealing with value judgments. When, moreover, we deal with deception in other societies, we engage in inter- and trans-cultural value judgments, which go against the tradition of descriptive relativism, strongly anchored within the discipline since the early twentieth century. There are exceptions, such as the anthropological concept of "trickster" (in French translated as *décepteur*), which is mainly analyzed in mythological and ritual studies and, as far as I know, not in economic anthropology.[2] In specific economic anthropological analyses such as those of "Big Man, Great Man" and chiefly exchange systems (Sahlins 1963, Godelier 1982, White and Lindstrom 1997), we speak of social inequality, but not of deception or self-deception. These latter terms are also not applied in the most recent debate on the trader's dilemma in small, Third World peasant communities although, as we will see, the underlying ideas of deception and self-deception are certainly implied. With the exception of Marxist (economic) anthropology,[3] deception and self-deception are not theoretical concepts in economic anthropology, probably for the reasons mentioned above.

I should say, however, that they are *not yet* theoretical concepts, because (1) social reality is full of deception and self-deception, (2) anthropology, with its particular research methods such as participant observation and the extended case method, is well equipped to identify and analyze ethnographic examples of this kind due to its grass roots approach to social reality, and (3) we still have our concept of asymmetrical exchange, characterized by unequal access to material resources and knowledge, and linked to a certain type of socially shared ideas or ideology. The concept of asymmetrical ideology, which I proposed in an earlier publication (Van der Grijp 1993, pp. 8–9, 207–10), is connected with social inequality.[4] Asymmetry between individuals or groups can be gauged from an interaction between individuals or groups which has the form of an unequal exchange of goods or services. Social asymmetry, or inequality, can exist at any of a number of levels within a society: between the sexes (the gender debate), between age and kinship categories, between classes, or between societies at the international level, such as the relations between Third World countries and the highly industrialized countries of the West. Furthermore, there are all kinds of connections and linkages between the various levels and fields of social inequality. Asymmetrical ideology can be seen as the system of ideas in which forms of social inequality are presented as self-evident and natural, or even as representing God's will. This definition of asymmetrical ideology (as the presentation of social inequality within a society as something self-evident) is intended to give the concept of ideology a heuristic value. If we are looking for an analytical equivalent of the concept of deception in economic anthropology, in my view, this could be the concept of asymmetrical ideology linked to that of asymmetrical exchange.

Concerning economic anthropology, I would like to specify three points.[5] First, most contemporary non-Western societies studied by anthropologists are societies with a mixed economy with both capitalist aspects such as commodity production, private property of the means of production, the use of money to "make" more money, and wage labor and, on the other hand, "traditional" aspects, which may be (a combination) of a subsistence, barter, and gift character (see, for example, Van der Grijp 1993; 2002b; 2003). The second point concerns the rise of a large middle class in both Western and non-Western societies in the twentieth and twenty-first centuries, which does not annihilate the contradiction and opposition between capitalist and working classes, but complicates the analysis (Van der Grijp 2004). My third point is that, nowadays, anthropological analyses, including economic anthropological ones, are no longer limited to non-Western societies (Plattner 1998, V. Smith 2001, Van der Grijp 2002a). In the past, too, anthropologists included (aspects of) Western societies in their analyses. Here, however, I am pointing at the more than incidental study of Western societies in (economic) anthropology. This obliges us to redefine our material object, and will be reflected in the choice of case studies in the present chapter.

A particular, contemporary debate in economic anthropology is that on the trader's dilemma in rural villages in parts of the Third World. The trader's dilemma is the quandary between the moral obligation to share wealth with kinsfolk and neighbors and the necessity for the trader to make a profit and accumulate capital (Evers and Schrader 1994, Van der Grijp 2003). The trader – as an individual or group – tries to find a solution for this. The dilemma may be found within two contexts: (1) the trader buys agricultural products in his village and finds himself morally obliged to give the other villagers a good price or even, eventually, to share his profit with them, although he often has to sell the same products outside the village at a market where laws of supply and demand exist and the profit margins are rather limited; (2) in his village shop, the trader sells imported (often industrial) products but, because of the low standard of living of the villagers, he sells them at a reduced price, sometimes even on credit. In both cases the trader is confronted with the risk of either losing his working capital – and, eventually, going bankrupt – or losing the respect and moral support of his neighbors and kinsfolk. Actually, these traders can only accumulate the necessary capital for their enterprise by cutting or circumventing the solidarity links with their social environment. This is a kind of deception in terms of custom. Analyzing this contemporary dilemma in the form of qualitative case studies in different societies may be one way of taking deception seriously, and may be a fruitful contribution to this debate on the interface of anthropology and economics. Originally, the model of the trader's dilemma was developed on the basis of societies in South East Asia. In this chapter, I will present an ethnographic example from the island of Wallis in western Polynesia. To this, I will add a second case study on tribal art traffic, a form of cross-cultural deception related to asymmetrical access to knowledge and markets in another part of western Polynesia, the Kingdom of Tonga. Main market forms for these kinds of art objects and other collectibles are auctions. My third case study deals with organized fraud during the auction process. Within this case we are dealing with forms of asymmetrical ideology and economic deception in Western societies. This also holds for the fourth and fifth cases concerning a contemporary art market in North America and an example of a particularly deceitful entrepreneurial relationship in Western Europe.

A prosperous supermarket owner in western Polynesia

My first example is based on recent fieldwork in Polynesia.[6] The entrepreneur Penisio Tialetagi was born on the western Polynesian island of Futuna, which is part and parcel of the French overseas territory of Wallis and Futuna.[7] After multiple technical training courses in New Caledonia, amongst others in cold-storage engineering, he went to work in telecommunications as an employee of France Cable on Wallis Island. In addition to his regular job, he had contracts with the two supermarkets and some smaller shops on the island for maintenance and repair of their cooling and freezing installations. The latter he did in the evenings and on weekends – he was the only cold-storage engineer at the time – until he realized he could earn more money doing that, than with his regular work for France Cable. Moreover, it became embarrassing that his clients continued to call him at the state enterprise for his lucrative sideline. In 1989, after nine years, he resigned from France Cable in order to start out for himself. Presently, he is the owner of the third largest supermarket (the other two are both controlled from New Caledonia), and combines this with several other commercial activities. He is also engaged in the construction of an even larger supermarket which would make him the owner of the largest supermarket in the French overseas territory of Wallis and Futuna. The creation of this local commercial empire is remarkable, also in view of the dominant subsistence, barter, and gift economy within this society (Van der Grijp 2002b; 2003).

In 1986, whilst still working for France Cable, Penisio Tialetagi ("Peni") had opened a grocery shop in his native village, Fiua, in the Futunan district of Sigave.[8] In order to avoid "administrative problems" with his regular job for the French administration, from the outset, Peni registered the shop in the name of his younger brother although, actually, he was the businessman. This may be seen as a (not uncommon) form of deception vis-à-vis his employer, the French state. At the time, it was still a small shop operated by his brother together with two saleswomen, and it was supplied by ship two or three times a month. Peni organized this from Wallis. During those years, Peni was increasingly able to expand the shop. After his voluntary resignation from France Cable, he started a nightclub on Wallis and, in 1994, a clothes shop. This he opened on the yard (*'api*), half-way up the hill, about 50 meters from the main road on Wallis Island. Since 1993, he practices commercial agriculture and also breeds pigs. He breeds hundreds of pigs each year, and also buys piglets in Noumea, and fattens these with formulated New Zealand pig feed supplemented with manioc and coconuts. Pigs are very much in demand on the islands as ceremonial gifts and Peni earns a great deal of money with this trade. In 1997, he started a petrol station and, in 1999, a supermarket in which he also sells his own agricultural products. Previously, his grocery trade was a type of annex to his gas station but, in the meantime, this has developed into the third largest supermarket on the island. His most recent operation is his maintenance garage behind the supermarket, and the catering service within. At present, Peni has 45 employees, 20 of whom are full-time employees. In the year 2000, his turnover was 160 million CFP on Wallis alone (100 CFP would be about 1 euro or 1 US$).[9] Behind and beside his supermarket, he is expanding further. It is likely his supermarket will become the largest on the island.

Many Wallisians wishing to set up in business are constantly inhibited by what is known in French as "la coutume" (*fakafenua* in Wallisian) to which they have to conform. Among other things are frequent requests by family members for contributions (*kole*) and, usually, as a consequence they have to renounce their business aspirations. Peni, too, is regularly confronted with this phenomenon:

> When family members turn up for the first time in order to borrow money, I usually give them 5000 or 10,000 CFP, not more. I'm not going to lend them 100,000 CFP. In this way, I limit the damage. When ordinary customers don't pay their debts, they may no longer buy anything from me. Their account is blocked automatically. At present, everything is computerized. I can't allow credit to people who don't pay. All those small shops around which went bankrupt, owe this to the credit system. I'm well aware of the basic idea: family members and acquaintances come over to ask for money when they need it, but when they have money themselves they do not know you anymore. My family is here next door. I work with my children and with my wife. My family is only there when we are at home, not here in the supermarket (personal comment, February 2001).

Thus, Peni is defending and legitimizing his position against "tradition-oriented" gift claims. In this case study, the focus is on the foundation of a successful shop combined with other commercial activities. Shops usually stand on a plot of land. Land tenure on Wallis is controlled by both principles of chieftainship and (cognatic) kinship. It is forbidden to sell land, whilst money plays an increasingly important role in the local economy. Peni could not obtain a loan from the bank because the buildings on his – by definition unsaleable – land do not represent mortgage value. Thus, the question comes to the fore how he obtained his land, both the land of his shop on Futuna and of his business on Wallis, and: what is the actual status of his land tenure? Peni's shop on Futuna is situated on the kaiga (that is, the Futunan word for yard, or 'api in Wallisian) of his father's home in the village of Fiua in the Sigave district. This plot of land together with others should be divided between himself and his brothers and sisters via palavers in family meetings. An important argument for ceding the plot in Fiua to Peni was that, later, his nieces and nephews, when they complete their studies, will have prospective employment in Peni's enterprise. The basis of Peni's business on Wallis is the yard ('api) of his wife. Peni explains the background:

> After I married my wife, I lived twelve years with her father, who was the owner of the land. All that time, I spoiled the old man (matua), and indulged his material fantasies, also in the end when he had to go to hospital. His children live in Noumea. I told him that he should transfer his land ('api) to me, so that I could place my

> investments there. He agreed and also convinced his children of this. They can't retract the last will of their father. It was a gift to his daughter, to me, and to our children. Because of this, I never had any problems. Ten years ago he died. After fifty years, only my name will be left, but my children, that is, my father-in-law's grandchildren, will be still active then. They will be – and are already at present – the owners of the land. I think that the old man has thought it up this way.

Thus, on both Futuna and Wallis, Peni is co-owner of the land, but he emphasizes that his children and the other grandchildren of his parents (-in-law) will be the future owners of the various enterprises. Interesting in the above quotation is the passage about the "material fantasies" of his father-in-law when the latter was still alive. Actually, Peni had to provide him several times with sums of money for air tickets to and from New Caledonia (as well as for the man's other children and grandchildren), a car, meals in restaurants, and other "luxury" goods and services. Was this a form of deception? Peni still has ambivalent feelings about this which is reflected in the words "material fantasies," words which he does not use when he makes an air trip or buys a new car for himself. Apparently, at this stage of his entrepreneurial career, he had to give in to the – for him – negative side of the trader's dilemma. Peni's business on Wallis only got off the ground after the death of his father-in-law who, in his last will, gave the green light for the exclusive use of his land. However, it remains a fact – and the attitude of the bank proves this – that, in legal terms, Peni's land tenure, and together with this the ownership of the buildings in which he runs his business activities, is precarious.

Peni had to ply his father-in-law with gifts with an eye to winning an inheritance from him, the land on which he could build his supermarket. This does not seem to be obviously deceptive, either with respect to his father-in-law (who received what he wanted) or to custom (to honor one's father-in-law with gifts). Nor does the need to give gifts to his father-in-law seem to represent the negative side of the trader's dilemma, since this normally involves the negative social repercussions of not making gifts to relatives. Indulging an aged relative in the hopes of receiving an inheritance (perhaps at the expense of other potential heirs) is a common phenomenon in Western societies as well. Peni emphasizes that his children and the other grandchildren of his parents (-in-law) will be the future owners of the supermarket and other commercial enterprises, but the second quotation from Peni does not seem to support the idea that he really expects the other grandchildren of his wife's father to benefit from the inheritance. Instead, he observes that it "was a gift to his daughter, to me, and to our children." When Peni says that "my children, that is, my father-in-law's grandchildren, will be ... the owners," he appears to be legitimizing his own children's status as the ultimate heirs by emphasizing that they are directly descended from his father-in-law (through their mother), but his children are not his father-in-law's only grandchildren. The deception and asymmetrical ideology is to be found in Peni's wording.

Tribal art traffic in Tonga

Our second example of deception concerns the so-called "tribal art" market related to the Kingdom of Tonga, also in western Polynesia, although similar examples may be found all over the Third World (Phillips and Steiner 1999). Ofa Fakatoa (a pseudonym) is a carver of wood, black coral, cow bone, and whale bone in Tonga.[10] For several years, he has had a stall at the local market of Tonga's capital Nuku'alofa, and not only sells his own woodcarvings and other self-made products to tourists and visiting Tongan emigrants, but also antiques such as the famous Tongan headrests (*kali*), kavabowls (*tano'a*), and stone adzes to collectors and dealers in tribal art (see Barrow 1972, Cartmail 1997, Edler 1990). Some years ago, he had found an old, particularly well-carved paddle on his home island in the central Tongan island group of Ha'apai. Ofa: "I have seen many paddles in Ha'apai, but this one had a different form. Several Tongan names were carved on it, probably from fishermen, not in a random way, but nicely ordered. It was a beautiful old piece, made by an extremely skilled carver" (personal communication 2003). At the time, Ofa sold many antiques to Jeffery Mitchell, a tribal art dealer from San Francisco. Jeffery also was a genuine collector of Tongan art, as witnessed one of Ofa's friends who visited Jeffery at home in San Francisco. Jeffery came to Tonga at least once a year and was an appreciated customer of Ofa. During his next visit, Ofa did not show the paddle to Jeffery at first, but only after he had bought nine headrests and several other antiques. Then, Ofa took out the paddle from a corner of his livingroom and showed it to Jeffery saying: "I also found this on my native island." Ofa did not say this so that Jeffery would buy this paddle on the spot, but in order to show him that he had something different from his usual merchandise. Jeffery held the paddle in his hands at least 15 minutes and looked at it from all sides. Ofa said to him: "You can buy it if you want, but you may also leave it until your next visit."

Jeffery answered that he would certainly buy it next time. In retrospect, Ofa thinks that Jeffery did not buy the paddle immediately because he already had filled up a container with merchandise, both old and new objects. The paddle was rather long and not easy to transport. One month later, another American dealer showed up and Ofa, who lacked cash as well as other antiques at that moment, sold the paddle for T$900 (about the equivalent of US$900 and 900 euros). Two months later, Jeffery to his great surprise, spotted the paddle at a tribal art auction in New York. He had a close look and realized that it was the same paddle as the one he saw in Ofa's house in Tonga. The paddle was sold at the auction for US$300,000. Back home, Jeffery gave Ofa a call immediately and asked him: "Did you sell that paddle?"

"Yes," answered Ofa, "I needed money and a man from Los Angeles bought it for T$900." Then, Jeffery informed him that his paddle made US$300,000 at the auction in New York. After he told me this story, I asked Ofa what he thought about this price difference. Ofa answered:

> I don't care about that. All these sorts of things happen behind an iron wall, and I don't know what is going on behind that wall. That man from Los Angeles who bought the paddle from me probably also had no idea that the paddle would make that huge sum. The price was only fixed at the auction at that very moment. If the starting-price of the paddle had been 5000 dollars and nobody had made a bid, the price would have remained 5000 dollars. Probably those people liked that particular paddle (ibid.).

When Ofa sold the paddle, he had already been informed that a Tongan war club was sold for a similar price at an auction in London. The man who sold the club, Keith St Cartmail, a good acquaintance of Ofa, was "not really rich," but had farm land in New Zealand and found the club somewhere in his country. Next he sold the club in London, which gave him an idea. He sold all his land and started collecting and dealing ancient Polynesian art professionally and also wrote the book The Art of Tonga (published after his death in 1997). Meanwhile, Jeffery has also died. He had told Ofa: "Ofa, don't sell anything to Americans, the best places to sell antiques are Paris, Tokyo, and London" (ibid.). Maybe, as Ofa now believes, Jeffery wanted to keep the United States clear for himself for later on. This is what Ofa understood of the strategy of this tribal art dealer. Ofa does not make a secret of his limited knowledge of the auction procedure. For him, this is a process behind closed doors ("a thick iron wall") of which he does not have any knowledge. We will return to that process below.

However, we do know that it is not very probable that a Tongan paddle sold at auction for US$300,000 would have had a starting price of US$5000. Auction houses appoint specialists with a rather good market insight in the items they are dealing with, in this case Polynesian and other non-Western ("tribal") artifacts and art, to determine the starting price. This is not a criticism on the Tongan woodcarver and antiques dealer Ofa Fakatoa, because he clearly indicated that he does not really know how the auction works. However, I would like to make another observation, which in my view is more important, related to deception. The American dealer who bought the paddle from Ofa Fakatoa for T$900 may not have been aware that this object would make US$300,000 at auction, but he probably did know that the paddle was worth much more than the amount he paid for it, a profit beyond every reasonable proportion. One might argue that 100 percent mark-up would be a reasonable profit, 3000 percent clearly is not. Concerning the access to this kind of knowledge about collecting and market value, apparently, there is structural inequality between inhabitants of non-Western societies such as Tongan society and Western societies such as Euro-American societies. Within this context, we might even speak about a form of intercultural swindle (deception), which is, strictly speaking, maybe not illegal, but leaves a lot to discuss in terms of morals. However, I am also concerned with another dimension here, that is, that this example is embedded in widespread and long-lasting traffic in non-Western art. Within this traffic, culturally meaningful objects are extracted from their society of origin and transported to the Western world, where they are identified and valued in terms of their society of origin. They are alienated from their original context, including the accompanying deception (based on unequal access to knowledge), and defined in terms of the market and collectibles.

For private collectors of tribal art, Polynesian objects in large Western museums are the ultimate reference points for artistic and cultural value attributed to these pieces and thus also of their collector's value.[11] Almost all ancient objects circulating between private collections end up at auctions and, ultimately, in museums, either by direct purchase, or by donations on the part of collectors or their heirs. The relationship between private and public collectors (that is, museums) is an ambivalent one. There is rivalry between them concerning knowledge of the objects collected: museums may call upon scientific, government paid specialists (such as anthropologists), and the objects in well-known museums are the ultimate references for private collectors (see Bonnain 2001), however, an important part of ancient Polynesian art is still in private collections and, through their collective purchasing power, private collectors dominate the trading network of the sources for these kinds of art objects.

Incidentally, Ofa Fakatoa and his colleagues sell Tongan antiques to representatives of Western museums (they mentioned well-known examples in Washington and Tokyo), but many more to dealers and private collectors of so-called tribal art. They never sell to the National Museum in Tonga for the simple reason that this museum does not pay reasonable prices – reasonable both in terms of the international and the local market. Within this context, I would point out a paradox: art objects have to be authentic enough to be on the tribal art market, but not so authentic that they may be removed from this market in order to be placed in autochthonous (national) museums. The latter presupposes the existence not only of international but also of national laws for the protection of cultural heritage. In Tonga, this is still not the case. There have been and there still are every now and then proposals for bills within Tongan parliament, but these lacked sufficient votes every time. At present, in Tonga there are hardly any restrictions to stop this kind of traffic, and the cultural heritage in the form of ancient artifacts and art objects of this genuine Polynesian country continues to be emptied, which in my eyes is an evident form of asymmetrical exchange and deception based on unequal access to knowledge and markets.

Tricky business at auction

The third example concerns some practices of auction houses, the large ones being concentrated in Western metropoles. Several forms of organized fraud or deception may occur at auctions for antiques, art (modern and tribal), and other collectibles. The first form of fraud is known as "revision." Just before the auction and after they have had a look at the items for sale, certain dealers come together with the catalogue in hand in order to decide between them who will make a bid on which items and until what price. By means of this revision, a kind of economic conspiracy, they eliminate competition among themselves, and can acquire the items for a much cheaper price.[12] A second form of fraud or deception at auction, a variety of the first one but more elaborate, is known as "the ring" (Learmont 1985, Smith 1989). In this case, a group of dealers chooses a representative who will make bids on all items in which group members are interested. By doing this, all competition between the members of the group can be eliminated and the group will be able to obtain the items for a considerably lower price than usual. Later, the same goods are auctioned again within the select group of the ring during a so-called knock-down auction. For the success of the operation it is crucial that as many dealers interested in the goods as possible are organized in the ring, in order to exclude as much competition as possible during the official auction. Non-members of the ring, both dealers and amateurs, are discouraged during the auction through a systematic strategy of overbidding. Thus, it may happen that the representative of the ring pays slightly more than normal for some items, but most items will be obtained far below the usual selling price.

During the second auction, exclusively for ring members and in a secret place, a hotel room for example, the starting price of the bidding is the price the ring representative paid during the official auction. Those with an interest in the item at stake make bids against each other until the item is knocked down to the highest bidder. The difference between the price paid for the item during the official auction (for example 100 euros) and that during the knock-down auction (for example 130 euros) is the "profit," which does not go to the original seller and the auctioneer, but to the ring as a whole. This money (30 euros in our example) is put down in the middle of the table. When, during this knock-down party, items are auctioned for which the ring representative had to pay a higher price than usual in order to overbid and discourage non-ring members (for example 150 euros), the starting price during the knock-down auction will be lower (for example 90 euros). If the highest price during the knock-down auction remains under the price paid during the official auction, the highest bidder still has to pay the price of the official auction but, then, he can take the difference between his own highest bid and the official auction price from the money in the middle of the table. At the end of this second auction, when everything is sold, the remaining money in the middle of the table is distributed among the ring members. Usually, this is a lucrative affair.

The long term operation of a ring can be disastrous for auction houses. In the long run, sellers will notice that the bids remain below the normal level and they will move to other auction houses, or refrain from selling at all. Moreover, rings are illegal.[13] Through the increasing activities on the antiques market and the rocketing prices on the art market, the auction circuit gained increasing interest in the media. According to Learmount (1985, p. 194), the apparent rest on the auction market is "something of a deception" because auction houses prefer to pretend to ignore active rings and remain quiet about certain occurrences because they fear getting a bad name.[14] Learmount (ibid., p. 195) does not doubt that "the rings continue to flourish in every part of the auction business" and, he adds, "the ring is alive and well and living very close to wherever auctions are taking place." We could close this subject with this not very cheerful message.

But, we may ask, is the auctioneer himself not to blame? The auctioneer does not buy or sell from his own possessions and would thus be impartial. There is, however, a practice which suggests differently and which we deal with here as the third form of auction fraud or deception, namely the practice of simulating bids in the auction room from time to time. This would be "a widely accepted trick ... perpetrated by all auction houses," according to a well-known Dutch auctioneer (Glerum 1991, p. 57; my translation, PvdG). This auctioneer, who has been the star of a popular television series on auctions for many years, gives the example of a painting which he values at 15,000 euros, and he agrees with the seller that the painting will not be sold for less than 14,000 euros. The starting price, however, is lower: 10,000 euros. When there are real bids during the auction, there is no problem, but when there are no bids at all, the auctioneer looks in different directions in the auction room and waves with his hammer and calls out: 10,500; 11,000; 11,500; 12,000. When there is still no real bidder at 12,000 euros, he knocks down his hammer, calls a fictive name or number to his assistant and says: "sold!" His assistant knows that actually the painting is not sold because they did not reach the minimum price. Even when there is a real bidder for 12,000 euros, the auctioneer continues simulating higher bids in order to push the only real bidder to the minimum price of 14,000 euros. In Dutch auction jargon this kind of simulation is called swimming (zwemmen), in English it is called "taking bids from the walls" or "taking bids from the chandeliers." Although the auctioneer concerned, who has been in the profession for several decades (among other things during 25 years at Sotheby's-Amsterdam), says that this way of doing business does not please him at all, he still legitimizes this current technique in auction practice. In his discourse we can distinguish three arguments:

1) Insiders know that it is not probable that a sought-after painting estimated at 14,000 euros would be sold for 10,000 euros;
2) every auction house will simulate that the goods are sold because, if it becomes evident several times that the auction goers are not responding to the goods offered, that would temper the atmosphere in the room and it might become difficult to sell other goods;
3) the auction house has the right to make bids on behalf of the seller (ibid., pp. 59, 58, and 59 respectively).

The first argument seems to suggest that non-initiates should not come to auctions, or should at least refrain from bidding. Such a message, however, is in complete contradiction to the set-up of auctions and the discourse of auctioneers. The second argument and the third defend the interests of the auction house and those of the seller, not those of the buyers. Here, there is not much left of the impartiality of the auctioneer mentioned above, at least not within the perspective of the only real bidder in the auction room. Within his perspective, the scenario in which he or she ended up may be seen as a form of pure swindle. The first two forms of organized auction fraud distinguished in this section are illegal, the third is probably not, or at least not when it remains within certain limits. However, it still is deception.

The fine art market in St. Louis

The fourth case study derives from an economic ethnography of the fine art market in the U.S. metropolitan area of St. Louis, which has about 2.4 million inhabitants. In St. Louis there are approximately 812 visual artists, 222 of whom are considered as real, active, and serious professionals (Plattner 1996, p. 82). In the 1970s and 1980s, there was an economic boom, accompanied by a boom in the number of art galleries and also in the sales of fine art; in the 1990s, this boom was over and the question comes to the fore of how gallery-owners are able to survive. The relationship between art galleries and painters can be problematic when it concerns payment after selling a work, because there are months that sales in the gallery may remain below cost level. What to do in such a case? A gallery-owner defends his point of view:

> But the lights and air conditioning ... goes on, and the tax bill goes on, and the employees have to be paid, and so on, so what do you do? Well, you try to pay your vendors slowly and spread it out. ... An artist expects that, if you get 1200 US$ for a sale on Tuesday, that they should get 600 US$ on Thursday. And they wonder why they're not. ... That's not the reality of the business world. But they don't understand that. And in fact they would consider it an infraction of their contract with me if I were to admit to them that there's a float, just like the banks used to have a float on their checks (ibid., p. 150).

The practice of this art dealer and also of the banks to which he refers corresponds with the first lesson I received at school from my economics teacher (not an anthropologist) long ago: how to act "economically"? My economics teacher's answer: by paying your debts as late as possible. Banks oblige you to pay interest (and prosper from that) but, usually, private persons do not ask for interest. To fill the gap of one debt, many small enterprises use the money from postponed payment of another debt, and may be able to survive via this strategy. From the point of view of the artist in the example above, however, withholding or delaying payment is immoral, a form of deceit. Most artists, according to Plattner, have experiences with postponed payments. Often, dealers legitimize this deception by stating that the artist did not need the money at the very moment of the sale, because the artist could not have foreseen the sale.

This is not only a form of asymmetrical ideology, but also a matter of power difference and asymmetrical exchange: the dealer is able to give priority to his (or her) need to keep the gallery running rather than the artist's subsistence needs In extreme cases it may also occur that a dealer does not pay the artist at all. Some artists have also experienced this kind of deception.

A shortsighted optician in a French town

The fifth and last example is about deception of one entrepreneur by another in contemporary France, thus one more situation in which problems of culture relativism do not occur. In France, the Afflelou company is the number one seller of spectacles. The president of the Afflelou Group represents the trade mark image of the enterprise with his personal name, *Alain Afflelou*, and also by playing the key role in frequent publicity spots on television. In the latter he tries to "de-dramatize" the fact of wearing glasses and "no longer consider them as a prosthesis." However, his real success, no doubt, is due to his competitive price strategy. With 486 shops, 2500 people working for him, and a 307 million euro yearly turnover he is the evident market leader in glasses.[15] I obtained this information via a special program on Afflelou on the French television series "Les coulisses de l'économie" (behind the scenes of the economy) on channel TF1 in October 2001. The program consisted of lengthy interview fragments with the successful entrepreneur, interrupted by short reports on spectacle amelioration, production, and distribution. With a reference to American interview techniques, the interviewers asked Afflelou for his favorite word. His answer was: *honesty* ('honnêteté'). Next, they asked him the word he detested most. Afflelou's answer: *treason* ('trahir'). The program also showed an interview with a former Afflelou franchise owner.

Before becoming a franchise owner ('franchisé'), this man had been working as an independent optician in a small town in the southwest of France. For several decades, he was the owner of one of the three optician shops in this provincial town. The advantages of becoming a franchise owner in the form of inexpensive purchase prices and wide publicity largely outweighed the 4.15 percent of his turnover (after tax-deduction) he had to pay as royalties.[16] The relationship with Afflelou was more than friendly, with regular lunches and dinners, and a personal exchange of friendly letters of which the man cited some striking examples. During the amicable relationship, Afflelou convinced the optician to open a second shop in the same town. Initially, the optician did not want to because, on the basis of longstanding professional experience, he knew that the market for spectacles in his town was already saturated by the three existing shops. Afflelou, however, continued to push his franchise owner, who finally ceded and invested all his personal means in a second shop, in the expectation that his economically powerful friend would support him in the case of failure. The second shop failed indeed. The expected support by Afflelou did not come and, actually, the small town optician was unable to get in touch with him during this difficult period. The second shop, in competition with his first shop, led to the optician's bankruptcy. His creditors obliged him to sell his two shops, which were bought by Afflelou. Soon, the second shop was closed down. For Afflelou too, this second shop, the fourth in this small town, turned out not to be viable.[17] Here, we clearly have another case of asymmetrical exchange and deception, related by a disappointed and bankrupt victim. All this would make an excellent case study in economic anthropology because it supplies the information allowing for an understanding of the motives of the actors of this social drama – although as anthropologists we usually would like to obtain more ethnographic details.

Conclusions

The various forms of deception in our case studies illustrate and underline the thesis that social reality is full of deception. The examples of deception are clearly of a different kind; and not only in terms of scale of analysis (*"échelle d'analyse"*). The case study of Penisio Tialetagi on Wallis illustrates (the model of) the trader's dilemma, where traders can only accumulate the necessary capital for their enterprise by cutting or circumventing the solidarity links with their social environment and which amount to forms of asymmetrical exchange and deception in terms of custom. Evers and Schrader (1994) introduced the model of the trader's dilemma in order to apply it to Third World societies, particularly South East Asia. In my first case study I extended this field of application to a part of Polynesia. The last two cases of actors on the St. Louis fine art market and the French market for spectacles, however, demonstrate that a similar conflict between the imperatives of profit-seeking and "traditional" social obligations may be found in Western economic settings as well. The type of asymmetrical exchange, asymmetrical ideology, and deception practiced by the New York gallery owners and the French optical-chain owner is the other side of the coin of that practiced by Third World village entrepreneurs. The difference is that the latter openly strive to impose a capitalist relationship that runs counter to the locally dominant ethic of solidarity, whereas the former lead their business partners (artists or the local optician) to believe they are bound by a link of solidarity only to cut that link in favor of the locally dominant capitalist ethic, which is a much clearer form of deception. In the second and third cases, on tribal art traffic and auction practices, I showed forms of asymmetrical exchange, asymmetrical ideology, and deception in particular market settings where either unequal access to knowledge (tribal art) or outright treachery (auctions) plays a crucial role.

The historian of economics Polanyi (1957) used to make a distinction between formalists and substantivists, a distinction well known and applied in economic anthropology. Formalists have an *idée fixe* of the *homo economicus*, and see human beings as rational actors who are able to make a (rational) choice in terms of costs-benefits between scarce means and expected results, in contrast to substantivists, who believe that every economy is rooted in its specific culture with specific social relationships and representations, and proclaim that the study of the economy in non-capitalist societies should break away from the theory of market economy. Striking about our case studies is that they demonstrate that Western (capitalist) businessmen themselves do not always perfectly embody the formalist's model of the *homo economicus*. Polynesian entrepreneurs, on the other hand, seem to be rational and self-interested and thus in line with the *homo economicus* model, although they still have to cope with the trader's dilemma within a mixed economy with strong gift-obligation dimensions. The originality of this paper, indeed, being that ethnographic case studies taken from non-Western (Polynesian) and Western (North-American and European) societies are juxtaposed. The theoretical justification for this juxtaposition is to be found in the actual modification and enlargement of the material object of economic anthropology: most contemporary non-Western societies studied by anthropologists are societies with a mixed economy with both capitalist and "traditional" aspects; the rise of a large middle class in both Western and non-Western societies; and, finally, the fact that anthropologists no longer limit their analyses to non-Western societies. In thinking about the (possible) application of the notion of deception within economic anthropology and, consequently, leaving behind a relativistic stance, we should take this all into account.

Notes

1 The shift in meaning to the French word *déception*, (a *faux ami*) which means disappointment and disillusionment, is probably due to "being deceived in the expectation" (*decipi spe*) (Van Veen and Van der Sijs 1991, p. 185).

2 Tricksters are ambiguous personages in North-American, Polynesian, and African myths (respectively the Coyote and the raven, Maui, and the rabbit) and European legends (Reynard the Fox, Tijl Uilenspiegel, Robin Hood) (see Radin 1956, Lévi-Strauss 1958, pp. 248–51). Jan Pouwer (1978) even suggested that the anthropologist himself is a "trickster's apprentice." See on verbal deception Fortier (2002); for an exceptional case of deception as a research method see Lauder (2003).

3 In Marxist anthropology, a theoretical current of the 1970s and 1980s (Godelier 1973, Kahn and Llobera 1981, Meillassoux 1975, Rey 1973, Seddon 1978), deception was used as an explicit analytical tool. In using the classical Marxist surplus value theory, prices fixed by "laws" of offer and demand within capitalism were clearly seen as deception.

4 The notion of ideology was inspired by Godelier's (1984) definition, the additional specification "asymmetrical" in asymmetrical ideology was mine. Linking the notion of asymmetrical exchange is a logical next step.

5 On contemporary economic anthropology see Caillé (2000), Dupuy (2001), Géraud, Leservoisier and Pottier (2000), Godelier (1984), Narotzky (1997), Plattner (1989), Wilk (1996).

6 In 2000–2001 on Wallis and Futuna. This was my seventh anthropological fieldwork in Polynesia since 1982.

7 Wallis and Futuna are Polynesian islands and they are French, but they are not part of that other French overseas territory known as French Polynesia (also including Tahiti). Wallis and Futuna are situated north of Fiji, northwest of Tonga and west of Samoa. A third French overseas territory in the South Pacific is New Caledonia. Many Wallisians and Futunans live in New Caledonia, even more than on their home islands.

8 On Wallis and Futuna, almost everybody knows Penisio Tialetagi via his abbreviated first name Peni, a custom maintained throughout this section.

9 In January 2001, 1 CFP equalled 0.00838 euro. The CFP, an abbreviation of "cour franc pacifique," is also used in French Polynesia and New Caledonia.

10 Information based on my eighth period of fieldwork in Polynesia, in 2003. Tonga is an independent Polynesian kingdom northeast of New Zealand and east of Fiji.

11 Compared to Melanesian objects, Polynesian objects are much more valued in this respect, also in monetary terms. This has to do with the considerably longer contact period of Polynesian societies compared to most Melanesian ones. For one-and-a-half centuries, most ancient Polynesian art objects and artifacts can be found in Western private collections and museums, and the very few objects which arrive on the market are quickly subjected to competitive bidding at extremely high prices.

12 In the literature, the phenomenon of the revision is mentioned, among others, by Geismar (2001, p. 40).

13 The English Auctions Bidding Agreement Act of 1927, for example, states that "if any dealer agrees to give, or gives, or offers any gift or consideration to any other person as an inducement or reward for abstaining, or for having abstained, from bidding at the sale by auction either generally or for any particular lot, or if any person agrees to accept, or accepts, or attempts to obtain from any dealer any such gift or consideration as aforesaid, he shall be guilty of an offence under this Act, and shall be liable on summary conviction to a fine not exceeding one hundred pounds, or a term of imprisonment for any period not exceeding six months, or to both such fine and such imprisonment" (cited in Learmount 1985, p. 186).

14 At the end of the 1960s, there were indications that several rings operated in the British auction circuit. However, it appeared to be a problem to provide concrete evidence of this. In a debate in the House of Commons in 1969, one of the parliamentarians pointed out the fact that the Auctions Act of 1927 had only resulted in one prosecution until then, namely in 1928.

15 All opticians in France together make a turnover of 2.89 billion euros with 29 million French citizens wearing glasses and 2.4 million wearing contact lenses. Statistically, a French wearer of glasses changes these every four years. There are not many new wearers of glasses, the market being rather stable.

16 Franchising is a form of enterprise in which a small dealer, against payment, uses the trademark, the reputation, and the experience of a larger company. According to Afflelou, an Afflelou shop makes three and a half times the turnover of an average French optician's shop.

17 As usual in the series, the television program was re-broadcast during a night hour two weeks later, but the story of the deceived optician in the provincial town was omitted for unstated reasons.

References

Barrow, T., *Art and Life in Polynesia* (Rutland, VT and Tokyo: Charles Tuttle, 1972).

Bonnain, R., *L'empire des masques: Les collectionneurs d'art premiers aujourd'hui* (Paris: Stock, 2001).

Caillé, A., *Anthropologie du don: Le tiers paradigme* (Paris: Desclée de Brouwer, 2000).

Cartmail, K. St., *The Art of Tonga* (Honolulu: University of Hawaii Press, 1997).

Dupuy, F., *Anthropologie économique* (Paris: Armand Colin, 2001).

Edler, C., *The Art of Polynesia* (Honolulu, HI: Hemmeter Publishing Corporation, 1990).

Evers, H.-D. and Schrader, H. (eds), *The Moral Economy of Trade: Ethnicity and Developing Markets* (London and New York: Routledge, 1994).

Fortier, J., 'The Arts of Deception: Verbal Performances by the Raute of Nepal', *Journal of the Royal Anthropological Institute*, 8 (2002), 233–57.

Geismar, H., 'What's in a Price? An Ethnography of Tribal Art at Auction', *Journal of Material Culture*, 6 (2001), 25–47.

Gellner, E., 'Anything Goes: The Carnival of Cheap Relativism Which Threatens to Swamp the Coming *fin de millénaire*', *Times Literary Supplement* (16 June 1995), 6–8.

Géraud, M.-O., Leservoisier, O. and Pottier, R., *Les notions clés de l'ethnologie: Analyses et textes* (Paris: Armand Colin, 2000).

Gerschlager, C., 'Introduction', in C. Gerschlager (ed.), *Expanding the Economic Concept of Exchange: Deception, Self-Deception and Illusions* (Boston, Dordrecht and London: Kluwer, 2001), pp. 1–24.

Glerum, J. P., *Veilen: Het hoe en waarom van de hoogste prijs* ('s-Gravenhage: BZZTôH, 1991).

Godelier, M., *Horizon, trajets marxistes en anthropologie* (Paris: Maspéro, 1973).

Godelier, M., *La production des grands hommes* (Paris: Fayard, 1982).

Godelier, M., *L'idéel et le matériel: Pensées, économies, sociétés* (Paris: Fayard, 1984).

Godelier, M., 'Is Social Anthropology Still Worth the Trouble? A Response to Some Echoes from America', *Ethnos,* 65 (2000), 301–16.

Kahn, J. and Llobera, J. (eds), *The Anthropology of Pre-Capitalist Societies* (London: Macmillan, 1981).

Lauder, M. A., 'Covert Participant Observation of a Deviant Community: Justifying the Use of Deception', *Journal of Contemporary Religion,* 18/2 (2003), 185–96.

Learmount, B., *A History of the Auction* (London: Barnard and Learmount, 1985).

Lévi-Strauss, C., *Anthropologie structurale* (Paris: Plon, 1958).

Meillassoux, C., *Femmes, greniers et capitaux* (Paris: Maspero, 1975).

Narotzky, S., *New Directions in Economic Anthropology* (London and Chicago, IL: Pluto Press, 1997).

Phillips, R. B. and Steiner, C. B. (eds), *Unpacking Culture: Art and Commodity in Colonial and Postcolonial Worlds* (Berkeley and Los Angeles: University of California Press, 1999).

Plattner, S., *Economic Anthropology* (Stanford, CA: Stanford University Press, 1989).

Plattner, S., *High Art Down Home: An Economic Ethnography of a Local Art Market* (Chicago, IL: University of Chicago Press, 1996.

Plattner, S., 'A Most Ingenious Paradox: The Market for Contemporary Fine Art', *American Anthropologist*, 100 (1998), 482–93.

Polanyi, K., 'The Economy as Instituted Processes', in K. Polanyi, C. M. Arensberg and H. W. Pearson (eds), *Trade and Market in the Early Empires: Economies in History and Theory* (Glencoe, IL: The Free Press, 1957), pp. 243–70.

Pouwer, J., 'The Anthropologist as the Trickster's Apprentice: Complementarity, Ambivalence and Dialectics', in G. A. Moyer, D. S. Moyer and P. E. de Josselin de Jong (eds), *Explorations in the Anthropology of Religion* (Leiden: Instituut voor Culturele Antropologie en Sociologie der Niet-Westerse Volken, 1978), pp. 206–45.

Radin, P. et al., *The Trickster: A Study in American Indian Mythology* (New York: Philosophical Library, 1956).

Rey, P.-P, *Les alliances des classes* (Paris: Maspero, 1973).

Sahlins, M., 'Poor Man, Rich Man, Big Man, Chief: Political Types in Melanesia and Polynesia', *Comparative Studies in Society and History,* 5 (1963), 285–303.

Seddon, D. (ed.), *Relations of Production: Marxist Approaches to Economic Anthropology* (London: Frank Cass, 1978).

Smith, C. W., *Auctions: The Social Construction of Value* (Berkeley: University of California Press, 1989).

Smith, V., 'Ethnographies of Work and the Work of Ethnographers', in P. Atkinson et al. (eds), *Handbook of Ethnography* (London: Sage, 2001), pp. 220–33.

Spiro, M. E., 'Postmodernist Anthropology, Subjectivity, and Science: A Modernist Critique', *Comparative Studies in Society and History*, 38 (1996), 759–80.

Van der Grijp, P., *Islanders of the South: Production, Kinship and Ideology in the Polynesian Kingdom of Tonga* [Verhandelingen 154] (Leiden: KITLV Press, 1993).

Van der Grijp, P., 'Passion and Profit: The World of Amateur Traders in Philately', *Journal of Material Culture*, 7 (2002a), 23–47.

Van der Grijp, P., 'Selling is Poverty, Buying a Shame: Representations of Work, Effective Leadership, and Market Failures on Wallis', *Oceania*, 73 (2002b), 17–34.

Van der Grijp, P., 'Between Gifts and Commodities: Commercial Enterprise and the Trader's Dilemma on Wallis Island (Western Polynesia)', *The Contemporary Pacific*, 15 (2003), 277–302.

Van der Grijp, P., *Identity and Development: Tongan Culture, Agriculture, and the Perenniality of the Gift* [Verhandelingen 213] (Leiden: KITLV Press, 2004).

Van Veen, P. A. F. and van der Sijs, N. (eds), *Etymologisch Woordenboek: De Herkomst van Onze Woorden* (Utrecht and Antwerp: Van Dale Lexicografie, 1991).

White, G. M. and Lindstrom, L. (eds), *Chiefs Today: Traditional Pacific Leadership and the Postcolonial State* (Stanford, CA: Stanford University Press, 1997).

Wilk, R. R., *Economies and Cultures: Foundations of Economic Anthropology* (Boulder, CO and Oxford: Westview Press, 1996).

Wilson, B. R. (ed.), *Rationality* (Oxford: Blackwell, 1970).

12

Gift Exchange, Play and Deception*

Marcel Hénaff

Abstract

The aim of this essay is to show how the concept of exchange, particularly in relation to the question of deception, must be carefully re-evaluated when applied to the realm of the exchange of gifts. This type of exchange, considered in its traditional – that is, ceremonial – expressions, is not primarily an exchange of goods, but a *procedure of public recognition* between statutory partners. I intend to situate this procedure within the framework of other types of recognition among primates. When considered in this manner, the nature of this type of exchange appears to be neither economical (it is not about profit) nor moral (in the philanthropic sense), but rather, political because it concerns, first of all, the ways in which we make conventions and alliances. Moreover, this procedure, based on risk and trust, (but not contractual in nature), implies original forms of playing and gambling and cannot be separated from specific types of deception that are very different from those found in the economical exchange. What is at stake is the issue of *trust*, which is still the central question of our modern societies and constitutes the primary way for them to relate to traditional societies.

Introduction

In order to problematize the concept of play in relation to the concepts of exchange and deception, I shall first propose to clarify the concept of exchange itself. This clarification mainly concerns the profound difference between the ceremonial exchange of gifts and the contractual exchange of goods. The first has been seriously misunderstood since the rise of political economy; it has been mistakenly conceived as help, barter, or mutual profit, or, on the contrary, as a moral gesture of charity; or it has been included in the realm of modern economy as an aspect of the social redistribution of goods.[1]

Since Marcel Mauss's essay, *The Gift,* (1924) a new field of interpretation has developed. But we have to understand (and that will be the aim of this essay) that the ceremonial gift is not about exchange of goods but about *reciprocal recognition.* Precious goods, as we will see, are not offered to enrich but to honor the partner (individual or group) in order to create or maintain a *public* relation. This involves challenge, expectation, alliance, promise, and prestige, leading to a strong social bond or to its symmetrical opposite: revenge as vindicatory justice.[2] This really is the universe of a certain type of risk and playing, which are of a different nature than those experienced in the contractual exchange[3] in the sphere of economy.

The logic of contractual exchange is indeed totally different. It is designed to avoid any uncertainty about the partner (such as the reversal of friendship into conflict); the contractual relation defines all of the partners' duties and limits (regarding goods and time). It is constructed in order to prevent unexpected attitudes or events; it is a precise procedure that generates complex strategies within legal boundaries. Because of these constraints – inseparable from the resistances it inevitably provokes – and because the contract's aim is to ensure a mutually profitable result, each partner is tempted to try by all means to take advantage of the formulation of the contract itself (hidden conditions, restrictions, lack of precision). Therefore, it seems obvious that the risk of deception is an intrinsic part of the contractual procedures. Playing in that case has to be invisible, hypocritical, and can be seen as a mere strategy of control. But, even though the ceremonial gift exchange appears in comparison as an open play which culminates in a festive celebration, the possibility of deception remains no less a constitutive dimension of the gift relationship, but for totally different reasons. The aim of this essay is to show that the two types of exchange are radically heterogeneous. However, the one does not exclude the other; the one is not an alternative for the other. The sphere of recognition cannot replace or be replaced by the sphere of the marketplace.

In order to bring to light the originality of deception in the case of ceremonial gift exchange,[4] my main objective is to propose a new hypothesis regarding the reason for this social practice. For that purpose it is important to first explain what the gift exchange is not.

Gift exchange does not belong to the field of economics

The reduction to economics of the rituals of giving is most often done by simply lumping different things together when describing "primitive exchanges." In a famous section of book I, chapter 2 of *The Wealth of Nations* (1993 [1776]), Adam Smith, presenting the origins of the "proclivity to making deals" inherent in mankind, mixes in an unquestioning manner all kinds of exchanges: services, words, gifts, useful goods. This is not surprising: every eighteenth-century author does the same. It is more surprising to find the same views in the works of such authors as Max Weber and Karl Polanyi. Weber, in his *General Economic History* (1981) described traditional exchanges among African tribal leaders or medieval princes as "trading through gifts." It seems that Weber did not perceive the self-contradictory character of the phrase. However, when referring to documents such as the Tell al-Amarna tablets (1400 B.C.), he was struck by the description of gifts without counterparts – except for the recipients' attitude of allegiance toward the givers – this type of giving was practiced among princes in the Middle East, especially between the Pharaoh and those who were obliged to him. Those were, after all, strange and unreliable practices: "Innumerable breaches of loyalty gradually led to the imposition of counterparts, so that this circulation of gifts became a trade subject to a precise accounting." (Weber 1981, p. 238) Thus, there was, Weber believed, a movement toward a greater rationality. Discussing the origins of currency, he wrote: "The function of currency as a means of universal exchange originates in foreign trading. Its first source is a steady trading consisting in giving to outsiders.... The state of peace between two kingdoms presupposes constant gift-giving between rulers; trade between leaders originates in these exchanges of a commercial nature" (ibid.). We shall find out that this was not the case, and that this confusion is precisely what must be avoided. Many examples could be given. Mauss himself, who illuminated this issue, often remained dependent on an inadequate vocabulary when presenting these exchanges as "a market before the institution of traders" (Mauss 1924, p. 4), even though his own analysis showed something different, even though he came to a radical questioning of the prejudices of *homo economicus*.

Karl Polanyi, who, among historians of economics, was one of the most attentive to anthropological research, wrote that the kula ring, the system of circulating gifts on the Trobriand Islands as described by Malinowski, was "one of the most elaborate trading transactions known to man," (Polanyi (1957 [1944], p. 50), and added, in a categorical manner: "We do say 'trade' even though no profit is obtained, either in currency or in kind ... even though every operation is entirely ruled by etiquette and magic. It is trade, nevertheless" (ibid.). It is true, Polanyi explains, that kula exchanges are reciprocal gifts: their aim is the prestige afforded by this ostentatious generosity, while the total effect of these movements of goods over great distances represents a considerable circulation of wealth: "The result is a stupendous organizational achievement in the economic field" (ibid.). Polanyi's thesis is a subtle one: he recognizes that what is involved is an exchange of gifts, but asserts that this movement of exchange has an economical value that goes beyond it and must be recognized. It can, indeed, be described as having unintended but real economical effects. However, Polanyi does not see that even from this point of view, some questions should be raised: this wealth comprises mainly ceremonial necklaces and bracelets; the time required to make and exchange them makes it impossible to describe this as a success in economical terms. If there is success, it is at an entirely different level, which Malinowski correctly identified as an exclusively social level: a powerful network of interpersonal bonds, as we shall soon see.

Thus, both Weber and Polanyi, who were most critical of economists' prejudices, nonetheless remained dependent upon the model of trade in their attempt to describe or explain reciprocal ceremonial gift giving. It is easy to guess what can be found in the works of other authors who are less demanding and attentive to data regarding traditional societies.

Starting in the early twentieth century, new ethnographic research on ritual reciprocal gift giving practices raised doubt on the barter interpretation. First came the great investigations made by Franz Boas and his team – which included George Hunt, a native – on the peoples of the American northwest (Boas 1969 [1895–1913]): their social organization, their narratives, and finally their practices of ceremonial exchange, of which the potlatch was the most spectacular. Yet Boas, concerned with assigning for the benefit of federal administrators – or even his own colleagues – an economic rationality to practices that did not seem to have one, added to his fruitful investigations comments that amounted to comforting the old prejudices.[5] Undoubtedly, things changed in 1922 when Malinowski published Argonauts of the Western Pacific, in which the surprising practice of reciprocal giving that make up the core of the social life of the peoples living on the Melanesian coasts of the Trobriand Islands are analyzed. Malinowski, unlike Boas, presents a very sophisticated reflection on the original character of those ritual exchanges; but, mostly, he clearly opposes prejudices reductive to economics: "The word 'trade' is used in current ethnography and in economic literature with so many different implications that a whole lot of misleading, preconceived ideas have to be brushed aside in order to grasp the facts correctly" (Malinowski 1961 [1922], p. 84). Malinowski also wrote of those prejudices: "We have to realize clearly that the kula contradicts in almost every point, the definition of 'savage trade'" (ibid., p. 85). What also makes Malinowski's analyses interesting is that they show that, apart from the kula, there is an ordinary trade – gimwali – which also has very complex forms, but that these barter operations are totally different from the exchanges of gifts (we shall return to this point, which Polanyi ignored).

Re-examining the work developed mainly by Boas and Malinowski, Mauss restated in a radically new way the general question of the ceremonial exchange of reciprocal gifts. He saw in it not only one of the major dimensions of social life, but its very institution. Mauss opens this debate in a context which was difficult for two reasons. First, because of the very old and widespread prejudices regarding supposedly "primitive" peoples, prejudices found even among the most open-minded thinkers (Mauss himself sometimes speaks of "backward peoples"). In addition, there is a universal reluctance to consider the practices of reciprocal gift-giving outside the framework of the exchange of goods in terms of economics, be it barter or monetary. Mauss, who did so much to denounce this reduction, sometimes gave in to the temptation of resorting to the vocabulary of trade, profit, or contract. True, his hesitations remained a minor failure considering how much he accomplished in such an unfavorable context. It was Mauss who made us realize that the practices of ceremonial gift dominate the life of traditional societies, including pre-modern, western societies (but modernity, let's affirm it clearly, does not imply disappearance of gift relationships). In spite of this, for Mauss, as for most anthropologists, the question of the gift does not seem separable, even from its opposite, from trade and profitable economical exchange. It is indeed important not to confuse these two questions; but, as we shall see, it is just as important not to place them along the same line of evolution. The gift is neither the ancestor of trade (both exist at the same time) nor an alternative to trade (they do not fill the same function). Both practices are entirely compatible. C. A. Gregory (1982) seems to have understood this well, as shown by his attempt to confront various modes of circulation of goods depending on different types of societies. Among these modes, he drew a particular distinction between those based on kinship and those based on economic interest. This leads to the distinction between commodities and goods associated with prestige. The first are alienable, while the latter are not. The first aims at maximizing profit, the latter, number of debtors. At this last point, we can no longer follow Gregory. It is clear that he was constructing a kind of model for two types of economies, as if the system of the exchange of gifts aimed at a personalized distribution of goods and brought about a system of debt tied to the inalienable character of the goods involved. This was a kind of reworking of Boas's explanations (in that Boas wrongly interpreted what he so accurately described) or, of the "trade" interpretation of Polanyi. Like these authors, Gregory could not help understand the practices of the ceremonial gift as an original version of an economic relationship, which is a sure way to miss their specificity. He was fascinated as they were, by the fact that goods are involved. Here lies the misunderstanding: gift and trade relationships are seen as two modes of exchange of goods, the difference between them being that the former, unlike the latter, would not be motivated by profit. Some goods would be freely given, others exchanged for profit. This view seems reasonable, but actually it is completely misleading.[6] The same could be said of F. Perroux's theory (1963), which interprets the economics of the gift as an alternative to the mere logic of capitalism or to state-controlled economy; he calls gift anything that is neither trade nor administrative constraint, like the invisible contribution to economy: competence, creativity, dedication; this would be an acceptable convention if he were not referring to Mauss (p. 156) based on an obvious misunderstanding. Another notable case of misinterpretation is found in G. Gilder in Wealth and Poverty (1981) This author assigns to capitalism from the outset a function of generous, contribution-creating demand, the source of subsequent productive activity; according to him, capitalism is led to constantly renewing its free supply in order to boost itself. This view deserves to be discussed, but presenting it as a fact supported by Mauss, as Gilder does, shows quite a distorted reading of *The Gift*. A comparison between capitalistic supply and the potlatch is a fraudulent analogy.

A misunderstanding needs to be avoided here. To say that the reciprocal ceremonial gift has no economic designs does not mean that it is unrelated to economic activities; indeed every society produces and exchanges goods for its material reproduction. It is therefore a mistake to oppose gift-giving societies to merchant societies. Moreover, the priority given to ceremonial exchanges has considerable effects on material production and useful exchanges. However, as Malinowski clearly explains when referring to the kula ring, this material production is not oriented toward its own growth, but aims at what is considered most important, that is, at obtaining precious goods for ceremonial exchange.[7] The ceremonial exchange is what matters most because it generates or maintains bonds between groups and shows the prestige of the partners.

As we shall see, ceremonial gifts generally aim at a public reciprocal recognition through the mediation of the goods offered. They do not prevent useful exchanges; they may express indifference toward usefulness, but they do not aim at denying it. Thus, there is an ordinary economics "embedded" within the social order (as Polanyi saw) and the social order may be dominated by relationships of ceremonial gifts as defining the priorities of the community as a whole as well as positions of authority. Both activities exist and coexist, but within very different realms in terms of function and importance. We must understand what they are.[8]

The ceremonial gift is not a moral gesture

Opposing the interpretation reductive to economics, one is often tempted, when trying to understand the ceremonial gift, to take as a starting point the modern gift and its different forms, be they individual in the gift, or institutional in humanitarian assistance; from that starting point, one goes back to ritual forms while keeping the same questions. One then returns to our modernity and shows how a whole system of generous assistance, of noble gestures, originating long ago, end up compensating for the ruthless system of the marketplace. Without being entirely wrong, this genealogy distorts reality because it projects the moral purpose of the modern gift onto the functioning of the ceremonial gift. On the contrary, it must be emphasized that the practice of ceremonial giving is no more a gesture of assistance or charity than it is an alternative to market relationships. In this case, the word gift is probably inappropriate (Mauss recognized this at the end of *The Gift*, p. 73). It would be better to speak of sumptuary offerings. What matters is not giving in itself, but launching or continuing a procedure of reciprocal recognition (as in *recognizing one another*) expressed through precious goods and services. If the gifts are directed toward an individual, what matters is not the individual as such, but what they represent. This has nothing to do with a generous act implying on the part of the giver an attitude of moral renouncement.[9]

The debate on the gift runs a constant risk of falling back into this old prejudice if a distinction is not clearly kept between the private forms of generosity (be it in moral or religious terms) and the ceremonial practice of the exchange of gifts. This is not a mere separation between past and present, archaic and modern. The ceremonial gift is still sufficiently present within western-type societies for us to be convinced of it: reciprocal dinner invitations, marriage or birthday presents, celebration of achievements, and so on. These practices are very different from gestures of gratification such as anonymous donations to charities, time dedicated to people in pain or other admirable gestures that stay away from public promotion. The latter are gestures involving decisions made by the donors alone. No custom accepted by all, no social expectation places pressure upon those who choose to give for the purpose of giving or helping others. In addition, the donors – especially if they remain anonymous – do not expect as a result of their gesture a strengthening of the social bond within a community; they aim for the well-being or acts to relieve people whom they often do not know.

The case of the ceremonial gift is entirely different. Not only must it be known, but if it were not it would miss its goal, which is precisely to bring about a reciprocal and public recognition, to create or reinforce the social bond. It can be characterized by the fact that it demands givers, receivers, things given, time and circumstances of the act be identified. In other words, this form of exchange involves neither personal virtue nor individual kindness, neither spiritual accomplishment nor pure and anonymous generosity, but foremost the bringing about of a solemn recognition of the other according to rules transmitted by tradition. It is a social form whose effect must be a social one and cannot be assessed using criteria applicable to moral gifts. This does not mean that the private act of obligation bears no relationship to the reciprocal gift as was said of the market relationship. There is indeed a common denominator, which is the generous gesture; there probably lies the source of the usual confusion, for neither act has the same function nor generates the same effects.

The ceremonial gift: offering, challenging, bonding

Mauss bases his account of the ceremonial gift on the requirement to return the gift, probably because, as was mentioned, this requirement is the most enigmatic one for us. Mauss relies on the interpretation based on indigenous characters, not, as Lévi-Strauss (1987) thinks, because he does not grasp the immediate unity of the three actions – actually he sees it quite well – but because it is difficult to come up with a general explanation of the very act of giving; thus he confesses his puzzlement regarding *kula* exchange: "Unfortunately we do not have a good knowledge of the rule of law that governs these transactions" (Lévi-Strauss 1987). This is what we must ask: before a gift must be returned, what required that a gift be made in the first place? Why give, and why is it an obligation? Some of Mauss's work shows an awareness that the problem lies in the use of the very term, gift. Its altruistic connotation remains so powerful that it is difficult for us to see how the ceremonial gift is not primarily meant to fulfill its recipient with goods as such but *to express consideration*, to honor him or her.

On this point Mauss's analysis, as well as much of later research, shows the lack of a more radical reflection on the practice of the ceremonial gift as the preferred expression among humans of the encounter between alien groups. However, in the very last pages of his essay, Mauss shows awareness of what seems to us to be at the core of the issue: "Over a considerable period of time, and in a considerable number of societies, men approached one another in a curious frame of mind, one of fear and exaggerated hostility, and of generosity that was likewise exaggerated, but such traits only appear insane to our eyes.... There is no middle way: one trusts completely, or one mistrusts completely; one lays down one's arms and gives up magic or one gives everything" (Mauss 1990 [1924], p. 81). It may be that the obligation to give is entirely contained in this paradoxical characteristic of human beings, who are at the same time all radically others and radically the same. This entails the question, who is this other – individual or group – that looks like us? Who are they, in this elsewhere that is like our here? How can one not be like us, who know quite well who we are? How can these others seem so close to us and not be some of us? Should they be deterred from entering our space, and forcefully repelled? Or should they be welcomed? How can we express our desire for an encounter or an alliance? How can we be sure they will accept it and not change their minds? How can we create a lasting bond?

Such are the questions implied in the act of giving; they involve neither economics nor morals, neither usefulness nor charity. They concern above all the demand to be recognized, not to be grateful. This seems to be at the core of the enigma of the ceremonial gift.

For an ethology of the encounter: the gift exchange as a symbolic gesture

> "Nobody ever saw a dog make a fair and deliberate exchange of one bone for another with another dog."
>
> Adam Smith (1993 [1776], p. 21)

Andrew Strathern, in his classical work on the circulation of the *moka* gifts in the Mount Hagen region of New Guinea, wrote that in the village of his informant – an old man who had witnessed the arrival of the first white men, representatives of the Australian administration – the question had been raised as to whether the strange creature that had come and visited them was a human being or one of those pale cannibalistic monsters mentioned in legends; they offered him pigs, and in return he gave them precious shells. That was when the natives decided that they were indeed dealing with a genuine man like themselves (Strathern 1971, p. xii).

This is an exemplary tale, in that it invites us to raise in a radical manner the ethological question of the recognition between humans, and to confront the modes of relation and encounter in our species with those observed in various types of animal societies. These relationships include many aspects and take on such predictable forms in every species that they have been considered as rituals. They involve colors, smells, sounds, visual forms, and attitudes. Of course, the most relevant ethological information is the one that concerns groups of apes, particularly gorillas and chimpanzees (Goodall 1986; De Waal 1989, 2001; Mc Grew, Marchant, and Nishida 1990; Premack 1994, pp. 350–65; Mc Grew 1992; Bard and Parker 1996). Modes of approach, recognition and acceptance are subtle and highly complex. Observers are unsure whether all of them should be considered as being programmed. Some kinds of "traditions" are specific to certain groups; however, the main modes remain stable within a species, and the forms they take only show a limited range of variation. The process of recognition includes at least two aspects (which often constitute two phases following each other). The first step is a recognition as an identification of the other as either alike or not; this is a moment of adequate perception (it is found in every living species). The second aspect is by far the more important one: it is a recognition as acceptance, as act of "respect" or even allegiance. It is also found in every mammal, and of course is more highly developed among primates. This acceptance is performed through a whole series of visual behaviors whose expression remains relatively unchanged.

On the contrary, human groups stand out because they display a considerable range of variation of these processes. It is as if the inventiveness in the modes of approach and contact were proportional to the degree of autonomy of living beings. These stabilized variations passed on from generation to generation are part of what is called cultures. However, an invariant stands out among these variations: the very fact that the recognition of the other (in its second step, as recognition granted to a partner), is performed through the reciprocal giving of objects that are considered as important; this is what is called presents. Something of oneself – a good of one's own – is presented and given to the other. The precious character granted to that thing makes it manifest that it is something of one's own that is equated to a part of oneself, something one holds dear, to which one assigns value, that one ventures to give: at the same time a guarantee and a substitute of the giver. And the other understands that the one or those who offer this good request a response of the same kind. This is why this process of encounter and exchange is marked by two characteristics that aim at emphasizing its importance. First, the act of presenting is not performed in a trivial or neutral way. It involves a great emotional charge; the moment is a solemn one, and feelings are ambiguous. There always is a concern that what is given might not be accepted or not be considered as adequate. But the wish to bond, the pleasure involved in being with one's chosen partners must also be expressed; hence the festive and consumption aspect of the event. Goods are offered along with courteous words, deferential gestures, sometimes dances, music, or delicacies. Second, all of this follows well-established protocols that work as conventions and aim at eliminating the risks that could be brought on by any awkward improvisation, which would also give an impression of carelessness. This formal aspect is what confers a kind of solemnity to the act of giving and its acceptance (thus, in kula, exchanges are announced with horn blows and everything takes place according to set stages and in an atmosphere of seriousness and mutual respect which doesn't preclude festiveness). Because of all this, the gift is said to be ceremonial according to Malinowski's definition: "I shall call an action ceremonial if it is: (1) public; (2) carried on under observance of definite formalities; (3) if it has sociological, religious or magical import, and carries with it obligations" (Malinowski 1961 [1922], p. 95).

The recognition of another human being or group always takes place through the act of holding out a mediating object to the other, presenting them with something that one is giving away as a part of oneself, chancing it into the alien space. This is what this act indicates: first, we recognize you as other humans, like ourselves; second, we accept you as possible partners; finally, once relationships have been established, we wish to remain bonded to you in the future.

It can be said that this act is symbolism if we accept that etymologically speaking a symbol is a physical element that stands for a pact; sum-bolon means literally what is placed together. In certain ancient forms of reciprocal commitments (used by Greeks and Romans) a piece of pottery or metal was broken and each partner kept half of it as evidence and guarantee of the agreement; each piece, matching the other, could vouch for the agreement at any time and often long afterwards. In this way, the symbol belongs to the realm of the alliance, of relationships of reciprocity; this does not mean that symbolism is necessarily of a social nature, but that symbolism always implies a system of differentiated elements that are related to each other according to a convention of exchange (Ortiques 1962, Sperber 1975).

If indeed giving is this unique, and specifically human, process of recognition, then it is crucial that the partners in the pact – the sumballontes – alternate actions; things offered by one side must respond to those offered by the other; the sum-bolon consists in the set made up by the giver, the thing that is given, the recipient and the response of the recipient giving something back. Symbolism is the fact of this triple implication and this double movement, either immediate as in the opening gifts, or extended through time as in already confirmed alliances. The exchange of reciprocal gifts cannot be reduced to the expression of a courteous sociality; it is the procedure that publicly institutes the act of honoring each other, be it individual or group, which begins or replays the founding act of the alliance. It is worth noting that in encounters and processes of approach between two human groups, even the friendliest bodily expressions are not sufficient to establish recognition – meaning acceptance. An additional element is required: this physical element, guarantee of good faith, offered as a token and substitute for the one who offers an alliance – the given thing. No such procedure is found in any primate group. At most, chimpanzees will share the flesh of an animal that was killed in a collective hunt, but they never show procedures of approach of a group by another through the offering of an object that would then be kept as testimony to the agreement and to which another object given by the partner would respond immediately or later on. Actually, acts of sharing among primates (such as holding out a piece of food to another) do not in themselves qualify as giving;[10] the ceremonial gift is not the sharing of a good; it is not an expression of altruism (altruism is a phenomenon that can indeed be observed in every primate society); it is not a mere benevolent giving away of what one owns; it is the granting of a guarantee that commits the giver, as a substitute of himself, and is presented as the conclusion of a pact. This gift – this risky gesture – does not aim at increasing the partner's possessions or at helping him. We must once again reject the economist's prejudice that always focuses on the consumable good and ignores the act of challenging the other, as well as the moral prejudice that promotes the act of helping while misunderstanding agonistic generosity.

It would be tempting to consider this guarantee as a mediation (and indeed it is one) that would express the opposition between subject and object – where the subject would assert himself in the thing presented. This interpretation appears to be consistent but it is only relevant to the logic of the contract (the aim of which is to separate the subject from the object); but when applied to the alliance and to the gift relation it confuses things, because what makes it possible for an object to become a guarantee and a substitute is that it is an extension of the very being of the ones who offers themselves through it, as a part of them that is mobile but not distinct from them. Such is the ceremonial – public – act that is called giving, which means, first and foremost: solemnly recognizing, accepting, and honoring each other, and above all establishing an alliance through the mediation of what is given to the other. And for this recognition, acceptance, and bond to be maintained and developed, reciprocal gifts, the most important being the matrimonial alliance, must be constantly renewed.

Thus, the reason for the initial obligation to give comes to light, as well as the obligation to accept and give back. Reciprocal ceremonial giving manifests a fundamental structure of reciprocity as a condition for all social life in the human species.[11] We can say, as Mauss did, that we have reached the "bedrock." Yet, at this point, we must be aware of the extreme complexity of the act and relationship of giving. What ensures that the gift will be accepted? What is implied in the relationship with another human being, another animal endowed with language? What does recognizing mean? What is the status of the thing that is given and what defines its significance for the partners? What is the nature of the bond thus formed? What does a denial of recognition or a misunderstanding in the exchange entail?

Challenge, generosity, and play

These questions probably imply the following: how can we understand the aspects of challenge and generosity involved in giving? Mauss sensed this: "There is no middle ground: either complete trust or complete mistrust; laying down the weapons and giving up magic, or giving everything" (Mauss 1990 [1924], p. 81). The challenge includes two aspects: the first merely involves inciting the other to respond. It solves the following problem: how to solicit without appearing to solicit. The challenge requires a response without having to request it. The very structure of the challenge rooted in the relationship between two equally autonomous living beings remains to be understood. The second aspect involves giving much or giving what is considered to be precious in order to make the challenge forceful enough, to oblige the partner. In this case, excess has a power of anticipation. It makes it possible to throw the arch of a bridge toward a still invisible shore and to ensure that from the other side the same action will complete the building. Without this challenge – this excessive gesture – the distance between positions, between one and the other, would remain insurmountable. But the approach itself would be inconceivable because one of the protagonists would have to give in. The challenge of the gift provokes and invokes. It provokes precisely in that it remains intractable. It invokes trust and reassures in that it gives everything: oneself in the guarantee presented, in the thing which is given.

The ceremonial generosity is not a moral one, or if it is, that is only as a supplement; it is the proof that while chancing into an alien space, one is prepared to establish an alliance. Groups and individuals know that the greatest temptation is to keep to oneself, to find well-being at home. At the same time, the greatest satisfaction lies in being recognized by others. There is pleasure in bonding with others, in knowing what is elsewhere. There is also the danger of being rejected or attacked. The gift solves this dilemma. As a challenge, it makes it possible to risk making a move toward the other while forcing the other to hazard a move toward us. It becomes a gamble on the possibility of going outside oneself under conditions of reciprocity.

This concept of challenge makes it possible to understand several aspects of the gift relationship. First of all, generosity must be ostentatious. As Boas and Malinowski keep reminding us, giving is glorious and brings prestige. This honor remains enigmatic. Should it be understood as a denial of material goods?[12] Leaving aside certain cases of exacerbated potlatch described by Boas,[13] what matters is not to destroy, but, on the contrary, to provide ample evidence of wealth in which the substance of the giver and their group are expressed. Exhibiting goods, offering them, displaying prodigality, does not amount to saying all this is nothing, on the contrary, it takes it for granted that it will be highly valued. Yet it must be clear that the first goal is to honor the recipient, to show them the highest possible consideration, even an excessive one, and in this lies the honor of the giver. To this aim, it is important for the action to be known and seen by all, spectacular if possible. This makes it easier to understand that what is involved is not charitable generosity but public liberality. Attempting this challenge, keeping it in front of all, is what brings prestige and glory in the relationship of recognition (which is profoundly different from the struggle for recognition according to Hegel).[14]

The challenge is not primarily a rivalry for a coveted object but a call and even a provocation for a response; however, there is rivalry, but in a playful or "athletic" sense, not one caused by envy; if this rivalry becomes exacerbated, that is because another element destabilizes the play of the challenge and the alternation between partners. But why call it play? More precisely, it belongs to the category of play that implies a principle of alternation; those are games played by two partners, each of whom has a turn in response to the others' (as in chess, card games, or many ball games). Such games are structured as duels or tournaments. They imply, as Huizinga (1986 [1937]) saw, a kind of spontaneous convention that is also an ethics: "to each their turn"; playing twice in a row is cheating. One must play in one's turn because every challenge must expect a response. Not to respond means losing. Or rather, it is a response by default, but a response nevertheless. With his usual insight, Mauss noticed this playful aspect of gift exchange rituals when he wrote (about peoples of the northwest coast of America): "On this subject, it would be necessary to study gambling which, even in European societies, is not considered to be a contract but a situation in which honor is committed and where goods are handed over that, after all, one could refuse to hand over. Gambling is a form of potlatch and of the gift system" (Mauss 1990 [1924], ch. 3, note 139, p. 112). A kind of equivalence is even found among the Tlingit and the Haida between game, potlatch, and warfare. One can win or lose everything (wife and children included). In this phenomenon of the game, there is always a challenge and a call, thrown out toward the unknown, a means of seducing the stranger. "Seducere" literally means drawing others toward oneself, bringing them in from elsewhere. But this bet that requests and even demands a response from the other (which means that the challenge has reached them, has crossed over to the invisible shore) calls for a reply, the return move that is so obvious in the practice of the game.

Roberte Hamayon (2001) studying populations of Siberian hunters, the Bouriats, especially their shamanistic practices, clearly showed that the game is tied to the ceremonial gift and the system of alliance. The major seasonal rituals of preparation for hunting take on the form of games; they constitute a kind of symbolic hunt, directed and mimicked in dances performed by the shaman with various animal masks. Moreover, this symbolic hunt is understood as a matrimonial union between the hunter-husband and the hunted animal; the shaman mimics the rutting male trying to seduce his animal spouse. The whole ritual revolves around the motif of the alliance which, in addition to the union with the animal, also includes one with the forest spirits and with other animals. All of these relationships are understood as relationships between partners who at the same time respect, provoke, attract, and please each other through their exchanges, which is why "games please the spirits." Thus, Hamayon says, the human community conceives of itself as forming a couple with the environment. This feeling of a kind of equal partnership is a very strong one; it finds its most powerful expression in the game, as a relationship of challenge and reply, giving and returning, enjoyment and obligation.

It may be that the potlatch already shows a break with this model; how can we explain the change operated from playful to exacerbated rivalry? Hamayon signals that when the world of the alliance is replaced with that of affiliation; when hunters become breeders, the ancestors who handed down the herd count for more than the forest spirits who give the chance to capture the prey. A hierarchical verticality replaces the horizontal relationship between equal partners. This is probably one of the key elements determining the appearance of a more hierarchical, more authoritarian world.

The possibility of deception

Because the relationship between partners in the reciprocal ceremonial gift implies in its principle a *risk* and includes an element of seduction, it also implies the possibility of *deception.* This possibility cannot be separated from the nature of the partners involved as fundamentally autonomous beings, jealously guarding their autonomy. This is only a possibility, not a necessary component. Yet, it may be said that, without this possibility, there would be no risk, and thus recognition itself would be worthless. It is well known that the first element of risk lies in the possibility for the partner to refuse the offer; in which case conflict arises. The second element lies in the possibility for partners to mutually accept the offer, but with manipulative intentions. In other words, there is deception. It may take various forms. The giver may be sincere but the receiver duplicitous, or the reverse, even if the goods offered are faultless. More commonly, the goods offered may be unsatisfactory. But in the end, what is at stake is always granting or refusing recognition, and its value is estimated by the yardstick of the honor involved.

It is noteworthy that this quasi built-in ambiguity was one of the first aspects recorded by Mauss when, at the beginning of *The Gift*, he quoted stanzas from the Havamál, one of the oldest poems of the Scandinavian Edda:

> "A man ought to be a friend for his friend and repay gift with gift. People should meet smiles with smiles and lies for treachery..."
> "Know – If you have a friend in whom you have sure confidence and wish to make use of him, you ought to merge your souls and exchange gifts with him and go to see him often..."
> "If you have another in whom you have no confidence and yet want to make use of him, you ought to address him with fair words but with a crafty heart and repay treacheries with lies..."[15]

This text, like so many other materials, very clearly supports our approach: what is at stake in the exchange of gifts is not the goods as such, but the relationship between the partners. Therefore, deception can only concern this relationship itself (in which goods act only as mediations). In the ordinary commercial exchange, deception concerns the goods as such: either their quantity or their quality. Even if a partner has been treated with much deference, they may consider that they have been injured if the goods that were the object of the transaction do not match the agreement reached. In the relationship, based on the gift, on the contrary, deception may take place not necessarily through reducing the value of the promised goods but, paradoxically, through offering goods more valuable than expected. An extravagant present, giving the other the delusion of great esteem or deference, may be the surest way of deceiving them about the relationship. What is at stake is recognition: granting it while refusing it, denying it through inappropriate presents. But, in a more subtle way, the logic of the obligation to return the gift may be pushed to the limit: forcing the partner to take on difficult or even deadly commitments by giving him presents that require an unavoidable conventional response. Good examples of this can be found in Homer. In the Iliad, Antimachus accepts sumptuous presents from Alexander, an ally of Priam the king of Troy, and by doing so becomes an ally of the latter and eventually finds himself forced to send his two sons to fight on Priam's side, and be killed.

Therefore, the logic of the reciprocal gift can act as a trap because the receivers must choose between refusing the gift and thus declaring themselves an enemy, or accepting it and finding themselves caught in a costly or even deadly obligation. They must therefore display cunning as great as the giver's, to be able to refuse the gift without offending them. It is important that the refusal be justified by conventions stronger than those requiring its acceptance. Thus, elsewhere in the Iliad, Achilles's young squire is offered a gold cup by Priam in exchange for his help; accepting it would make him indebted to the old King and would amount to betraying Achilles who, with other Greeks, is besieging Troy. He must therefore refuse the gift, but he must do so for reasons that will be recognized on both sides as imperative. Such reasons exist. He reminds Priam that, because of his young age, he cannot receive presents without his master's permission. He must therefore turn down the offer. On the other hand, he voluntarily grants the requested favor: to guide the old king during his visit to the besiegers' encampment. Homer's readers are not surprised by the young man's cunning: under the squire's disguise lies the god Hermes, the master of ruse and counter-ruse, acting in support of Achilles.

Even though at the beginning of *The Gift* Mauss quotes a document (the Scandinavian poem mentioned above), showing the splendor of the gift associated with the possibility of deception, he failed to consider this duality in his subsequent analyses. This does not mean that he failed to understand the issue; on the contrary, he had explicitly addressed it in a short article, "Gift, gift," published in the same year (Mauss 1969 [1924]), shortly before *The Gift*. He emphasized the remarkable fact that the same term means gift in English and poison in German; he noted that the Dutch language has kept both meanings. The common origin of this double meaning seemed fairly obvious to him: among Indo-European peoples, especially Celts, Germans, and Scandinavians, exchanges of presents and libations of beverages both occurred during feasts. "The gift-drink," he wrote, "can be a poison; typically, outside of grim circumstances, it is not; but it can always become so. In any case, it is always an enchantment (the word gift has kept this meaning in English) that forever binds the communicants and can always turn against one of them if he were to breach the law. The kinship in meaning between gift as present and gift as poison is therefore easy to explain and seems natural" (ibid., p. 49). In a way, the partner is ingested with the drink, for the better if possible, but also for the worse if he is duplicitous. This ambiguity also appears in the Greek notion of dosis, which means the act of giving but also the medical "dose" akin to poison (hence antidosis: antidote); and in the Roman notion of potio, which includes both remedy and magical drink, or even poison, but without a direct link to the realm of the gift.

Why does Mauss not return to these questions in *The Gift*? Did he consider them in the end to be too marginal, relative to the central question of the triple obligation to give, receive, and return the gift – that "total social fact" of traditional societies? Maybe. However, there is another hypothesis: in spite of the novelty of his approach, Mauss remained to some extent trapped within the standard explanation that sees the movement of reciprocal gifts as a circulation of goods. Indeed, although Mauss occasionally used terms taken from the vocabulary of trade, he clearly understood that gifts aim at ensuring status, increasing the prestige of the giver, and are meant for luxury consumption. But he did not see that these goods are only of secondary importance: that they are above all the expression of a recognition offered and returned under conditions involving risk and uncertainty; and that, for this very reason, the possibility of deception remains part of the process. What matters is to create or renounce trust. This trust is personal, and intense; the goods offered are nothing but tokens and guarantees of it, since one gives oneself in what one gives. The matrimonial alliance is its most accomplished and institutional expression: it indexes the reciprocal commitment with the reproduction of life itself and the alternation of generations. But the risk of a breach and conflict remains because the autonomy of the partners is constantly reasserted.

The trade exchange and the model of the contract

Mercantile exchange aims at reducing this risk by doing away with the primary requirement of personal recognition in the movement of goods. Even if the partner is granted some esteem, that is not the purpose of the transaction, which aims at acquiring or selling those goods as such; they are what has to be appreciated and evaluated. If there is a deception, it will concern these goods regardless of any friendly or deferent attitude of the seller.

When acquiring or providing goods, and not recognizing a partner, money makes it possible to set fair equivalences. Such exchanges imply precise and efficient procedures of reciprocal commitment. Such is the contract, which, in its forms and implications, is the exact opposite of the reciprocal ceremonial gift. This is precisely why it provides a guarantee of fairness and independence. Before attempting to describe its characteristics, we may note that Mauss made a surprising use of this term in the context of exchanges of ceremonial presents.

In *The Gift* (Mauss 1990 [1924]) the term "contract" is often used to describe commitments made between partners: "exchanges and contracts take place in the form of presents" (p. 3); "we shall describe the phenomena of exchange and contract in these societies" (p. 4); "there is total service in the sense that it is indeed the whole clan that contracts on behalf of all" (p. 6); "this system of contractual gifts in Samoa ..." (p. 8). The sacrifice is also considered a relationship of this type with the gods ("we can begin at this point a theory and history of the sacrifice as contract..." [p. 15]). The choice of the concept of contract is clearly inappropriate in the case of the ceremonial gift, but first, we must understand why Mauss is using this term. At least two reasons can be considered. One is general: Mauss broadly resorts to this notion to designate any type of commitment between different partners; he might as well have used the term pact, which he sometimes does. "Contract" thus refers to a form of mutual commitment between partners. But there is another, more crucial reason: in the practices of gift exchanges, the obvious element of constraint can only be compared to that of a contract. Indeed, Mauss's interest in the question of the gift started with his work on the origins of the contract and certain archaic forms of the law (Roman, Scandinavian, and Hindu). At the same time, another sociologist, Georges Davy, who had been his student, was working on these questions and in 1922 published a book on this topic entitled *La foi jurée* (1975 [1922]), which focuses primarily on the Kwankiutl, Tlingit, and Haida potlatch. From the start, the ceremonial gift is situated or rather pre-interpreted within a legal framework stemming from European culture. At first, Mauss seems to adopt this approach, because using the paradigm of the contract to interpret the ritual gift enabled him to recognize the two central characteristics of any "social fact" according to Durkheim: that is, being coercive and being immediately collective. However, several reticent references made by Mauss to Davy (in *The Gift* or elsewhere) render his discomfort obvious. Besides placing the potlatch within an evolution that would lead to the modern contract, what made Mauss most uncomfortable was that the agonistic character of the potlatch makes it incompatible with the very concept of contract. Or, rather, for Mauss, the contract is only related to the compulsory aspect of the gift, which is not a variant of the contract nor its ancestor, but a specific fact, it is even a "total social fact." A passage of *The Gift* clearly outlines the different status of the contract with respect to the phenomenon of the game or gambling "which, even today, is not considered contractual, but rather comprised of situations in which honor is engaged and where property is surrendered even when it is not absolutely necessary. Gambling is a form of potlatch and a part of the gift system."[16] In short, even when Mauss still uses the term contract, he does not want to consider the ceremonial gift in terms of legal criteria, as does Davy following an evolutionist model, but intends to help us understand one of its crucial characteristics: obligation. His whole essay clearly aims at bringing forth the irreducible originality of the reciprocal gift exchange.

We can now try the reverse approach by quickly indicating the main characteristics specific to the model of the contract and distinguish it from the model of the traditional gift. Since our purpose is to underline the contrast with ceremonial exchange, we shall restrict our consideration to the contract of sale and purchase. We can state the following: 1) such a contract implies a negotiation between partners in view of obtaining the greatest mutual advantage; this negotiation may be easy or on the contrary harsh and even hostile, each partner attempting to defend their interest; 2) even if the contract is made between individuals (generally two, be they actual persons or institutions; but also contracts of association – called partnership contracts – which may imply several members), it is not of a personal nature; it involves persons not as particular subjects but as subjects in the law; the contract thus has an impersonal form; if something is bought from or sold to a friend, the friendship may be recorded but cannot as such be part of the grounds of the contract (one cannot commit oneself by contract to remain friends, nor define love relationships); 3) in a contractual exchange, the goods exchanged are defined and described exhaustively; the transaction concerns those goods and not others; thus the object of the contract is strictly limited; 4) by hypothesis the goods involved in a contractual procedure of sale are alienable (persons, honors, or public functions, for instance, cannot be sold by contract, without an immoral decision contrary to law); 5) the obligation contracted by the partners is public and legally defined; breaches of commitments are subject to sanction by law (fines, physical constraint, loss of rights); and 6) finally – this is a crucial point – the specificity of the contract comprises being limited in time; it is in force over a defined duration and becomes null and void after that.

We can see that each of these points profoundly contradicts the logic of the gift exchange. The sale contract is a procedure whose aim is not to request recognition by the partner. It aims at a clear, efficient, measurable exchange of goods. This is why the monetary instrument suits it so well. This is also why it is important to distinguish it from the gift relationship. The Protestant ethics firmly established this distinction by instituting a radical separation between the universe of the gift – that of grace – left solely to God, and that of business – the realm of men – and the object of the "inner-world." Conversely, one can show, as Clavero did,[17] how Catholic ethics has allowed a contamination between these two logics.

Trust and risks calculation

Modern economic theory – as everyone knows – is based on the hypothesis that the system of production and the realm of the marketplace have become autonomous. For over three centuries, economic theory has been constructing the figure of the *homo economicus*, now called the rational economic agent. By considering traditional gift relationships as mere archaic mercantile exchanges, it has also proposed doing away with such practices. Economic activity claims to belong to a clear and efficient mode of operation, the very mode defined by contractual relationships. Every economic theory was developed against the background of this strict rationality whose most accomplished figure is probably that of the calculating agent outlined in *game theory*. That agent operates choices based solely upon their own interest; that theory presupposes as an unquestionable truth that the selfish aim is natural and thus legitimate. Individual interest is taken to be the ultimate horizon of rational behavior. This is also why game theory has been able to provide powerful conceptual tools to society's various models of interaction. These models make it possible to coordinate the total sum of rationally directed individual choices within a social organization that is itself understood as the total sum of interactions. Hence the agent's every action is a strategic relational choice.

However, it soon became a suspicion that the rational actors, constantly busy working out their "moves," might be nothing more than fictional figures that would be hard to identify within ordinary social experience. Granted, it is a model which, as such, is entitled to being an abstraction; it still remains that the model must be operational. Yet it is far from being so when the particular character of interactions is taken into account.

Interactions do not amount to mere moves within a neutral space. We have come to better understand that rational choice theory (especially with reference to the famous prisoner's dilemma) implies the central question of trust. What does this mean? It is not enough to demonstrate, based on game theory, that in the end agents have everything to gain by cooperating and even by being altruistic, in short by granting trust to their partner. When understood that way, trust remains purely strategic, a mere element in the computation of interests, as Williamson (1993) and Hollis (1998) have shown.

We must then understand where this trust, which is crucial to the very logic of rational choices, originates; either it is generated by these very choices and it remains, in the end, a parameter in the calculation of interests; or it precedes them and makes them possible, in which case it is important to identify its origin and manifestations. The oversimplifications (and sometimes the impasses) of game theory when confronting the problem of trust within interactions come from a failure to realize this: trust can only appear at the local level in a particular "move" because it is not a mere parameter that may or may not come into play, but a founding element of any relationship between individuals. A shortcoming of social analysis (regarding the concrete conditions of trust) combines at this point with an epistemological one (regarding the consideration of the diversity of parameters). Yet the question of trust must be articulated at two different levels of social depth. At the first level, it must be situated within the whole set of collective mediations that make it operational within a given society; in traditional societies, such mediations are closely tied to ethnicity, rituals, ways of living, religious beliefs; in modern societies, they may be legal, ethical, or tied to reputation (which does not exclude a powerful continued influence of ethnic or religious elements). In short, the granting or refusal of trust cannot be separated from what constitutes a community: its rules, values, and traditions. Economic agents always make their decisions within such situations. In other words, even if in any given case agents may theoretically choose their own attitude and calculate their own interest, it remains that what empirically determines their choices and incites their trust is a whole set of parameters tied to representations shared within their community.

This, in any case, is the objection most frequently raised against the interaction model based on game theory. It signals a kind of return to Durkheim's position; or at least it proposes to correct the individualistic aim through a holistic interpretation. This correction seems necessary because it makes it possible to integrate a fuller and more complex set of parameters. It aims at accounting for a socially and culturally defined agent, rather than a pure model of interaction. Yet this is not sufficient. Something remains unexplained, which must now be examined: the second level of social depth that was mentioned above.

Conclusion: trust, deception, and social bond

It is not enough to state that game theory is located at too abstract a level and that the cases it deals with – such as the prisoner's dilemma – can only be verified for a theoretical model, since this drawback is inherent in any model. It is thus not enough to say that in actual interactions the guarantee of trust can be provided by cultural conditions whether they are religious or ethical ones, or based on any collective value system strongly internalized by the agents. The question must be raised in a more radical way: What is trust itself? Why does it constitute the foundation of social relationships as such? In that light, deception itself appears not merely as one possible form within the framework of strategic relationships, but as a risk inherent in the social relationship as such.

The attitude that is called trust undoubtedly belongs to the emotional realm. It is a powerful bond of a particular kind between agents. But what are emotions themselves? On this question, Dumouchel (1999 [1995]) provides a convincing and innovative analysis in which emotions are understood as being, in essence, processes of coordination between living beings within each species and, in the case of the human species, what constitutes the social bond itself:

"Emotions are social in that they are not the means but the state of humans living together. The fact that we have an affective life is not a cause of but is the fact that, as beings, we are not completely independent of each other. ... This is why the way in which emotions are social is primary. It is not derived. Our affective life makes us social animals. It constitutes the social for us. ... The adjective social does not take on a special meaning when it is applied to emotions; on the contrary, all the other senses of the word are, or should be, based on that meaning. To say that emotions are social is to say what the social is" (p. 84).

Thus, according to the same author, it is important to understand the various expressions of emotions (anger, astonishment, joy, envy, sorrow, desire, worry, trust, defiance, and so on), not as types that may be considered in isolation, but as salient moments within the emotional continuum constituted by the process of coordination between agents. Trust must be located within this continuum. This is the background against which the act which we defined above as the ceremonial gift, based on an ethologics of the encounter, takes on its meaning, namely the act through which an object is offered to the other as something of oneself, a guarantee and substitute of oneself, chanced into the other's space, witness to the recognition that is offered and counterpart of the one that is expected, but with the concern that this bet might be a losing one, that the other may fail to respond, or respond inadequately. Mistrust – and deception – may, as well as trust, stand out as a mode of the relationship. Hence the ritual form taken up by the relationship, its observance of a conventional process that makes it possible to avoid improvisation, misunderstandings, and mistakes, constitutes the procedure which is meant to preempt this very risk. Once again, it is clear that traditional gift relationships are not primarily exchanges of goods but modes of the institutionalization of the social bond, through which trust is generated or confirmed.

More precisely, the ceremonial gift exchange is the specific mode of public reciprocal recognition in traditional societies. For them, this exchange constitutes the very way of establishing conventions and making alliances, the most important of which being the matrimonial one, because it involves the entire network of public relationships based on kinship. This defines the political level in these types of societies precisely, because it concerns their public life: their forms of justice and their structure of power. However, in societies where a central authority has emerged, public recognition is guaranteed by law and inscribed in the various institutions of a justice system. This circumscribes a field of rights, but not personal behavior. Each citizen or public authority can sue an offender. The law guarantees only a civil status, but does not take the place of the gesture of recognition. But we still have to perform that gesture, at least at two major levels: the first is that of social relationships, which are defined by public civilities and local expressions of courtesy; the second involves the agent in a more personal way: it concerns ethical attitudes of respect and trust toward other agents.

This trust is the prior ground which allows contractual relationships and commercial exchanges to develop. It now seems clear that trust as a mode of the social bond cannot be reduced to a mere parameter within game theory; it cannot be a mere strategic element in the computation of rational self-interest presupposed by that theory. For the same reason, deception in commercial exchange is not a strictly localized behavior within a set of operations aiming at maximizing the profit of the agent who manipulates their partner or partners. The mistrust implied by this deception undermines the social bond and the requirement of reciprocal recognition that is an integral part of it. In this way also, the issue is necessarily an ethical one.

Notes

* Translated by Jean-Louis Morhange with the collaboration of Anne-Marie Feenberg

1 This includes all forms of institutionalized compensations known as the welfare system. But it could also include the most recent forms of corporate philanthropy, often defined as "gift economy." See on this issue: Dowie (2001), Himmelstein (1997).

2 The analysis – later on in this essay – of the ceremonial, reciprocal exchange of gifts will help us to understand this expression. In traditional societies (of lineage or segmentary-type, for instance), the justice system takes the form of what we improperly call "vengeance," which is indeed a precise ritual of compensation among allied groups. See Verdier (1980–86).

3 By contractual exchange, we understand all kinds of trade made within the frame of juridical rules. It is not limited to reciprocal business; any form of legitimate trade presupposes the acceptance of such rules.

4 I do not intend to address the issue of deception in commercial exchange, which is discussed by most of the other contributors to this volume. Later on, I will briefly outline the main features of contractual exchange to contrast it with gift exchange.

5 Boas wrote: "The economical system of the Indians of British Colombia is largely based on credit, as that of civilized peoples. ... Incurring debts on the one hand, paying debts on the other, makes up the potlatch. ... Those who receive presents during the ceremony receive them as loans, which they use in their current enterprises, but after a lapse of a few years, they must return them with interest to the giver or his heir," *12th Report on the North Western Tribes of Canada*, pp. 54–5.

6 This confusion is so widespread that in most social anthropology textbooks or treatises, the question of the ceremonial gift is most often dealt with in the chapter on exchanges in general and as an interesting form of the circulation of commodities, whereas it belongs to the field of institutional forms of authority and assignment of status.

7 We can find a good example still today in New Guinea: money earned through salaried work allows more and more men who are no longer warriors to obtain the privilege of organizing festivities, which secure one's reputation and make marriages possible; this is the case,

for instance, of the ceremonial exchanges called "moka" in the Mount Hagen region. See Akin and Robbins (1999).

8 On the specificity of the phenomenon of the gift, one can refer to the wealth of information (studies, debates) presented by Alain Caillé and collaborators in *La Revue du MAUSS*, 1re série: N° 11, 1991, "Donner, recevoir et render" N° 12, "Le don perdu et retrouvé" 2e série: N° 1, 1993 "Ce que donner veut dire," N° 8, 1996, "L'obligation de donner." See also Jacques Godbout (1998 [1991]), Caillé (2000).

9 Irwin Goldman rightly remarks: "Kwakiutl have no sense of charity: for them, a genuine donor can give only to a genuine recipient." (Goldman 1975, p. 104).

10 Therefore, I cannot endorse the views of Craig Stanford on this particular point, despite my interest in his excellent analysis: "The Ape's Gift," in De Waal (1989).

11 This analysis confirms C. Lévi-Strauss'views on what he calls "the principle of reciprocity" (1969). See my comments in: Hénaff, (1998), pp. 36–67.

12 Following the very Hegelian interpretation put forth by Claude Lefort in his well-known text (1986).

13 Recent research has put this "crazy potlatch" (which fascinated Georges Bataille) into perspective. We now know that this very exacerbated form appeared rather late, that is, in the last decades of the nineteenth century. This is when the drop in the demographic level had considerably reduced the availability of prestigious positions. At the same time, the great increase in trade with white colonists had created important new sources of revenue and hence spending resources. Moreover, the ban on tribal wars, imposed by the Canadian government, contributed to displacing the rivalry onto potlatch alone. Barnett (1938), Codere (1950), see also Mauzée (1986).

14 This Hegelian view is also the frame proposed by Axel Honneth ([1992] 1995).

15 In Mauss, (1990 [1924]), p. xiv. (These are short excerpts of a long poem).

16 Mauss (1990 [1924]), p. 101, n. 119. The notion of rhythm also developed by Mauss is very helpful in order to understand the very source of the drive to play. "Man is a rhythmic animal" he writes in his *Manuel d'ethnographie*, (1988), p. 85.

17 Clavero 1991. See my comment on this essay in Hénaff 2002, pp. 368–80.

References

Akin, D. and Robbins, J., *Money and Modernity: State and Local Currencies in Melanesia* (Pittsburgh, PA: University of Pittsburgh Press, 1999).

Bard, K. A. and Parker, S. T. (eds), *Reaching into Thought: The Minds of the Great Apes* (Cambridge: Cambridge University Press, 1996).

Barnett, H. G., 'The Nature of the Potlatch', *American Anthropologist*, 40 (1938), 349–58.

Boas, F., *Contribution to the Ethnology of the Kwakiutl* [1895–1913] (New York: Am Press, 1969).

Caillé, A., *Anthropologie du don* (Louvain: Desclée de Brouwer, 2000).

Clavero, B. A., *Anthropologia católica de la economía moderna* (Milan: Dott A. Giuffre, 1991).

Codere, H., *Fighting with Property: A Study of Kwakiutls Potlatching and Warfare 1792–1930* (New York: J. J. Augustin, 1950).

Davy, G., *La foi jurée. Etude sociologique du problème du contrat: la formation du lien contractuel* (Paris: Félix Alcan, 1922; New York: Arno Press, 1975).

De Waal, F. B. M., *Peacemaking among Primates* (Cambridge, MA: Harvard University Press, 1989).

Dowie, M., *American Foundations: An Investigative History* (Cambridge, MA: MIT Press, 2001).

Dumouchel, P., *Emotions. Essai sur le corps et le social* (Paris: Les Empêcheurs de penser en rond, 1995; reprinted 1999).

Gerschlager, C. (ed.), *Expanding the Economic Concept of Exchange: Deception, Self-Deception and Illusions* (Dordrecht and Boston: Kluwer, 1995).

Gilder, G., 'The Return of the Giving', in G. Gilder, *Wealth and Poverty* (New York: Basic Books, 1981).

Godbout, J. (with A. Caillé), *The World of the Gift* (Montreal: McGill Queen's University Press, 1998; orig. *L'esprit du don*, Paris: La Découverte, 1998).

Goldman, I., *The Mouth of Haven: An Introduction to Kwakiutl Religious Thought* (New York: Wiley, 1975).

Goodall, J., *The Chimpanzees of Gombe: Patterns of Behavior* (Cambridge, MA: Harvard University Press, 1986).

Gregory, A. C., *Gifts and Commodities* (London: Academic Press, 1982).

McGrew, W. C., *Chimpanzee Material Culture: Implication for Human Evolution* (Cambridge: Cambridge University Press, 1992).

McGrew, W. C., Marchant, L. F. and Nishida, T. (eds), *Great Apes Societies* (Cambridge: Cambridge University Press, 1990).

Hamayon, R., *La Chasse à l'âme* (Paris: Société d'Ethnologie, 1990).

Hamayon, R., 'Tricks of the Trade or How Siberian Hunters Play the game of Life-Exchange', in C. Gerschlager (ed.), *Expanding the Economic Concept of Exchange: Deception, Self-Deception and Illusions* (Dordrecht and Boston: Kluwer, 2001).

Hénaff, M., *Claude Lévi-Strauss and the Making of Structural Anthropology* (Minneapolis: University of Minnesota Press, 1998).

Hénaff, M., *Le Prix de la vérité. Le don, l'argent, la philosophie* (Paris: Seuil, 2002).

Hénaff, M., 'Religious Ethics, Gift Exchange and Capitalism', *European Journal of Sociology*, 44/3 (2003), 293–324.

Himmelstein, J. L., *Looking Good and Doing Good: Corporate Philanthropy and Corporate Power* (Bloomington: Indiana University Press, 1997).

Hollis, M., *Trust within Reason* (Cambridge: Cambridge University Press, 1998).

Honneth, A., *The Struggle for Recognition: The Moral Grammar of the Social Conflict* (Cambridge, MA: Polity Press, 1995).

Huizinga, J., *Homo Ludens: A Study of the Play Elements in Cultures* [1937] (New York: J & J Publishers, 1986).

Lefort, C., 'Exchange and the Struggle of Mankind', in C. Lefort, *The Political Forms of Modern Society: Bureaucracy, Democracy, Totalitarianism* (Cambridge, MA: Polity Press, 1986).

Lévi-Strauss, C., *The Elementary Structures of Kinship*, ch. 5 (Boston, MA: Beacon Press, 1969).

Lévi-Strauss, C., *Introduction to the Work of Marcel Mauss* (London: Routledge and Kegan Paul, 1987); trans. by F. Baker from M. Mauss, *Anthropologie et sociologie* (Paris: PUF, 1950).

Malinowski, B., *The Argonauts of the Western Pacific* [1922] (New York: E. P. Dutton & Co., 1961).

Mauss, M., 'Gift-Gift' [1924] in *Oeuvres* (Paris: Minuit, 1969), pp. 46–51.

Mauss, M., *Manuel d'ethnographie* (Paris: Payot, 1988).

Mauss, M., 'Essai sur le don' [1924], in *The Gift,* trans W. D. Halls (New York: W.W. Norton, 1990).

Mauzée, M., 'Boas, les Kwakiutl et le potlatch: éléments pour une réévaluation', *L'Homme*, 4/26 (1986).

Ortigues, E., *Le Discours et le symbole* (Paris: Aubier, 1962).

Perroux, F, *Economie et société. Contrainte, Echange, Don* (Paris: PUF, 1963).

Polanyi, K., *The Great Transformation* [1944] (Boston, MA: Beacon Press, 1957).

Premack, D., 'Why Animals Have Neither Culture nor History', in T. Ingold (ed.), *Companion Encyclopedia of Anthropology* (London: Routledge, 1994).

Smith, A., *An Inquiry into the Nature and Causes of the Wealth of Nations* [1776], I, ch. 2; ed. K. Sutherland (Oxford: Oxford University Press, 1993).

Sperber, D., *Rethinking Symbolism* (Cambridge, Cambridge University Press, 1975).

Stanford, C., 'The Ape's Gift', in F. De Waal (ed.), *Tree of Origin. What Primate Behavior Can Tell Us about Human Evolution* (Cambridge, MA: Harvard University Press, 2001).

Strathern, A., *The Rope of Moka: Big-Men and Ceremonial Exchange in Mount Hagen New Guinea* (Cambridge: Cambridge University Press, 1971).

Verdier, R. (ed.), *La Vengeance*, 4 vols (Paris: Editions Cujas, 1980–6).

Weber, M., *General Economic History* (New Brunswick and London: Transaction Books, 1981).

Williamson, O., 'Calculativeness, Trust, and Economic Organization', *Journal of Law and Economics*, 36 (1993), 453–86.

Index of Authors

Index of Subjects